NATO
after
FORTY YEARS

NATO
after
FORTY YEARS

Edited by
Lawrence S. Kaplan
S. Victor Papacosma
Mark R. Rubin
Ruth V. Young

A Scholarly Resources Inc. Imprint
Wilmington, Delaware

The paper used in this publication meets the minimum requirements of the American National Standard for permanence of paper for printed library materials, Z39.48, 1984.

Scholarly Resources Inc.
104 Greenhill Avenue
Wilmington, DE 19805-1897

Cover design printed by permission of Information Directorate, North Atlantic Treaty Organization, Brussels, Belgium

Library of Congress Cataloging-in-Publication Data

NATO after forty years / edited by Lawrence S. Kaplan . . . [et al.].
    p. cm.
    Includes index.
    ISBN 0-8420-2366-6. — ISBN 0-8420-2367-4 (pbk.)
    1. North Atlantic Treaty Organization—History. I. Kaplan, Lawrence S.
II. Title: NATO after 40 years.
    JX1393.N67N33 1990
    355'.031'091821—dc20   90-8817
                                                CIP

Contents

Preface and Acknowledgments

This volume grew out of an international conference, sponsored by the Lyman L. Lemnitzer Center for NATO Studies with the support of the NATO Information Service, held at Kent State University on 18–20 April 1989 to commemorate the fortieth anniversary of the signing of the North Atlantic Treaty. The format of this volume resembles, but does not duplicate, *NATO after Thirty Years*, the first of six books on NATO published by Scholarly Resources.

The intention of the participants was to deal with NATO's historical record and its significance for the present and future. For this purpose the early chapters concentrate on such issues as the relations of the larger and smaller nations with NATO and with the United States over the forty-year span. The latter half of the book centers on the continuing issues of the alliance, including relations with the Third World and with the European Community, as well as with such central concerns of the organization as conventional versus nuclear defense, the place of détente in NATO's history, and the record of arms control negotiations with the Warsaw Pact. Two chapters look to the future of NATO from differing perspectives. While there was no intention of including a representative from every member nation among the authors, there has been an effort to draw from perspectives of a variety of NATO constituencies. Finally, given the rapidly changing events in the forty-first year of NATO's history, the editors invited Thomas H. Etzold, a member of the conference group, to close the volume with an essay appropriately titled "NATO at Middle Age: An Unexpected Midlife Crisis."

The editors wish to express their appreciation for the special contribution of Professor Robert W. Bowie, director of the Policy Planning Staff of the State Department during the Eisenhower administration. His perceptive remarks on the durability of NATO were presented in a dinner address to members of the conference and friends of the Lemnitzer Center.

The editors also owe a large debt to the many commentators who participated in the proceedings. They include Martin S. Alexander, UK; Harry C. Allen, UK; Philip J. Briggs, USA; Joseph I. Coffey, USA; Alex Danchev, UK; Lynne Dunn, USA; John English, Canada; Thomas H. Etzold, USA; Hans-Joachim Giessmann, German Democratic Republic; Colin Gordon, UK; Daniel C. Helmstadter, USA; Morris Honick, Belgium; Richard H. Immerman, USA; Robert S. Jordan, USA; Joseph Kruzel, USA; Bruce R. Kuniholm, USA; Ronald Landa, USA; Allan R. Millett, USA; Olav Riste, Norway; Jacquelyn Y. Silson, USA; E. Timothy Smith, USA; David S. Sorenson, USA; Douglas T. Stuart, USA; Laurent Wehrli, Switzerland; and Benedict K. Zobrist, USA.

The editors are grateful for the continuing interest of NATIS and Scholarly Resources in our activities. Additionally, we wish to thank faculty and student associates who contributed time and effort to this project: Boleslaw A. Boczek, Robert W. Clawson, Lawrence S. Kaplan, and S. Victor Papacosma, who chaired sessions; James Bado, transportation director, assisted by Brian Hollinger, Richard Haluska, and Sean Kay; Fred McCandless, Special Services; and hostesses Shari Duren, Elizabeth Williams, and Elizabeth Zurzolo. The preparation of the book has benefited from the services of Edward Krzemienski, editorial assistant. Invaluable services also were provided by Sandy Baker; the center's secretary. Our special gratitude is extended to the center's administrative coordinator, Ruth Young, who once again displayed her marvelous organizational abilities and enthusiasm and without whose efforts the conference could not have succeeded and this volume could not have appeared.

Introduction

The conditions that made the Atlantic Alliance a necessity in 1949 have changed dramatically over forty years. Then, only American power could shelter a Europe devastated by World War II from the one nation, the Soviet Union, that could challenge American dominance. Although its strength was not equal to that of the United States, its Communist ideology, backed by the largest army in the world, appeared to be on the brink of embracing all of Europe. NATO was the instrument initiated by European leaders to bring the United States out of its isolationist history and into an entangling relationship with the Old World. The result was an alliance and organization designed first to contain Communist expansion and, second, to facilitate the reorganization of Western Europe as an integrated political and economic entity that would assume an equal partnership with the United States. The history of the first forty years of the alliance reflects these objectives.

In 1989 it appeared that NATO had been successful in both areas. Not only had the Soviet Union failed to control Western Europe through subversion or through conquest, but also Soviet society under the leadership of Mikhail Gorbachev was on the threshold of being transformed along the lines of a Western democracy. Whether or not communism will even survive was open to question. The military threat of the past had receded. Less dramatic, because the time span was longer, is the transformation of the European allies into an integrated community. Indeed, Western Europe now has the potential of equaling, if not surpassing, both superpowers in the future.

However, these are not the only changes in forty years. New nations, in what came to be called the Third World, have risen to change the bipolar balance of the globe. Some of these nations, such as Taiwan and South Vietnam, have been wards of one or the other of the superpowers, but some—India and Pakistan, for example—have maintained their independence. The world of 1989 was larger than an arena of East-West competition, or even of West-West problems, which have been the major concerns of the alliance. The peace and stability of the world may now depend on countries of Latin America, Asia, or Africa as much as on Europe or North America.

In light of both the achievement of older goals and the presence of new challenges, it is not surprising that critics speculate about the alliance's future. The authors in this book deal implicitly with the relevance of the alliance for the 1990s and with the rivalry of the superpowers throughout the first forty years. Other subjects considered are the conflicts between the United States, with its tendencies toward unilateralism, and its fifteen allies, each with grievances against the United States.

In some respects, intra-alliance issues dominate NATO's history, which is not surprising in a free association of nations in which each member has to balance national interests against common interests. NATO frequently has different meanings for different countries. Canada's position is unique, for example. It is not a European nation, but it is a neighbor to the most powerful NATO ally and, as such, has found both opportunities and dangers in the alliance. NATO's transatlantic character has diluted American pressures, but, at the same time, Canada has been concerned about being neglected in an organization that perhaps draws the United States excessively into European issues. Alan Henrikson finds that insufficient recognition has been given to the contributions Europe has made and can make to North American security. Concentration on a northern rim of NATO would minimize geostrategic distinctions between Europe and America.

NATO has held various meanings for the major West European members, who are different from the Americans and Canadians, and from each other. For the United Kingdom, as Geoffrey Warner points out, NATO has been a means of ensuring a "special relationship" with the United States. The British have never achieved the preeminence that they had anticipated in 1949, but they have been able to win a position as primus inter pares among the allies. France, at least for the first few years, was suspicious of the Anglo-American condominium in control of the alliance, weighing the security offered by the alliance against the loss of independence and inferior position it would hold within the organization. It has rejected the organization while keeping its role as an ally. On balance, as Pierre Mélandri observes, the French, for all their ambivalence toward the senior partner, preferred a strong America to a weak America. According to Werner Kaltefleiter, NATO has been indispensable to the security and prosperity of the German Federal Republic. For West Germany, geography has permitted no choice other than NATO. Kaltefleiter presents a picture of Gorbachev's new foreign policy as a greater threat to the alliance and to Germany than the predictable hostility of his predecessors.

From a very different angle of observation, the members from Scandinavia and the Low Countries have expressed their discontent with American behavior in the alliance. The United States has been a more frequent target of their emotions than has the Soviet Union, if only because their major ally has been within reach. The endemic failure of the United States to consult with allies has been a subject of constant discussion, as in the North Atlantic Council's admonitions. Cees Wiebes and Bert Zeeman see a need to restructure the alliance to give greater voice to the smaller members' concerns.

Other members of the alliance offer alternative perspectives. None is more distinctive than Italy's. As Raimondo Luraghi sees it, the Mediterranean arena has been neglected by NATO headquarters, despite the fact that potential for Soviet mischief has been greater there than in northern or central Europe. Both low-intensity conflict and terrorism reflect a dangerous volatility that deserves more attention than it has received.

In the foregoing papers there is a recognition that, for all the problems with the superpower as an ally, NATO remains important to its members. The underlying sense of optimism in these accounts appears as well in Reimund Seidelmann's view of NATO's relations with the European Community. Since the EC's members are all European NATO powers (except for Ireland), the connections are important. In the short run, there will be continuing conflict, not only within the community itself but also between the EC and the United States over possibilities of exclusion from a fortress Europe. The growth of an integrated Europe could mean the dissolution of NATO, but it need not. Seidelmann's recommendation is for a reformed NATO that would take into account European integration and use the strength of the European pillar in resolving global issues.

Scott Bills's examination of NATO's record with respect to "out-of-area" issues, especially in the Third World, is less enthusiastic. NATO has always been Eurocentric, and the organization's efforts to include out-of-area problems have usually failed, either because of unilateral American conduct or because of incompatible interests among the member nations in a particular area. Action in the Third World has been the source of many of the strains that have weakened the alliance over the past forty years. There is little prospect for change in the future.

Détente, like arms control, has been subjected to cycles over the past forty years, with tension and relaxation succeeding each other. Anton DePorte finds limits to both tension and détente. The 1962 Cuban missile crisis was the highest point of Cold War conflict between the blocs, and the prospect of mutual destruction was serious enough to have made subsequent periods of tension more restrained than they were during the first fifteen years of the alliance's history. On the other hand, no matter how well developed détente may become in the future, it is unlikely that it will lead to the termination of the alliance. Despite events of 1990, Europe is still divided.

The unraveling of the alliance is a theme in Luc Reychler's treatment of arms control negotiations. The author claims that there is room for skepticism, given the snail's pace at which negotiations had proceeded over the past generation. The Gorbachev initiatives raise dangers as well as hopes for the process. Western failure to respond coherently could be destructive to the future of the alliance. But the record also offers reasons for optimism. Despite periodic setbacks, there has been overall progress in the development of arms control mechanisms, particularly in the second half of NATO's forty-year history. More may be expected in the next decade if the allies can build, as Reychler puts it, "a 'European House' without destroying the détente and the 'Atlantic House.' "

William Park concentrates on the trouble the alliance has faced in the past over differing nuclear defense strategies in Europe. If NATO has had a recurring problem in finding consensus over crises in the Third World, there have been even more vexatious troubles between the United States and its European partners over how and when to use nuclear weaponry. Europeans welcomed the principle of "massive retaliation" and its consequent low threshold for the use of nuclear weapons, while the United States since the Robert McNamara period has emphasized a higher threshold accompanied by more expensive conventional forces. Park asserts that the allies have never fully distinguished deterrence from defense. The alliance has been unable to come up with a satisfactory response in the event that deterrence should fail. If nuclear defense is increasingly unsatisfactory, then the alternative of conventional defense is too expensive. There is little likelihood that Europe will fill the gap that a reduction in the numbers of American troops in Europe would create. While progress in arms control negotiations, combined with the lessening of the Soviet threat, may resolve the question of nuclear defense, it also may lead to decoupling of the United States from Europe.

Chapters by S. I. P. van Campen and Ronald Steel develop scenarios about the future that are substantially different from those of the other authors—and from each other's. Both essays question the survivability of the alliance. Van Campen sees an uncertain future as a consequence both of the inability of the Western allies to cope with Gorbachev's tactics and of the inability of the North Atlantic Council to coordinate a common policy. If the Soviet Union is a potential instrument of NATO's demise because of its new foreign policy, the United States is a contributor through its past and present unilateral policies followed at the expense of the alliance's credibility. Steel also sees possibilities of a termination of NATO but would welcome, rather than reject, the prospect of it being no longer necessary for the restoration of Europe's power or for the containment of Soviet power. He recommends a gradual withdrawal of both Soviet and American forces and a dissolution of both blocs in an orderly fashion.

Finally, Thomas Etzold considers NATO in the context of the recent upheaval in Eastern Europe. He explains why the alliance has been successful for its first forty years, what is currently happening in the world to change NATO's ability to work as before, and what might be expected in the 1990s.

Forty years after the North Atlantic Treaty was signed there is still no united Europe, and the nuclear weapon has not been tamed. Changes in the Soviet Union—*perestroika* in particular—are not necessarily permanent. There is sufficient uncertainty in East-West relations to make the alliance meaningful in the foreseeable future. Even if a lesser role for the United States is likely in the 1990s, the American presence inside NATO is important not for the numbers of troops or missiles that it must control but for the stability that it has provided in the past and in the present.

Nonetheless, the tumultuous events of the forty-first year of NATO's history may make this prognosis invalid. The pace of *perestroika* has advanced so fast that the chain reaction following the rapid changes in Eastern Europe, particularly the upheaval in the East German regime that began in November 1989, could leave the Atlantic Alliance in tatters. What hostility from the Soviet bloc and dissidence within NATO could not accomplish, the unraveling of the Communist system could, namely, the dissolution of the alliance. If this should come about early or late in the 1990s, it could be seen as a supreme irony. Success in containing Soviet expansion, in exposing the hollowness of the Communist system, and in advancing the cause of a united Europe could result in the separation of North America from Europe and break the transatlantic ties that were the hallmark of the past two generations. NATO would be irrelevant in the post-Cold War era.

If that scenario should happen, the ending of both the West and East blocs could fulfill Ronald Steel's projection. There are enough signals abroad to make such an outcome credible at the beginning of this century's last decade. Such an end to NATO, if not to history, would also fit a goal that the Soviet Union has visualized since the 1950s, when the Rapacki Plan promoted a neutralized Germany and the removal of U.S. and Soviet troops from central Europe and, in the American case, from the European continent itself. This, and other Soviet proposals in the late 1950s, was dismissed by Americans and West Europeans alike as an insidious Communist ploy. A generation later, such an arrangement could be made without eliciting the suspicions of the past. The difference lies in the putative existence of a strong and united Europe that would be equal, if not superior to, the power of America and the Soviet Union.

Is this an accurate image of the future? Other scenarios may be drawn that might make the Atlantic Alliance more necessary than in the past, even if its structure might be changed over the next few years. What would be the reaction in the West if Gorbachev should not survive and should be succeeded by a reactionary dictatorship in control of the powerful military machine the Soviets have built over the last twenty-five years? There could be panic in the West if NATO were no longer present to counter a Russian, if not Communist, imperial presence in Europe.

A united states of Europe could calm such concerns. But such an entity does not exist in 1990, and it probably will not be created by 1992. The European Community has not progressed to the point of possessing the political and military cohesion to complement its still incomplete economic unity. The presence of the United States could be a stabilizing force in NATO—that is, if its role were played out as discreetly as S. I. P. van Campen would have it. Genuine consultation among equals through a larger delegation of powers to the NATO secretariat would be particularly appropriate as the military face of SHAPE (Supreme Headquarters Allied Powers Europe) decreases in significance.

Even if post-Communist Russia, beset by the internal problems of its economy and its restive nationalities, were to pose no threat to the stability of the West, the presence of a united Germany might give all Europeans pause. Not that revanchism or Prussian militarism or a neo-Nazi revival are likely consequences of the changing scene in the 1990s; rather, a much stronger German economy, already the dominant entity in the European Community, could diminish the roles of other major European nations and through its strength in the community press for an *Ostpolitik* that would serve a German, rather than European, interest. Germany could sit astride Europe from the Atlantic to the Urals by virtue of its economic, not military, strength.

While such a vision is exaggerated, it is not unthinkable, as is evident by the considerable attention being paid it by Europeans. Given Germany's destabilizing effect, the United States still would have a part to play in Europe, as a buffer to German, if not to Soviet, power. NATO is the only vehicle for a continuing American presence in Europe, a presence that might be welcomed by Russians as well as by West Europeans. As talk of the reunification of Germany increased after the removal of Erich Honecker from power in East Germany in November 1989, Gorbachev cautioned both East and West that "now is not the time to break up established institutions." It is reasonable to suggest as well that a restructured NATO, with its original political function predominant, would be a check against the tendency in America to turn its back once again on the European continent.

Lawrence S. Kaplan

About the Contributors

SCOTT L. BILLS is associate professor of history at Stephen F. Austin State University. He received his Ph.D. from Kent State University and is the author of *Empire and Cold War: The Roots of U.S.-Third World Antagonism* (1990), as well as more general articles concerning U.S.-Third World relations in the era after World War II. He is also the editor of *Kent State/May 4: Echoes through a Decade* (rev. ed., 1988) and a contributor to two previous volumes in the Lemnitzer Center series.

ANTON W. DEPORTE is currently a visiting scholar at the Institute of French Studies, New York University. He earned his doctorate from the University of Chicago and served as a career officer in the U.S. Department of State from 1955 to 1980. Positions held there included membership on the Policy Planning Staff and directorship of the Office of Research on Western Europe. His publications include *DeGaulle's Foreign Policy, 1944–1946* (1968) and *Europe between the Superpowers—The Enduring Alliance* (2d ed., 1986).

THOMAS H. ETZOLD was assistant director of the U.S. Arms Control and Disarmament Agency (1984–1986). He served previously as professor of strategy at the U.S. Naval War College, and in other executive positions with the Navy and Defense departments. He is now president of the Ivy Group, a firm consulting in defense, energy, advanced technology, and intelligence matters, and is senior research fellow of the Atlantic Council of the United States.

ALAN K. HENRIKSON is associate professor of diplomatic history at the Fletcher School of Law and Diplomacy, Tufts University, where he teaches American and European diplomatic history and international negotiation. He also is Counselor on Canadian Affairs at Harvard University's Center for International Affairs. He did undergraduate and graduate work in history at Harvard and also holds degrees from the University of Oxford, where he studied as a Rhodes scholar. He has published extensively in the field of U.S. foreign policy and was a contributor to the Lemnitzer Center book *East-West Rivalry in the Third World: Security Issues and Regional Perspectives* (1986).

WERNER KALTEFLEITER is professor of political science and director of both the Institute of Political Science and the Institute of Security Studies at the University of Kiel, in West Germany. He is the author of numerous articles and books, including *The Peace Movements in Europe and the United States* (1985).

LAWRENCE S. KAPLAN is university professor of history and director of the Lyman L. Lemnitzer Center for NATO Studies at Kent State University. He received his Ph.D. from Yale University and has written numerous articles, monographs, and books on U.S. diplomatic history and NATO affairs, including *A Community of Interests: NATO and the Military Assistance Program, 1948-1951* (1980), *The United States and NATO: The Formative Years* (1984), and *NATO and the United States: The Enduring Alliance* (1988). He has also served as coeditor for four earlier volumes in the Lemnitzer Center series.

RAIMONDO LURAGHI is professor of American history at the University of Turin and Director of its Center for Defense Studies. His Ph.D. is from the University of Rome. He is President of the Italian Association for Military History and has many publications in this area, including *Storia della Guerra Civile Americana* (1966). Earlier, he coedited the Lemnitzer Center volume *NATO and the Mediterranean* (1985).

PIERRE MÉLANDRI, who studied at the Ecole Normale Supérieure and Harvard University, is professor of contemporary history at the University of Paris X. His main fields of interest are American history and international relations, and he has been a research scholar at Princeton, the Johns Hopkins School of Advanced International Studies, and the Wilson Center. He has published seven books, including *L'Alliance Atlantique* (1979), *Les Etats-Unis face à l'Unification de l'Europe, 1945–1954* (1980), *Une Incertaine Alliance. Les Etats-Unis et l'Europe: 1973–1983* (1988), and *Reagan: Une Biographie Totale* (1988).

S. VICTOR PAPACOSMA is professor of history and associate director of the Lyman L. Lemnitzer Center for NATO Studies at Kent State University. He received his Ph.D. in Balkan history from Indiana University and has published widely in the area, with a concentration in twentieth-century Greek politics. Among his publications are *The Military in Greek Politics: The 1909 Coup d'Etat* (1977) and a coedited volume in the Lemnitzer Center series, *Europe's Neutral and Nonaligned States: Between NATO and the Warsaw Pact* (1988).

WILLIAM H. PARK is a principal lecturer in the Department of History and International Affairs at the Royal Naval College, Greenwich, UK, and a visiting lecturer at the City University of London. He authored *Defending the West: A History of NATO* (1986) and is currently working on a book on changing patterns of European security.

LUC REYCHLER is professor of international relations, peace research, and strategic studies at the Catholic University of Leuven. He was educated in Belgium and received his Ph.D. from Harvard University. He is the author of *Patterns of Diplomatic Thinking* (1979) and coauthor of *Supermächten: USA* (1985), *NATO's Northern Allies* (1985), *Directory Guide of European Security and Defense Research* (1986), *In Search of European Security* (1986), and *European Security beyond the Year 2000* (1987).

MARK R. RUBIN is associate professor of French, administrative director of the Center for International and Comparative Programs, and associate director of the Lyman L. Lemnitzer Center for NATO Studies at Kent State University. His doctorate is from Princeton University. He has written on French and Swiss military affairs and coedited two earlier volumes in the Lemnitzer Center series.

REIMUND SEIDELMANN is professor of international relations at the University of Cologne, in West Germany, having also taught earlier at the University of Giessen and Georgetown University. His many publications are in the fields of international relations theory, security policy, and European integration. His most recent book is *Auf dem Weg zu einer westeuropäische Sicherheitspolitik* (1989).

RONALD L. STEEL is professor of international relations at the University of Southern California and author of several books on foreign policy, including *The End of Alliance: America and the Future of Europe* (1964), *Pax Americana* (1967), and *Walter Lippmann and the American Century* (1981). He is a frequent contributor to such magazines as *New Republic* and the *New York Review of Books*.

S. I. P. VAN CAMPEN holds his doctorate in political and social sciences from the University of Amsterdam. He has served as special adviser for policy planning to the secretary general of NATO (1966–1971) and as director of the Private Office of the NATO secretary general (1971–1984). He has published several articles and books on problems of foreign policy and international relations.

GEOFFREY WARNER is professor of European humanities at the Open University in the United Kingdom. Educated at the University of Cambridge and the Fondation Nationale des Sciences Politiques in Paris, he has published *Pierre Laval and the Eclipse of France* (1968) and *Iraq and*

Syria, 1941 (1974), as well as many articles and essays on European and international history since 1945.

CEES WIEBES is a university lecturer at the Department of International Relations and International Law of the University of Amsterdam. He has published *Indonesische Dagboeknotities van Dr. H. N. Boon* (1986) with Bert Zeeman, *Affarer till varje pris* (1989) and *Peittelyn Taito* (1989) with Gerard Aalders, and numerous articles on postwar international relations. He is currently preparing with Bert Zeeman a study on Belgium, the Netherlands, and military alliances, 1940–1949.

RUTH V. YOUNG, administrative coordinator, has been a member of the Lyman L. Lemnitzer Center staff since 1982.

BERT ZEEMAN is a reference and acquisitions librarian at the University Library of the University of Amsterdam. With Cees Wiebes as coauthor, he has published *Indonesische Dagboeknotities van Dr. H. N. Boon* (1986). He also has authored many articles on postwar international relations and is currently researching Belgium, Netherlands, and military alliances, 1940–1949, with Cees Wiebes.

NATO AND ITS
MEMBER STATES

The North American Perspective: A Continent Apart or a Continent Joined?

Alan K. Henrikson

To what extent can the history of the participation by the United States and Canada in the North Atlantic Treaty Organization be explained by their need—and perhaps even other allies' need—to defend North America itself? There seems to be a conceptual disconnection in the North American involvement in NATO between the imperative of self-protection, termed "continental defense," and the larger, almost altruistic purpose of "the defense of the West," a commitment too often taken to mean essentially a security guarantee of and for Western Europe. Geopolitically, North America is viewed as a continent apart.[1]

A recent example of the curious scholarly neglect of North American defense as a theoretical and historical subject is the otherwise very informative and graphically effective book by Laurence Martin, *NATO and the Defense of the West: An Analysis of America's First Line of Defense.* The focus of Martin's work is on the central front in Europe and, to a lesser extent, NATO's northern and southern flanks. The defense of North America, arguably at least a part of "America's first line of defense," is scarcely mentioned. At the end of a section describing the elaborate command structure of NATO, Martin notes: "Outside these commands there is also a Regional Planning Committee to discuss joint Canadian-American concerns." Even his discussion of the bipolar U.S.-Soviet relationship centers on Europe. Although he observes that the United States and the Soviet Union are "closest geographical neighbours in the North Pacific and, significantly in the missile age, across the Arctic," he also contends that "the projection of American military power in NATO places the most important confrontation between the Superpowers in Europe and makes it the strategic centre of the world."[2]

Why is the defense of the North American region within the formal treaty area of NATO so often overlooked? Possibly the best single explanation, covering the thinking of many Americans and Canadians and perhaps many Europeans as well, is the regnant historical interpretation of the involvement by the United States in Europe's defense as an abandonment of "isolationism."[3] In political terms, this means a rejection of unilateralism; in geostrategic terms, it means a rejection of continentalism. The ancient dogma of the self-sufficiency of the New World bastion, or Fortress America, usually is renounced as if it were a form of heresy, its policy temptations forever to be forgotten.

At the time of NATO's founding, these so-called isolationist impulses, unilateralism and continentalism, despite the apparent paradox actually contributed to the Atlanticism that for Americans and Canadians has motivated the North Atlantic security commitment. This is the hypothesis here proposed: The U.S. and Canadian security interest in protecting North America, if the logic of that geostrategic premise is developed to its widest implications, dictates much the same "overseas" involvement as a more explicitly Europe-first alliance—that is, a transatlantic pact conceived of as essentially a commitment to action on the central front in Europe, as well as on Europe's northern if not also its southern flank.

Interestingly, some early U.S. advocates of an American security guarantee to Western Europe tried to present the Truman administration's novel peacetime political and military commitment to the Old World as, in effect, simply an eastward extension of the Monroe Doctrine. This was done in part for tactical political purposes. The argument was used to diffuse the proposals, made by Senator Robert A. Taft and others, to replace the formal treaty of alliance then being negotiated with a mere unilateral offer of American support for Europe, such as the Truman Doctrine or, perhaps better, a congressionally initiated declaration of America's intent.[4]

The importance of this point, then and today, is that concern about the security of North America is perhaps the best guarantee of U.S., and also Canadian, involvement in NATO. It may be, in the sense of deepest, as well, the best explanation of why these countries joined it forty years ago. Thus, far from being inimical to the transatlantic institution of NATO, "the North American perspective" may be its geostrategic and political foundation.[5]

This is by no means the whole story, however. In addition to the logic of "continental defense," as the first imperative may be called, there were at the time of NATO's founding two other rationales, relevant if less geostrategically immediate to inhabitants of North America. The second imperative concerned the European "balance of power"—to restore the situation in Europe so that equilibrium could be maintained there without the need for North American involvement or assistance in emergencies.

Americans (several years after Canadians in each case) twice had helped to put out fires in the house of Europe, and they did not want to have to do so again. The third imperative, somewhat more theoretical, was the logic of "collective security," a normative as well as a strategic rationale. The idea was to create a network of obligations, a general system of security, whereby the safety of all nations could be preserved. Any violations would arouse the ire and incur the sanctions of the entire international community, in which the formerly isolationist Americans as well as the more internationalist Canadians now believed they were permanently included.

These three concepts—"continental defense," "balance of power," and "collective security"—have worked together in forming the alliance connection between North America and Western Europe. It tends to be assumed, however, that too close an analysis of the separate motives behind formation of the transatlantic security system would be counterproductive. This apprehension, owing to the variety of security interests within the alliance, is not altogether unfounded.

Nonetheless, such analysis actually can serve to strengthen the alliance's cohesion. The partial, although not perfect, congruence of the strategic objectives behind NATO as viewed from the U.S. and Canadian perspectives, demonstrate the extent to which the organization and the policies of the present transatlantic defense arrangement are "overdetermined." That is, there are more than enough causes or reasons for doing what has been done, and is being done, in NATO. When one ally wishes to withdraw from a particular function, for its own individual purposes, others may wish to carry it out for their own reasons. Whether or not this occurs is perhaps the best test of a "security community."[6] Analyzing how much the separate strategic motivations of alliance members do not coincide may suggest guidelines for reform of NATO, or for restructuring the organization and redistributing some of its responsibilities.

Continental Defense, Balance of Power, and Collective Security

Although they are distinguishable, the three above-mentioned concepts and associated logics that have animated the American and Canadian strategic involvement in NATO are seldom distinguished. Before considering how, during successive phases of the participation of the United States and Canada in transatlantic defense, the three rationales interacted, it would be well to present a more detailed description of the essential purposes and programmatic contents of each.

The first and most basic concept is the imperative of continental defense. Its origin is in U.S.-Canadian plans for securing the North American continent and its outposts just before and during the Second

World War. On 18 August 1938, at the time of the Czechoslovak crisis, President Franklin D. Roosevelt stated in an address at Kingston, Ontario: "I give you assurance that the people of the United States will not stand idly by if domination of Canadian soil is threatened by any other empire." The Canadian prime minister, William Lyon Mackenzie King, replied two days later that Canada's territory would not be a base for aggression against the United States. "We, too, have our obligations as a good friendly neighbor," he said, "and one of these is to see that, at our own instance, our country is made as immune from attack or possible invasion as we can reasonably be expected to make it, and that, should the occasion ever arise, enemy forces should not be able to pursue their way either by land, sea or air, to the United States across Canadian territory."[7] When the two North American leaders met at Ogdensburg, New York, in August 1940, they announced the formation of the Permanent Joint Board on Defense (PJBD), an institution based on their shared view that North American defense constituted a single, indissoluble problem. This conception has lasted to the present day.

The next year, in April 1941, Prime Minister King visited President Roosevelt at his home in Hyde Park. There the two announced that, in mobilizing the resources of the continent, "each country should provide the other with the defense articles which it is best able to produce, and, above all, produce quickly, and that production programs should be coordinated to this end."[8] Although it lacked the status of a formal treaty relationship, this agreement, like the earlier Ogdensburg accord, substantiated the principle of joint defense planning. There would be functional specialization in military manufacture and coordinated if separate deployment of forces on the North American continent.

The security of the North American outposts of Alaska, the Aleutians, Greenland, and Iceland preoccupied King and Roosevelt and their associates. It was primarily the United States that actually sent military forces to protect these marginal areas on the Pacific and Atlantic fronts during the war. Both areas saw some action. The Japanese briefly occupied the outer Aleutian Islands of Kiska and Attu in 1942, at the time of the Battle of Midway. The Germans periodically made landings on the coast of Greenland, mainly to collect and report weather data, until they were definitively driven off by the U.S. Army and Coast Guard in the summer of 1944. Within the interior zones of the North American defensive framework, the PJBD kept itself busy with logistical projects such as the aerial Northwest Staging Route and with construction tasks such as the fortification of Newfoundland, which was then still a British colony. Canada was prominent in both of these efforts, as well as in supplying shipments for transatlantic convoys.[9]

The essential point is that, although their roles were differentiated, both Canada and the United States from this period on regarded the defense of

North America, including their own outer islands and the nearby insular territories belonging to European countries, as a shared problem, inherently and enduringly "joint." This fundamental realization carried over into and lasted throughout the whole post-Second World War period, even though the urgency of North American defense waned before it, later, again waxed.

The second strategic concept, also deriving from the experience and logic of the Second World War, concerned American and Canadian interest in helping to reestablish a European balance of power. The usual formulation is that the two North American countries would "back up," or reinforce, not actually "join," or become integral to, a reconstituted European equilibrium. This mechanism would serve, indirectly, as a protection to them, as well as to the whole Western Hemisphere. For most of its history, as Walter Lippmann and other realistic commentators argued, the physical security of the United States had depended on the inner workings of the European balancing system.[10] The breakdown of that structure had been a major factor in permitting the German kaiser's, and later Adolf Hitler's, aggression toward the West. Joseph Stalin's expansion in that direction seemed entirely possible, too, if nothing were done to prevent it. No longer was it sufficient, many Americans and Canadians realized at war's end, for North America to be able to mobilize its vast resources to defeat an aggressor in Europe. Their two countries should give timely assistance to like-minded European nations in peacetime to deter aggression as well as, if necessary, to defend against it.

Powerful new technological developments reinforced the reasoning behind this new doctrine of deterrence: the airplane and the A-bomb. Revolutionary advances in aircraft design, jet propulsion, rocketry, and, most ominously, nuclear physics brought about a new world within which no country, no matter how geographically remote, could consider itself invulnerable. The "hard-shell," or territorial, state was a geopolitical feature of the past.[11] The North American continent was no longer, as isolationists once had assumed, physically impregnable.[12] North America's natural shield of time and space soon would be obliterated. The United States and Canada then would have what most European countries long had possessed: "live" frontiers.

As President Harry S. Truman's Air Policy Commission, chaired by Thomas K. Finletter, reported in 1948, the traditional peacetime strategy of the United States would have to be "changed radically." The Finletter Commission warned: "We can no longer count on having our cities and the rest of our mainland untouched in a future war. On the contrary, we must count on our homeland becoming increasingly vulnerable as the weapons increase in destructiveness and the means of delivering them are improved." Moreover, the North American target would be much more valuable and attractive. The commission advised that "if future aggressors will have learned anything from World Wars I and II it will be that they must never let United States industrial power get under way; they must destroy it at the outset if they are to win."[13]

Not only could this logic be used to justify a substantial buildup of the North American continent's own defenses, particularly its air defense, but it also pointed to the need for an effort to establish security on the European continent. Even before the United States entered World War II, there had been Americans who favored a self-interested effort to contribute to the military balance of Europe. The name of William Allen White's allegedly pro-British group expressed the idea: Committee to Defend America by Aiding the Allies. The threat of a transatlantic attack against North America had to be prevented even from arising. In this sense the central front of NATO became, by the end of the 1940s, part of "America's first line of defense," somewhat as Great Britain had been pictured by some anti-isolationist Americans at the beginning of the decade. Most Canadians had held this view consistently, not because they believed in the centrality of Europe but because of their primary preoccupation with the safety of North America. The close connection between the framework of continental defense and European security made Americans realize, not merely from altruism or Anglophilia, that the European power-balancing system—"my neighbor's home," as Franklin Roosevelt metaphorically referred to the British part of it—must somehow be protected.[14]

In 1945 the European structure appeared to have collapsed. Where there was once a familiar international system of states, there now seemed to be a continental vacuum ("Now Europe balanced, neither side prevails; For nothing's left in either of the scales," in Alexander Pope's epigram).[15] The primary U.S. effort to fill this void was the European Recovery Program (ERP), or Marshall Plan. Canada contributed too, partly in the form of grain shipments purchased with ERP funds. It also assisted through its work in the United Nations Relief and Rehabilitation Administration (UNRRA) and with a large postwar loan to Great Britain.[16] By offering to help restore Europe's economic strength and hence its political balance, the United States and Canada, using their own huge reserves before rather than after another European conflict, hoped that they would safeguard North America itself.

The third concept by which the United States and Canada could be assured of future safety was collective security. This would shield the North American continent by creating an organized sense of "community" around it, hemispherically and globally. Collective security provided for a systematic protection of the two North American neighbors. Canada saw more clearly how its own individual security might thereby be defended, partly against an overbearing United States. As the Canadian diplomat John Holmes wrote with characteristic directness and candor, the Canadian enthusiasm for "multilateral creation" after the war was in part "a wish to make continental institutions unnecessary." By entwining North America in such multilateral relationships as the commitments of the UN Charter, Canada hoped to gain diplomatic flexibility, cultural breathing space, and political counterweight. Holmes confessed that Canada had an "almost ideological antipathy" to mere regionalism in international institutions. This reflected worries about the "North American region" into which it might be cast. Consistent with this multilateralist logic, the Canadian government was one of the few governments to insist on the ultimate international authority of the UN Security Council, so that regional organizations such as the Pan-American Union "could not be managed by a regional superpower."[17]

Canada already had accumulated considerable experience in multilateral diplomacy, as a "senior commonwealth" within the British Empire and also as a member of the League of Nations. Its postwar strategy in dealing with its southern neighbor-suddenly-become-"superpower" reflected its historic reliance on another device to preserve its freedom of maneuver: the "North Atlantic triangle."[18] Within this imagined formation, Canada was *tertius gaudens*, an influential although not decisive third party in a balance between the United States and the United Kingdom. As a makeweight, it fancied, it might be able on occasion to tip the transatlantic scales in its own interest, as well as in the larger Atlantic interest.

One product of this three-way conception of Atlantic security was the pre-Pearl Harbor Canadian defense agreement with the United States, Joint Basic Defense Plan No. 2, or ABC-22. This was not directed toward hemispheric defense as an end in itself but rather was intended to supplement agreements being reached in U.S.-British staff conversations.[19] The aim of this strategic accord, from the Canadian point of view, was to bring against Nazi Germany the combined might of the British Commonwealth and the United States, if and when America itself entered the war. Under this scheme, Newfoundland, for example, assumed a role not only in continental defense but also in transatlantic offense. Military aircraft would be catapulted from it to the British Isles, there to be hurled against Hitler's *Festung Europa*. This pattern of U.S. and Canadian strategic planning, initiated within the framework of North American continental defense but oriented toward Europe, powerfully informed the participation of the two continental neighbors later in the North Atlantic Treaty Organization.

The North American Regional Allies

The United States and Canada, although neighbors, had distinctly different self-images and outlooks, which naturally produced differing conceptions of how to organize their joint defenses in the postwar period. Americans constantly have needed to be reminded of Canada's variant, nonidentical North American perspective. A later Canadian government publication on the subject of national security succinctly expresses this fundamental point: "Defence Is Spelled with a C."[20]

Intellectually, and politically, the United States and Canada have not even belonged to the same hemisphere. The "Western Hemisphere" within which Americans traditionally locate themselves is a cartographer's convention.[21] The U.S. foreign policy with which this concept is associated, the Monroe Doctrine, faces mainly toward Latin America and not upward toward Canada. The U.S. view encompasses an "inter-American system" of states, of which Canada long refrained from joining. In a marked departure, Canada finally joined the Organization of American States (OAS) in November 1989.[22] This will not wholly change Canada's geographical self-image. "Canada's hemisphere," the Canadian political geographer Andrew Burghardt has pointed out, "is not a circle but an ellipse, foreshortened toward the south and north, extended toward the east and west." Canadians sometimes speak of living in a "Northern Hemisphere."[23]

Following the Second World War the U.S. government expressed interest in having Canada join the inter-American defense scheme that it was then organizing. At the military level, an Inter-American Defense Board already existed that could perform strategic planning for such an organization.[24] In May 1946, President Truman sent Congress a bill titled "The Inter-American Military Cooperation Act." As he pointed out, "The collaboration authorized by the bill could be extended also to Canada, whose cooperation with the United States in matters affecting their common defense is of particular importance."[25] In truth, however, the involvement of Canada in Latin American security matters was not at all urgent at that time. Even Canada's cooperation with the United States in arranging for the defense of the North American continent was not considered crucial then.[26]

Canadian responses to these American overtures regarding participation in a Pan-American system were polite, but basically negative. When the possibility of participation in the Rio de Janeiro Conference on hemispheric defense came before the cabinet in Ottawa in April 1947, Lester Pearson, undersecretary in the Department of External Affairs, advised against it, arguing that Canadian defense was more concerned with the Northern Hemisphere. Moreover, he pointed out, it would be difficult "to formalize participation in United States Inter-American Defence Arrangements while we have been unwilling to formalize those within the Commonwealth."[27] The argument, reflecting Canada's common-law heritage and its resistance to British efforts to centralize imperial defense, may have seemed somewhat tendentious, but it had the weight of Canadian political tradition behind it.

Thus Canada did not sign the Inter-American Treaty of Reciprocal Assistance, also called the Rio Treaty. It refrained as well from participating in the conference at Bogotá, Colombia, in 1948 that established the Organization of American States. This was in part because the OAS was to be a voting organization and would be dominated, politically, by a Latin American majority. It refused also because, if the facts be stated frankly, most of South America—beyond the English- and French-speaking islands of the Caribbean—was at that time beyond the ken of most Canadians. While a few officials in Ottawa imagined that Canada usefully might play a mediating, moderating role within an inter-American system, helping Latin American countries to counterbalance the Colossus of the North, most sensed wisely that, as Holmes expressed it, it was "in the Canadian national interest to have as few rows as possible with the United States administration and Congress."[28]

Canadians also had, curiously, a somewhat foreshortened picture of the northernmost reaches of the continent, the "undefended roof" of North America, as some referred to it. While U.S. strategists, using the North Pole-centered maps that came into fashion toward the end of the Second World War, increasingly became preoccupied with the possible exchange of air assaults with the Soviet Union across the world's top, Canada's "arcticians," mostly explorers and scientists, understandably wished to minimize that possibility.[29] Canadians realized, however, that their country possessed an increasingly important "Arctic frontier," which was not only largely unexploited but also largely unprotected.

This vast expanse of northern Canada seemed to the American military, then taking steps to expand its own wartime facilities in Alaska and in Danish-controlled Greenland, to be a dangerously wide "gap" in the North American continent's defenses.[30] Urged by Washington either to close this gap themselves or to enlist U.S. help in doing it, Canadian officials, concerned by the implied threat to their sovereignty, alert to the danger of giving provocation to the Russians, and unconvinced of the military need for Arctic defense, resisted this American pressure. Lester Pearson, in an article in *Foreign Affairs*, sharply stated that his country did not "relish the necessity of digging, or having dug for her, any Maginot Line in her Arctic ice."[31]

Partly to deflect, or at least to diffuse, this disconcerting American scrutiny of positions in its high north, the government in Ottawa sought a wider, multilateral context for continental defense cooperation. Initially, it was hoped, the United Nations organization might provide a suitable setting. When the Canadian section of the bilateral U.S.-Canadian PJBD produced plans for a revision of ABC-22, Pearson and Arnold Heeney, secretary of the Privy Council, objected that this joint defense plan had not been part of the UN planning for international security. Their view was that the multilateral framework had priority and that any bilateral plans that might be necessary should be fitted into it. Ideally, as some Canadian diplomats and politicians apparently thought, the UN system of security would obviate the need for any bilateral defense measures with the United States.[32]

Within official Canadian decision-making circles, there understandably was some division over such important matters. The officials' differences over technical issues concerning the formality, size, and scope of international cooperation can be summed up in two general words: "federative" and "functional." The former point of view was best represented by the philosophy of Pearson's second-in-command at Ottawa, Escott Reid. So federationist was Reid in his thinking about transatlantic security that he even believed that there should be a North Atlantic parliament, similar to the UN General Assembly. Within such a body, a two-thirds majority would adopt conventions that, when ratified by two thirds of the member governments, would be binding upon them.[33] The more realistic, functionalist perspective was most clearly exemplified by the diplomatic approach of the Canadian ambassador in Washington, Hume Wrong. Functionalism stressed the importance of cooperating in areas in which cooperation was possible and productive. Wrong, a practical man, conditioned his recommendations to Ottawa according to his assessment of what kinds of international arrangements the U.S. Congress would, and would not, accept. During the talks regarding formation of a North Atlantic system of security, Wrong at one point rebukingly emphasized to Reid: "We are creating not a federation but an alliance."[34]

Canada was a primary participant in the negotiation of the North Atlantic Treaty from the very first stage of deliberation, the phase of the "United States-United Kingdom-Canada security conversations" held secretly at the Pentagon in March 1948.[35] The inclusion of Canada in these discussions was in a sense an outgrowth of the tripartite deliberations initiated by Field Marshal Bernard Montgomery following the war. As chief of the Imperial General Staff, Montgomery had visited Canada and the United States in 1946 and secured consent at the highest level in both North American nations for the commencement of American-British-Canadian consultations regarding future weapons standardization, operation procedures, and even war planning. As Montgomery visualized his unexpected diplomatic achievement, it ensured "the continued functioning of the machinery of the Combined Chiefs of Staff." It would bring about, he hoped, "the unification of the defence policy and plans of the British Empire and the United States *before* another war."[36] The Canadians no doubt saw this arrangement in more strictly triangular terms.

From the beginning of the transatlantic security conversations of 1948, the conception that governed Canadian diplomacy was that of a broad

Atlantic community, as distinct from a one-way, military-focused, aid-to-Europe scheme. The importance of this distinction is that, in the former arrangement, Canada would be more or less the equal of most other partners, all around the Atlantic. In the latter, Canada would be no more than the junior partner of the United States. Pearson, then Canada's secretary of state for external affairs, envisioned a *"North Atlantic Regional System for security and progress"* within whose framework *"the decisions which affect all will be taken by all."*[37] In this arrangement one clearly can see his, and Reid's, "community" ideal. The vehicle for the Canadian vision was Article 2 (the "Canadian" article) of the proposed North Atlantic treaty. This provision encouraged cooperation in nondefense fields, including economic collaboration, to make an Atlantic pact "more than a military alliance."[38]

The main rival to this Canadian conception, other than the Monroe Doctrine-modeled idea of a unilateral guarantee by the United States of Europe's security, was the "two-pillar" image of a transatlantic alliance. Also later known as the "dumbbell" idea (considered by some of its critics an indication of its intellectual worth as well as its notional shape), the two-pillar scheme featured an alliance between two strong entities at opposite sides of the Atlantic.[39] This concept was favored by Americans who were nostalgic for the days of isolation and who believed that hemispheric leadership was the proper vocation for the United States. It also was supported by Americans, more ideologically internationalist and integrationist, who wished to give encouragement to those Europeans, notably the French economic planner Jean Monnet, who dreamed of a "United States of Europe."[40]

This pro-European reasoning had such strong idealistic appeal that it was difficult for Canadians to oppose it. But they tried to do so nonetheless, believing that they had to in order to preserve a triangular or even more complicated multiangular transatlantic system that would keep a balance in North America. Pearson has confessed that an "Atlantic alliance composed of two pillars, groups, or poles—one European, one North American—would have created an unenviable position for Canada in our relations with the United States."[41] Reid further explains, putting the issue even more starkly: "If ever the Atlantic alliance became a partnership between the United States of America and a United States of western Europe or of Europe, Canada might have to choose between applying for membership in one of the federations or withdrawing from the alliance."[42]

This Canadian insistence on a truly collective North Atlantic treaty, with the principle of reciprocity built into it, was a major factor in making the language of Atlanticism that of multilateralism, rather than bilateralism or unilateralism. Article 5 of the North Atlantic Treaty, which eventually was signed in Washington on 4 April 1949, proclaims the agreement of all the parties that "an armed attack against one or more of them in Europe or North America shall be considered an attack against them all."[43] No differentiation is made between the continents, and the commitments made by each ally to the others are fully mutual. The ten original European members, in theory, were as obliged to respond to aggression against Alaska or the Yukon territory as the two North American members were pledged to help militarily if Sicily, Bavaria, or Finnmark were assaulted.

The practical reality of the situation was different. In the actual organization of the North Atlantic Treaty alliance structure authorized by Article 9, the distance between North America and Western Europe, perhaps inevitably, reemerged. Five regional planning groups were formed. One of these was the Canada-United States Regional Planning Group (CUSRPG), to be headquartered in Arlington, Virginia. This group the Canadians were glad to join, partly as it offered an alternative to the existing military relationships between Canada and the United States. These bilateral arrangements, it was hoped, would be fitted into a multilateral context, reestablished on a multilateral basis, or perhaps even entirely replaced by multilateral structures.

Canadian officials were more ambivalent, however, about participating in the West European planning group, which the United States joined. Canadians were inclined to think that some of the alliance's other bodies, such as the Military Supply Board, appropriately might be placed in North America. They were persuaded by U.S. officials, however, that the Military Supply Board should be located in Europe, so that the Europeans would feel a greater weight of responsibility for their own future needs.

These decisions left the United States and Canada almost completely free to work out their own military-supply arrangements directly between themselves. As the PJBD had preceded NATO, it was incumbent upon the planners to decide how to relate it to that structure. Whereas Canada's diplomats and politicians tended to find the multilateral cover of NATO attractive, the Canadian military, in contrast, was inclined to share the U.S. military's distaste for overseas "interference."[44]

In 1946 a Canadian-U.S. Military Cooperation Committee (MCC) was established under the wing of the PJBD to consider the military factors in revising the wartime defense plan.[45] The Canadian Chiefs of Staff in 1949 considered making this entity the Regional Planning Group under NATO. The American Joint Chiefs strongly objected to such a transformation, arguing that the PJBD system was permanent, whereas the NATO agreement had been established only on a twenty-year basis. Moreover, the NATO treaty centered on the Atlantic, whereas the Joint Board was concerned with security on the Pacific side of the continent as well. Territorial and coastal defenses were regarded as national matters, outside the scope of NATO entirely.[46]

Air defense already had been accepted as a joint matter; there were "no boundaries upstairs."[47] The Canadians considered air defense a possible NATO activity within the CUSRPG. American officials were extremely sensitive about this subject, however. They did not want the European NATO partners to insist on having air-defense facilities on the scale of what they were planning for North America. Resources were limited, and the Pentagon did not want to rearm Europe at the expense of U.S. defense stocks. They were concerned, furthermore, about the reliability of the Europeans as sharers of classified technical and other information, and they wanted the Europeans to have nothing to do with the new Strategic Air Command (SAC), the strategic retaliatory force.

The Canadian military had little choice but to concur. Despite multilateralist arguments from External Affairs for greater NATO involvement in North American defense, it was decided finally to leave continental defense pretty much as it was, a matter of North American interest and responsibility. No further effort was made to integrate the PJBD into NATO. The CUSRPG, whose membership was virtually identical with that of the MCC (which in effect did its work), was reduced to making periodic vague reports to NATO about North American defense arrangements. NATO seemed to be only for Europe.[48]

To the most multilaterally minded statesmen of Canada, the confirmation of this pattern in the early 1950s was a profound disappointment. In the mind of Pearson, NATO was not a one-continent arrangement. Its European members should accept responsibility, and not only in principle, for the security of North America, just as Canadians and Americans were contributing, directly and materially, to the security of Europe. In particular, he regarded the future defense of the North American Arctic, owing to the rise of the prospect of atomic war, as a matter of alliancewide concern. He favored the involvement of European troops in North American defense, to make the North American sector "an integral part of the North Atlantic defence structure." Canadian forces sometimes took part in military exercises in northern Norway; so, too, should Norwegian contingents operate "in our Arctic."

Nonetheless, "nothing effective could be done," Pearson recognized then and in retrospect. He lamented that "the Americans would have none of this concept which, they thought, would interfere with their own control. Our own service people also, I suspect, preferred bilateral dealings and arrangements with Washington." Canadians, having twice fought on European soil in world wars, had become accustomed to "serving overseas" in Europe. Reciprocally, "the idea that even token European contingents might share the responsibility of our continental defence was a novelty unworthy of serious consideration." To the European allies, and to most Americans and probably even most Canadians, North America remained a continent apart. "Thus, the Canada-United States regional group," Pearson stated with regret, "was merely a formal part of the North Atlantic Treaty defence structure."[49]

The Bomber Threat, SAC, and NORAD

The structure of North American defense thus became continentally solidified. The explosion of a Soviet atomic bomb in August 1949, fully two years ahead of most Western expectations, raised the specter of a devastating attack on North America, as well as on U.S. and Canadian forward positions in Europe. The most acute danger, however, still was considered to be some time away, as the Soviet Union had not yet developed an effective air-delivery capability. An important report of 14 April 1950 to the National Security Council, NSC-68, estimated that "within the next four years, the U.S.S.R. will attain the capability of seriously damaging vital centers of the United States." Although it was insecure, the North American position nonetheless was considered safer than many base areas overseas. NSC-68 raised the question, in particular, of "whether Britain with its present inadequate air defense could be relied upon as an advance base from which a major portion of the U.S. attack could be launched."[50]

When, on 25 June 1950, war broke out in Korea, American and Canadian anxieties greatly increased. The Communist challenge to the balance of power in Asia (and possibly Europe), and also to the general system of collective security, caused them to pay increased attention to remedying their own physical exposure. Even as they enlisted soldiers for the UN force in Korea and, as a major precaution, added new divisions to the NATO shield in Germany, they had to respond to the primary security imperative of continental defense.[51] The technological problems inherent in covering such a vast space as North America were formidable, however. Moreover, there was little expert agreement on how it should best be done, or to what extent. The doctrinal preference on the part of all three branches of the two countries' military establishments—land, sea, and air—was for taking the offensive rather than for holding defensive positions. Continental defense was a vital but distinctly secondary mission.[52]

It nonetheless was believed by North American strategists, Canadian no less than American, that the old mobilization system, which relied on reserves and auxiliaries rather than on fully trained and equipped "forces in being," was outmoded. If nuclear weapons were going to be available at the outset of a conflict, recalled General Charles Foulkes, chairman of the Canadian Chiefs of Staff Committee, "the defensive forces must be on the spot, trained and ready to fight."[53]

The final result of these several factors—the impending bomb threat direct from the Soviet north, the need to withdraw some U.S. Strategic Air Force aircraft from vulnerable bases overseas, and the increase in international political tension caused by the outbreak of the Korean War— was a crash program in the United States and Canada to provide North America with an effective air defense network. Much of the technical thinking behind this emergency effort was carried out by the Lincoln Laboratory at the Massachusetts Institute of Technology. The undertaking, initiated in 1951, was conceived, in the words of U.S. Air Force Secretary Thomas Finletter, as the "Manhattan Project of air defense."[54]

In part because of the continuing improbability of guaranteeing destruction of a sufficiently high percentage of incoming Soviet planes, North American defense emphasized warning as much as it did defense with fighter aircraft. Air defense was indispensable to the mission of strategic deterrence. This was the NATO-approved but operationally almost independent function of the SAC, headquartered since 1948 at Offutt Air Force Base near Omaha, Nebraska.

Technical advances in aircraft, combined with the new vulnerability of bases overseas, required that this strategic force be located mainly within the continental United States. When SAC was founded after the war its mainstay was the B-29 and, later, its modification, the B-50. Subsequently, SAC acquired the huge eight-engine B-36, and then the six-jet B-47. As the SAC commander, General Curtis E. LeMay, has explained, the development of air-refueling techniques gave the B-47 a wide range, but initially it was necessary to use overseas bases for it to reach targets in the Soviet Union. These were gradually withdrawn to continental North America. With the production of the eight-jet B-52, LeMay recalls, "propeller-driven bombers were dropped from the inventory and SAC became an all-jet nuclear force capable of world-wide attacks."[55]

To safeguard this formidable striking force, giving it adequate warning time to respond, a series of radar fences was extended across the North American continent. The first was the Pinetree line in southern Canada, intended to cover the most likely enemy approaches between Labrador and the Great Lakes. Next came the McGill, or mid-Canada line, which was constructed at the Canadian government's expense. The U.S. government took principal responsibility for designing the more sophisticated distant early warning (DEW) line, which stretched high across northern Canada to Alaska and Greenland. During the same period, in the mid-1950s, the U.S. Air Force extended the continent's warning system outward into the Pacific through the Aleutians. The U.S. Navy brought the system as far as Midway in the Pacific and also extended the monitoring line in the northern Atlantic. Pacific and Atlantic Barrier commands were organized to manage these facilities.[56]

Although it was a rather piecemeal and patchwork process, this U.S.-Canadian effort at aerial offense and defense nonetheless secured almost the entire free-world sector of the Northern Hemisphere. It would be hard to imagine a strictly Europe-based alliance doing more. The culmination of the effort was the formal establishment in May 1958 of the North American Defense Command (NORAD), located under Cheyenne Mountain near Colorado Springs, Colorado. This unique arrangement, a joint U.S.-Canadian undertaking, provided for continental air surveillance and coordinated air defense action for the northern part of the continent. Unlike the old PJBD, NORAD is not bicameral, with separate U.S. and Canadian sections. It is a unitary entity, with a single headquarters. Although the NORAD commander so far has been an American officer, the deputy commander, consequently a Canadian, can activate, under certain circumstances, and direct U.S. as well as Canadian air defense forces. No "comparably integrated military organization" exists anywhere, as Melvin A. Conant has noted.[57]

Although the establishment of NORAD aroused some controversy at the time, especially in Canada, it was essentially a technical and institutional working-out of a conceptual commitment to North American security made by the two countries during and just after World War II. As General Foulkes has stressed, "The decision for joint air defence was taken in 1946 not 1958, as some of the critics claim when discussing NORAD."[58] Concluded during the Progressive Conservative government of John Diefenbaker (1957-1963), NORAD was nonetheless an authentic outgrowth of the Liberal period of government. The controversy, such as it was, was not mainly partisan.

The wider international issue, still not wholly resolved, was the broader question of the relationship between NORAD and the Atlantic commitment, that is, NATO. Was NORAD a part of NATO? Could Canada influence the military strategy and behavior of the United States bilaterally, within NORAD, as well as it could have done multilaterally? There is also the Pearsonian question of whether the European members of NATO can and should assume an interest in the defense of North America, if only by releasing Canada from some of its financially burdensome commitment to keep troops in Europe after the war. As Pearson said to U.S. Secretary of State John Foster Dulles, Canada was anxious to show that the North American surveillance systems were "an important part of NATO defence, because without such effective early warning arrangements the retaliatory power of the United States might be destroyed and, in present circumstances, this would be as fatal for Europe as for America."[59]

No European government or even the United States government was willing to credit fully Canada's indirect commitment to the defense of Europe. Its role in NORAD did not even qualify as its contribution to the

CUSRPG, the regional planning group. NATO had no direct connection to the CUSRPG. This did not deter Prime Minister Diefenbaker, however, from claiming such a connection. NORAD, he told the Canadian House of Commons, was an "arrangement within the Canada-United States planning group" and "a further step in achieving the agreed NATO objectives for the CUSRPG." The U.S. military, which was opposed to establishing a NATO command for North America, rejected any such notion, and would allow the CUSRPG to transmit only very general information to NATO about North American air defenses. Diefenbaker, not surrendering the point completely, finally said to the House of Commons: "Without discussing the connection between NORAD and NATO I wish to say that I believe, whether it is part of NATO or not, it does strengthen NATO, which is all that matters."[60]

Had NORAD been institutionally integrated into NATO, as some Canadians had proposed at the time of the very first discussion of a North American air defense system, it might have proved far more beneficial politically and diplomatically for the government of Canada. "Our contribution to North American defence has been undertaken largely for political reasons," the Canadian historian and foreign affairs commentator, James Eayrs, has written; it has had "less to do with Canadian-Soviet relations than with Canadian-American relations."[61] It also has had a great deal to do with Canadian security relations with Europe, but Europeans did not seem to take much notice. They should have done so.

A further benefit of a formal linking of NORAD and NATO in 1956–1958 might have been a substantial easing of Canada's conscience about its participation in decisions regarding nuclear weapons. "The Canadian willingness to accept these weapons into their forces assigned to NATO," as Melvin Conant has speculated, "might well have been extended automatically to embrace its defense forces stationed in North America."[62] Without such an automatic conforming of Canadian policies in the American and European hemispheres, a double standard emerged: Canadian forces would use nuclear weapons abroad, but not at home.[63]

The Diefenbaker government was brought down over the nuclear weapons issue in 1963. Wishing to have it both ways, he and his colleagues had acquired weapons meant for atomic arming—the CF-101B *Voodoo* interceptor, the *Bomarc* antiaircraft missile, the *Honest John* close-support rocket, and the CF-104G *Starfighter*—but had not yet loaded them. Diefenbaker's Liberal successor, Lester Pearson, agreed to honor the Progressive Conservative government's commitments to equip Canada's continental air defense forces for nuclear battle by allowing them to carry U.S. atomic weapons. But he also wanted to renegotiate the Conservative agreement with the United States. This ambivalent sense of national obligation did not last, however, and Canada's nuclear employment arrangements, in both the American and European theaters, have since been dropped.[64]

Sputnik, the Third Option, and Star Wars

Just as the American and Canadian ideas about organizing their common defense seemed to be solidifying by the late 1950s, a number of developments occurred that began to dissolve them. On 4 October 1957 the Soviet Union launched an orbital satellite, *Sputnik*, thereby demonstrating its probable technical ability to shoot nuclear weapons intercontinentally as well. Here again, General Foulkes reflects, Moscow made a technological breakthrough—the ballistic missile—considerably earlier than had been predicted. Consternation reigned in North American defense circles. "It reduced the warning time from four or five hours to fifteen or twenty minutes and created a defence problem which seemed to defy solution," wrote Foulkes. "I submit that there is no direct defence for Canada no matter how much we are prepared to spend."[65]

General LeMay, too, was dismayed. Of distant French-Canadian heritage, he had flown with Canadians since early in his career.[66] Countless practice contests between SAC and NORAD, with Canada's air force participating, had sharpened "both our offensive and defensive swords" to near perfection, he recalled a decade later with some pride, and not a little hyperbole. "Not only did we feel secure at home from aerial attack, but we were convinced that we could destroy the entire military capacity of the Soviet Union without losing a man to their defenses. But then Soviets outflanked our vast air defense system with thermonuclear ballistic missiles. We had no defense for these weapons. *We still do not.*"[67]

The effect of this grim realization on American and Canadian military planners was to require them to concentrate almost exclusively on strategic deterrence. The vulnerability of North America, like that of other regions in the larger NATO treaty area, made emphasis on defense, except against strictly local aggression, seem pointless. Primary reliance would have to be placed on the psychology of the Soviet Union's leaders, who, it was hoped, would recognize and believe the Western willingness and ability to use nuclear weapons.

The Cuban missile crisis of October 1962 put the deterrence theory of security to a severe test. On 22 October, President John F. Kennedy announced publicly that offensive missile sites were being prepared in Cuba. These appeared to be of two different types, one for medium-range ballistic missiles and the other for intermediate-range weapons. The latter category of sites, not yet completed, appeared to be designed for weapons "capable of striking most of the major cities in the Western Hemisphere, ranging as far north as Hudson Bay," Kennedy said. He declared that it would be the policy of the United States to regard "any nuclear attack launched from Cuba against any nation in the Western Hemisphere as an attack by the Soviet Union on the United States, requiring a full retaliatory response upon the Soviet Union."[68]

Simultaneously, the forces of NORAD were put by presidential order on the third rung of the five-rung ladder of alert conditions (Defcon 3). The Canadian government endorsed this action two days later, 24 October, by which time the purpose of the action largely had been achieved. In the meantime, however, Minister of National Defence Douglas Harkness had approved, without the knowledge of Prime Minister Diefenbaker, the raising of portions of the Royal Canadian forces, including those in NORAD, to an alert condition comparable to that of American forces. Diefenbaker had demurred, in order to consult the cabinet and also the British government. Perhaps he sensed that precautionary measures were being taken without his express permission. "Not much escaped the Diefenbaker antennae," recalled a close associate.[69]

Although these responsive steps showed, arguably, that Canadian-U.S. defense coordination succeeded rather than failed during a time of crisis, there were Canadians who protested against the unilateral moves and peremptory demands of the U.S. president and other American officials. NORAD's uniquely integrated character meant that Kennedy's alert order implicated Canadian forces. "Yet Canada was consulted no earlier and no more fully than the European allies," the Canadian foreign affairs analyst Peter Dobell has pointed out.[70]

Canadians also differed with Americans over the issue of Vietnam, which further undermined the North American strategic consensus. Since the Geneva agreement of 1954, representatives from the Canadian government together with Polish and Indian officials had been trying, thanklessly, to maintain some semblance of peace in Southeast Asia as members of the International Commission for Supervision and Control (ICSC) for Vietnam.[71] Inevitably, this formal responsibility produced friction with the U.S. military, which increasingly became committed to ever-more-massive engagement on the side of the South Vietnamese government. The Canadian government also met with frustration in trying to interest the European NATO allies in peacemaking in Vietnam. Not all Canadians were unsympathetic with American purposes, of course, but many were. NORAD and even NATO became targets of their antiwar criticism. The apparent receptiveness of the Canadian people to American war protesters and draft dodgers generated considerable resentment in U.S. official circles. Speeches by Prime Minister Pearson and External Affairs Minister Paul Martin calling for a bombing halt increased American annoyance.[72]

When, at the very height of the American involvement in Vietnam, in 1968, the new Liberal party leader, Pierre Elliott Trudeau, came to power in Canada, U.S.-Canadian security relations could have taken a serious turn for the worse. Trudeau was not formed by the experience of World War II, in which he did not serve. He was skeptical of military solutions. His intellectualized approach to policymaking, and his declared need for a reassessment of Canada's world roles, implied a sharp reduction in Canada's international commitments, including even the distinctive peacemaking mission in which Canadian forces had developed such expertise and earned such regard. His Liberal predecessor, Lester Pearson, had won the Nobel Peace Prize for organizing the UN Emergency Force (UNEF) that had helped to resolve the Suez debacle in 1956. Many Canadians felt that the prize had been awarded to them.[73]

The continuing Canadian postwar commitment of troops to Western Europe also would be cut back under Trudeau. On 3 April 1969 his office announced that Canada, in consultation with its NATO allies, would "take early steps to bring about a planned and phased reduction of the size of the Canadian forces in Europe," ultimately, a 50 percent reduction (from 10,000 to 5,000). This was a compromise between the "stand-pat" position of some officials in the Departments of External Affairs and Defence and the recommendation of his closest adviser, Ivan Head, that there be no Canadian forces in Europe at all. The Trudeau government made no significant cuts, however, in the forces dedicated to NORAD, which had been the object of much of the internal criticism of Canada's military policy. The 3 April statement seemed to accord the highest priorities to home defense and the defense of North America. "We shall maintain appropriate defence forces," it said, "which will be designed to undertake the following roles: (a) the surveillance of our own territory and coast lines, i.e., the protection of our sovereignty; (b) the defence of North America in cooperation with United States forces; (c) the fulfillment of such NATO commitments as may be agreed upon; and (d) the performance of such international peacekeeping roles as we may from time to time assume."[74] He perhaps judged the function of North American defense to be related, in a direct and immediate way, to the Canadian national interest.

Somewhat inconsistently his government, in 1972, in order to counteract "the continental pull" of the United States, sought to diversify Canada's international relationships by extending them extracontinentally. This may be seen as a variation of traditional Canadian balance-of-power thinking, expanded from an Atlantic to a global scale. Rejecting the two policy choices of, first, a continuation of "more or less our present relationship" with the United States and, second, a move toward "closer integration" with it, the Trudeau cabinet selected the so-called Third Option: promotion of new connections. These would be with the major countries of

Western Europe, East Asia, and other regions, including Latin America. By reducing the vulnerability of the Canadian economy to possible U.S. policy shifts, which were likely to be disruptive because of the dependence of Canada on American capital and markets, this strategy of wide international diversification was expected to strengthen Canada's sovereign independence and national identity.[75] When the Federal Republic of Germany was approached with a Canadian request for a "contractual link" with the European Community, Chancellor Helmut Schmidt is alleged to have told Prime Minister Trudeau bluntly: "No tanks, no trade."[76] For political as well as for basic economic reasons, the Third Option amounted to very little.

The 1984 return to power of a Progressive Conservative government, under Brian Mulroney, put back in place a number of the neglected or rejected elements of Canadian national security policy. Prominent among these intended restorations, which the Trudeau government itself finally had begun to make, was a strengthening of the Canadian military presence on the central front in Europe (to 7,500 troops). The Canadian Mechanized Brigade and Air Group in southern Germany were scheduled for major improvement. Eventually, as a result of a decision to withdraw from a logistically questionable commitment of a Canadian Air-Sea Transportable (CAST) Brigade Group and two Rapid Reinforcement fighter squadrons to Norway in crisis situations, additional troops and equipment were made available for an enlarged Canadian force, of division size, in southern Germany. A previous decision to commit a battalion group to the Allied Command Europe Mobile Force, which would be available for use in NATO's northern region in emergencies, was confirmed.

The political as well as the purely military purpose of this consolidated commitment of Canada's forces to Europe, emphasizing its central region, was made clear in a government white paper, *Challenge and Commitment: A Defence Policy for Canada*: "The presence of Canadian armed forces in Western Europe contributes directly to the defence of Canada, and, what is more, ensures that we will have a say in how key security issues are decided."[77] The paper made clear the Conservative government's intention to reinforce the idea that Canada would seek its security within the NATO structure.[78]

Of even greater relevance to the direct defense of Canada was cooperation with the United States in shielding the North American continent. At the "Shamrock Summit" with President Ronald Reagan in Quebec City on 17 March 1984, Prime Minister Mulroney joined in announcing a U.S.-Canadian agreement on the modernization of the North American air defense system. A new radar line, the north warning system (NWS), would be built in the Canadian north as a replacement for the nearly thirty-year-old, and outmoded, DEW line. NWS would consist of a fence of long- and short-range radars across the Canadian Arctic at approximately the 70th parallel, supplemented by over-the-horizon backscatter (OTH-B) radars along the eastern and western coasts of Canada and the United States, and also a series of dispersed bases for airborne warning and control system (AWACS) aircraft. The new radar in the high north, unlike the old one, would be partly paid for and wholly operated by Canadians.[79]

This increased financial commitment reflected a heightened concern among the Canadian people about their nation's sovereignty in the Arctic zone, which was becoming the scene of increased petroleum-exploration activity and even seemingly more sinister movements, such as the transit through the Northwest Passage in August 1985 of the U.S. Coast Guard icebreaker *Polar Sea*. Submarine operations, conducted by the United States and possibly also by the Soviet Union, caused anxiety as well. These concerns prompted the Canadian government, through an announcement to the House of Commons by External Affairs Minister Joe Clark on 10 September 1985, to declare the waters in question "internal" to Canada. "The policy of the Government," Clark said, "is to maintain the natural unity of the Canadian Arctic archipelago and to preserve Canada's sovereignty over land, sea and ice undiminished and undivided."[80]

Sovereignty requires surveillance. For that purpose, as well as for more basic, defense-related ones, the Mulroney government planned to build ten to twelve nuclear-powered submarines to endow the Canadian maritime forces with extended under-ice capability. Canada, as *Challenge and Commitment* emphasized, is a three-ocean country. Its coastlines touch Atlantic, Pacific, and Arctic waters. "In all three oceans, underwater surveillance is essential to monitor the activities of potentially hostile submarines," the paper explained. Through their "mere presence," nuclear-powered submarines could deny an opponent the use of Canada's sea areas, thoroughfares leading not only to Canada but also to the Atlantic and the Pacific. The paper ambitiously stated: "SSNs [nuclear-powered attack submarines] will complement aircraft, destroyers and frigates in a vivid demonstration of Canadian determination to meet challenges in all three oceans."[81]

The need for such surveillance and control arose partly from revolutionary developments in military technology, a factor that has driven defense requirements in North America perhaps more than in other regions of the NATO alliance. The geographical focus of the new technology transformed world strategic environment in the Arctic. As the Canadian white paper grimly recognized, "what was once a buffer could become a battleground."[82]

Even more apocalyptic was the U.S. program for "Star Wars" or, more formally, the Strategic Defense Initiative (SDI), which promised in theory to project a shield over the continent's upper zone, General LeMay's vertical flank. Dramatically announced by President Reagan on 23 March 1983, this ambitious enterprise, which followed the renaming in 1981 of NORAD as the North American Aerospace Defense Command, caused some people in Canada to fear "annihilation without representation." Their fear was just the opposite of that of some Europeans at the time, namely, that a defensive umbrella over North America might allow U.S. decision makers to imagine their country invulnerable again and accordingly to "decouple" the strategic retaliatory commitment to Europe. Canadians felt all too closely "coupled," fancying that U.S. strategists might think it feasible to use their futuristic defensive shield as a barrier behind which to launch a preemptive strike against the Soviet Union. The issue for a time produced almost as much controversy in Canada as did the installation of intermediate-range nuclear forces (INF) in Europe in the early 1980s. The debate there over association with SDI has been called "Canada's INF."[83]

The Canadian submarine program and, quite possibly, SDI are today defunct, owing to huge costs, technical problems, and, above all, the conceivable end of the Cold War with the Soviet Union itself.[84] To be sure, the technological realities and strategic necessities of possible warfare over the North American continent have not fundamentally changed, but the economic, political, and psychological conditions of continental defense have altered profoundly. Nonetheless, if and as East-West tensions ebb further, the likelihood is that the relative emphasis in both countries on continental security concerns will increase. The strategic choices that the United States and Canada have had to make among 1) providing for North American defense, 2) sharing in the maintenance of a European balance of power, and 3) contributing to UN collective security efforts may remain, but the outcome may be obvious. As Douglas Bland and John Young of Queen's University suggest, "All indicators point to a closer Continental functionalism whatever the eventual structural overlay. While it has been a tenet of Canada's postwar security policy that a 'dumbbell' or two-pillared Alliance configuration would be inimical to Canadian interests, the dumbbell will likely have to suffice in coming years."[85]

What manifestly is needed today is a conceptual reintegration of the security interests of both North American NATO countries with those of Western Europe and the larger international community—a rejoining of continents comparable to that envisioned by the American and especially the Canadian founders of NATO. U.S. statesmen, preferring to act unilaterally and on a Western Hemisphere basis, generally have been able to secure their national military interests, and even those of the alliance, by means of an extended continental North American strategy, stretching out far over the Atlantic and also the Pacific. The wings of the American eagle have spread wide. Canadian officials, preferring to act multilaterally and on a vaguely Northern Hemisphere basis, have not felt equally secure in their achievement. The wings of the stately Canada goose often have been folded. Nonetheless, through alliance membership, rather than through the neutralism that some occasionally have considered a Canadian option, Canada, to the extent that its characteristic form of Atlanticist multilateralism has been pursued actively, has expanded its own horizons and also those of its North American partner. It has helped to teach the United States, naturally a solitary bird, to fly somewhat more in formation.

If Canadians had chosen not to participate jointly in the defense of North America within the North Atlantic Alliance framework, U.S. officials surely would have provided for the defense of the continent themselves. This would have put even greater pressure on Canada's independence and identity than the existing NATO-NORAD arrangement, however awkwardly it has developed. This is "the perplexing paradox" of a lesser power facing a neighboring superpower, as one commentator, Michael Tucker, has called it. In the case of Canada, "alliance commitments have been as much a source as a derogation from its sovereignty."[86]

What Canada has not yet succeeded in demonstrating is that a widening of the alliance space—opening up the defensive arrangements of the North American continent to direct participation by Western European allies— would secure its national interests even further. The geostrategic unity of the "Northern Rim," from the Barents Sea to the Bering Strait, in fact implies just such a need for greater Allied cooperation in defending Atlantic Alliance interests, economic as well as strategic, in the Arctic.

The international interests of the North American and West European members of NATO, and also of Japan, are even more interdependent now than they were when the North Atlantic Alliance was formed. The organization of the alliance and the strategic outlook of most of the allies, however, have not yet reflected that reality. NATO never has been what Lester Pearson considered a genuine two-continent alliance, a true security "community." During most of NATO's history, North America has been a continent apart. As its future unfolds, it may gradually become a continent joined.

Notes

1. William T. R. Fox, *A Continent Apart: The United States and Canada in World Politics* (Toronto: University of Toronto Press, 1985), 6.
2. Laurence Martin, *NATO and the Defense of the West: An Analysis of America's First Line of Defense* (New York: Holt, Rinehart, and Winston, 1985), 8, 12.
3. See, for example, ibid., 8.
4. Alan K. Henrikson, "The Creation of the North Atlantic Alliance," in John R. Reichart and Steven R. Sturm, eds., *American Defense Policy*, 5th ed. (Baltimore: Johns Hopkins Press, 1982), 296–322, esp. 300, 303–4, 310–11. The way in which

the Monroe Doctrine was reshaped rhetorically to cover the western part of Europe is shown by Lawrence S. Kaplan, "NATO and the Language of Isolationism," *South Atlantic Quarterly* 57, no. 2 (Spring 1958): 204–15.

5. For the Canadian government, especially, the motivation behind the formation of NATO had a strong economic component. This was expressed, albeit weakly, in Article 2 of the North Atlantic Treaty. See Robert Bothwell, Ian Drummond, and John English, *Canada since 1945: Power, Politics, and Provincialism*, rev. ed. (Toronto: University of Toronto Press, 1989), 119–21.

6. See Walter Lippmann, *U.S. Foreign Policy: Shield of the Republic* (Boston: Little, Brown, and Company, 1943), chap. 7, "The Atlantic Community," and Karl W. Deutsch et al., *Political Community and the North Atlantic Area: International Organization in the Light of Historical Experience* (Princeton: Princeton University Press, 1957), 5–7.

7. Colonel Stanley W. Dziuban, *Military Relations between the United States and Canada, 1939–1945* (Washington, DC: Office of the Chief of Military History, 1959), 3–4.

8. "Declaration by President Roosevelt and Prime Minister Mackenzie King regarding Co-operation in War Production, 20 April 1941," ibid., appendix D.

9. U.S.-Canadian cooperation in protecting the North American continent and its approaches is described in detail in ibid. and, somewhat more broadly, in Stetson Conn and Byron Fairchild, *The Western Hemisphere: The Framework of Hemisphere Defense* (Washington, DC: Office of the Chief of Military History, 1960), and Stetson Conn, Rose C. Engelman, and Byron Fairchild, *The Western Hemisphere: Guarding the United States and Its Outposts* (Washington, DC: Office of the Chief of Military History, 1964). Naval cooperation is discussed by Patrick Abbazia, *Mr. Roosevelt's Navy: The Private War of the U.S. Atlantic Fleet, 1939–1942* (Annapolis, MD: Naval Institute Press, 1975); Marc Milner, *North Atlantic Run: The Royal Canadian Navy and the Battle for the Convoys* (Toronto: University of Toronto Press, 1985); and idem, "Anglo-American Naval Co-operation in the Second World War, 1939–45," in John B. Hattendorf and Robert S. Jordan, eds., *Maritime Strategy and the Balance of Power: Britain and America in the Twentieth Century* (New York: St. Martin's Press, 1989), chap. 11. The influence of the United States on Newfoundland, where American base rights were obtained as a result of the U.S.-U.K. destroyer-bases deal of September 1940, is described in David MacKenzie, *Inside the North Atlantic Triangle: Canada and the Entrance of Newfoundland into Confederation, 1939–1949* (Toronto: University of Toronto Press, 1986).

10. Lippmann, *U.S. Foreign Policy*, 100–13; Carl Joachim Friedrich, *Foreign Policy in the Making: The Search for a New Balance of Power* (New York: W. W. Norton and Company, 1938); Nicholas John Spykman, *America's Strategy in World Politics: The United States and the Balance of Power* (New York: Harcourt, Brace and Company, 1942).

11. The implications of these developments for the territorial state are analyzed in John H. Herz, *International Politics in the Atomic Age* (New York: Columbia University Press, 1959). Many Canadian officials, including Lester Pearson, concluded that only international control of the atomic weapon henceforth could provide individual countries with security. See, for example, his memorandum, "On Atomic Warfare," 8 November 1945, in J. A. Munro and A. I. Inglis, "The Atomic Conference 1945 and the Pearson Memoirs," *International Journal* 29, no. 1 (Winter 1973–74): 90–109.

12. Manfred Jonas, *Isolationism in America, 1934–41* (Ithaca, NY: Cornell University Press, 1966), 121–29.

13. *Survival in the Air Age: A Report by the President's Air Policy Commission* (Washington, DC: Government Printing Office, 1948), 12; "Defence Discussions with the United States," memorandum from Under-Secretary of State for External Affairs to Prime Minister, 23 December 1946, *Documents relatifs aux relations extérieures du Canada/Documents on Canadian External Relations*, vol. 12, *1946*, 1723.

14. Samuel I. Rosenman, *Working with Roosevelt* (New York: Harper and Brothers, 1952), chap. 15, "Lend-Lease: Arsenal of Democracy, 1940–1941." The ambivalence of American military support for Britain before the U.S. entry into the war is well articulated in David Reynolds, *The Creation of the Anglo-American Alliance, 1937–41: A Study in Competitive Cooperation* (Chapel Hill: University of North Carolina Press, 1981).

15. Hajo Holborn, *The Political Collapse of Europe* (New York: Alfred A. Knopf, 1963); "The Balance of Europe," in Bonamy Dobrée, ed., *Alexander Pope's Collected Poems* (London: J. M. Dent and Sons, 1959), 387; Martin Wight, "The Balance of Power," chap. 7, in Herbert Butterfield and Martin Wight, eds., *Diplomatic Investigations* (Cambridge, MA: Harvard University Press, 1966).

16. John W. Holmes, *The Shaping of Peace: Canada and the Search for World Order, 1943–1957*, 2 vols. (Toronto: University of Toronto Press, 1979), 1:33–34, 181–83; Bothwell, Drummond, and English, *Canada since 1945*, chap. 6, "A Strategy for Economic Survival."

17. Holmes, *Shaping of Peace* 1:160.

18. John Bartlett Brebner, *North Atlantic Triangle: The Interplay of Canada, the United States, and Great Britain* (New Haven: Yale University Press, 1945).

19. Conn and Fairchild, *Framework of Hemisphere Defense*, 383–85.

20. *Canada Today/d'aujourd'hui* 9, no. 3 (1978): 1.

21. S. Whittemore Boggs, "This Hemisphere," U.S. Department of State *Bulletin* 12, no. 306 (May 1945): 845–50; Alan K. Henrikson, "The Map as an 'Idea': The Role of Cartographic Imagery during the Second World War," *The American Cartographer* 2, no. 1 (April 1975): 19–53.

22. Colin MacKenzie, "Democratic Principles Praised as Canada Formally Joins OAS," *Globe and Mail* (Toronto), 14 November 1989. The Canadian secretary of state for external affairs, Joe Clark, represented the move as "a decision to become a partner in this hemisphere." Canada had accepted permanent observer status at the OAS in 1972.

23. Andrew Burghardt, "Canada and the World," chap. 18 in John Warkentin, ed., *Canada: A Geographical Interpretation* (Toronto: Methuen, 1968), 571; H. Ian Macdonald, "Canada in Two Hemispheres," *Behind the Headlines* 23, no. 6 (July 1964), 2–4.

24. On the origins and development of inter-American defense cooperation, see John Child, *Unequal Alliance: The Inter-American Military System, 1938–1978* (Boulder, CO: Westview Press, 1980); and Alan K. Henrikson, "East-West Rivalry in Latin America: 'Between the Eagle and the Bear,' " in Robert W. Clawson, ed., *East-West Rivalry in the Third World: Security Issues and Regional Perspectives* (Wilmington, DE: Scholarly Resources, 1986).

25. Quoted in Holmes, *The Shaping of Peace* (Toronto: University of Toronto Press, 1982), 2:80.

26. A National Security Council document, for instance, placed Canada as no more than eighth, following Italy, on a list of countries ranked according to their "importance to our national security" and only sixteenth, after the Philippines, on a list of countries ordered according to their "importance to United States security and the urgency of their need in combination." "United States Assistance to Other

Countries from the Standpoint of National Security," JCS 1769/1, 29 April 1947, in Thomas Etzold and John Lewis Gaddis, eds., *Containment: Documents on American Policy and Strategy, 1945–1950* (New York: Columbia University Press, 1978), 71–83. Joseph Jockel correctly notes the "sharp differences" in U.S. and Canadian accounts of planning for continental defense in the early Cold War period: U.S. military writers stress "the sanguine view" of the direct Soviet air threat until 1948 or even later, and Canadian writers recall "pushy U.S. airmen" being intent on securing the Canadian Arctic as early as 1945. Joseph T. Jockel, *No Boundaries Upstairs: Canada, the United States, and the Origins of North American Air Defence, 1945–1958* (Vancouver: University of British Columbia Press, 1987), ix.

27. Quoted in Holmes, *Shaping of Peace* 2:81.

28. Ibid., 288.

29. Henrikson, "The Map as an 'Idea.' "

30. Acting Secretary of State Dean Acheson wrote President Truman on 1 October 1946 that "the planning and application of joint defense measures remains the most active of our current relations with Canada. Our military authorities are naturally insistent on closing the gap between Alaska and Greenland." Quoted in Jockel, *No Boundaries Upstairs*, 22.

31. L. B. Pearson, "Canada Looks 'Down North,' " *Foreign Affairs* 24, no. 4 (July 1946): 638–47. Canada then still was talking with the Soviet Union about postwar international cooperation regarding the Arctic area.

32. Holmes, *Shaping of Peace* 1:173.

33. Escott Reid, *Time of Fear and Hope: The Making of the North Atlantic Treaty* (Toronto: McClelland and Stewart, 1977), 220–23.

34. Holmes, *Shaping of Peace* 2:113.

35. The four stages of intergovernmental discussions are well described in Reid, *Time of Fear and Hope*, 45–49.

36. *The Memoirs of Field-Marshal the Viscount Montgomery of Alamein* (New York: Signet, 1958), 393–98; General Charles Foulkes, "Canadian Defence Policy in a Nuclear Age," *Behind the Headlines* 21, no. 1 (May 1961): 2–3.

37. John A. Munro and Alex I. Inglis, eds., *Mike: The Memoirs of The Right Honourable Lester B. Pearson* (New York: Quadrangle, 1973), vol. 2, *1948–1957*, 53 (emphasis in original).

38. Reid, *Time of Fear and Hope*, chap. 11, "More Than a Military Alliance."

39. Ibid., 129–30.

40. George W. Ball, *The Past Has Another Pattern: Memoirs* (New York: W. W. Norton, 1982), chap. 6, "Jean Monnet"; Merry and Serge Bromberger, *Jean Monnet and the United States of Europe*, trans. Elaine P. Halperin (New York: Coward-McCann, 1968).

41. Munro and Inglis, eds., *Mike*, 51.

42. Reid, *Time of Fear and Hope*, 132.

43. *The North Atlantic Treaty Organization: Facts and Figures* (Brussels: NATO Information Service, 1984), 264–66.

44. Holmes, *Shaping of Peace* 2:278.

45. The senior U.S. Army member of the PJBD, General Guy Henry, initiated a proposal for CANUSA—the Canada-United States of American Chiefs of Staff. This ambitious scheme alarmed the Canadian government and also the U.S. Joint Chiefs of Staff, for a CANUSA might have set a precedent for a comparable undertaking with every one of America's allies. Nothing came of the idea. Jockel, *No Boundaries Upstairs*, 14–17.

46. Holmes, *Shaping of Peace* 2:278.

47. Foulkes, "Canadian Defence Policy," 2.

48. Holmes, *Shaping of Peace* 2:278, 280; Jockel, *No Boundaries Upstairs*, 96–97.

49. Munro and Inglis, eds., *Mike*, 84.

50. "NSC-68, A Report to the National Security Council, 14 April 1950," *Naval War College Review* (May-June 1975): 81–82.

51. The Canadian government "decided not to denude the country of its trained troops but to raise and train additional forces for Korea, leaving the Mobile Brigade Group and the air defence forces to deal with any threat to Canada." Foulkes, "Canadian Defence Policy": 5–6. A brigade group and an air division (eleven, later twelve, squadrons of fighter aircraft) were sent to Western Europe. Altogether, Canada's armed forces doubled in size. Bothwell, Drummond, and English, *Canada since 1945*, 123.

52. Samuel P. Huntington, *The Common Defense: Strategic Programs in National Politics* (New York: Columbia University Press, 1961), 326–28.

53. Foulkes, "Canadian Defence Policy," 5.

54. Huntington, *Common Defense*, 329.

55. General Curtis E. LeMay, with Major General Dale O. Smith, *America Is in Danger* (New York: Funk and Wagnalls, 1968), 38–39.

56. Foulkes, "Canadian Defence Policy," 6; Melvin A. Conant, *The Long Polar Watch: Canada and the Defense of North America* (New York: Harper and Brothers, 1962), 39–41; Huntington, *Common Defense*, 340; Jockel, *No Boundaries Upstairs*, chaps. 3, 4, maps 1–3.

57. Conant, *Long Polar Watch*, 48.

58. Foulkes, "Canadian Defence Policy," 2; Holmes, *Shaping of Peace* 2:285–86.

59. Munro and Inglis, eds., *Mike*, 84.

60. Jockel, *No Boundaries Upstairs*, 111–17.

61. James Eayrs, "Military Policy and Middle Power: The Canadian Experience," in J. King Gordon, ed., *Canada's Role as a Middle Power* (Toronto: Canadian Institute of International Affairs, 1966), 83.

62. Conant, *Long Polar Watch*, 186.

63. Foulkes, "Canadian Defence Policy," 15–17.

64. Joseph T. Jockel and Joel J. Sokolsky, *Canada and Collective Security: Odd Man Out* (New York: Praeger, 1986), 28: "The nuclear role in Europe was dropped in 1972 and the last of the nuclear weapons in Canada was removed in 1984, leading many Canadians to take satisfaction with what they saw as their country's restored nuclear purity."

65. Foulkes, "Canadian Defence Policy," 8, 9.

66. Thomas M. Coffey, *Iron Eagle: The Turbulent Life of General Curtis LeMay* (New York: Crown Publishers, 1986), 11–12, 185–86.

67. LeMay, *America Is in Danger*, 40 (emphasis in original).

68. Text in Robert A. Divine, ed., *The Cuban Missile Crisis* (Chicago: Quadrangle, 1971), 32–37.

69. H. Basil Robinson, *Diefenbaker's World: A Populist in Foreign Affairs* (Toronto: University of Toronto Press, 1989), 287–88.

70. Peter C. Dobell, *Canada's Search for New Roles: Foreign Policy in the Trudeau Era* (London: Oxford University Press, 1972), 27.

71. James Eayrs, *In Defence of Canada—Indochina: Roots of Complicity* (Toronto: University of Toronto Press, 1983); Douglas A. Ross, "The Dynamics of Indochina Diplomacy: Pearson, Holmes, and the Struggle with the Bureaucratic Right 1955," in Kim Richard Nossal, ed., *An Acceptance of Paradox: Essays on*

Canadian Diplomacy in Honour of John W. Holmes (Toronto: Canadian Institute of International Affairs, 1982), 56–85.

72. Bothwell, Drummond, and English, *Canada since 1945*, 260–61, 262–64.

73. Alastair Taylor, David Cox, and J. L. Granatstein, *Peacekeeping: International Challenge and Canadian Response* (Toronto: Canadian Institute of International Affairs, 1968).

74. Dobell, *Canada's Search*, 5, 36. For an authoritative account of the background of the Trudeau government's decisions regarding Europe, by the deputy chairman of the External Affairs Department's Special Task Force on Europe (STAFEUR) and, later, Canadian ambassador to NATO, see John G. H. Halstead, "Trudeau and Europe: Reflections of a Foreign Policy Adviser," *Revue d'intégration européenne/Journal of European Integration* 12, no. 1 (1988): 37–50. To NATO's new supreme allied commander in Europe, General Andrew Goodpaster, the Canadian reduction in forces represented a major organizational challenge, for the Canadian troops, though relatively few in number, were highly trained, and a Canadian withdrawal might become a precedent for other, smaller NATO members. He succeeded in moderating the extent and the effect of the Canadian action. See Lewis Sorley, "Goodpaster: Maintaining Deterrence during Détente," in Robert S. Jordan, ed., *Generals in International Politics: NATO's Supreme Allied Commander, Europe* (Lexington: University Press of Kentucky, 1987), 127–29.

75. Mitchell Sharp, secretary of state for external affairs, "Canada-U.S. Relations: Options for the Future," *International Perspectives*, special issue (Autumn 1972); Allan E. Gotlieb, "Power and Vulnerability: Canadian and American Perspectives on International Affairs," with commentary by Alan K. Henrikson, in Elliot J. Feldman and Neil Nevitte, eds., *The Future of North America: Canada, the United States, and Quebec Nationalism,* Harvard Studies in International Affairs, no. 42 (Cambridge, MA: Center for International Affairs, Harvard University; Montreal: Institute for Research on Public Policy, 1979), 109–39.

76. Jockel and Sokolsky, *Canada and Collective Security*, 53. Schmidt, with whom Trudeau developed a "close and confident personal rapport," helped to convince the Canadian premier of the importance of maintaining the conventional deterrent in Europe. Halstead, "Trudeau and Europe," 44.

77. Department of National Defence, *Challenge and Commitment: A Defence Policy for Canada* (Ottawa: Supply and Services, 1987), 6.

78. Douglas L. Bland and John D. Young, "Trends in Canadian Security Policy and Commitments," *Armed Forces and Society* 15, no. 1 (Fall 1988): 113–30, esp. 124–27.

79. Department of National Defence, *Challenge and Commitment*, 55–59.

80. The text may be found in Franklyn Griffiths, ed., *Politics of the Northwest Passage* (Kingston and Montreal: McGill-Queen's University Press, 1987), appendix. The traditional position of the U.S. government, which recognizes Canada's interest in securing its northern area from unwanted extrahemispheric intrusions, is that the Northwest Passage is an international waterway. Many Canadians fear that, at best, the United States might be willing "to uphold Canada's national claims against everybody but themselves." Peter C. Newman, "Uncle Sam's Sovereignty Promise," *Maclean's* 100, no. 13 (March 1987): 33.

81. Department of National Defence, *Challenge and Commitment*, 49, 52–53. A widely discussed possible challenge was a Soviet naval effort to outflank NATO's main line of defense in the North Atlantic—the Greenland-Iceland-United Kingdom (GIUK) barrier—by sending submarines directly under the Arctic ice cap through the Davis Strait into the Atlantic. See, for example, Eric Margolis, "Will Canadian

Waters Become the Next Maginot Line?" *Wall Street Journal*, 21 February 1986. In U.S. official circles there was some initial suspicion that the planned Canadian submarines were mainly "sovereignty weapons" directed against the United States. The Canadian government's genuine defense motives, including contributing to alliancewide "collective defense in the north," are emphasized in Joel J. Sokolsky, *Defending Canada: U.S.-Canadian Defense Policies* (New York: Priority Press Publications, 1989), 46–47.

82. Department of National Defence, *Challenge and Commitment*, 6.

83. Jockel and Sokolsky, *Canada and Collective Security*, 21, 22.

84. Paul Lewis, "Military Buildup in Canada Falls Victim to Budget Cuts," *New York Times*, 30 September 1989; Michael R. Gordon, " 'Star Wars' Fading as Major Element of U.S. Strategy," ibid., 28 September 1989.

85. Bland and Young, "Trends in Canadian Security Policy," 127.

86. Michael Tucker, *Canadian Foreign Policy: Contemporary Issues and Themes* (Toronto: McGraw-Hill Ryerson, 1980), 150.

The Anglo-American
Special Relationship[*]

Geoffrey Warner

On 26 May 1950, Britain's foreign secretary, Ernest Bevin, told his Cabinet colleagues that the United States increasingly regarded the North Atlantic Treaty as the focus for the further development of the Western world. Britain's future relations with the United States would largely be determined, therefore, by the success of the collaboration between the two countries in the Atlantic alliance. "Since it is the kernel of their policy," Bevin argued, "it must also be the kernel of ours."[1]

Without calling Bevin's sincerity into question, it would be quite wrong to conclude that the North Atlantic Treaty Organization (NATO) has always been at the center of the so-called special relationship between Britain and the United States. Indeed, it could be argued that one of the things that is special about it is the way in which it has transcended the obvious focus of common interest in the security of Western Europe. Both countries have had worldwide interests and commitments and have consciously sought to harmonize them. Any discussion of the special relationship must take its global aspect into account, not least because most of the major rifts in it have occurred outside the NATO area.

As far as Britain was concerned, the need for a special relationship with the United States arose from an awareness of its diminished strength in the postwar world. A report dated 29 June 1945 from the Post-Hostilities Planning Staff, the body charged with assessing Britain's postwar security requirements, observed that even a united British Empire would be

*Reprinted from "The Anglo-American Special Relationship," *Diplomatic History* 13, no. 4 (Fall 1989): 479–99. Copyright 1989 by Scholarly Resources Inc. Reprinted by permission of Scholarly Resources Inc.

incapable of securing its interests against the most likely potential aggressor, the Soviet Union, without the support of powerful allies. It was therefore "vital to ensure the full and early support in war of the U.S.A." A few weeks later, on 14 August, the new Labour Cabinet was warned by economist John Maynard Keynes of the likelihood of a cumulative deficit of U.S. $5 million on the country's balance of payments for the period 1946–1949. This could only be offset by American aid. Without it Britain would face the prospect of "a financial Dunkirk" that would entail not only "a sudden and humiliating withdrawal" from its overseas commitments but also "an indefinite postponement" of the government's ambitious reform program.[2]

Britain's aim, therefore, was quite simply to harness the much greater military, political, and economic power of the United States in support of its own objectives. Despite the difficulties involved, it was felt that superior British diplomatic skill could bring this about. As an anonymous Foreign Office official patronizingly put it in March 1944: "If we go about our business in the right way we can help to steer this great unwieldy barge, the United States of America, into the right harbour. If we don't, it is likely to continue to wallow in the ocean, an isolated menace to navigation."[3]

It has been argued by some scholars that the years 1945–1947 saw something of an uphill struggle by the British government to gain the support of the U.S. government.[4] It should not be forgotten, however, just how much was achieved during this period. Although it was unpopular in many quarters, the American loan to Britain at the end of 1945 was vital to the latter's economic reconstruction. In June-July 1946 the little-known Spaatz-Tedder agreement, under which the RAF (Royal Air Force) agreed to prepare some of its airfields in East Anglia to accommodate American heavy bombers capable of carrying out both conventional and atomic strikes against the Soviet Union, paved the way for the much more highly publicized transfer of B-29s to Britain during the Berlin crisis of 1948. In 1947 the still classified UKUSA agreement on the exchange of intelligence was concluded; it provided for the extension and development into the postwar period of the extremely fruitful pooling of information, particularly signals intelligence, or SIGINT, that had existed during the Second World War. Finally, the "Pentagon talks" on the defense of the Middle East at the end of the same year were regarded by the British as a great success in winning American backing for their position in what they saw as the most crucial overseas area from the point of view of imperial defense.[5]

These successes, however, have to be offset by the breakdown of the intimate wartime collaboration between the two countries on the development of nuclear weapons. The McMahon Act of August 1946 greatly restricted the exchange of information on atomic matters between Britain and the United States. The Attlee government promptly resolved to press ahead with the development of Britain's own atomic bomb. "We could not afford to acquiesce in an American monopoly of this new development," Bevin told the other members of the highly secret Cabinet committee that took this decision in January 1947.[6]

These sentiments showed that while a special relationship with the United States was still desirable, it was important not to allow Britain to become too dependent on it. For the Labour government this was partly a question of ideology. As Bevin put it to the Cabinet's defense committee in March 1946, Britain was "the last bastion of social democracy," a philosophy that was quite different from both "the red tooth and claw of American capitalism and the Communist dictatorship of Soviet Russia."[7] At the back of the foreign secretary's plan for a "Western Union" in 1948 there undoubtedly lay the long-term objective of a vast Eurafrican bloc, consisting of the Western European countries and their colonial territories and backed by the Commonwealth, which would be able to assume if not a neutral at any rate a genuinely independent position between the Soviet Union and the United States.[8]

A number of factors were responsible for the gradual decline of this concept: the continued weakness of the British economy culminating in the devaluation of sterling in September 1949, which bound Britain more closely to the United States; the reluctance of the Commonwealth to pursue a joint policy under British direction; the hijacking of the movement for West European unity by the federalists, whose ideas were regarded as totally impracticable by Bevin; and opposition from within the Cabinet and civil service to what were seen as his own unrealistic schemes.

Most important, however, was the intensification of the Cold War. The negotiations that led to the North Atlantic Treaty began in March 1948 with Britain playing a leading role. The essential requirement, as Bevin told the Cabinet on 2 November 1948, was an American commitment to respond at once to any Russian attack upon Western Europe. "[Al]though the European powers must necessarily hold the front in case of aggression," the foreign secretary stated, "it was not possible for Great Britain to repeat the role that she had played in 1914 and 1940. . . . It was essential that everybody should be brought into the war at the same moment. The security of Western Europe required a regional pact which committed the trans-Atlantic as well as the continental Powers." The North Atlantic Treaty was of course concluded in April 1949, but it was not until December 1950 that this objective was finally achieved, when the United States agreed to the appointment of General Dwight D. Eisenhower as supreme commander of the alliance's forces and to the placing of the reinforced American contingents in Europe under his command. Bevin, who had only a few months left to live, is reported to have said on this occasion that he had nearly died three times during the previous year but had kept himself alive "because I wanted to see this North Atlantic Alliance properly launched."[9]

At the same time, Britain itself moved in the direction of a great commitment to the defense of Western Europe. The chiefs of staff, in their global strategy paper of May 1947, had listed the "three pillars" of British security as the defense of the United Kingdom, the control of the essential sea communications, and the holding of the Middle East. By July 1948, under the impact of the Brussels Treaty, which linked Britain, France, and the Benelux countries in the West European Union, the Berlin blockade, and the negotiations for an Atlantic alliance, the chiefs had added the defense of Western Europe as far to the east as possible. At this stage the expectation was still that Britain's own contribution to this defense would be mainly aeronaval, but in March 1950 the Cabinet's defense committee approved the dispatch of two infantry divisions to reinforce the British occupation forces in Germany. Two months later, in another global strategy paper, the chiefs of staff announced what they described as "a most important change" in the relative importance that they attached to Western Europe as opposed to the Middle East. "If we lost the Middle East," they now argued, "we would still survive: if we lost Western Europe, we might well be defeated."[10]

Any suggestion that Western Europe, with or without the support of the Commonwealth, could even in the long term constitute a meaningful "third force" in the world now seemed to have been abandoned. Even with the help of the Commonwealth, Bevin told the Cabinet on 8 May 1950, Western Europe was not strong enough to confront a military threat from the East. Britain and Western Europe must henceforth rely upon "the English-speaking democracies of the Western Hemisphere," and "the wider concept of the Atlantic community" must begin to be substituted for the earlier concept of Western union. In response to American requests after the outbreak of the Korean War in June 1950, the British government put its money where its mouth was by launching a massive rearmament program.[11]

In return for their efforts in Europe and elsewhere, the British hoped for and expected a privileged position as the United States' principal ally and partner. To some extent this was conceded, as is shown most convincingly at the working level by the regular but informal consultations between U.S. Secretary of State Dean Acheson and the British ambassador in Washington, Sir Oliver Franks, during which the whole range of international issues was discussed. Nevertheless, there remained disappointment in London that Britain was still insufficiently differentiated from the rest of Western Europe and that, in the words of one Foreign Office official, the Americans "were not prepared to encourage us to think that we could establish, through any special relationship with them, an alibi for our duties in respect of European integration."[12]

American pressure for closer integration with Western Europe was a sore point with the British government, and not just for the well-known reasons: the Commonwealth, the sterling area, the different political and economic structures of Britain and the Western European countries, and the psychological gulf that separated one of the victorious "Big Three" of the Second World War from those who had been defeated and occupied. There was also a rarely expressed and therefore rarely noticed fear that closer integration with Western Europe would increase Britain's dependence upon the United States. As Bevin remarked on 24 April 1950, if Britain surrendered its sovereignty to a European organization the Americans would be able to influence British policy indirectly by means of the financial pressure they could bring to bear upon the weaker member of the organization in which Britain would always be a minority.[13]

There was a major crisis in the special relationship at the end of 1950, but not untypically it arose in Asia rather than in Europe. At a press conference on 30 November, President Harry S. Truman conveyed the impression not only that he was about to authorize the use of the atomic bomb in Korea, where allied forces were under severe pressure from the Communist Chinese, but also that he would entrust the decision to his "mad satrap" General Douglas MacArthur, the local commander in chief. Since the modus vivendi of January 1948, the British government had lost its right of veto and even of consultation over the use of American nuclear weapons that President Franklin D. Roosevelt had accorded to Prime Minister Winston Churchill in October 1943. The Foreign Office already had become concerned at the implications this had for the launching of nuclear strikes from the USAF bases in Britain, which had grown in number since the first B-29s had crossed the Atlantic during the Berlin crisis of 1948. Truman's press conference widened the area of concern and caused considerable anxiety among the general public, so that when Clement R. Attlee flew to Washington on 3 December 1950 for urgent consultations with the president, one of his principal objectives was to secure a general American commitment on prior consultation before any use of the atomic bomb. Truman gave him a verbal assurance, but when the prime minister suggested that he might care to write it down, the president retorted "that if a man's word wasn't any good it wasn't made any better by writing it down."[14]

Further efforts were made by the British government during 1951 to secure a specific commitment concerning atomic bombs launched from bases on British soil. Eventually the two sides came to an agreement, according to which the use of American air bases in Britain in an emergency was a matter for the joint decision of the British and U.S. governments "in the light of the circumstances prevailing at the time." This agreement was revealed in the House of Commons on 5 December 1951, exactly one year after Attlee's visit to Washington, by the new Conservative prime minister, Winston Churchill, whose party had been returned to power in the general election at the end of October. It had, however, been prepared by the Labour government and was thus an impressive example of the continuity of British foreign policy.[15]

Another example of continuity in the NATO context concerned the rearmament of West Germany. It was widely known that the alliance's force goals could not be reached without a German contribution, but, in view of the experience of the Second World War, this would clearly give rise to severe political problems. In September 1950 the British Cabinet reluctantly agreed to the principle of West German rearmament because the Truman administration had made it clear that full American participation in the defense of Western Europe was conditional upon it. The French, for whom domestic political implications were even more difficult than they were for the British, initially dug in their heels and refused, but subsequently they produced a plan for a European army organized along the same supranational lines as the recently proposed Schuman Plan for the integration of Western Europe's coal and steel industries. The British and Americans were horrified by the French plan. Both regarded it as militarily unworkable and as a device to delay German rearmament. In addition, the British had no sympathy with its federalist implications. By mid-1951, however, the Americans had come round to supporting the European Defense Community (EDC), as the European army plan was now known, because they believed that it was the only way in which German rearmament would ever be achieved.

In these circumstances both the British Labour and Conservative governments were prepared to give the EDC their general blessing, but neither was prepared to join what Churchill once called "a sludgy amalgam." The question became progressively more acute after 1951, and the Churchill government made great efforts to produce a satisfactory solution to the problem of Britain's relationship to the EDC. Every concession prompted fresh demands from the importunate French, who were terrified that without British help their creation would eventually fall under the domination of the historic German enemy. When the French national assembly finally voted down the EDC in August 1954, it was the British foreign secretary Anthony Eden who, even if he did not quite dream up the idea in his bath one morning, persuaded the interested parties to accept the alternative solution of an expanded West European union combined with a pledge to keep British forces on the Continent so long as its members desired. This was a remarkable diplomatic achievement, especially in view of the almost total and inexplicable paralysis on the part of the United States, and one that undoubtedly merited the tribute subsequently paid by the Belgian foreign minister, Paul-Henri Spaak, to its architect: "In 1954 and 1955 [Eden] saved the Atlantic alliance."[16]

Winston Churchill was of course the great proponent of the special relationship. If he did not actually coin the expression himself, he certainly gave it the widest publicity in his famous Fulton speech in March 1946. In a meeting shortly before his inauguration in January 1953, President-elect Eisenhower recorded that Churchill had "an almost childlike faith" that the answers to all foreign policy problems were to be found in the Anglo-American partnership. Eisenhower saw this notion as "completely fatuous" and wistfully expressed the hope that the aged British prime minister would soon hand over the reins of power to someone younger, a sentiment shared by many of Churchill's own colleagues.[17]

Far from improving during the Churchill government, however, it might seem that the special relationship actually deteriorated. This is certainly the impression one would gain from reading the relevant volume of the memoirs of then Foreign Secretary Sir Anthony Eden, which, as Eden's successor Selwyn Lloyd remarked after reading the first draft, was permeated throughout by "a strong anti-American bias." But Eden was writing in the aftermath of the Suez crisis, which ended his political career, and historians must be careful not to fall victim to his bitterness. Although there were disagreements between the British and Americans at this time, notably over the Middle East and Indochina, there was considerable cooperation too. Even in the Middle East the two governments were able to join forces in organizing the overthrow of the Mohammed Mossadegh regime in Iran in 1953, while the U.S. government paid the greatest possible tribute to its British partner in April 1955 when it agreed to announce its willingness to participate in summit talks with the Russians precisely in order to secure the return of the Conservatives in the general election held later that month.[18]

The new prime minister was Sir Anthony Eden. If he had "saved the Atlantic alliance" in 1954 and 1955, did he come close to destroying it in 1956? The answer is almost certainly "no," but the Suez crisis of that year did mark the greatest rift in the special relationship since the end of the Second World War. The Americans were angry that the British had deceived them, that they had distracted the world's attention from the Russian invasion of Hungary, and that they had rendered the newly emerging nations more susceptible to Communist propaganda concerning "Western imperialism." The British were furious that the Americans, whom they regarded as their most faithful friends and allies, should have stabbed them in the back precisely when they felt most passionately that their vital interests were at stake.

This paper is not the place for a detailed history of the crisis, but it is important to describe the kinds of pressure that the United States applied to

Britain, since these illustrate the inherent one-sidedness of the special relationship. First, there was the economic and more especially the financial pressure that was undoubtedly the principal factor in compelling the British to bring their military operation to a halt. "We must stop, we must stop," Chancellor of the Exchequer Harold Macmillan told a junior Foreign Office minister shortly before the cease-fire was decided, "or we will have no more dollars left by the end of the week." This pressure, moreover, continued after the cease-fire in order to compel the British to withdraw their forces from Egypt. It was so ruthless and relentless, in fact, that both Eden and his foreign secretary, Selwyn Lloyd, later agreed that the government should have resigned at the end of November 1956.[19]

Second, there was the cutoff in the supply of intelligence information. This was virtually total from 31 October, the day after the Anglo-French ultimatum to Egypt and Israel, until 6 November, when channels were partially reopened in order to transmit a reassuring American assessment of what, on the face of it, was a Soviet threat to launch a missile attack on Britain and France.[20] This, incidentally, was also the date of the cease-fire in Egypt.

Third, there is some intriguing but incomplete evidence of American connivance in and encouragement of the plans of Macmillan and R. A. Butler, the two most obvious candidates for the succession, to force the resignation of Eden as prime minister.[21] Eden did resign in January 1957 and was duly succeeded by Macmillan.

If Eden's premiership witnessed the nadir of the special relationship, the first phase of Macmillan's almost certainly saw its apogee. Unlike many of his fellow-supporters of the Suez operation—and he was one of its most enthusiastic advocates—the new prime minister saw no point in crying over spilled milk. An internal postmortem on Suez, written in the Cabinet office, concluded among other things that the episode had exposed the limitations of British strength and that Britain "could never again resort to military action outside British territories, without at least American acquiescence."[22] The corollary, therefore, was to reestablish Anglo-American relations on a sound footing, a task that Macmillan set about immediately and with great energy. Fortunately, the Americans were receptive. At the height of the Suez crisis, President Eisenhower had written a friend that "Britain not only had been, but must be, our best friend in the world," and less than two weeks after Macmillan took over as prime minister, Eisenhower invited him to a meeting in either Washington or Bermuda. Macmillan appreciated what he later called the president's "delicacy" in proposing the latter location. "For us," he wrote, "Bermuda—British territory—made the whole difference."[23]

The meeting took place from 21–24 March 1957, and the prime minister reported to his Cabinet colleagues that he did not see how it could have gone better. On 14 October, Lloyd recorded the penitent reflections of John Foster Dulles, the archvillain of the Suez crisis from the British point of view. He and the president believed, Lloyd cabled, that there should be a reexamination of the whole structure of Western cooperation and that the Anglo-American alliance must be at the core of this process. Dulles believed that there had possibly been "too much 'take it or leave it' and 'we know best' spirit" on the American side, while the president felt he had been "quite wrong" to abolish the combined chiefs of staff organization at the end of the Second World War. Would the prime minister care to come to Washington to discuss all of this?[24]

Indeed, he would. Moreover, on 28 October 1957, Macmillan reported triumphantly to the Cabinet that, as a result of his conversations in the U.S. capital (on 23–25 October), the two governments had agreed to concert a common policy in order to counter Soviet encroachment, not only by the military but also by political, economic, and propaganda means; and that the U.S. government had agreed to adopt and apply a policy of pooling resources concerning the development and production of new weapons, in pursuit of which the president had undertaken to request Congress to amend the McMahon Act. All that Britain had to do in return for what the prime minister described as these "substantial and valuable concessions on the part of the United States government" was not to press for a change in Chinese representation at the United Nations without prior American agreement. No wonder Lloyd felt able to conclude that "largely as a result of the personal friendship between the Prime Minister and President Eisenhower, we had now succeeded in regaining the special relationship with the United States which we had formerly enjoyed."[25]

Due mainly to their shared experiences in the Mediterranean theater during the Second World War, Macmillan and Eisenhower were personal friends, but the roots of the Anglo-American rapprochement after Suez went much deeper than this. They were embedded in the changing military balance between East and West. Both the United States and Britain were now thermonuclear powers, having exploded their first hydrogen devices in October 1952 and May 1957, respectively. Largely on grounds of economy, both had adopted defense policies based upon strategic nuclear deterrence as opposed to more costly conventional forces, the United States with the "new look" in 1953 and Britain with the Sandys white paper in 1957. (In Britain's case it is important to emphasize that this quite consciously involved a reduction in its commitment to NATO. An immediate consequence of the new British defense posture was the withdrawal of some of the forces that the government had promised would remain in Western Europe under the London and Paris agreements of 1954.) The Soviet Union, however, was also a thermonuclear power, and it was imperative for the West to maintain its superiority, not least in respect to nuclear weapons delivery systems. The Americans were particularly anxious to deploy the first generation of intermediate-range ballistic missiles in Europe, whence they could reach targets inside Russia, and President Eisenhower formally offered them to Macmillan at Bermuda in March 1957. Although the warheads would be under control of the United States, the delivery vehicles would be owned by Britain and operated by British personnel. They thus constituted a valuable contribution to the modernization of Britain's own nuclear deterrent, especially after it developed its own thermonuclear warheads.

The situation became even more pressing in October 1957, when its launch of the first artificial satellite, *Sputnik*, indicated that the Soviet Union might soon be able to deploy intercontinental ballistic missiles capable of hitting targets in the United States. The British government was well aware that *Sputnik* was largely responsible for the American enthusiasm for the special relationship demonstrated at the Washington meeting. One consequence was a proposal, accepted at the meeting of the NATO Council in December 1957, for the deployment of American intermediate-range ballistic missiles (IRBM) on the territory of other alliance members. The detailed agreement for the stationing of IRBMs in Britain was eventually concluded in February 1958 and provided for a "dual key" mechanism whereby the missiles could not be launched without the approval of both the British and U.S. governments. On 2 July 1958, President Eisenhower signed a revised version of the Atomic Energy Act and the administration followed it up the very next day by signing a new agreement on nuclear collaboration in the field of defense with the British government.

The changing military balance between East and West was paralleled by the first signs of a shift in the balance of power within the Western alliance. In 1950, Britain, although a long way behind the United States, was unquestionably the second most powerful country in the Western world. Its gross domestic product stood at $20.3 billion, compared with France's $8.8 billion, West Germany's $10.6 billion, and Japan's $4.8 billion. At 689,000, Britain's armed forces were larger than those of any other member of NATO save the United States. By 1957–58, however, the situation had begun to change. West Germany's economic miracle was well under way—its rate of economic growth was almost three times that of Britain during the 1950s—and the first contingents of what would eventually become the largest military force in Western Europe were recruited in 1957. France's economy, too, had been growing much faster than Britain's, and its armed forces had overtaken in size those of its cross-Channel neighbor in 1958. Admittedly this latter phenomenon was due to the war in Algeria, but it was likely to endure given Britain's decision to abolish conscription, which was announced in the Sandys white paper. In June 1958, moreover, France acquired a strong man in the shape of General

Charles de Gaulle, who was determined to end the chronic political instability that had characterized the Fourth Republic and had been a major contributing factor in the relatively low level of French influence in world affairs. Finally, both France and West Germany were at the core of a new and potentially powerful politico-economic grouping, the European Economic Community (EEC), which had been launched in March 1957.

It is revealing that no serious thought was given at the time by the British government to joining the EEC. There was, it is true, considerable concern at the economic divisions it would cause in the Western world, and strenuous although unsuccessful efforts were made to offset these, first by the proposal for a Europe-wide free trade area. After this was turned down by the French at the end of 1958, the formation of the European Free Trade Association (EFTA) was designed to act as a bridge between the EEC and the rest of Western Europe. The idea that the EEC might develop into a rival focus of power within the Western alliance and the world generally does not seem to have occurred to British policymakers in the late 1950s. Its own resources, plus of course its special relationship with the United States, seemed more than enough to secure Britain's accustomed place in the sun.

By 1960, however, the British government was beginning to have second thoughts. The principal catalyst was undoubtedly the failure of the Paris summit in May, which was a bitter blow to Macmillan, who for more than eighteen months had invested a great deal of time and energy in his more or less self-appointed role as honest broker between East and West. "Shall we," he wondered in one of his gloomier moods, "be caught between a hostile (or at least less and less friendly) America and a boastful, powerful 'Empire of Charlemagne'—now under French but later bound to come under German control[?] Is this the real reason for 'joining' the Common Market . . . and for abandoning (a) the Seven [EFTA], (b) British agriculture, (c) the Commonwealth? It's a grim choice."[26]

Britain finally took the plunge in July 1961 and applied for full membership in the EEC. Macmillan told Commonwealth leaders in September of the following year that one reason for his government's decision was that he thought it inevitable that, given the realities of power, the United States would attach growing importance to the views of the EEC and that there would also be a developing tendency for the Americans and the EEC to "concert policy on major issues without the same regard for our views and interests such as our present relationship with Washington affords."[27]

This belief was undoubtedly encouraged by the policies of the Kennedy administration, which had come to power in the United States in 1961. Despite the close personal friendship that seemed to exist between Macmillan and John F. Kennedy, the whole thrust of the new administration's policy toward Western Europe and NATO was in the direction of deemphasizing the special relationship with Britain in favor of the grand design, which it was hoped would appease the growing restlessness of France and West Germany while at the same time maintain the dominant position of the United States within the alliance.

Nowhere was this clearer than in the field of defense. Macmillan's defense minister from 1959 to 1962, Harold Watkinson, has made no secret of his distaste for the McNamara regime in the Pentagon compared to the more easygoing attitudes of the Eisenhower administration. He wrote that "by 1962 [and the context makes clear that he was thinking of the early part of the year] I became convinced that Britain should seek to strengthen her future defense through her ties with Europe, rather than by seeking to preserve what looked increasingly impossible to achieve, namely a special defense relationship with the United States."[28]

What Macmillan described as "McNamara's foolish speech" at Ann Arbor in June 1962, in which Secretary of Defense Robert S. McNamara attacked independent nuclear deterrents, only served to make matters worse. The new administration was anxious to reduce what it saw as NATO's excessive dependence upon nuclear weapons in favor of a policy of flexible response. This involved the elimination of the British, and now also the French, independent deterrents and an attempt to allay the European allies' anxieties by selling them American missiles. "In NATO," Macmillan recorded, "all the allies are angry with the American proposal that we should buy rockets to the tune of umpteen millions of dollars, the warheads to be under American control. This is not a European rocket. It's a racket of the American industry."[29]

For Britain, however, the most alarming demonstration of the direction in which American thinking was moving came at the end of the year with the Skybolt affair. To ensure an independent nuclear delivery system in the missile gap, the British government had been working on an IRBM called Blue Streak. In February 1960, Blue Streak was canceled on grounds of cost and vulnerability. In the spirit of the special relationship, the Eisenhower administration had offered to sell Britain an American air-to-ground missile, Skybolt, which would have prolonged the life of the RAF's strategic bomber force. The British believed that they also had secured a gentleman's agreement whereby, if Skybolt failed to come up to the mark, they would be permitted to buy Polaris, a submarine-launched missile then being developed for the U.S. Navy. In return, the British had agreed to provide base facilities for the American Polaris submarines.

By late 1962 the Pentagon had concluded that Skybolt was unlikely to be successful and should be canceled. Moreover, it aired its doubts in public without consulting the British. As if this were not bad enough, the administration initially showed no inclination to honor the alleged gentleman's agreement entered into by its predecessor regarding Polaris. Such missiles, it insisted, would only be made available in the context of a multilateral, mixed-crewed submarine force under NATO control. On hearing the news, Macmillan is reported to have exclaimed incredulously: "You don't expect our chaps to share their grog with the Turks, do you?" But much more was at stake than the Royal Navy's rum ration. The future of Britain's independent nuclear deterrent was in the balance, and so was the special relationship. It took tough negotiations between the two sides at Nassau from 18–21 December 1962 to reach a compromise whereby Britain did receive its own Polaris missiles but pledged in return to allocate them to NATO, "except where . . . supreme national interests are at stake."[30]

Just over three weeks after the Nassau agreement, on 14 January 1963, President de Gaulle vetoed British entry into the EEC. It seems reasonably certain from the evidence that the former did not give rise to the latter. De Gaulle never wanted Britain in the Common Market, partly because he did not relish a possible rival for its leadership, and partly because the rhetoric of the special relationship led him to suspect that Britain would play the part of an American "Trojan horse" in an organization that he firmly believed should develop in increasing independence from the United States. Macmillan was shattered. "All our policies at home and abroad are in ruins," he lamented in his diary.[31]

The Conservative government survived for nearly two more years, although ill health forced Macmillan to resign in October 1963. The thirteen years of Conservative rule were marked, as we have seen, by both the heights and the depths of the special relationship. Even if the latter had again begun to decline after 1961, it was still a reality, as no one who reads Macmillan's account of his frequent and intimate exchanges with President Kennedy during the Cuban missile crisis of October 1962 could gainsay.[32] Moreover, after de Gaulle's veto of its entry into the EEC, Britain had nowhere else to go. Macmillan's realization of the changing balance of power within the Western alliance had come too late.

At the general election of October 1964 a Labour government under Harold Wilson was narrowly returned to power. Labour had been in opposition for so long that there was some uncertainty as to precisely where it stood in the field of foreign policy. (The Conservative government had warned the United States that if it failed to deliver the goods at Nassau it "might have to deal with a more neutralist and less pro-American Labour government!"[33]) Any anxieties on that score, however, were soon dissipated. Despite his left-wing reputation, Wilson was no neutralist. In any event, his majority in the House of Commons was wafer thin, and the pound was under constant pressure. He needed all the help he could get, and the most obvious source was the United States. Although the details remain obscure, recent research has shown that in the course of 1964–65 some sort of deal was struck between the British and U.S. governments whereby, in return for American support of sterling, Britain agreed to retain a military presence east of Suez. According to Britain's new secretary of defense, Denis Healey, the Americans took the view that British forces were "much more useful to the alliance outside Europe than in Germany."[34]

With its growing involvement in Vietnam, it was not surprising that the United States felt the need for reliable support elsewhere in an increasingly turbulent Third World. It was also the case that the U.S. Treasury believed that the pound was the first line of defense for the dollar. The British government, for its part, was happy to oblige. Wilson and the majority of his colleagues did not want a Labour government to be saddled with the opprobrium of a third devaluation (after 1931 and 1949), and even if British troops had not already been engaged in confrontation with Indonesia in defense of Malaysia, a continuing presence east of Suez would have fed the prime minister's delusions of grandeur.

The new government also swiftly abandoned its preelection pledge to phase out Britain's independent nuclear deterrent. The Nassau agreement, which had been the subject of much Labour derision when it was originally concluded, was now eagerly embraced and steps later were taken to update the Polaris missiles supplied under its terms. There was still, however, the problem of the proposed NATO multilateral force, which some enthusiasts in the U.S. administration continued to favor. It had hardly any advocates in Britain, and, when Wilson went to Washington in December 1964 for his first meeting with President Lyndon B. Johnson, he took with him an alternative proposal that, as Healey candidly admitted later, was deliberately "devised . . . as a means of scuppering the M.L.F. [multilateral force]."[35] It succeeded, too.

After greatly increasing his parlimentary majority in the general election of March 1965, Wilson carried out another reversal in policy. Hitherto a skeptic about if not an opponent of British membership in the EEC, the prime minister now began to mobilize support for a second application to join. His own motives are unclear, although it is likely that he was greatly influenced by the civil service, which, after having strongly opposed closer links with Europe in the 1940s and 1950s, had now evidently come to regard them as the answer to the country's problems. One thing is certain: The Cabinet, like the Labour party itself, was bitterly divided. The internal debates that took place in the second half of 1965, and of which we are fortunate in possessing a number of detailed accounts, provide a fascinating insight into the fundamental political assumptions of those involved, and the continuing relevance of the special relationship was never far from the center of preoccupation.

One of the most enthusiastic "Europeans" was George Brown, the right-wing deputy leader of the Labour party and foreign secretary from August

1966. Before taking over his new office Brown had confided to one Cabinet colleague that, after the recent American bombing of Hanoi, "the time had come when we had to reassess our entire foreign policy and look again at the close relations with America. As it was, we were getting separated from the United States without really establishing any close relations with Europe."[36] If all the right-wingers had argued like Brown, the divisions within the government might have been less acute. The left-wing minister, Barbara Castle, told her colleagues in October 1966 that, if Britain truly intended to abandon the special relationship and pursue a Gaullist policy of détente with the Soviet Union, she might be interested in an approach to Europe, but since it was her understanding that the main purpose behind the proposed second attempt to join the EEC was "to fight for links with the U.S. and for NATO," she was not interested.[37]

Tony Benn, a future leader of the Labour left whose views were then still evolving, wondered whether the special relationship was not worth a great deal more to Britain than was entry into Europe. As the minister responsible for Britain's nuclear program, among other things, Benn was well aware of just how close the special relationship was in the nuclear field. "Not only do we have defence relations [he noted in his diary]—as a result of which all British atomic security is vetted and overseen and double checked and approved by the Americans—but we also owe a tremendous amount to them in the sphere of technology." Indeed, one of his senior civil servants told him in June 1967 that he did not believe a British approach to Europe would succeed unless the government was prepared to make a nuclear deal with the French, which would involve a break in the special relationship and changing sides in the NATO battle—joining the French against the Americans.[38]

This view may have been overly melodramatic, but it seems that the British government did make one important shift in its policy at least partly in order to accommodate the anti-American prejudices of General de Gaulle. According to the then chancellor of the exchequer, James Callaghan, one reason for rejecting the long-term package for the protection of sterling put forward by the United States in February 1967 was that the political conditions attached, which included the familiar demand for a continuing military presence east of Suez, would have complicated efforts to convince the French leader that Britain was sincere in its European vocation.[39]

The main reason for the rejection of the package, however, lay in the growing conviction that Britain could simply no longer afford a world role. In July 1967 a defense white paper announced an almost total withdrawal of British forces from east of Suez by 1977. The shock of devaluation, which took place in November 1967, compelled an acceleration of this timetable. In January 1968, Wilson told the House of Commons that the date of withdrawal had been brought forward to 1971, and the defense white paper of February 1968 summed it all up with the words, "Britain's defence effort will in [the] future be concentrated mainly in Europe and the North Atlantic." The Americans were deeply upset. U.S. Secretary of State Dean Rusk described the British government's decisions to George Brown as "opting out" and "the end of an era." Six months later Rusk told the National Security Council that the United States and Britain were now "working on fewer real problems" and that "[t]he concept of Atlantic cooperation could replace the special relationship," and Defense Secretary Clark Clifford further explained that "the British do not have the resources, the backup, or the hardware to deal with any big world problem. . . . They are no longer a powerful ally of ours because they cannot afford the cost of an adequate defense effort."[40]

By a supreme irony the enforced concentration of Britain's defense effort on Europe coincided with General de Gaulle's second veto of British entry into the EEC. In February 1969 the general seemed to show some sign of relenting when he suggested to the British ambassador in Paris, Christopher Soames, that he was willing to discuss a new and looser form of European association, politically controlled by Britain, France, West Germany, and Italy, which would take the place of both NATO and the EEC. What was essential, however, was that this new association must be truly independent of the United States. However sincere the French president's proposals may have been, the Foreign Office saw them as a cunning trap designed to lure Britain into a position in which it would be discussing the destruction of an organization to which it already belonged (NATO) and another that it professed to wish to join (the EEC). This fact could be disclosed to the other interested parties at any time, thereby causing the greatest possible embarrassment to the British government. The Foreign Office therefore revealed de Gaulle's proposals itself, first to the other EEC governments and the United States, and then to the world at large by means of a deliberate "leak" to the press. De Gaulle was furious, and Anglo-French relations sank to new depths of acrimony and suspicion.[41]

The inconsistent and unhappy record of the Wilson government is partially offset by the successes enjoyed in NATO itself by Denis Healey, whose six-year tenure at the British ministry of defense from 1964 to 1970, combined with his considerable energy and debating skills, gave him a position of great influence within the alliance. Thus Healey played an important part in the December 1967 decision to adopt the so-called revised strategic concept concerning the proper balance between NATO's conventional and nuclear forces. He also was instrumental in April 1967 in setting up the nuclear planning group, which discussed the thorny issue of the use and control of thousands of tactical nuclear weapons deployed in Western Europe. Finally, in 1968, Healey proposed the formation of a separate caucus within NATO that would coordinate the views of the European members of the alliance, an idea that came to fruition in the shape of the "Eurogroup."[42]

The Labour government was defeated in the general election of June 1970 and was succeeded by a Conservative administration under Edward Heath. Henry Kissinger, who as President Richard M. Nixon's national security adviser and secretary of state worked with Heath, subsequently penned the following portrait of him:

> Of all British leaders Heath was probably . . . the least committed emotionally to the United States. It was not that he was anti-American. Rather, he was immune to the sentimental elements of that attachment forged in two world wars. . . . The United States was a friendly foreign country, entitled to the consideration that reflected its power and importance, but the special relationship was an obstacle to the British vocation in Europe. Heath was content to enjoy no higher status in Washington than any other European leader. Indeed, he came close to *insisting* on it.[43]

The contrast with, say, Attlee, who proudly informed his colleagues after his talks in Washington in December 1950 that Britain had been "lifted out of the 'European queue' and treated as the United States's 'principal ally,' " was almost total.[44]

With single-minded dedication, Heath mounted the third attempt to take Britain into the EEC and, thanks in large part to the rapport he succeeded in establishing with Georges Pompidou, de Gaulle's successor as president of France, he achieved his objective. His solidarity with his fellow Europeans sometimes embarrassed and annoyed the United States, as for example when he joined France and other European countries in disassociating himself from American policy at the time of the Yom Kippur War, in October 1973. Indeed, he revealed thirteen years later that he had refused permission for the United States to use bases in Cyprus during the crisis, although he failed to mention one of the consequences: namely, that in retaliation and on only the second known occasion since the conclusion of the UKUSA agreement in 1947, the United States cut off the flow of intelligence to Britain for a week.[45]

Nevertheless, it would be quite wrong to assume that the Heath government and the British entry into Europe marked the end of Britain's special relationship with the United States. As Kissinger has also recorded, it was not easy to end because it was so informal and intangible in the first place. It is also clear that the old habits of consultation and cooperation persisted at the working level. Kissinger himself cites an excellent example of this when he describes the role of the Foreign Office official, Sir Thomas Brimelow, in the preparation and drafting of the U.S.-Soviet agreement on the prevention of nuclear war signed in Washington on 22 June 1973.[46]

Moreover, the Heath government was in power for less than four years. The Wilson-Callaghan Labour government of 1974–1979 and the

Conservative Thatcher government, which has been in power since 1979, have pursued a much more traditional policy in which the special relationship looms large. Indeed, as the British prime minister's most recent and best biographer has observed, "The Reagan-Thatcher axis was the most personal alliance in the Western world throughout the 1980s. From Moscow to Pretoria, from Tripoli to Buenos Aires, no theatre of global conflict failed to feel its effects. It eclipsed, where it did not determine, many of the details of Mrs. Thatcher's performance in the diplomatic field."[47]

There were differences of course—over Grenada, over SDI, and over the Reykjavík summit for example—but these were soon composed and were in any case overshadowed by a broader identity of views. There was certainly no danger of Europe replacing the United States in Margaret Thatcher's affections. "Winning the battle over Britain's contribution to the Community budget," writes Hugo Young,

> did not herald a new era of Euro-minded leadership. The country remained hooked on its special relationship with the United States, and a combative relationship all points east of Dover. In June 1988, President Reagan paid his last visit to Britain, and the occasion was dominated not by the future but by the past, with president and prime minister drenching each other in sentiment about the Second World War. At no point did Britain position itself in concerted fashion to intervene as West Germany continued to grow closer to France. Britain, instead, appeared not to want to lead. With the single European market beckoning in 1992, Britain's role was to spoil the party and set a firm limit to the measures of unification it would tolerate.[48]

Paradoxically, the prime minister's attachment to the special relationship has been paralleled by a marked shift away from it in the perceptions of the public at large. There has traditionally been strong support for NATO and the American alliance on the part of British public opinion. However, there has always been an underlying degree of apprehension about alleged American impetuosity in foreign affairs. This feeling has undoubtedly been strengthened by the presidency of Ronald Reagan who, in the words of an American student of British public opinion, was widely regarded in Britain "as a simplistic (though personally amicable) dunce whose poor grasp of the issues could do much damage," and this has in turn had an important effect upon attitudes toward Britain's relations with the United States. The same author cites Gallup opinion poll data to the effect that, whereas only 22 percent of respondents in March 1981 felt that these relations were too close, by March 1984 the proportion had risen to 34 percent, and by April 1986 (the month of the U.S. air strike against Libya from bases in Britain) the figure was 47 percent. Over the same period the proportion that felt that they were not close enough more than halved, from 15 to 7 percent.[49]

Depending on one's point of view, the Labour opposition in recent years has either expressed this growing concern or whipped it up. It has been extremely critical of American foreign policy in the Third World, and, while its official policy in the last two general elections has been to remain a member of NATO, it has espoused a nonnuclear defense policy of abandoning Britain's independent deterrent and insisting upon the withdrawal of all U.S. nuclear bases. There is also a powerful current of opinion on the Labour left that would like to withdraw from NATO and adopt a neutralist foreign policy. The party has, however, lost three elections in a row and, for reasons that have as much to do with the configuration of British domestic politics as with defense and foreign policy, will not find it easy to regain power. Even if it does, it could well modify its views as it has done in the past when moving from opposition into government.

There are many on the left who, feeding upon the comments of members of the U.S. administration to the effect that Labour's defense policy is incompatible with NATO security and the revelations of Peter Wright concerning alleged CIA-MI5 "dirty tricks" to "destabilize" the Wilson government in the 1970s, are convinced that no American administration would tolerate a government in Britain that genuinely sought to break its defense links with the United States and NATO. A recent and highly successful fictionalized version of the likely consequences of the election of a neutralist Labour government has the American president telling his advisers, "We lost China in 1949 and got by. We lost Vietnam in 1973 and got by. But if we lose Britain, we're done for."[50]

It is certainly true that although Britain has become a much less powerful ally for the United States since its armed forces and military commitments were drastically reduced in the 1960s and since other allies such as West Germany, France, and Japan overtook it economically in the same period, it still performs an important, if not vital, function in terms of American security. In the mid-1980s there were over 130 U.S. bases and military facilities of various kinds on British soil. The most obvious of these are the air bases—approximately one fifth of U.S. Air Force personnel stationed abroad are in Britain—and the nuclear submarine bases, but probably the most important are the electronic intelligence installations such as those at Menwith Hill in Yorkshire and Chicksands in Bedfordshire.[51] It remains a matter for speculation as to what the United States would do if the existence or operation of any of these was threatened by the actions of the host government.

Ultimately, however, Britain's special relationship with the United States and its membership in NATO have always depended upon successive governments' perception of the threat from the Soviet Union. There have been earlier hopes of East-West détente, notably after Joseph Stalin's death in 1953 and again in the 1970s, but the advent of Mikhail Gorbachev and *perestroika* are in a class by themselves. While professing admiration and sympathy for Gorbachev's policies, the Thatcher government is proceeding extremely cautiously insofar as the consequences for the Western alliance are concerned, as can be seen in its strong support for the modernization of NATO's theater nuclear weapons. Even if the Soviet Union is no longer a threat, the argument runs, it still has the capability to become one again.

As in its attitude toward the United States, the government's perception of the Soviet Union seems to be lagging behind that of public opinion. In March 1981, 70 percent of respondents to a Market and Opinion Research International poll stated that they thought the Soviet Union wished to extend its power over other countries, while only 31 percent said the same about the United States. Eight years later the two superpowers are running about neck and neck in the expansion stakes, with only 35 percent now believing that the Soviet Union wanted to extend its power compared with 33 percent thinking it of the United States.[52] Mrs. Thatcher may not be, to use one of her own expressions, "for turning" as a result of such sentiments on the part of the electorate. But if détente between the two superpowers continues, she could well find that, to use another of her favorite phrases, "there is no alternative."

Notes

1. C.P. (50) 118, 28 May 1950, *Documents on British Policy Overseas*, 2d ser. (London, 1984–), 2, no. 113 (hereafter *DBPO*, 2d ser., with volume and document numbers).
2. P.H.P. (45) 29 (O) Final, 29 June 1945, CAB 81/46, Public Record Office, Kew, England; C.P. (45) 112, 14 August 1945, *Documents on British Policy Overseas*, 1st ser. (London, 1984–), 3, no. 6 (hereafter *DBPO*, 1st ser., with volume and document numbers).
3. Unsigned memorandum, 21 March 1944, Record Class FO 371/38523/AN1538, PRO.
4. See, for example, Terry H. Anderson, *The United States, Great Britain, and the Cold War, 1944–1947* (Columbia, MO, 1981); and Robert M. Hathaway, *Ambiguous Partnership: Britain and America, 1944–1947* (New York, 1981).
5. Documents on the American loan are printed in *DBPO*, 1st ser., 3; and in U.S. Department of State, *Foreign Relations of the United States, 1945* (Washington, 1969), 6:1–204 (hereafter *FRUS* with year and volume number). For the Spaatz-Tedder agreement see Simon Duke, *US Defence Bases in the United Kingdom: A Matter for Joint Decision?* (London, 1987), 20–25, 195–98. For the UKUSA agreement see James Bamford, *The Puzzle Palace: A Report on America's Most Secret Agency*, rev. ed. (New York, 1983), chap. 8. For the "Pentagon talks" see William Roger Louis, *The British Empire in the Middle East, 1945–1951: Arab Nationalism, the United States, and Postwar Imperialism* (Oxford, 1984), 109–11.
6. GEN.163/1st Meeting, 8 January 1947, CAB 130/18, PRO. See also Margaret Gowing, *Independence and Deterrence: Britain and Atomic Energy, 1945–1952*, 2 vols. (London, 1974), 1:92–111.
7. D.O. (46) 40, 13 March 1946, CAB 131/2, PRO.

8. For a fuller development of this thesis see Geoffrey Warner, "The Labour Governments and the Unity of Western Europe," in *The Foreign Policy of the British Labour Governments, 1945–1951*, ed. Ritchie Ovendale (Leicester, 1984), 61–82; and idem, "Britain and Europe in 1948: The View from the Cabinet," in *Power in Europe? Great Britain, France, Italy, and Germany in a Postwar World, 1945–1950*, ed. Josef Becker and Franz Knipping (New York, 1986), 27–46.

9. C.P. (48) 249, 2 November 1948, Record Class CAB 129/30, PRO. For Britain's role in the formation of NATO see Nicholas Henderson, *The Birth of NATO* (London 1982), which is in fact a classified contemporary account. Bevin's alleged remark in December 1950 is cited in Geoffrey Warner, "The British Labour Government and the Atlantic Alliance, 1949–1951," in *Western Security: The Formative Years: European and Atlantic Defence, 1947–1953*, ed. Olav Riste (Oslo, 1985), 263.

10. D.O. (47) 44, 22 May 1947, printed in Julian Lewis, *Changing Direction: British Military Planning for Postwar Strategic Defence, 1942–1947* (London, 1988), appendix 7. The original is still classified. See also D.O. (50) 5th Meeting, 23 March 1950, CAB 131/8; and D.O. (50) 34, May 1950, cited in *DBPO*, 2d ser. 2, no. 43, fn. 2 (the document is still classified).

11. C.M. (50) 29, 8 May 1950, *DBPO*, 2d ser. 2, no. 74; Warner, "The British Labour Government and the Atlantic Alliance," 256–62.

12. Evelyn Schuckburgh letter, 21 June 1950, *DBPO*, 2d ser. 2, no. 117. See also Dean Acheson, *Present at the Creation: My Years in the State Department* (New York, 1969), 323–24.

13. Kinna minute, 24 April 1950, Ernest Davies MSS (in private possession). Mr. Davies was a parliamentary undersecretary of state for foreign affairs at the time. I am most grateful to him for showing me this document, which has not been published and which I have been unable to locate in the Public Record Office.

14. Jessup memorandum, 7 December 1950, *FRUS, 1950* (Washington, 1978), 5:1452. See also Gowing, *Independence and Deterrence* 1:308–13.

15. *FRUS, 1951* (Washington, 1979), 1:880–94, 900. See also Gowing, *Independence and Deterrence* 1:315–18.

16. Paul-Henri Spaak, *Combats Inachevés* [Unfinished struggles] (Paris, 1969), 1:315. For the Labour government's policy toward EDC see Geoffrey Warner, "The Labour Governments and the Unity of Western Europe," 74–79; for that of the Conservative government see John Young, "German Rearmament and the European Defence Community," in *The Foreign Policy of Churchill's Peacetime Administration, 1951–1955*, ed. John Young (Leicester, 1988), 81–107.

17. Robert H. Ferrell, ed., *The Eisenhower Diaries* (New York, 1981), 222–24.

18. Lloyd letter, 8 August 1959, Record Class FO 800/728, PRO. See also Anthony Eden, *Full Circle* (London, 1980), passim; Brian Lapping, *End of Empire* (London, 1985), chap. 4; and C. D. Jackson log, 11 July 1955, *FRUS, 1955–1957* (Washington, 1989), 5:304.

19. Douglas Dodds-Parker, *Political Eunuch* (Ascot, 1986), 111–12. See also Lloyd memorandum, 30 May 1958, FO 800/728.

20. Chester Cooper, *The Lion's Last Roar: Suez, 1956* (New York, 1978), 173, 197–200. Cooper was the CIA's liaison officer with the British.

21. This question was first explored in David Carlton, *Anthony Eden, A Biography* (London, 1985), 456–65. A fuller account may now be found in W. Scott Lucas, "Suez, the Americans, and the Overthrow of Anthony Eden," *L.S.E. Quarterly* 1 (September 1987): 227–54.

22. Millard memorandum, August 1957, FO 800/728.

23. Eisenhower letter, 2 November 1956, in *Ike's Letters to a Friend, 1941–1958*, ed. Robert Griffith (Lawrence, 1984), 175; Harold Macmillan, *Riding the Storm, 1958–1959* (London, 1971), 240–41.

24. Lloyd telegram, 16 October 1957, PREM 11/246, PRO.   See also Macmillan telegram, 25 March 1957, FO 371/129330/ZP28.

25. C.C. 78 (57), 28 October 1957, CAB 128/31(2).

26. Harold Macmillan, *Pointing the Way, 1959–1961* (London, 1972), 316.

27. Harold Macmillan, *At the End of the Day, 1961–1963* (London, 1973), 531.

28. Harold Watkinson, *Turning Point: A Record of Our Times* (Salisbury, 1986), 144–52.

29. Macmillan, *At the End of the Day*, 335.

30. Ibid., 555; George Ball, *The Past Has Another Pattern, Memoirs* (New York, 1982), 262–68. See also Macmillan, *At the End of the Day*, 341–44, 355–62, 553–55.

31. Macmillan, *At the End of the Day*, 367.

32. Ibid., chap. 7.

33. Ball, *Past Has Another Pattern*, 266.

34. Richard Crossman, *The Diaries of a Cabinet Minister*, 3 vols. (London, 1976), 1:95. See also Clive Ponting, *Breach of Promise: Labour in Power, 1964–1970* (London, 1989), chap. 3.

35. Bruce Reed and Geoffrey Williams, *Denis Healey and the Politics of Power* (London, 1971), 172–73.

36. Tony Benn, *Out of the Wilderness: Diaries, 1963–1967* (London, 1988), 449.

37. Barbara Castle, *The Castle Diaries, 1964–1970* (London, 1984), 178.

38. Benn, *Out of the Wilderness*, 480–81, 503. See also Crossman, *Diaries of a Cabinet Minister* 2:84.

39. James Callaghan, *Time and Change* (London, 1987), 211–12.

40. Reed and Williams, *Healey*, 229; Castle, *Castle Diaries*, 354; Ponting, *Breach of Promise*, 59.

41. Michael Stewart, *Life and Labour: An Autobiography* (London, 1980), 224–26. See also Joe Haines, *The Politics of Power* (London, 1977), 74–81.

42. Reed and Williams, *Healey*, 254–58.

43. Henry Kissinger, *White House Years* (Boston, 1979), 933.

44. Attlee telegram, 10 December 1950, FO 800/817.

45. Henry Kissinger, *Years of Upheaval* (Boston, 1982), 709–17; Heath, speech to the House of Commons, 16 April 1986, Parliamentary Debates (House), 6th ser., vol. 95, col. 891; Duncan Campbell, *The Unsinkable Aircraft Carrier: American Military Power in Britain*, rev. ed. (London, 1986), 345.

46. Kissinger, *White House Years*, 90; idem, *Years of Upheaval*, 278–85.

47. Hugo Young, *One of Us* (London, 1985), 249.

48. Ibid., 541–42.

49. Dean Gordon, "British Attitudes towards the United States," in *British Security Policy and the Atlantic Alliance: Prospects for the 1990s*, ed. Martin Holmes et al. (Washington, 1987), 101, 113.

50. Chris Mullin, *A Very British Coup* (London, 1988), 161. The author is a Labour M.P.

51. Campbell, *Unsinkable Aircraft Carrier*, 286–96; Duke, *US Defence Bases*, appendix 3.

52. *The Times*, 5 April 1989.

France and the United States

Pierre Mélandri *

To create a public image in France, one must choose between the "Lafayette sauce" or the "de Gaulle sauce," Michel Jobert observed a few years ago.[1] This remark, by a prominent political figure, suggests the omnipresence of America as a point of reference in French politics. Even if aspects as fundamental as transnational economic, technological, and cultural realities are set aside, Franco-American political relations are essential for France. This explains the difficulty of the choice alluded to earlier: On the one hand, the Lafayette sauce is as unavoidable as is solidarity among Westerners; on the other, with such a powerful partner, the desire to exist triggers a reflex to resist. That is indeed the principal innovation introduced by World War II into relations between France and the United States.

It is true that during most of the 1930s political relations between the two countries were nonexistent, or almost so.[2] The war quickly changed that state of affairs. First, Pearl Harbor proved to Americans that, willingly or not, they were living in a world too small for them to remain on the sidelines; second, the 1940 defeat convinced Franklin D. Roosevelt of the decadence of France. Thus, after maintaining diplomatic relations with Vichy for two years, the American president took a long time to accept the legitimacy of General Charles de Gaulle, whom he tended to consider an aspiring dictator or an adventurer. Of course, amid the joy of liberation in 1944, Americans received an enthusiastic welcome from the French. But the French also saw them as partners with whom they would have to fight continuously in order to guarantee the legitimacy of Free France and of the Resistance and to recover the country's earlier status, which had been compromised during the war.

---

* Translated by Françoise Massardier-Kenney and Mark R. Rubin.

The Fourth Republic

An obvious paradox characterized the relations between Washington and Paris during the Fourth Republic. Whereas after 1947 the alliance with the United States was perhaps the only real constant in the policy of French leaders, they, and even more so the French public, often felt distrustful or irritated by their powerful ally. When choosing a camp, France was, in fact, only yielding to the inevitable. Ultimately, France's choice remained a bitter reminder of the vanity of its illusions at the end of the war.

Beyond sovereignty, it was status that de Gaulle thought he had recovered for the French during the war's last months. To him, that success was a victory over Roosevelt, who for a while actually had wished to see France disarmed. However, his suspicions toward the Americans were not allayed. His somewhat distorted vision of Yalta would keep on haunting him. The general could not forget that the Americans opposed the French on two key questions: Germany and the French Empire.

It was not the general's departure from office in 1946 that modified Paris's policy objectives. For a while, France continued to attempt to pursue a balanced policy between the Soviet Union and the United States, a policy that it saw as its best guarantee for an independent diplomatic policy. From 1947 to 1950, however, the illusion of France maintaining a position equidistant from the two Great Powers completely disappeared. The replacement of the old European order by a world system dominated by Washington and the Kremlin, portended by the Soviet establishment of a security buffer zone but slowed for a time because of American hesitation in assuming worldwide responsibilities, was hastened. Politically weak, in desperate shape economically, France appeared in 1950 to be less an independent country than the "unwilling satellite" of one of the two great powers.[3]

On the whole, the American announcement of the Marshall Plan was well received by Paris, for the plan was supposed to ensure the reconstruction of the French production system and to allow a modernized France to recover a large measure of its independence in just a few years. But this intention did not take into account a fateful chain reaction that superimposed strategic preoccupations onto economic difficulties. The first link in this chain was the Soviet Union's refusal to participate.

For France, the consequences of that refusal were catastrophic. Communist ministers were dismissed from the Paul Ramadier cabinet in May 1947, but it was quite a long time before they gave up the hope of resuming their responsibilities. At the end of the summer, however, that possibility was no longer realistic, and, with the creation of the Cominform in the fall, the game was up. After working toward the French recovery effort in a substantial way, the French Communist party at this point tried to undermine it. The quasi-insurrection that broke out at the end of the year may have indirectly facilitated the granting of "temporary aid," which the government so desperately needed. But it also spread feelings of anxiety that were exacerbated two months later by the events of Prague. As early as February 14, Hervé Alphand remarked: "There is a lot of talk about the Prague events which put Czechoslovakia under the communist hold and which are an uncanny reminder of the March 15, 1939 events—except that the Soviets are more skillful than Hitler. Instead of sending in their armed forces, they use the Marxist ideal and allow the Czech Communist Party to carry out its coup d'état."[4] On 4 March 1948, Foreign Minister Georges Bidault wrote to General George C. Marshall, asking him to "strengthen collaboration between the old and new worlds, already so closely linked in their devotion to the only civilization worthy of that name, both on the political, and as quickly as possible, on the military front."[5]

The French minister must have hoped that the Americans would accede to his request, especially since he was then making concessions on some of the fundamental points on which France's German policy had been established. Already, during the preceding summer, Paris had been obliged to yield to the Anglo-American accords raising the steel production ceiling. The most serious incident occurred at the end of the year when, during the London quadripartite conference, the breakdown of negotiations turned Germany into a key stake and made its integration into the Western camp a high priority. From then on the creation of a West German government seemed unavoidable.[6]

To the French, this sequence of events involved a double danger: in the short term, the risk of a violent reaction from the opposite camp; and, in the long term, the threat of a Germany with restored power and sovereignty. From then on the birth of the West German state and the creation of the Atlantic Pact were closely intertwined. As early as 23 April 1948, British Foreign Secretary Ernest Bevin reminded the Americans that "a system of Atlantic security is probably the only way to convince the French to agree to the rebuilding of Germany."[7] Not only was the French Senate called upon to approve the "London Recommendations" only after the "Vandenberg Resolution" was passed, but also the North Atlantic Treaty's signature was to be followed by an agreement that diminished the constraints imposed on vanquished Germany.

For France, the abandonment of its German policy was not the only sign of its dependence. That status seemed to be embodied in the conditions under which Marshall Plan aid was granted: The French government had to pledge to do "its best" to stabilize its currency, to balance its budget at the earliest time, to ease restrictions on its exchanges with other countries, and, possibly, to grant the United States privileged access to strategic materials that the French overseas territories might have at their disposal. Most importantly, the use of "counterpart funds" would have to be authorized by the representatives of the Economic Cooperation Administration in Paris.

The conclusion of the Atlantic Pact also bespoke French dependence on the United States. France was unable to exact an "automatic" commitment from its new ally, it was obligated in the name of mutual assistance to furnish bases to its allies, and it was to obtain, at least at the outset, only a small part of the military assistance on which it had counted. As a poignant reminder of America's situation when it had to negotiate a treaty with the French king at the end of the eighteenth century, the pact was a superb example of the role reversal between the two allies.[8] That situation also was symbolized by the practice of French government leaders visiting Washington almost immediately upon their appointment, as though they required a stamp of authenticity from a power without whose aid it would be difficult for them to govern.

Was this dependency harmful to French interests?[9] The answer is extremely delicate. First, the relationship furnished France with a considerable amount of desperately needed aid.[10] France did not recover its independence in large part because it had to devote more resources than it anticipated to its security spending, and also because its colonial conflicts added to its budgetary deficits. American aid allowed France, because of Jean Monnet's influence, to carry out most of the modernization plan that he had conceived. Second, as early as 1952, Antoine Pinay, then finance minister, judged France to have recovered sufficiently to reject as unacceptable a memorandum in which the American ambassador suggested corrections to his budget proposal. If it is true that the Atlantic Pact solidified France's dependence in security matters, at least it gave France the American security guarantee that it had so sorely lacked after 1918.

How, in this case, can we explain the bitterness still elicited by American domination and best expressed by President Vincent Auriol on 17 November 1952 in an ultrasecret message addressed to Henri Bonnet: "The French . . . are wondering whether really the only reason we are part of the Atlantic pact is to be the target of humiliations?"[11] Two forces predominate: the tactlessness of many Americans, in particular of the press, who tended to treat the French as beggars and to compare them constantly and unfavorably to the Germans; and the rise of the United States, which seemed to correspond too closely to the decline of France. For the French, Americans did not come out stronger because of the decline of Europeans; rather, Europe's decline had resulted from America's desire for power. Had not the Americans made every effort to frustrate every French attempt to carry a bit more weight?

To be heard, Paris thought that it had leverage at its disposal. It had its status as a Great Power, which its participation in the Standing Group of NATO would solidify. However, the Americans did not intend to treat a country with precarious stability and reliability, and which, moreover, did not have a sufficiently large military force at its disposal, in the same way that they treated Britain. In January 1949 the French cabinet called on its ambassador to Washington, Henri Bonnet, to request the creation of an American-British-French "Special Defense Council" within the framework of the future alliance. But the U.S. Joint Chiefs of Staff objected that, unlike Britain and the United States, which had worldwide responsibilities at the strategic level, the French "have basically only European and North African responsibilities and inadequate strength to play any role in other theaters and therefore are not entitled to participate in consideration of global strategy."[12] Eventually, a compromise was devised: "to give France full membership in whatever was the real controlling body from the military point of view of the Pact, but at the same time confine the functions of any of the organizations under the Pact to the immediate question of the implementation of the Treaty."[13]

Despite repeated attempts, France never obtained the extension of the Standing Group's responsibilities outside of the treaty area. Quite to the contrary, its privileged status was gradually eroded by the adoption of a nuclear strategy emphasizing the primacy of the United States and the United Kingdom. In spite of French aspirations to a status like Britain's, France's partners always seemed to be comparing it to Italy.

For many Frenchmen, their empire should at least have been able to compensate for an excessively lopsided balance of forces. In a way, the Cold War at first impelled the Americans to help them. Nonetheless, few French leaders saw any reason to thank the Americans for their financial support in Indochina, after the victory of Mao Zedong. They mainly viewed that support as a cheap way for Washington, having signed an armistice in Korea as recently as July 1953, to allow another country, much less wealthy and much smaller, to wage the struggle that America should have been leading against the opposite camp. The conditions of U.S. aid extinguished France's hope to reaffirm its presence and its power.

Nonetheless, a united Europe, under French leadership, would at least have bolstered Paris's influence vis-à-vis the United States, especially since the Americans from 1947 had continually declared themselves in favor of such a French initiative.[14] It is true that French attempts to form a "third force" with the British met with indifference, if not hostility, but the March 1950 launching of Jean Monnet's Schuman Plan seemed clearly to reconcile the opposing points of view. This plan, which combined a supranational system likely to reassure the French with an offer of the "equality" to which the Federal Republic of Germany aspired, was interpreted by American officials as the unexpected proof of a French "renaissance." In the estimation of Dean Acheson, Monnet and Robert Schuman would from then on become privileged partners.

Unfortunately, that promising but delicate balance had hardly been reached when it was swept away by the Korean War, which refocused attention on matters of security and dealt European integration a blow from which it never quite recovered. France's leadership would never be as Atlanticist as it was during the weeks following the beginning of the war. In the hope of linking the United States more closely than ever to their security, the French proposed the creation of an integrated army. The Americans, in endorsing that plan, used it to extract a new concession from a crippled French government: Germany would have to be rearmed.

Monnet's bold plan for a European Coal and Steel Community was not successful in resolving this problem. The announcement of the Pleven Plan in October 1950, followed by its American-influenced metamorphosis into the European Defense Community (EDC) in May 1952, indeed provoked widespread French distrust toward a plan that the Americans, after a period of initial skepticism, were now zealously backing. For Paris, European military integration had been a way for France to use German potential to its advantage and to be more clearly heard by Washington. But now it seemed to be resulting in a community where the Germans could well become the dominant force and the French army would be placed under the authority of an allied (American) commander in chief. The situation changed rapidly following Joseph Stalin's death, after the July 1953 armistice quelled the panic created by the Korean War, and after McCarthyism tainted the image of those who had liberated Europe from nazism. In spite of the many concessions or admonitions proposed by American leaders, the French would not yield. By stressing the dichotomy between atomic powers and other alliance members, the new doctrine of massive retaliation exacerbated French fears that their status as the third "great" Western power would be not reinforced but instead called into question by the EDC. On 30 August 1954, under the Pierre Mendès-France government, Paris finally rejected the plan that it had itself put forward.

This flurry of resistance concealed a state of dependency and impotence. Not only had Germany been rearmed but also, in Indochina, the Americans seemed in a hurry to replace the French, thus confirming the suspicions of all those who denounced the hypocrisy of the pious speeches of Americans about the colonies' right to independence.

Between 1954 and 1958, colonial problems constantly fueled French suspicions of Washington. The idea had already been advanced in 1951 under the René Pleven government, then again in 1954 under Mendès-France, and Guy Mollet's government advocated for a third time the necessity for a tripartite dialogue. From 1955 on, following the mass entry of the newly independent colonies into the United Nations and the shifting of the Cold War toward the less developed world, along with the "balance of terror" American anticolonialism became increasingly intense. The Suez crisis of 1956 thus left lasting scars.

The French claimed that the Americans were largely responsible for the crisis that broke out during that summer through their refusal to finance the Aswan Dam. Worse still, the Americans encouraged Gamal Nasser's resistance by arbitrarily ruling out any use of force. To the United States, the Franco-British expedition was completely "senseless"; Washington was further angered at not having been warned about it. Not only did "gunboat diplomacy" discredit the West in the eyes of newly created countries, but it also effectively prevented the successful exploitation of Soviet repression in Hungary for propaganda purposes. Thus the Americans voted against their allies and with Russia in the United Nations. It is now known that President Dwight D. Eisenhower was ready to help his allies in the event of a Soviet attack.[15] But when, after Nikolai Bulganin's threat of a nuclear strike against Western Europe, the French turned to their ally, the response they received scarcely clarified matters for them. According to Christian Pineau, that response could be summarized in the following way: "The United States will honor its obligations to the Atlantic Alliance in case of a Soviet attack in Europe. However, the alliance can only come into play in the Middle East if Nasser is first to attack the Franco-British forces. In the event, they were the first ones to open fire; consequently the American guarantee does not apply."[16] According to André Fontaine, Secretary of the Treasury Douglas Dillon left open the question of what would happen if Franco-British forces ran into Soviet "volunteers" in Egypt.[17]

In France the crisis triggered anti-Americanism and a strong nationalist reaction. The desire to escape a restrictive dependency on the United States renewed the appeal of European integration, as well as in that of a French nuclear arsenal. As early as 30 November, a protocol defining the objective of a nuclear defense program was signed. At the same time, it became clear that the Common Market, until that time in a precarious state, was to be approved by the National Assembly. As Pineau noted, "The union of Europe was not only a noble dream; for a growing number of people, it was becoming a vital necessity."[18]

Those two strategies—European and nuclear—occasionally were combined. After *Sputnik* in October 1957, when the long-term reliability of American protection began to be disputed, the building of a bomb was decreed by the Félix Gaillard government (on 11 April 1958), and the old EDC plan was momentarily revived. The so-called Strauss-Chaban-Delmas agreement, which General de Gaulle was to cancel as soon as he came to power, was signed. This agreement provided for financial aid from the Federal Republic of Germany (and probably from Italy as well) for construction of French isotopic separation plant at Pierrelatte; in return,

France was to share information, some of which could have military significance, with those two countries.[19]

Nothing, however, better displayed the frustrations felt by the Fourth Republic toward the United States than the dissensions and suspicions raised by the Algerian War, the very cause of the republic's demise. The war so depleted the national treasury that by 1958 all gains realized from past economies were lost. The government once again found itself in the humiliating position of begging, particularly in Washington. Moreover, throughout the conflict, the French were irritated and their feelings were hurt by what they sometimes considered a betrayal, or at least a lack of solidarity, on the part of their allies. François Mitterrand suggested on 30 September 1957 that "we must explain to our allies that they have not understood—because we perhaps did not make it clear enough to them— that it is now the Mediterranean, and no longer the Rhine, that is central to our security."[20] But Eisenhower believed that the conflict impaired the participation of France in the integrated Atlantic army and that, by putting the United States in an impossible situation vis-à-vis the recently emancipated nations, it would be likely to make the opposite camp's task easier.

If, on the whole, the Americans were publicly hesitant to abandon an ally that seemed to be on the verge of collapse, the pro-Arab activism, real or supposed, of American oil companies, of their union activists, and of their secret agents gave rise among the French to the worst suspicions. The French indeed tended to think that their allies were impatient to take their place in the Mediterranean as they already had done in Indochina. However much American officials attempted to dissociate themselves from Senator John F. Kennedy's famous 2 July 1957 speech advocating Algerian independence, they never managed to dispel Paris's suspicions.

Charles de Gaulle

Those who identified the arrival of General de Gaulle with the retention of French control over Algeria were often to feel betrayed. That was certainly not true of those who saw him as the best defense against the intrusive influence of the United States. His foreign policy can largely be interpreted as a struggle against a hegemony that was considered a threat to Paris's independence and an obstacle (along with the analogous ascendancy of the Soviet Union) to the strengthened integration of Western Europe. For him, the principal errors of the Fourth Republic's officials were their failure to understand that France's dependence on the United Kingdom between the wars had turned out to be a handicap and their repetition of the same mistake when they accepted the leadership of the United States after 1945. In his view, Paris's mission was to fight the bloc system inherited from the war, which he described as a "misfortune coming after other misfortunes" for the European countries. In this, his policies showed remarkable continuity, although his approach was flexible. At the start the general limited himself to lending an air of success and credibility to the strategies of his Fourth Republic predecessors. But, from the middle of the decade until 1968, he concentrated on challenging the United States in a new and daring manner.

When he came to power, de Gaulle realized that his margin of maneuver was limited by the Warsaw Pact's aggressiveness and by the weakness of French resources. As a Westerner he could not, for the moment, consider distancing himself too far from the United States. Soviet adventurism ruled that out. But France had to rebuild its strength if it wanted to resist the Americans in any significant way. At the end of 1958 an austerity program and the first really successful devaluation of the franc allowed France to participate actively in the Common Market and to free itself of its foreign debt. In February 1960, its entry into the nuclear club gave new credence to its claim to equality with the United States and Britain. Most of all, the establishment of a stable administration, based on a strong executive, restored authority to a country that had been ridiculed for the instability of its government. The end of the Algerian war, and the badly needed budgetary relief that this provided, also liberated French diplomacy in many ways.

The Americans, who had been puzzled by de Gaulle's rise to power, were relieved. De Gaulle turned out to be the most steadfast of their allies against the power plays of the Soviet Union. During the second Berlin crisis, it was he who was most determined in his support for a hard line toward the Kremlin. During the abortive summit of 1960 as well, Eisenhower found him to be his strongest ally. Finally, although he went out of his way to point out that he had not been consulted, only informed, the general did not hide from Dean Acheson, Kennedy's envoy, the fact that he unconditionally supported Kennedy's determination to resist the positioning of Soviet nuclear missiles in Cuba. However, even if relations between the two countries were for a long time better than had been foreseen and if, as a result, in April 1960, the general was able to make a triumphant trip to the United States, the period of calm in Franco-American relations was coming to an end. Indeed, the general very soon showed his desire to see the status quo radically altered.

Atomic questions were at the center of Franco-American relations during these years. It is true that the tone was set at the very beginning, in July 1958, when John Foster Dulles met with the new French head of state. The American diplomat proposed to equip France with nuclear weapons with a two-key system. "We know," he reportedly told him, "that you are on the verge of developing your own atomic weapons. But, instead of your spending great sums on research and development, as well as on manufacturing them, wouldn't it be better if we supplied them to you?"[21] For the general, this proposal held no interest because of its two-key provision. The primary reason behind his desire for a nuclear capability was to give France a back-up insurance policy.[22] But he also wanted to ensure that France would have full independence. Thus, he refused any aid with strings attached. That is not to say that de Gaulle could accept Washington's incomprehensible (for him) attitude: "The McMahon law!" he exclaimed, when Eisenhower invoked it to justify his position. "I changed the French Constitution when I found that it was no longer workable."[23]

In 1961 the Kennedy administration concluded an agreement providing for an exchange of information on nuclear armaments in coordination with operational military imperatives. But this innocuous agreement was probably intended more to discourage the French national effort than to encourage it. Indeed, under Kennedy, Washington intended less than ever to provide any aid that would not subordinate the French nuclear strike force to American decision making. To the general's mind, the "great plan" was suspect from the start: Its goal seemed to be to integrate all of Europe into a large Atlantic free-trade zone whose security would be the exclusive responsibility of the United States.

Strengthened by an exceptional national recovery but, most importantly, freed by the evolution that Nikita Khrushchev's ouster and Leonid Brezhnev's arrival on the scene seemed to indicate, the general felt both capable and obliged to combat what he perceived then as the true danger: the propensity of a country whose power, which seemed more than ever to be unequalled, to dominate everything. That the spirit in which the challenge was made was perhaps more defensive than is generally acknowledged is indicated in Georges Pompidou's remark to Cyrus Sulzberger at the beginning of 1968: "He [de Gaulle] sees that Russia is on the defensive everywhere. The biggest weight, the greatest power is by far that of the United States. As for us, and especially in France, we must take care not to be swallowed up by the United States, In fact, I am gradually beginning to think that that is bound to happen anyway, but you know what we are trying to do."[24]

At a time when the United States was discovering that it could not simultaneously wage the war in Vietnam and the war against poverty, and when the Soviet Union had embarked upon a program of armament intended to ensure "parity," this obsession may seem unjustified. Nonetheless, that the recovery of France came at a time when it was being excluded from direct relations between the Soviet Union and the United States, probably illustrates not only the limits of the power of de Gaulle's worldview but also the reality of the danger that the general was combating. He denounced his big ally's role in the Vietnam War as hegemonic, while reminding everyone that he had warned Washington against involvement in the hornets' nest that was Indochina. He was sincerely convinced that France had to offer the underdeveloped world an alternative among the industrialized democracies. He believed that France had been able to do for Algeria what the United States had not succeeded in doing for Cuba after the revolution, namely, to prevent a nationalist movement from going over to the Soviet side. He also believed that the West had to envisage something beyond liberalism, whose dangers were evident, if it wanted to solve what seemed to him to be perhaps the most important problem of the second half of the twentieth century, the development of the world's most backward countries.

Similarly, that the American economy coped with the difficulties facing it did not at all diminish the danger for the allies. First, the United States might have been more than ever tempted to take advantage of the monetary privileges that it had obtained, at the risk of jeopardizing the entire system. Second, the phenomenal expansion of American multinational firms during those years occurred in the most technologically sophisticated fields, causing widespread anxiety.[25] Those technological advances, immortalized by the best-seller *The American Challenge*,[26] had serious effects; the American refusal to sell a giant computer necessary for the nuclear strike force to France in 1963 is the best example of that. Last, the worldwide expansion of English as an international language threatened the cultural influence of French.

In 1964 the first milestones of the new policy were set when initial contacts with the Soviet bloc were made; when the general made two trips to Latin America, considered by the United States as part of its private domain; when, during the first UN Conference on Trade and Development (UNCTAD) meeting, France supported the stabilization of raw material prices; and, especially, when Paris extended diplomatic recognition to the People's Republic of China. One year later the attacks were already less indirect. Not only did the general affirm his hostility toward the American intervention in the Dominican Republic but also, after evoking the possibility of a European solution in which "blocs" would be eliminated, he mounted a virulent attack against the dollar. Hervé Alphand remarked on 10 April:

> The general's January declarations about the gold standard, plus some large gold transactions made by Paris, had done more to increase Washington's bitterness than any other previous crisis. . . . This time, the majority of the public had been alerted and thought that the evil general wanted, in some satanic way, to attack their pocketbooks. In this country, nothing matters anymore besides the dollar.[27]

A few days later Maurice Couve de Murville admitted that Franco-American relations had never been at such a low ebb. But one year later a second initiative provoked a still more dramatic crisis: the early 1966 announcement of France's withdrawal from Supreme Headquarters Allied Powers Europe (SHAPE), whose creation France itself had requested of the United States during the summer of 1950. The shock effect was tremendous, even though de Gaulle had warned the Americans for several years about his intention to be done with an "integrated" system that France judged to be incompatible with its sovereignty, and even though the technical consequences of the act were greatly attenuated by the February 1967 conclusion of the Lemnitzer-Ailleret agreement. De Gaulle's solemn visit to the Soviet Union in the same year made his decision all the more troubling. Shortly thereafter, in Phnom Penh, he inveighed loudly against America's Indochina policy, repeating the criticisms that the United States had whispered to France during the Algerian troubles.

The offensive seemed to lose momentum in 1967. De Gaulle's "Long live Free Quebec" and the position taken during the Israeli-Egyptian war disconcerted many Frenchmen. Although the "all-directions defense strategy" outlined in December 1967 in the *Revue de Défense nationale* by General Charles Ailleret reflected the thoughts of the French president, it troubled even some of his closest advisers and was quickly abandoned. Yet in spring 1968 the general seemed to be on the verge of success. The United States was supporting the policy of détente, which he was advocating, and the Prague Spring seemed to portend liberalization in the opposite camp. The March monetary crisis in the United States demonstrated the extent of the danger that de Gaulle had been the first to denounce, and the choice of Paris by Hanoi and Washington for their negotiations exemplified the moral authority wielded by France. However, a few months later, the limitations and failure of de Gaulle's grandiose designs were brutally revealed. First, the entry of Warsaw Pact tanks into Prague in August quickly chilled its "spring." Second, the aftermath of the May 1968 uprising displayed the fragility of the economic base on which the fight against the dollar was founded. Most important, France had been saying aloud what many in Europe only dared think, although in so doing it took the risk of becoming isolated by taking excessively daring positions.

General de Gaulle seemed to have recognized that possibility since, from the end of 1968 on, his policy appeared to be closer to the one he had first pursued. At first, a kind of rapprochement with the United States was achieved. While the election of Richard Nixon, of whom de Gaulle had always had a high opinion, made that easier, it would seem that things already had begun to improve under Lyndon Johnson. After all, the Texan had offered to help the French government when it decided not to devalue the franc at the end of 1968. Although de Gaulle pursued his efforts to make France into an alternative model of industrialized democracy for the underdeveloped world, it was principally through a regrouping of European states that he sought to counterbalance the excessive influence of the United States. His successors also pursued this dual strategy, albeit with differences in style.

Georges Pompidou

The evolution of relations between France and the United States under Georges Pompidou can seem baffling. At first, both sides desired to cooperate. Despite advice to the contrary, President Pompidou insisted on going to the United States in 1970 to avert a further deterioration in relations between the two allies. He personally facilitated the success of the negotiations that North Vietnam and the United States held in Paris, and he made no secret of his interest in the nuclear cooperation that Washington seemed to be promising him. On the other side of the Atlantic, Nixon and Henry Kissinger on several occasions chose Pompidou as an emissary for their dialogue with other allies. Washington and Paris shared the same distrust of West German Chancellor Willy Brandt's *Ostpolitik*, and Britain was too absorbed by the problems caused by its entry into the European Economic Community to be able to play that role adequately.

Still, at the end of Pompidou's life, in 1974, Franco-American relations again fell into a state of exacerbated tension. Indeed, beginning with Michel Jobert's assumption of the post of minister of foreign affairs, the rhetoric between the two partners became increasingly heated. But the decision to toughen the French position already had been made, and the Elysée had opted for a confrontational political strategy.

The personal feelings toward Pompidou doubtless impinged on this situation. His illness, for example, made him more pessimistic and more intransigent. He also had bad memories of his trip to the United States and of the affront that he thought his country, in the person of his wife and himself, had received. In all likelihood, he came to doubt that the French should expect very much from their efforts to reach an understanding with their powerful ally.

French independence and the construction of a powerful Europe were his highest priorities. Although he did not feel much warmth for Brandt, Pompidou was nonetheless pleased with his decision to allow Great Britain to present once again its candidacy for the Common Market. A few months later Edward Heath's rise to power began an unusual period in which Britain, when pulled in opposite directions by France and the United States, now decided in favor of the former.

For Nixon and Kissinger it was important to subordinate everything to the Atlantic Community. They were convinced that only the United States could effectively take on the leadership of industrialized democracies, all the while acknowledging that its material means, more limited than in the past, forced them to redefine their strategy on a more cynical basis. Consequently, they demanded virtually exclusive freedom in the management of détente with the Soviet bloc and a more equitable redistribution of the Western defense burden.

Differences of approach eventually surfaced. At first the Vietnam War preoccupied the Nixon administration. Furthermore, it was unable to get the Soviet Union to agree to its new strategic vision before its breakthrough in China. Thus, at the beginning, it seemed to have no interest in alliance affairs. But on 15 August 1971 this era of benign neglect suddenly ended when, confronted with the first American trade deficit since 1893, Nixon withdrew the dollar from the gold standard. A rude awakening for the Japanese as well as for the Europeans, this action set into motion a controversial period of conflicting monetary policies that strained relations.

It is in this context that one must place the chilling reception the French gave to the "Year of Europe" plan put forward by Kissinger in 1973. To the French, Kissinger was particularly suspect, since he seemed motivated by a crucial American concern to avoid the creation of a Europe intent upon defining its principal political orientation without prior consultation within the Atlantic context. Nixon and Kissinger attempted repeatedly to undertake a privileged dialogue with French officials to forward their goal. It is true that Michel Jobert had established excellent relations with Kissinger during his tenure as Elysée chief of staff, and, even at the height of their rivalry, the two men seemed to share a certain complicity. The Atlantic Declaration (26 June 1974), which ended the whole episode a little more than one year later, was actually written almost exclusively by the Americans and the French.

In the meantime, tempers flared and the dispute reached a high point. Jobert wanted to take advantage of everything that was happening in order to advance his real agenda: the emergence of a Europe conscious of its specificity and cooperating in all areas, especially in that of security. He even stated that "the French nuclear strike force is at the disposal of France and of Europe."[28]

The October 1973 war added yet another reason for French restiveness; it gave the initiative back to the Americans. For a while, the war and its repercussions for the oil market seemed to favor the French game by making public the difference of interests in the Middle East between the Americans and their allies. However, the European declaration of 6 November in favor of the Arab side did not reflect the new autonomy of the community as much as it revealed its extreme vulnerability, which was underscored by the quadrupling of oil prices at the end of the year. Thus, during the Washington Conference (February 1974), Kissinger had little difficulty in isolating France from its European partners. In their desire for a rapprochement with the United States, they were even ready to renege on their commitments to Paris. However, up to the last minute, Kissinger considered making important concessions in exchange for last-minute cooperation by the French, and Jobert, who later was identified with this intransigence, was instructed by the Elysée not to give in on anything.[29]

During the following weeks, France once again denounced American "hegemony," and Kissinger vilified what he considered Paris's unilateral maneuvers to undermine his efforts both in the Middle East and in the energy crisis. A few months later, however, the signing of the Atlantic Declaration ended this critical phase. By that time, Georges Pompidou, as well as Willy Brandt and Edward Heath, were no longer in office. Their departures coincided with the end of an era in which European history had become synonymous with expansion and prosperity, and, in retrospect, seemed to portend another era, one fraught with difficulty. In French foreign policy, economic constraints weighed even more heavily than previously. Not only were French financial resources diminished but also commercial considerations, particularly with respect to oil-producing countries, played a greater role than before. The United States faced a crisis over Watergate and Nixon's resignation, which diminished its resources. Probably the conviction that only a strategy of dialogue and conciliation toward the Soviet Union could serve the interests of a weakened West explains Valéry Giscard d'Estaing's policy toward the United States.

Valéry Giscard d'Estaing

From 1974 to 1981, relations between the two countries more than ever could be explained by the double modification of the context in which they were evolving. On the one hand, in 1974 preoccupations were focused on the energy crisis and its possible consequences for the economy, the "governability" of democracies, and the elaboration of a new order, consistent with the interests of the democracies and acceptable to poorer countries. On the other hand, détente was not being called into question, and military problems were not occasioning much anxiety. In 1981 the news was dominated by the renewal of tensions, the rise of the European peace movement, and the growing fear of nuclear war. The evolution of the military situation underlined Europe's dependence upon the United States, so that its desire for independence sometimes seemed to resemble a sort of Finlandization. Additionally, the French president's policy toward the two superpowers can be partially explained by the disillusionment with which his previous policy of rapprochement with the United States must have left him.

Giscard d'Estaing's policy certainly was not an abrupt break with the past. Elements of continuity were such that the Americans would sometimes be tempted to think that he was only a well-mannered Gaullist.

Indeed, the Gaullist heritage seemed to prevail. The return to the integrated army was not mentioned even once, and in December 1979 the French president avoided any involvement with the allied double decision that he had nevertheless helped to develop. Last, probably because his candidacy in 1974 had received the open support of the Soviet Union, and also because he saw détente as the best assurance of autonomy from the United States, the French president took the utmost care to maintain good relations with the Kremlin.

Were the French then becoming America's Cubans? To think so would be to misunderstand the spirit of Giscard d'Estaing's political strategy. For the French president, facing the unrelenting reality of the crisis and a renewed instability in the underdeveloped world, the West doubtless had to reaffirm its solidarity, but that could only come about with reciprocal advantages that everyone could hope to draw from it. During this period, American assistance to the French nuclear program, assistance that the Jimmy Carter administration would later increase, was defined. What Giscard d'Estaing probably aimed for were real compromises that would allow France and Europe to profit as much as the United States.

It is in that context that Giscard d'Estaing and West German Chancellor Helmut Schmidt took the joint initiative to propose a summit of the large industrialized democracies in November 1975 at Rambouillet. Moreover, it was in that spirit that what can be considered as the "great compromise" between France and the United States was defined from 1974 to 1975. On the one hand, the Americans endorsed the idea of a North-South conference, so dear to the French. But, on the other hand, France made a much more far-reaching concession to the United States: Giscard d'Estaing agreed to the International Monetary Fund's (IMF) abandonment of gold and, most importantly, to the final acceptance of floating exchange rates. He probably thought that the return to fixed parities had been made unworkable by the first oil crisis. Perhaps he also thought that he could count on assurances reportedly given to him in secret by the Americans that the commitment made by governments to intervene to "avoid erratic fluctuations of their currencies" would be followed up with tangible actions.

In brief, Giscard d'Estaing took the risk that Pompidou had abandoned, to trust the United States and its sense of responsibility. However, in spite of its internationalist pronouncements, the Carter administration proved unable to resist acting in accordance with the most selfish American interests. The result was a lax policy. Moreover, put at a disadvantage by the hostility generated among moderate Arab states by the Camp David accords, the Carter administration was incapable of saving the shah of Iran or of replacing him with a government favorable to American interests. In short, far from preventing it, the United States seems to have precipitated the second oil crisis.

These events had far-reaching consequences. They forced the Carter administration to reverse itself completely on monetary policy, a change confirmed by Paul Volcker's arrival at the head of the Federal Reserve Board. They also indicated the growing inability of the United States to control the instability of the underdeveloped world and emphasized America's weakened position vis-à-vis the Soviet bloc. The lessons learned from these developments by Frenchmen and Americans appear to differ almost completely from one another. For the French, since everything—including a resounding speech by Kissinger on 1 September 1979—suggested that the American security guarantees were being inescapably eroded, the most important priority was to maintain détente in Europe.

As early as 1977, Giscard d'Estaing was concerned about the consequences that the new Carter human rights policy would have for détente, since détente was coming under increasing criticism from the U.S. public and Congress. The discovery of the formidable rearmament effort being made by the opposite camp, accompanied by a string of successes in, for example, Saigon, Angola, and Ethiopia, led an increasingly large number of Americans to wonder whether, for the Soviet Union, détente was a one-way street. Arms control became suspect. The Strategic Arms Limitation Talks (SALT II) accord, signed in June 1979, came under vigorous attack almost immediately. The chances of its ratification had apparently all but vanished when the Soviet invasion of Afghanistan dealt its death blow.

This time, the Kremlin's aggression did not impel a rapprochement between French and Americans. The American tendency to take a hard line, after years of arms reduction, appeared unduly blunt, and even primarily inspired by electoral considerations. The French perceived that the disparity between America's rhetoric and its real capabilities could give rise to dangerous situations. When speaking to economic journalist Jean Boissonnat in 1981, Giscard d'Estaing confided that "he would say in his *Mémoires* exactly at what specific moment the weakness of Carter's America put the world on the edge of disaster."[30]

In short, for Europe the moment had come to remind the world of its existence and to define its interests. This time France was not alone. Schmidt's reaction to Carter was irritation and impatience. Moreover, the French president and the West German chancellor were encouraged by the success of their first effort, the international monetary system, that they had established to compensate for their ally's decline. But the shift of priorities toward new domains soon revealed the limits of European autonomy, especially in matters of security.

The Venice Declaration on the Middle East illustrated the limits of the old Continent's influence. Moderate Arab states mostly expected that the Europeans would put pressure on the Americans. Moreover, Giscard d'Estaing's entire policy, based as it was on attacking the system of superpower blocs, seemed to be increasing tensions, rather than eliminating them as intended. Its corollary—the desire to maintain an increasingly necessary dialogue—played into the hands of the adversary. The Warsaw summit showed how it could lead to total failure.

Electoral preoccupations and economic considerations also must have played a part in the French refusal to follow the United States blindly. President Giscard d'Estaing may have thought that the Kremlin would favor, as it had previously, his continuing at the head of the French government; his refusal to apply the economic sanctions decreed by the United States allowed France to become the second largest supplier of the Soviet Union, after West Germany. But what the crisis showed most of all was that, within the context of the prevailing geostrategic system, the consequences of a weak America were even more alarming than were those of an overly dynamic one. Shortly thereafter, the Americans discovered that the French could be at the same time the most irritating and the most reassuring of allies.

François Mitterrand

In 1981 the contrast could not have been greater: on the one hand, Ronald Reagan and, on the other, François Mitterrand. The situation was ripe for disagreements; however, in the long run, the Americans finally came to appreciate the unparalleled support that the new French president gave them, even if they sometimes were aggravated by what they considered his ideological aberrations or his nationalistic crowing.[31]

Divergences, centered around economic and Third World policy, had never been so pronounced. Weakened by an isolated economic recovery, France was hard hit by the rise of the dollar and of interest rates resulting from Federal Reserve Board policy combined with Republican supply-side economics. The French were even more irritated with the United States because its policies seemed to have only negative effects during the first two years of the Reagan administration. Not economic recovery but a crisis unprecedented since the war coincided with the adoption of the Reagan program by Congress. The difficulties confronting the American administration prompted it to formulate an increasingly aggressive trade policy toward the European Community, combining attacks against its agricultural policy with quotas on steel. Worse still, Washington's apparent unilateralism appeared, in the long run, to jeopardize the global economic fabric by ignoring the lessons of the 1930s and thus undermining the financial system.

Washington also was increasing the risks of instability in underdeveloped countries and fueling the conflict that pitted French against

Americans on this subject. The French believed that Washington had a dangerous obsession about the East-West aspect of Third World problems. According to the Americans, Paris was blind to the dangers of the Soviet bloc's expansionism. This was compounded by an even greater difference of opinion than there had been in the past about what should be done to alleviate the extreme poverty of the less developed countries: The Reagan administration bristled at the socialist-leaning proposals made by the French, and the French remained extremely distrustful of the blessings that might come out of the unimpeded application of a free market economy in those parts of the world.

Friction from then on increased. In Central America, the two governments analyzed the situation in El Salvador and Nicaragua in diametrically opposite manners. In Cancun, they elaborated completely divergent approaches for aiding the less developed countries. Moreover, France viewed Libyan expansionism differently from the United States and thought that the American policy might well throw Libya into the arms of the Soviet Union.

On two issues, American and French positions became noticeably closer: Mitterrand did not like the Venice Declaration, which he found unbalanced. Additionally, Camp David was not to be dismissed, because it constituted a step in the direction of peace. Thus, Franco-American cooperation was possible in two arenas, with different degrees of success: in the multinational Sinai force and in the peacekeeping force in Lebanon after the "peace in Galilee" operation.

At that time, there were still Communist ministers in the French government, but their presence was no longer an important problem for Franco-American relations. At first their inclusion had alarmed an administration for which socialism could not, as a matter of principle, be identified with anything good and which greatly feared that Italy would follow in the footsteps of France. However, it did not take the Americans long to discover the subtleties of French politics. Because he was such an experienced politician, the new president was not likely to be hoodwinked by the French Communist party. To balance his having invited them into the government, he made it a point of honor to display clearly his allegiance to the West. He convinced his Communist partners, even before they joined the government, to call the Kremlin's deployment of SS-20s into question.[32]

One of Mitterrand's very first actions was to express France's support of the allies' two-track decision. Toward the Warsaw Pact's military threat, he became the most trustworthy ally of the United States. That was not, however, obvious from the start. In 1980, before becoming president, he spoke of the "double threat" when asked to "choose" between Washington and the Kremlin. Thereafter, he was doubtless preoccupied by the Kremlin's military effort. He also perhaps appreciated the assurance that

American Ambassador Arthur Hartman reportedly gave him that secret American aid to the French nuclear program would be continued. In any case, in January 1983 he pleaded the cause of deployment before the West German Bundestag and, in June, the Atlantic Council was hosted by Paris for the first time since 1966. But it was, perhaps, from July 1981 on that the French president most clearly showed his loyalty to his great ally when he showed Reagan his "farewell file," a unique set of documents on the installation and activities of the KGB, which only France possessed.[33]

The intensity of the trade dispute separating the two allies from the fall of 1981 to the fall of 1982 may seem surprising, but Reagan and Mitterrand had not been in office long enough at that point to be able to make compromises. As a result, the incompatibility of their ideas intensified. Moreover, compounding these problems, the economic crisis exacerbated the situation and increased the bitterness of the French. Finally, the imposition of martial law in Poland reinforced the power of the hard-liners in Washington and brought the delicate question of trade with the Kremlin back into the spotlight. The French government was already sensitive to the issue of military technology transfers to the Soviet Union, but it did not support a trade policy aimed at depleting that country's economy. After all, the Americans themselves seemed ready to be more flexible where their wheat exports were concerned. Thus, the French led the organized resistance against American efforts to impose stringent controls on trade with the opposite camp. At the Versailles summit in June 1982, a compromise seemed to have been reached, but it was shattered shortly thereafter. The Americans reduced the commitment that the French thought they had extracted from them concerning intervention in exchange markets. France retorted by diminishing the application of the agreement to trade with the Soviet Union. Reagan's establishment of sanctions, which clashed with the allies' policy, raised tensions to an extremely high level. After a few months, a compromise was worked out on the basic issues, but the crisis had not been solved before a new dispute arose between Paris and Washington: France refused to be party to an agreement that appeared to be like a concession to what was for it a unilateral guarantee.

Tensions thereafter subsided, probably because from 1983 on, the American economic recovery generated a more encouraging atmosphere although it did not diminish French protests against the excessively high dollar and U.S. interest rates. The two partners' positions had changed over time. On the one hand, the Mexican crisis had led to a relative relaxing of American monetary policy and economic approach; the rise of protectionism ended in 1985, with Washington's conversion to the philosophy of foreign-exchange market interventionism, which France had so long supported. Moreover, now that its military position was stronger, the American administration seemed ready to open a dialogue with the

Soviet Union. On the other hand, in March 1983, the French president defined the exterior conditions necessary for France's prosperity when he finally decided to end Libyan expansionism in Chad, traditionally a zone of French influence. And, perhaps because he could not understand the logic of Sandinista politics, or perhaps because Mexico was no longer in a position to provide assistance, he rather quickly gave up on his direct unilateral policy in Central America in favor of a more European regional approach.

A double continuity, however, was emerging on the central issues. On the economic level, the customary irritation over America's domination underscored one of the most systematic French demands: the return to a less erratic monetary system in which the dollar would not regularly provoke disturbances of the entire world economy, often as the result of American domestic policy. In that regard, the parallel with the Pompidou era is striking. First, perhaps, because it was again Michel Jobert, foreign trade minister in the Pierre Mauroy government, who reminded the GATT (General Agreement on Tariffs and Trade) in November 1982 of the necessary linkage between tariff negotiations and monetary stabilization. Second, the tension provoked between François Mitterrand and West Germany's Helmut Kohl by that position during the 1985 Bonn summit was a reminder of the tension that had existed between the former foreign minister and Schmidt in February 1974 in Washington.

Another line of continuity emerged beginning in 1985, with the American Strategic Defense Initiative (SDI) and the assumption of power in the Soviet Union by Mikhail Gorbachev, that would lead the French president to return in large measure to the policy of his predecessors.[34] The same concern for European balance that had moved de Gaulle to distance himself from the Americans led Mitterrand to oppose the development of defense systems, such as SDI, that would largely neutralize the British and French arsenals and widen the American technological advance over the Europeans.

On one level, obviously, little had changed. Indeed, the principal obstacle was the obvious asymmetry between American and French power and, consequently, the disparity between their ambitions and resources. On the one hand, the French government pursued a political strategy seeking to transform France into the "opposite pole," or "alternative" among the democracies. On the other hand, in order to give its political approach more strength and credibility, it had to promote European integration. Instinctively, it acted as if its historical mission was first to personify European identity, and then to free it from the shadow of its powerful ally.

Conclusion

The French political approach has long been simple although not easy to implement. While simultaneously reaffirming its solidarity with its allies, France's strategy has generally stressed its ultimate independence from them. But today France can no longer ignore that the forces that are threatening NATO, such as the increasing possibility of West German accommodation with the Warsaw Pact and the American aversion to first use of nuclear weapons, as symbolized by the Reykjavík summit, have created a new situation in which the dream of a united Europe could be shattered. The danger is no longer the irresistible domination of the United States but instead a helter-skelter race to reach agreement with the Soviet Union. It is doubtless the awareness of this new danger—or new opportunity—that explains the extremely gradual rapprochement that the French government has initiated with the allied defense system. Like its efforts toward nuclear collaboration with Britain and toward military cooperation with the Federal Republic of Germany, this shift, which manifests itself at many levels, is the price France probably has to pay for continued German allegiance to the Western bloc. In the final analysis, while France worries as much about America's possible disengagement from European affairs as about its wielding of undue influence, it is to its dream (or, as some would say, utopia) of European unity that France seems to look increasingly for the solution to its uncertainties vis-à-vis the leader of the West.

Notes

1. Mary Kathleen Weed, "L'Image publique d'un homme secret: Michel Jobert et la diplomatie française" (Ph.D. diss., Institut d'Etudes politiques de Paris, January 1982), 49. A shortened and updated version of this dissertation was published under the same title (Paris: Fernand Lanore, 1988). This latter version will be cited hereafter.
2. On this subject, and on Roosevelt's relations with de Gaulle and Vichy, see Jean-Baptiste Duroselle, *La France et les Etats-Unis des origines à nos jours* (Paris: Seuil, 1976), 145–78.
3. Ibid., 197–221.
4. Hervé Alphand, *L'Etonnement d'être: Journal, 1939–1951* (Paris: Fayard, 1977), 206.
5. Georgette Elgey, *La République des illusions, 1945–1951* (Paris: Fayard, 1965), 382.
6. René Massigli, *Une Comédie des erreurs, 1943–1954* (Paris: Plon, 1978), 105.
7. Harry S. Truman, *Memoirs, vol. 2, 1946–1951* (New York: New American Library, 1965), 282.
8. See Lawrence S. Kaplan, *The United States and NATO: The Formative Years* (Lexington: University Press of Kentucky, 1984), 14–29.

9. See Annie Lacroix-Riz, *Le Choix de Marianne* (Paris: Messidor/Editions sociales, 1985).

10. $312 million was supplied under the "temporary aid" program; then, from 1948 to 1951, $2.5 billion was given under the Marshall Plan and, from 1951 to 1955, $2.7 billion under the Mutual Security Law. See Gérard Bossuat, "L'Aide américaine à la France après la seconde guerre mondiale," *Vingtième Siècle, Revue d'histoire*, no. 9 (January-March 1986): 17–35; and idem, "La Modernisation de la France sous influence: Premières étapes de l'appel à l'étranger, 1944–1949" (Thèse nouvelle, Université de Paris, April 1988).

11. Vincent Auriol, *Journal du septennat*, vol. 5, *1952* (Paris: Colin, 1978), 713–14.

12. Memorandum, director of the Office of European Affairs (Hickerson) to secretary of state, 17 February 1949, U.S. Department of State, *Papers Relating to the Foreign Relations of the United States, 1949* (Washington, DC: Government Printing Office, 1975), 4:121.

13. Memorandum, counselor of the Department of State (Bohlen) to secretary of state, 31 March 1949, ibid., 256.

14. See Pierre Mélandri, *Les Etats-Unis face à l'unification de l'Europe, 1945–1954* (Paris: Pédone, 1980).

15. Stephen Ambrose, *Eisenhower: The President* (New York: Simon and Schuster, 1984), 368.

16. Christian Pineau, *1956: Suez* (Paris: Robert Laffont, 1976), 175.

17. André Fontaine, *Histoire de la guerre froide*, vol. 2, *De la guerre de Corée à la crise des alliances, 1950–1971* (Paris: Fayard, 1967), 280.

18. Pineau, *1956: Suez*, 212.

19. John Newhouse, *De Gaulle and the Anglo-Saxons* (New York: Viking, 1970), 66–67.

20. Alfred Grosser, *La IVe République et sa politique extérieure* (Paris: Colin, 1972), 386.

21. Charles de Gaulle, *Mémoires d'espoir*, vol. 1, *1958–1962* (Paris: Plon, 1970), 220.

22. Jean Lacouture, *De Gaulle. III: le souverain* (Paris: Seuil, 1986), 353.

23. Ibid., 352.

24. Quoted in Cyrus Sulzberger, *L'Ere de la médiocrité* (Paris: Albin Michel, 1974), 286.

25. Direct investments made by the Americans in France increased from $364 million at the end of 1957 to $1.240 billion at the end of 1963, $1.904 billion in 1967, and $2.590 billion by the end of 1970.

26. Jean-Jacques Servan-Schreiber, *Le Défi américain* (Paris: Denoël, 1967).

27. Alphand, *L'Etonnement d'être*, 477.

28. Weed, "L'Image publique d'un homme secret," 90.

29. Samy Cohen, *La Monarchie nucléaire* (Paris: Hachette, 1986), 108.

30. Jean Boissonnat, *Journal de crise, 1973–1984* (Paris: J. C. Lattes, 1984), 204.

31. See Evan G. Galbraith, *Ambassadeur de choc* (Paris: Stock, 1986), 167.

32. Grosser, *Affaires extérieures*, 289.

33. Thierry Wolton, *Le KGB en France* (Paris: Grasset, 1986), 241–42.

34. See the analysis by Samuel F. Wells, Jr., "Les Politiques étrangères de Mitterrand: Bilan d'un premier septennat," *Commentaire*, no. 43 (Autumn 1988: 655–66.

NATO and Germany

Werner Kaltefleiter

The year 1989 brought a double anniversary for the Federal Republic of Germany (FRG): the fortieth anniversary of its founding and the fortieth year of NATO's existence. This Western alliance is the basis of the Federal Republic's integration into the West, although the prospect of an integrated European Community in 1992 diverts attention from both anniversaries. NATO deserves higher priority because it includes the United States and thus presents the only credible and effective guarantee of security for European democracies, in general, and for the FRG, in particular.

The incorporation of the Federal Republic into the Western international community began in 1951 with the treaty on the European Coal and Steel Community (ECSC) and reached its first peak with the FRG's entry into NATO in 1955. This is yet another anniversary worth noting, because after five years the sovereignty of the young West German democracy became linked with this major military alliance. With the Treaty of Rome in 1957, which established the European Economic Community, West German integration reached a new level, even though the organization of this common market and the efforts to increase political cooperation have dominated integration policy since then and will continue to do so in the foreseeable future. The incorporation of the Federal Republic into the community of Western democracies contained from the very beginning both a foreign and domestic policy dimension.

The Foreign Policy Dimension

A glance at the map of Europe highlights the reality that the FRG, whatever efforts it may make, cannot defend itself alone. The postwar decision to establish a free democratic society in the area of West Germany posed a contrast to the Communist regimes in the Soviet bloc and raised the question of national security for this newly formed state.

This vulnerable situation was not, however, restricted to the FRG. In principle, it was true for all West European countries, although this may be less clear, for example, from a Portuguese or an Irish perspective. In this analysis, one must accept the law of geopolitics that rimlands can only preserve their independence from the heartland if they have the support of the opposite shore. Also, one must differentiate between NATO's initial phase and its later years. After World War II the states of Western Europe were clearly in no position to defend themselves, due to the destruction of their economies, among other problems. One of the major results of the Second World War was the fall of the traditional European Great Powers from a position of dominance in world policy. However, after a vigorous West European development period, resulting in the successful reconstruction and achievement of a standard of living never before enjoyed in the history of Europe, security matters have become more complex. Two issues must be discussed within this context.

First, it is indisputable that, in view of West Germany's geopolitical position and its demographic, economic, technological, and military resources, viable European defense is only possible with the inclusion of the Federal Republic. The integration of the Federal Republic into the Western international community today, in contrast to thirty-five years ago, is not just due to a West German concern for survival; it is also in the interest of the other West European states and in the interest of the United States, as well. Without the Federal Republic and a free Western Europe at its side, the United States would only be in an inferior position in its global rivalry with the Soviet Union.

Second, in contrast to the preceding situation, other scenarios are conceivable for a European defense capability, if the necessary defense efforts are provided. This prospectus, however, can lead one politically astray. At issue is not the question, so frequently posed in the United States, of why 240 million Americans should defend 320 million Europeans. This query overlooks the true function of the Atlantic Alliance, which is also the central prerequisite for West German membership in it: the prevention of war and the ability to endure successfully a potentially long-term defensive battle. Within this context, two institutional elements of the alliance are important: First, in an alliance of democracies, only defensively oriented politics will find a consensus; second, in view of the geopolitical position of the Federal Republic, this means that defensive combat operations will take place on German soil. The approximately 100-kilometer area west of the West German-Czechoslovakian border contains one third of the Federal Republic's resources and 25 percent of its population. Even the extremely optimistic assumption that a defense would take place only within this 100-kilometer zone demonstrates that such a concept is politically unacceptable for the FRG. If this is true for exclusively conventional defense, then the use of tactical nuclear weapons in this area would be virtually unthinkable for West Germany.

From this it follows that, on the one hand, the concept of forward defense, the absolute border defense, is the conditio sine qua non of West German membership in the alliance. On the other hand, the high mobility of modern forces means that actual forward defense is operatively almost impossible. Instead, it would include at least the 100-kilometer zone and an analogous territory in East Germany. Consequently, the prevention of war has absolute priority for the FRG.

What relationship does this strategy have to the presence of American troops in Europe? Deterrence is NATO's policy, in accordance with the political necessity of war prevention. However, deterrence is a matter not only of military means but also, and foremost, of political credibility in the will and capability to defend. Herein lies the meaning of the American presence. Stationing U.S. troops near the border and having 300,000 of these soldiers and their dependents located in Europe guarantees immediate American engagement in a European conflict. The American presence provides the guarantee of credible deterrence, the basis of every strategy. The question is thus not whether Europeans can defend themselves but one of how the absolute futility of an attack can be demonstrated to the Soviet Union. The effective response to this query rests in the strategic positioning of American troops. This, in turn, carries with it two related issues. The first relates to the continual conflict within the alliance over burden sharing, and the second concerns discussion of the so-called nuclear threshold.

A simple glance at the ratio of defense expenditures to gross national product quickly leads to the claim raised again and again in the United States that Europeans should spend more for their defense. However, it can be argued, at least statistically, that defense efforts are not expressed solely by this index and that the differences between a professional army, with high personnel costs, and a military with compulsory service must be evaluated. Other issues for serious consideration are the expenditures for the maintenance of West Berlin, the disturbance to the population from training maneuvers, the high concentration of troops, low-level flights, and other negative realities. These points nonetheless are not the central problem: No 1 or 2 percent increase in defense appropriations in the Federal Republic or in any other West European state can compensate for the political role played by the American presence, which augments the credibility of NATO's deterrence capabilities. Whether such increases are necessary is another question, but they cannot substitute for America's positioning in the heart of Europe.

Discussion about the nuclear threshold conceals fundamental differences between the nuclear world power, the United States, and its European allies, especially the FRG. After almost a decade of intra-alliance discussion, the twenty-year-old strategy of "flexible response" still lacks precise meaning. In view of the risk of escalation connected with any military conflict, it is in the interest of the global nuclear power, the United States, to limit every conflict regionally and to conventional weapons. This would guarantee that the United States and the Soviet Union would remain sanctuaries in such a war. However, for any country involved in conflict, which in the case of Europe would assuredly be first and foremost West Germany, this situation not only means that the fighting will be carried out on its own territory, but it also provides an invitation for the Soviet Union to attempt such a conflict. If Moscow can be certain of regional and conventional limitation, the risk of military action for the USSR is far less than it would be if it had to fear nuclear escalation and an accompanying threat to its own territory.

As a result of this merging of superpower interests, the United States has continually demanded a strengthening of conventional forces in order to raise the nuclear threshold, which means nothing more than increasing the chance to limit conflicts. In contrast, it has been in the interest of Europeans, in general, and Germans, specifically, to plan for the earliest possible initial use of nuclear weapons in order to increase the effect of deterrence. A further conclusion is that the Intermediate-range Nuclear Forces (INF) Treaty complies with American interests, but not with those of Europeans. That the Europeans nevertheless have been pressured into a celebration of this treaty is due not to foreign policy considerations but primarily to the competitive structures of the domestic party systems.

The Domestic Dimension

The French author Ernest Renan has written that democracy is a plebiscite daily repeated. This is true not only for the legitimacy of the system but also for central areas of policy, which clearly include security and alliance considerations. The founding of the Atlantic Alliance forty years ago and the FRG's entry into it five years later were domestically possible in the member countries concerned only because the political understanding was based on a clear perception of threat. That is, the existence of the free societies in Europe was threatened by the Soviet Union or, more accurately, by the existence of a structurally expansive Communist realm. The sequence of events following the close of the Second World War—the founding of Communist dictatorships in the wake of the Red Army, the coup d'état in Czechoslovakia, the Berlin blockade—reached a peak with the invasion of South Korea, vividly substantiating this threat perception.

There was still another motivating factor for the FRG. Chancellor Konrad Adenauer led the young German democracy into the free international community not just for foreign policy reasons. Adenauer, whose character was considerably shaped by the experiences of the Weimar Republic's fall and the Nazi period, was deeply skeptical of whether it was possible to anchor democratic institutions effectively in German political culture. He thus underestimated the meaning of well-functioning political institutions. This skepticism resulted in his program to include "free" Germany in the circle of democracies with the purpose of stabilizing and securing democracy in Germany.

It is pointless to argue whether this skepticism was justified. Democratic stability in the FRG is not questioned today, although occasionally German loyalty to NATO is. The concerned voices that could be heard in Washington, London, and Paris when Willy Brandt introduced the "new *Ostpolitik*" are memorable. These apprehensions were repeated during the peace movement's protests against the 1979 NATO dual-track decision and its subsequent implementation in 1983. There appears to be no dearth of occasions on which to express these doubts anew. How founded or unfounded these doubts may be, based on domestic policy developments, remains disputable. It is indisputable, however, that the freedom of each West German government to act in East-West relations is dependent on its NATO membership.

The substantial changes during the forty years of the alliance and the Federal Republic of Germany include a fundamental shift in threat perception. How much of the population feels threatened by the Soviet Union has always fluctuated. Since Mikhail Gorbachev came to power, however, these changes have taken on a new dimension. Whereas the figures in the past were between 50 and 70 percent, today only 20 percent of the population feels threatened by the Soviet Union. The Soviet leader was more popular in West European countries than was Ronald Reagan at the end of his term.

The security policy agenda in the FRG in 1989 focused on such problematic questions as: How can the strength of the German armed forces be maintained in view of demographic changes, how can the modernization of central weapons systems be financed, and should the modernization of short-range nuclear missiles be part of a general arms control policy? These all-important issues are but secondary to the overriding question of how to reach consensus about the necessity of alliance membership despite an almost nonexistent threat perception.

It is true that approximately 80 percent of the population favors West German membership in NATO. Almost as many are in favor of the presence of American troops. However, these are accustomed rituals. If these questions are posed in the context of a burden or sacrifice, even if it is only the noise from low-level flights, then a consensus is no longer recognizable.

The causes for this development are manifold, and it would be inappropriate to trace them all to the behavior of Gorbachev. The political leadership of Germany is confronted with a demanding test. The erosion of consensus in security policy in the FRG in recent years makes clear that the political leadership has apparently not fulfilled its task. In a democracy the effectiveness of the approach toward problems of foreign and security policy, political areas in which most citizens cannot claim any personal experience, depends on how these issues are portrayed by the political elite and then repeated in the mass media. Consequently, consensus on security issues is not solely a problem for a party, but for the party system as a whole. Thus, there are different—although basically parallel—developments on both sides of the German party system.

The erosion process began after 1980 when Chancellor Helmut Schmidt could no longer hold the Social Democratic Party (SPD) to a security policy consensus on rearmament, which had been reached in 1979 not only in the North Atlantic Council but also among a large majority at the SPD party conference in Berlin. One can accuse Schmidt of basing his public position on rearmament solely on the deployment of the SS-20 missiles, only because he did not believe that he could communicate the more complex aspects of security policy. This judgment, however, does not address the real causes of this situation, which developed from the emergence of the Greens, their fusion with the peace movement, and the resulting competition between the Greens and the SPD for the same electorate.

Neutralist-pacifist approaches mixed with a great deal of anti-Americanism and trust in the Soviet Union have always existed in the Federal Republic of Germany—as they have in other West European democracies. Believers in such approaches, up to 10 percent of the population, are not a problem as long as they are not represented by a separate political organization. Since the late 1970s this section of the electorate has organized its own party, and the party of the center-left, the SPD, has lost the chance of governing if it cannot win over this segment. The SPD has reacted by adopting the Greens' symbolic positions, thereby contributing to the demise of West German consensus on security policy issues. In place of threat perception the concept of security partnership has appeared, linked to the assumption that a threat is not based on political systems but rather on the existence of weapons. From this reasoning also follows the premise that the elimination of weapons will become an end in itself and that the Soviet Union will no longer be perceived as an ideological threat to the West.

At the special SPD party conference in November 1983 in Cologne, where Helmut Schmidt together with some two dozen loyal followers comprised a small—some would say radical—minority on the question of rearmament, it became apparent that the SPD, and thus a large part of public opinion led by this party, had abandoned the alliance consensus on security policy.

On the other side of the West German party system, two other parties also competed for the same electorate. The Christian Democratic Union (CDU) and the Christian Socialist Union (CSU) both claim the tradition of Konrad Adenauer, and together they present themselves as the reliable party of Western integration, the Union. This position is reflected in all of its programmatic statements and in the convictions of its political leadership, now headed by Chancellor Helmut Kohl. However, because majorities and not convictions produce the opportunity to govern, situations can emerge in which compromises appear necessary. A CDU/CSU policy with compromises is for NATO interests a lesser evil than an SPD-Green government. The necessity for compromise, however, is directly related to the Free Democratic Party (FDP) and its broker role.

The FDP as a coalition partner, regardless of whether it sides with the SPD or the CDU/CSU, requires some areas in which it can maintain its own identity for the purpose of improving its electoral prospects. Foreign and military policy issues are appropriate, since they do little harm to voter interests and generally polish images. This orientation guides the FDP's strategy in the coalition relationship. Prior to 1982 the party was in coalition with the SPD, which, increasingly in competition with the Greens, abandoned security policy consensus. Therefore, until 1982 the FDP, under Hans-Dietrich Genscher, sought to project itself as the guarantor of Atlantic loyalty.

In the FDP's coalition with the CDU/CSU since 1982, this strategy has been impossible because the Union and its chancellor were matchless in their Atlantic solidarity and friendship with the American president. As a result, Genscher and the FDP have sought to acquire prominence by pursuing a policy of arms control and accommodation with the Soviet Union, reflecting a party tradition dating back to the 1950s. So the FDP has come closer to the SPD, which welcomes this shift for reasons of power politics. Even if the threat of a coalition change is not credible at the present, every inclination toward the opposition increases the concern of the Union about the longevity of the CDU/CSU-FDP coalition and thus its own hold on power.

The results of this distribution of power became evident during the debate that, in the end, led to the INF Treaty, and continue to be shown in the present discussion surrounding the modernization of short-range nuclear missiles. Every Soviet suggestion, whatever its consequences for the security interests of the FRG and the Western alliance, is emphatically welcomed by the Greens. The SPD has also adopted this general position, and the FDP, after careful consideration, finds acceptable elements in it that, upon further discussion, may lead to general acceptance. The Union, although it is the strongest party, is in a minority position. In light of the 1990 elections and after some hesitation, it has adopted positions that have been accepted by the other parties. Thus, there is now no political party that convincingly and publicly expresses the security interests of the FRG and NATO.

This is not to imply criticism of the resoluteness and firmness of individual politicians such as Chancellor Kohl. On the contrary, the degree of steadiness that Helmut Kohl has shown since his election in October 1982 on the question of rearmament is remarkable, particularly with the prospect of the federal elections in March 1990. However, a resolute position on numerous issues cannot be maintained over years except with the greatest difficulty, particularly if there is no support from the other Western allies—as in the case of the INF Treaty. One must understand that policy is the result not of personal characteristics but of competitive relationships within the German party system.

Perspectives

German domestic developments have reflected changing appraisals of Soviet policy. If, as Adenauer stated in his last speech before a CDU conference, in 1967, the Soviet Union has entered the community of peace-loving people, then the change in the threat perception and the articulation of problems based on it by the German parties is only an adaption to a new reality, one that will enable scarce resources to be assigned to other areas of concern than security policy. However, the experiences since Adenauer's speech—the invasions of Czechoslovakia and Afghanistan, the events in Angola, Mozambique, and Nicaragua, the second Vietnam War against the United States and the third Vietnam War in Cambodia, and the military buildup of the Soviet Union, unequalled in history—call for skepticism. They temper current hopes in Western democracies that a fundamental change has occurred in Soviet policy under Gorbachev. Even if there were no doubts about the Soviet leader's intentions, skepticism would be justified on two grounds. First, Gorbachev's declared policy does not match the Soviet Union's political behavior. For example, the withdrawal of six thousand aged tanks from central Europe, which Gorbachev announced to the United Nations, was preceded by the deployment of ten thousand of the most modern tanks since Gorbachev's accession to office. Second, the chance that Gorbachev can carry out his policy within the system of the Soviet Union is estimated by politicians and Sovietologists to be less than 50 percent.

It follows from both of these points that the long-standing principle that security policy must be based on worst-case assumptions maintains its validity. However, a commensurate consensus is needed in the affected democracies, and foremost in the Federal Republic of Germany.

It is unrealistic to assume that the party system of the FRG will easily pull itself out of the quagmire of security policy issues. In the past, the Soviet Union frequently contributed to the stability of the security policy consensus through its obviously expansive actions. Experience with Gorbachev since 1985 indicates that, at least for the foreseeable future, such provocative behavior is very unlikely. The Western alliance, therefore, must come to a new security policy consensus on its own, and this is the decisive challenge for the next decade.

West Germany's domestic problem is not unique. Other NATO countries face similar challenges in varying degrees. Consequently, the restoration of consensus within NATO is a prime duty of the alliance. If the domestically pressured political leaderships, and this is true beyond party lines, express a realistic threat perception together in the alliance, there is a chance to break the domestic shackles that result from the competitive circumstances of the respective party systems.

Konrad Adenauer's vision of stability for the West German democracy through membership in the community of democracies thus takes on a new dimension: the stability of a security policy consensus in the democracies through cooperation between democratic governments in the alliance.

Political Consultation during International Crises: Small Powers in NATO

Cees Wiebes and Bert Zeeman *

Prologue

Small Power meets Big Power at a cocktail party in Washington. *Dutch Foreign Minister Joseph Luns*: "I am pleased to meet you at last."

U.S. Admiral Hyman G. Rickover: "So you are the man who for years has been weeping and crying about not having received an atomic submarine from us. I have therefore taken a lot of handkerchiefs with me in order to wipe your tears, because our assistance you will not get."

Dutch Foreign Minister Luns: "I don't need your handkerchiefs. Why do you refuse atomic submarines to the Netherlands?"

U.S. Admiral Rickover: "You are wholly dependent for your existence and survival on the United States. Right? Therefore we and not you will decide what type of warships you may possess and you should know that you are far too small and poor ever to be able to build or to run atomic submarines. . . . I know all your arguments and I am sick and tired of them."[1]

In 1966 the Atlantic Institute in Paris published *Crisis Management: The New Diplomacy* by Alastair Buchan. According to Buchan, the Atlantic

---

* The authors gratefully acknowledge the cooperation of the Dutch Prime Minister's Office and the Dutch Ministry of Foreign Affairs in the preparation of this paper. We would like to thank the following persons for their comments on an earlier version of this article: Duco Hellema, Henk Houweling, Jan Melissen, and Joseph Jockel.

Alliance was in considerable disarray: Old alliance mechanisms developed ten or fifteen years earlier were clearly out of date.[2] His assessment was widely held in the mid-1960s. With ominous titles such as *The Troubled Partnership, The End of Alliance*, and *NATO in Quest of Cohesion* other commentators, including Henry Kissinger, Ronald Steel, and Karl Cerny, also pointed to fundamental weaknesses in the transatlantic partnership.[3]

Given the state of the alliance, Buchan thought that "considerable modification" of the alliance was essential if NATO was to survive. In order to overcome the problems involved in crisis management, he advocated a Washington-based system of long-term contingency planning, a North Atlantic Policy Planning Council, and a standby system for high-level crisis consultation. His suggestions seemed to be especially aimed at America's principal European allies—Britain, France, and West Germany— because, as Buchan himself noted, "small allies . . . she can probably retain indefinitely for they have little freedom of choice. But to retain the support of the major allies means finding a common objective with them." Buchan was aware of possible difficulties with the smaller NATO allies, who would not be too happy with his prescriptions. Nonetheless, to be effective "the reality of power" had to be confronted.[4]

Buchan expected the smaller allies to be especially sensitive about inroads into their national autonomy. However, for small allies there are other factors involved in the centralization of consultation mechanisms. Consultation, and hence the opportunity to influence or restrain other allies, is generally considered one of the benefits of joining an alliance, especially for smaller nations. That influence also can be used to limit one of the negative consequences of joining an alliance, that of entrapment or the fear of being dragged by the major allies into a larger military conflict.[5] Robert W. Russell has observed that, for the Netherlands, political consultations within NATO have compensated for being small and lacking any automatic claim to a special relationship with the United States.[6]

Buchan's suggestions have not been implemented. Nevertheless, NATO has survived, plagued by recurring crises.[7] The issues that Buchan confronted are still apparent today: Crisis management, political consultations, and the role of the smaller powers remain unresolved issues forty years after NATO's birth. Among the central unresolved questions are: To what extent did political consultation take place at times when the alliance needed it most? What effects did the lack of consultation have on the loyalty of the smaller allies and hence on the cohesion of the alliance? Answers to these questions are important for at least two reasons. First, from a historical perspective, they will clarify the role of the smaller allies within NATO. Is NATO still, as Johan Galtung once remarked, a feudal alliance, hierarchically ordered with rather limited horizontal interaction among its lower-ranking members? Second, from a policy perspective, the answers will provide us with some leads regarding the future course of NATO. The Cuban missile crisis (1962), the Soviet-orchestrated invasion of Czechoslovakia (1968), and the downing of the Korean airliner, KAL 007 (1983), are useful crises to study. These events are very dissimilar. However, this diversity allows us to assess the process of consultations and crisis management under different circumstances. These events also have in common certain traits usually associated with international crisis: explicit threat, a short time span, and surprise.

The Cuban crisis, an obvious East-West confrontation, provoked an infringement of the tacit Soviet-American understanding. Although this crisis, centering on Fidel Castro's island, was on the edge of the territorial scope of the North Atlantic Treaty, it had threatening implications, especially for the situation in Berlin. The assault on Czechoslovakia did not infringe upon European spheres of influence or bloc structures. Nonetheless, it had direct implications for the workings of the Western alliance because it threatened to destabilize the complex military and political environment at the demarcation line between NATO and the Warsaw Pact. The downing of the Korean airliner was an out-of-area problem. Although the incident offered no direct threat to the security of any of the parties, it was dealt with in such a serious fashion and with such rhetorical overkill that it could have caused a severe threat to international peace and security.

In addressing these three crises, we are dealing with just one aspect of the central problem that confronts the smaller allies in NATO. However, it is a cardinal one in an alliance. The ability to deal with crises is of paramount importance to NATO. The feeling among small allies that their interests also should be taken into account in crisis management is fundamental to alliance harmony. Allied loyalty and alliance cohesion are at stake. In our conclusions, we will try to put our findings in the broader context of interallied relations, the problems and roles of smaller powers, and the future of the alliance.

Given the different regulations regarding the declassification of federal records in NATO member states and in NATO itself and the relatively more liberal situation in the Netherlands, our research is primarily based on Dutch sources. Our findings therefore should be evaluated as a first, but necessary, step toward a better understanding of political consultations between larger and smaller allies during international crises.

Political Consultation in the First Decade

In the area of political consultation with the smaller allies, NATO did not have a very propitious start. Unknown to their future allies the United States, the United Kingdom, and Canada settled the principal features of the

North Atlantic Treaty in the ultrasecret Pentagon negotiations of March 1948. When France and the Benelux countries joined the negotiations in the summer of 1948, the three Anglo-Saxon conferees decided to keep their agreement secret, which, on a number of occasions, seriously hampered the negotiating process. After the text of the treaty was completed, in the spring of 1949, Norway, Denmark, Iceland, Portugal, and Italy were invited to become members of the alliance on a take-it-or-leave-it basis. The distribution of power within the alliance was aptly demonstrated in the discussions on Article 5, the core article of the treaty, in which the United States pledged its political and military support of Europe. In the end, domestic considerations clearly were more important to the Truman administration than were the wishes of its prospective partners.[8]

Political consultation was firmly engraved in the North Atlantic Treaty. Article 4 states that the "Parties will consult together whenever, in the opinion of any of them, the territorial integrity, political independence or security of any of the Parties is threatened." The negotiators left no room for doubt; Article 4 was applicable "in the event of a threat in any part of the world, to the security of any of the Parties, including a threat to the security of their overseas territories."[9] Thus, the North Atlantic Treaty closely resembled, but went beyond, the stipulations of the 1948 Treaty of Brussels. This forerunner of NATO had explicitly limited the scope of its assistance clause to the territory of the signatories in Europe, whereas the NATO consultation clause knew no geographical limits.[10]

However, in the first years of NATO's existence, these solemnly agreed-upon provisions proved to be idle words. The North Atlantic Council was created, but its main business usually consisted of the United States asking its European allies for increased defense spending and the Europeans pleading with their big brother for more aid. The Western reaction to the outbreak of the Korean War registered the fact that political consultation hardly existed. The Truman administration, without consulting even its closest ally, Britain, decided to intervene in Korea on behalf of the free world. Most of America's NATO allies ultimately followed suit by sending military contingents to the Korean battlefields.

In 1951 a committee was instructed to recommend ways and means to enlarge the scope of political consultation. While acknowledging that each government was entitled to full freedom of action, the NATO Committee on the North Atlantic Community advocated increased consultation in order to strengthen the alliance, adding that while all members of NATO have a responsibility to consult with their partners on appropriate matters, a large share of responsibility for such consultation necessarily rests on the more powerful members of the Community."[11] The implication was clear: To foster alliance cohesion, political consultation was imperative, and the smaller allies were entitled to generous treatment by the greater ones.

Despite this recommendation the situation did not improve very much during the next five years. Political consultation only occurred ad hoc.[12] As the North Atlantic Council assessed progress in this area during its meeting of May 1956, the allies decided to set up a Committee on Non-Military Cooperation that, once again, made recommendations to improve and extend nonmilitary cooperation. The Suez crisis of November 1956 amply demonstrated the need for such measures. The lack of consultation among the principal allies during this heated period reverberated in the report of "the three wise men"—Halvard Lange, Gaetano Martini, and Lester Pearson: "It is easy to profess devotion to the principle of political—or economic—consultation in NATO. It is difficult and has in fact been shown to be impossible, if the proper conviction is lacking, to convert the profession into practice. . . . There is a pressing requirement for all members to make consultation in NATO an integral part of the making of national policy. Without this the very existence of the North Atlantic Community may be in jeopardy."[13]

The fundamental dilemma of reconciling the right of each government to act unilaterally with the need for allied consultation and common policies was papered over in the recommendations of the three wise men. The "essential thing" for each ally was to keep in mind always the interests of the alliance and not to adopt firm policies before "adequate advance consultation" had taken place, unless "circumstances" made this impossible. And they added that the interests of the alliance members were "not confined to the area covered by the Treaty."[14]

Five years later, on the eve of the Cuban missile crisis, this dilemma was still not resolved. The North Atlantic Council debated in May 1962 in Athens the plans of U.S. Secretary of Defense Robert S. McNamara for a changed nuclear strategy based on flexible response. The European allies lukewarmly accepted this concept of a controlled nuclear war. Great Britain and the United States promised to consult all allies before taking recourse to nuclear weapons, but the guidelines left, according to Harlan Cleveland, a loophole almost as wide as the commitment: time and circumstances permitting.[15] Five months later, NATO's political consultation mechanisms were put to the test seriously.

The Cuban Missile Crisis of October 1962

According to Dean Rusk, Cuba was the "most dangerous crisis the world has ever seen," the only time when both superpowers came "eyeball to eyeball." An American diplomat told his Dutch colleague that the United States "looked through a barrel of a gun." Lawrence Kaplan judges that it could have been a casus belli. Only because Nikita Khrushchev backed away from the brink, a major war between the Soviet Union and the United

States (and thus NATO) was averted.[16]   In a strict sense, the Cuban missile crisis was not a crisis directly threatening NATO.   Cuba is situated just south of the Tropic of Cancer, outside the territorial scope of the alliance. However, the potentially grave repercussions of this confrontation clearly made it a crisis threatening not just the United States but also its European allies, thereby necessitating political consultation under Article 4.

Furthermore, the crisis erupted at a critical moment in the existence of NATO.   Allied unity had been under the severe strain of centrifugal forces caused by the Berlin crisis of 1961, French President Charles de Gaulle's challenges to America's leadership, and the problems of nuclear sharing. West German Chancellor Konrad Adenauer bitterly resented the lukewarm and feeble U.S. reaction to the building of the Berlin wall.   De Gaulle shared Adenauer's sentiments.   He abhorred European subservience to the United States and tried to reconstruct Western Europe under French leadership.   Plans to make NATO the fourth nuclear power were intended to counteract these centrifugal tendencies in the alliance.   In December 1960 the North Atlantic Council put under study a plan to create a multilateral nuclear force (MLF) jointly owned and manned by the European allies, but the control of the nuclear warheads was to remain in U.S. hands.   Instead of appeasing Europeans, the MLF exacerbated U.S.-European differences. Given this tense situation in interallied relations, it was clear that the Cuban missile crisis could have grave repercussions for the alliance.

The Cuban crisis demonstrated again that the American administration attached little importance to meaningful consultations with its NATO allies. When President John F. Kennedy announced the blockade of Cuba in his speech on 22 October, the allies were informed only forty-five minutes beforehand about the important developments that led to this drastic decision.   They had been told nothing about the discoveries by U-2 planes of the Soviet rocket launchers on Cuban soil.   The Dutch embassy in Washington reported before the broadcast of the speech that there was frenzied political activity in Washington. Embassy officials had quickly consulted the British and French ambassadors, who complained that they also were being kept in the dark.   Undersecretary of State George Ball brought the NATO ambassadors up to date only immediately before the president's speech.   Dean Acheson, who had been sent on a special mission by Kennedy, briefed the North Atlantic Council at the same time.[17]

This form of consultation, dubbed by Cleveland as "consent-building notification after the fact,"[18] created almost universal resentment among the allies.   In London the Dutch ambassador, Baron Adolph Bentinck, learned from the permanent undersecretary at the Foreign Office, Sir Harold Caccia, that Prime Minister Harold Macmillan had been only partly informed by U.S. Ambassador David Bruce. The Foreign Office was particularly worried about the possible consequences for Berlin. Bentinck concluded that the British cabinet had been unpleasantly affected by the American measures.[19]

The Adenauer government was similarly very disturbed about the lack of consultations and information before Kennedy delivered his major speech. Bonn feared that the United States would provoke the Soviet Union into a major action involving Berlin. Roving Ambassador Acheson had to calm down Adenauer. In France, de Gaulle was concerned that the U.S. administration might perhaps compromise with Moscow at the expense of Europe. As Acheson began to brief him just before Kennedy's speech, de Gaulle asked a preliminary question, as if to get the record straight. " 'May we be clear before you start,' he said. 'Are you consulting or informing me?' Acheson confessed that he was there to inform, not consult."[20] Nonetheless, de Gaulle gave his support as an independent but loyal ally.

Smaller allies reacted similarly. For instance, Italian Prime Minister Amintore Fanfani strongly castigated Kennedy's behavior and was critical about the lack of consultations. He was joined by his Canadian colleague, John Diefenbaker, and by Belgian Foreign Minister and former Secretary General of NATO Paul-Henri Spaak. Diefenbaker was so fearful of entrapment that he barred U.S. Strategic Air Command bombers from the utilization of Canadian airfields during the crisis and initially refused to put Canadian air defense forces on full alert. For Ottawa it was a particularly uneasy experience because the North American Defense Command Agreement (NORAD) stipulated direct and immediate consultations. In this case Ottawa, just like the other allies, was informed barely one hour prior to Kennedy's speech. The Turkish government was outraged and extremely worried because they feared that Kennedy would be wheeling and dealing with the *Jupiter* missiles.[21]

Did the Dutch enroll in this chorus of criticism? The day after Kennedy's speech the Dutch NATO representative was instructed not to pledge "absolute solidarity" with the Americans but only to show his "understanding and support." Foreign Minister Luns told Prime Minister Jan Eduard de Quay that he disagreed with American policy. De Quay was unable to comment on Kennedy's speech in parliament, because he did not have a copy of its text. On 25 October the cabinet held a special meeting that Luns did not attend because he refused to break off his holiday. This attitude contrasted starkly with the air of urgency and panic in other Western capitals. The Dutch cabinet did not fear a major escalation and decided, in its capacity as a loyal ally, to support Kennedy's policy, although it expressed disapproval over his speech. Several members were puzzled about why the president had not mentioned NATO and criticized America's failure to brief the North Atlantic Council in advance. The cabinet recognized that Cuba was outside NATO's scope, but the crisis could have severe repercussions in Berlin. De Quay reported that the same strong criticism had been voiced during a meeting of the North Atlantic Council on 24 October and that the U.S. representative had promised to keep the allies up to date regarding future developments.[22] From the meeting notes of the Dutch cabinet secretary, one can even infer that the ministers debated the idea of not supporting Kennedy at all. However, Luns later observed that if the other allies had dissociated themselves, the Soviet Union would have gained a major psychological victory.[23]

One is forced to conclude that neither advance consultations nor a flow of information to the allies occurred. The United States directed this operation, and the allies, large or small, were forced to look on from the sidelines and could only hope for the best. Therefore, it is not surprising that the American suggestion that NATO should go on a high level of alert did not meet a favorable response. All NATO members held the same view, and consequently NATO forces did not mobilize.[24]

The lack of consultation also applied to the crucial and secret American decision to remove missiles from Turkey in the wake of the Cuban crisis. The decision was more political than military. The missiles lacked real military value and were quite obsolete with their old, liquid fuel systems. Nobody could even be sure that they were operable. However, the missiles represented an integral part of America's NATO commitment and, as George Ball correctly notes, Washington "could not trade off equipment committed by NATO to serve interests of its own without undercutting the confidence of our Western allies." This was especially true, because the actual turnover of the *Jupiters* to the Turkish army had taken place only on 22 October 1962.[25]

Although the Dutch ambassador in Washington was told unequivocally that Kennedy would never tear down this obsolete base near Soviet territory, the American administration proceeded to follow exactly this course. Kennedy gave a hedged promise to the Soviet Union to withdraw the *Jupiters* at a future date, again without advance consultations with the other allies. Even the Turks were not consulted, despite Washington's fears that the removal of the missiles might lead to the fall of the Turkish government.[26]

Accordingly, several scenarios circulated. One option was that, without notifying NATO in advance, Washington would arrange a secret agreement with the USSR on the *Jupiters*, although it knew beforehand that a formal swap would frighten the German, British, Turkish, and Dutch governments and confirm de Gaulle's earlier evaluation. It would undermine NATO's political morale. Nevertheless, the White House decided not to consult NATO, and Ambassador Thomas Finletter received explicit instructions not to "hint of any [U.S.] readiness to meet [the] Soviet Jupiter proposal."[27]

In its final analysis of the crisis the Dutch Ministry of Foreign Affairs concluded that the U.S. government had been successful in its efforts not to make Cuba a crisis to be dealt with in NATO. The other allies were neither adequately informed nor consulted about Kennedy's speech, the removal of the *Jupiters*, or the contents of the secret Kennedy-Khrushchev correspondence (at least eight letters).[28] The Dutch unequivocally deplored the American attitude because, in their opinion, a major crisis in East-West relations should have been dealt with in the framework of NATO. But, as Frank Costigliola concludes, "The President saw no need for such consultation."[29]

In retrospect, political consultation during the Cuban missile crisis was evaluated in dramatically different ways. Former NATO Secretary General Manlio Brosio considers the Cuban episode "a brilliant example of timely sharing of information by the United States." James Nathan, however, concludes: "In spite of European gestures of support, the alliance received a shock from which it did not recover."[30]

One has to conclude that in 1962 the relationship between the smaller allies and the largest power in the alliance was hierarchically structured. Even the British reached this conclusion. The power imbalance between the United States, on the one hand, and its fourteen allies, on the other, exercised a major limitation on the influence that smaller allies could exert in the beginning of the 1960s. In his "Annual Review for 1962," the British ambassador in The Hague, Andrew Noble, aptly summarized the state of the alliance: "The Dutch realize even more clearly than we do that in 1963 the lesser Powers, to which we now both belong, have little influence on the policies and actions of the nuclear giants. Cuba made that very clear."[31]

This state of affairs, however, did not lead to closer interallied consultations among the lesser powers and thus to a more independent posture. Except possibly for the French, there was not yet room for this. Kennedy's policies undoubtedly reinforced de Gaulle's conviction that France had to shrug off American dominion—preferably in concert with its West European neighbors but, if necessary, alone. Paradoxically, de Gaulle's independent posture created a result opposite from the one that he wanted. For instance, Dutch fear of de Gaulle's intentions prevented the creation of a continental grouping. The Dutch clearly preferred American dominance over French. European maneuverability in foreign policy was also rather limited. A small ally like Norway soon experienced this reality: Shortly after the crisis and the imposition of American countermeasures against Havana, two Norwegian ships sailed for Cuba with grain and oil. The U.S. ambassador in Oslo, Clifton R. Wharton, made all too clear that these ships should alter their course or else. The Norwegian foreign minister asked, "Or else?" Wharton told him flatly that Washington would otherwise cut off the deliveries of weapons.[32]

To summarize, political consultation hardly took place during the Cuban missile crisis. The United States acted unilaterally, only notifying its smaller allies if and when the administration considered notification politically expedient. Regarding the *Jupiters*, notification was not considered essential. Alliance cohesion did not suffer immediately. U.S. action was resented but had to be accepted, given the distribution of power and the fact that the crisis had erupted in America's own backyard. Although the crisis accentuated dramatically the dependence of the smaller allies on the United States, it did not stimulate moves toward closer cooperation among them. On the contrary, France's more independent stance forced some of the lesser allies even closer into American arms.

The Soviet Invasion of Czechoslovakia

By the time the crisis in Czechoslovakia erupted, the international political scene had changed fundamentally from that of 1962. Kennedy's "Atlantic Partnership" had failed to materialize, and interallied relations were more strained than ever before. France had left the military structure of NATO in 1966, forcing the relocation of NATO's military and political infrastructure to Belgium and the Netherlands. The MLF never came into existence. To grant the smaller allies some influence in NATO's nuclear policymaking, the North Atlantic Council had decided in December 1966 to create the Nuclear Planning Group.

U.S. policy in Vietnam caused much resentment in Western Europe, whereas criticism of Europe's share in the defense burden led to Senator Mike Mansfield's call for American troop withdrawals from Europe. Nuclear parity between the United States and the Soviet Union gave rise to new political concepts. In December 1967, NATO adopted the Harmel Report, which called for defense as well as détente. Bilateral contacts with the Warsaw Pact countries intensified, only to receive a severe setback within a few months.

The Soviet-orchestrated invasion of Czechoslovakia during the night of 20–21 August 1968 caught NATO off guard, although for some months reports had been coming in on troop movements near the Czech border. In the beginning of August the Supreme Allied Commander in Europe (SACEUR), General Lyman L. Lemnitzer, asked the NATO Council for political guidance with respect to possible measures, but the council decided not to go on higher alert. Afterward, political experts concluded that "political-strategic warning notwithstanding, NATO had practically no tactical warning of the move."[33] Dutch military sources indicate, however, that NATO forces in West Germany were withdrawn from the Czech border region some hours before the invasion in order to prevent any misadventures.[34]

This invasion, on the threshold of NATO's eastern flank, produced conflicting responses in the alliance. The three nuclear powers reacted in a rather low-key fashion. President Lyndon B. Johnson condemned the events but recognized that Czechoslovakia was within the Soviet sphere of influence and refused to endanger the prevailing détente. He merely postponed, but only briefly, his scheduled meeting with Soviet Prime Minister Alexei Kosygin on limiting strategic arms.[35] The British considered the invasion "an offensive defensive operation" aimed at the reconstruction of Warsaw Pact cohesion, which constituted "no additional threat to NATO." Prime Minister Harold Wilson expounded his worry during an emergency session in Parliament, but no extra measures were contemplated. The French, the third member of the nuclear club, blamed the whole episode on Yalta. Foreign Secretary Michel Debré made the offhand comment that the invasion was no more than a "traffic accident."[36]

The West Germans reacted in the strongest way. President Heinrich Lübke considered Prague to be the prologue to World War III. Chancellor Kurt Georg Kiesinger and Foreign Minister Willy Brandt repeatedly asked Washington for additional military measures, primarily as a political gesture. The negative American response left Bonn feeling abandoned. German worries lessened only when Washington announced publicly on 17 September that an incursion into Germany would result in a direct response by NATO. For the time being, Bonn decided not to sign the Non-Proliferation Treaty (NPT).[37]

Most of the smaller allies reacted rather guardedly. The Norwegians and the Danes expressed their deep concern about movements by Soviet troops and ships in the Baltic and on the Kola Peninsula. When the Dutch minister of defense, Den Toom, visited Norway, he conferred with the king and with his Norwegian colleague, Otto G. Tiedemand. Both expressed their anxiety about Kola and pointed to a possible rapid Soviet operation in the north of Norway. Italian Foreign Minister Giuseppe de Medici voiced disappointment about NATO's silence. Prime Minister Giuseppe Saragat later sent a personal message to Johnson, complaining that the president seemed to have more anxiety about Israel than about Berlin or Western Europe.[38] But despite the fact that the invasion seemed to threaten directly NATO's central front, the alliance, as a whole, reacted cautiously.

The North Atlantic Council and the Military Committee convened immediately after the first reports of the invasion reached Western capitals. Consultation between the allies was seriously hampered by "the tendency of governments which get crisis information to hatch it themselves for a while before telling their allies." The American delegate received authorization to tell his colleagues what the U.S. government knew only minutes before the council session. His British counterpart was instructed to disclose information only if the Americans would do likewise, and the French delegate did not even get that much leeway from Paris.[39] The allies decided, however, not to go on high alert. Even the proclamation of "military vigilance" was not considered necessary. SACEUR General Lemnitzer thereupon placed allied military installations and forces immediately and covertly on emergency alert. The NATO Council disapproved bilateral contacts with Warsaw Pact countries and decided not to withdraw any troops from Europe in the near future, even if Romania were to be the next victim of the Brezhnev Doctrine.[40]

The possibility of such an assault troubled all allies. However, the council acknowledged that any formal NATO statement on Romania could provoke a Soviet reaction. If Moscow responded with force, then the alliance would have to take steps. In a way, according to Dutch Foreign Minister Luns, mutual assured destruction (MAD) produced a kind of paralysis. He therefore rejected any plans of assistance to Romania. Likewise, a possible Soviet intervention in Yugoslavia created similar problems for the NATO allies. The Yugoslav ambassador approached Luns and queried how The Hague and NATO would respond to an attack. Luns replied that if the Yugoslav forces would defend the country for some time, then aid would not be inconceivable. The American chargé accosted Luns with the same question on explicit instructions from President Johnson. Luns later declared unreservedly during a cabinet meeting that the U.S. administration was not prepared to drop Yugoslavia.[41]

Apart from the deliberations in Brussels the smaller allies tried to arrange political consultation at a higher level. After an abortive German attempt to convene a special meeting of the foreign ministers of NATO (torpedoed by the argument that such a meeting would only lead to a meaningless political statement), the smaller allies took the lead. Norway's Tiedemand, supported by the Dutch, asked for an emergency meeting of the defense ministers, only to be rebuffed by the larger powers. Den Toom tried to organize a meeting of the Nuclear Planning Group with even less success. Their only accomplishment came in the form of a promise for a special meeting of NATO foreign secretaries in New York during the UN General Assembly on 7 October, more than six weeks after the invasion.[42]

The lack of high-level political deliberation and doubts about the American position led to unexpected consequences. Western Europeans tried to organize their own consultations. Only two days after the invasion, Brandt and de Medici proposed an emergency session of the Consultative Council of the Western European Union (WEU). Luns supported them, but the proposal came to naught owing to French resistance. Paris, in turn, tried to arrange expanded consultation within the framework of the European Economic Community (EEC), but it had to face the traditional Dutch resistance against such proposals. Belgian Foreign Minister Pierre Harmel thereupon tried to work out a special provision for political consultations in the WEU without France.[43]

In mid-September, Dutch Prime Minister Piet de Jong and Luns went to Bonn for talks with Kiesinger and Brandt. During their meetings the Dutch encouraged their hosts to behave like a big power and to loosen ties with Paris because de Gaulle endangered their mutual security. Bonn was urged to take the lead vis-à-vis Paris. This suggestion did not fall upon deaf ears. Only one week later Brandt told the British ambassador in Bonn that he was interested in the formation of a European caucus within NATO, even if the French would not take part. It was not exactly what the Dutch had meant, but to them it was still a clear step forward.[44]

The Germans, however, quickly retreated from their new position. On 28 and 29 September, de Gaulle visited Bonn, and the two governments closed ranks. De Gaulle reiterated his belief that the U.S. administration would never use nuclear arms in support of Europe. To be sure, he could not give Kiesinger the guarantee that France would do so, but he promised the chancellor that in the event of aggression "que nous serions ensemble." Kiesinger was indebted to the French for this pledge. It signified the resumption of close relations between Paris and Bonn, rather to the dismay of the Dutch government.[45]

Given the French-German agreement, the Harmel initiative for the WEU was doomed. Harmel kept pushing for political consultations without France, which, of course, infuriated de Gaulle. Despite fierce French resistance, there were several gatherings, but Bonn and London did not wish to provoke de Gaulle and risk his wrath over Britain's application for entry into the EEC. The entire enterprise finally died silently.[46]

When the NATO foreign ministers finally met on 7 October in New York, Secretary of State Dean Rusk stated unequivocally that an attack on Austria or Yugoslavia would be unacceptable to his government. Luns supported him, declaring that the strategic importance of neutral and nonaligned European states to the West was greater than NATO's legal obligations; he clearly implied thereby that the scope of Article 5 was too narrow at that moment. The foreign secretaries decided to hold their regular yearly ministerial meeting of NATO in Brussels one month early on 15 and 16 November.[47] During this meeting, Rusk repeated that Austria and Yugoslavia clearly belonged to the alliance's military sphere of interest, but at his explicit request this pledge was not mentioned in the final communiqué. The Consultative Council agreed that an incursion into Romania would not cause direct consequences for NATO. The allies warned the Soviet Union about any other military adventures, but concurrently declared that the process of détente had to continue. Tranquillity returned to most European capitals, and a few months later these very same nations were urging Washington to resume talks with the Soviet Union.[48]

For the smaller allies the handling of the Czech crisis did not differ fundamentally from that of the Cuban affair. Consultation mechanisms within the framework of Article 4 did not function adequately. The larger powers rebuked requests by the smaller states for high-level consultations. When the foreign ministers finally convened in New York, six weeks after the invasion began, the crisis, in fact, had passed. In the meantime, the U.S. administration decided unilaterally, and without consulting its allies, to send two destroyers into the Black Sea. According to the Americans, it was just a routine visit, previously scheduled and therefore not requiring consultations, which, in any case, had never taken place in the past over such deployments. Not all of the allies accepted this explanation without criticism.[49]

Not only had the alliance's political apparatus not functioned properly, but also the same judgment could be leveled against intelligence gathering. The surprise that the invasion caused in Western capitals has already been pointed out. It took more than three weeks before NATO's Military Committee started its analysis of the crisis and the consequences for the alliance. Differences of opinion and basic rivalry between the political and military experts caused the delay. SACEUR General Lemnitzer secured no political guidance from the NATO Council and, as he later recalled, this silence was "one of the most serious breakdowns in the political-military mechanisms of the Alliance that occurred during my tenure as SACEUR."[50]

According to Kaplan, General Lemnitzer's exasperation was not wholly justified. The severity of the Soviet repression sobered NATO. However, this can be disputed: One can certainly expect the alliance to perform appropriately at the height of a severe military crisis that occurs right at its borders. This is all the more the case given the need for political consultations recognized in Article 4. Harlan Cleveland maintains that "NATO was readier for round-the-clock crisis management than it had ever been before." But our findings point to the fact that there was hardly any "crisis management" that could be depicted "as the whole range of co-ordinated diplomatic, economic, military and other efforts aimed at solving an international crisis or at least preventing it from escalating into an armed conflict." Crisis management was one of the refinements of the strategy of flexible response, which had been officially adopted in 1967. It was supposed to apply, as a Dutch expert accurately notes, to situations short of war, such as Czechoslovakia in the summer of 1968.[51]

Given this situation the smaller European allies made an early start with discussions about some sort of grouping within NATO. These talks faltered primarily because of French resistance and the problems arising from Britain's bid to enter the EEC. These feeble attempts to organize a kind of European caucus foreshadowed the problems that were to plague all other such attempts in the 1970s and 1980s. First, membership in both WEU and the EEC did not encompass all the Western nations; in both organizations southern and northern states were not represented. Second, European NATO members were, and still are, dependent for their political and military intelligence on American sources. Third, every attempt to Europeanize NATO gave Washington a justification for cutting down its military presence in Europe. Nevertheless, the creation of the Informal Group of NATO European Defence Ministers (EUROGROUP) in 1968, safely within NATO, was not entirely a coincidence, given the developments of the preceding years. This group consisted of the ministers of defense of all the European allies minus France, but its purpose did not stretch into the political realm.

Subservience to the wishes of the American protector was still paramount. Discussions on increased defense spending after the Czech invasion indicate this relationship clearly. Although the final NATO analysis of the invasion concluded that it was a defensive Soviet action not aimed at the alliance, that the invasion and the ensuing internal dissent weakened the Warsaw Pact, and that détente should still be the number one priority of the alliance, all the European allies promised to increase their defense budgets in order to please the American government. The problems of burden sharing and European criticism of the U.S. intervention in Vietnam already had created widespread resentment in Washington. Rusk responded to French criticism of Johnson's policy in Vietnam by telling Luns: "One cannot be whore in Vietnam and at the same time virgin in Europe."[52] As long as the United States was a "virgin" in Europe, the other allies had to be content with both the advantages and disadvantages of the alliance.

Nevertheless, growing doubts about the American security pledge slithered into NATO. Mounting European disenchantment over the war in Indochina contributed to initial signs of divisiveness. NATO states questioned more and more key elements of alliance policy, assessing critically the actions of its most powerful member. Distrust in Western Europe of American intentions heightened to such an extent that President Richard Nixon had to send a message to the other alliance leaders in January 1972 concerning his visit to Moscow in May. Nixon reassured them that the American administration had "no intention of dealing over the heads of its friends and allies in any matter where their security interests might be affected."[53] Such a message would have been almost unthinkable during the earlier Dwight D. Eisenhower, Kennedy, and Johnson administrations.

The Downing of KAL 007 in 1983

The period from 1968 to 1983 offers further evidence of strains in the alliance. The Vietnam War, the brutal Portuguese repression of the population in its African colonies (Guinea Bissau, Angola, and Mozambique), the military dictatorship in Greece, the U.S. role in the overthrow of Salvador Allende in Chile, and Greek-Turkish conflicts over Cyprus and the Aegean provided a succession of internal crises. Alliance members no longer hesitated to castigate each other in public. The position of NATO as the most important focus for security consensus eroded further and further. Nonetheless, membership in the alliance itself was, apart from Greece and Turkey, not a matter of controversy in the societies of the smaller powers. What caused tension were the positions taken by the alliance on specific issues and even on strategic guidelines.[54]

The end of 1973 saw a low ebb in consultation among the allies. The period from 1977 to 1983, however, after President Jimmy Carter's announcement of plans to deploy neutron bombs in Europe and the decision in 1979 to modernize its medium-range nuclear weapons, was one of the most critical in the existence of NATO. Dangerous diseases such as "Hollanditis" (the "extreme form" of nuclear pacifism) and "Denmarkization" (the underpayment of one's share of the collective defense burden in NATO) became widespread. Burdened with this disability, NATO entered the era of Ronald Reagan and its preoccupation with the "evil empire."

In the early morning hours of 1 September 1983 a Soviet fighter pilot, seated in an SU-15 interceptor, shot down a Korean Air Lines jumbo jet over the Sea of Japan near the Soviet island of Sakhalin. KAL 007 was on its way from Anchorage, Alaska, to Seoul, Korea. It had flown off course for several hours over one of the most militarily sensitive areas of the Soviet Union and had not responded to repeated Soviet warnings. About one minute before KAL 007 would have passed into the safety of international airspace, it was struck by a heat-seeking missile and exploded, killing all 269 passengers and crew members on board.

During a press conference that same day, Secretary of State George P. Shultz announced the American version of the events surrounding the KAL 007 incident. Shortly after the plane's downing, international press agencies spread the news that the airliner had been forced to land on Soviet territory, but Shultz's press conference ended this rumor.[55] The secretary stated that at least eight Soviet fighters had been in the vicinity of KAL 007 at one time or another and that the fighter that finally shot down the Korean airliner was "close enough for visual inspection." According to Shultz, there was no evidence that the Soviet Union had tried to warn the Korean plane, although it had been tracked by Soviet radar for some two and one-half hours. He therefore concluded that there was "no excuse for this appalling act."

Until Shultz's press conference the allies had been in the dark as to the real fate of KAL 007. The Dutch embassy in Tokyo faithfully confirmed the messages of the international press agencies that the Boeing jet had been forced to land on Soviet territory.[56] This dependence upon American information continued in the first few days after the incident. Assistant Secretary of State Richard Burt briefed the Western allies on 2 September. He told them that the United States had recorded the conversations between Soviet ground control and the KAL pilot during the twenty-five minutes before the shootdown (information that was officially denied) and that the possibility could not be ruled out that Soviet ground control had confused KAL 007 with an American intelligence-gathering plane, a modified Boeing 707 dubbed RC-135. Two days later a different picture was presented: The Americans made an official announcement that an RC-135 had been on assignment off the coast of Kamchatka at the time that Soviet radar picked up KAL 007 and that the plane had flown in the vicinity of the civilian jet. In addition, Washington tried to mislead the allies. For example, they were told by Assistant Secretary of State for European Affairs Lawrence Eagleburger that RC-135 aircraft did not enter Soviet airspace, despite the well-known fact that RC-135s sometimes penetrated Soviet airspace to record radar responses.[57]

The U.S. government had been forced into this claim by the propaganda offensive of the Kremlin. The Soviet Union, after having remained silent for a few days, decided to present its side with full force. The RC-135 proved to be a godsend to them. U.S. Air Force Intelligence (USAFI) established that the Soviet pilot had failed to identify the Korean Boeing, but it never passed on to the allies its important conclusion that there was no "specific evidence showing that the Soviets had knowingly shot down an airliner." The other intelligence agencies and the White House Special Group squelched this information provided by USAFI.[58] The Special Group (including Vice President George Bush, Secretary of Defense Caspar Weinberger, CIA Director William Casey, and Shultz) decided to take a harsh, rhetorical stance vis-à-vis the Soviet Union, brushing aside information that did not fit in with this public position, but not in a manner to endanger current talks with the USSR in Geneva (on arms limitations) and Madrid (the Conference on Security and Cooperation in Europe). Weinberger especially advocated harsher measures, but President Reagan sided with Shultz.

Up to this point the American administration had been trying to make the KAL 007 affair an exclusively U.S.-Soviet problem, but now there was a shift. On the morning of 3 September, Assistant Secretary of State Burt again briefed the Western allies. This time he stressed that the downing of KAL 007 created a problem for the whole international community. The State Department therefore wanted close consultations and cooperation with the allies in order to prevent these kinds of dramas in the future. The cooperation had to take shape, in the first place, in the UN Security Council. Burt then announced the submission of a UN resolution condemning the

Soviet act and asking for a fact-finding mission as well as an investigation by the International Civil Aviation Organization (ICAO).[59]

The first discussions in the Security Council already had taken place on 2 September. Most of the delegates condemned the Soviet action. "A wanton, calculated, deliberate murder," "incredible and atrocious brutality," and a "flagrant and serious attack on the safety of international civil aviation" were some of the accusations leveled against the Soviet Union, but no action had yet been taken. Needless to say, these accusations were based on raw and disputed intelligence data, much of which was still being withheld from the allies.[60] A new meeting was scheduled for 6 September.

In preparation for that meeting, Burt again briefed America's allies on 5 September based on a National Security Decision Directive approved by Reagan that same day.[61] This directive outlined the measures to be taken against the Soviet Union. The basic American goal was to show the world once and for all the contrast between Soviet words and deeds. The USSR therefore had to admit its responsibility for the disaster, had to be isolated in the area of civil aviation, and preferably had to be condemned by an impartial investigation. Burt stressed that "the critical element is that we act in concert to demonstrate visibly and firmly the unanimity of revulsion in the civilized world to the Soviet action and conduct."[62]

U.S. Ambassador Jeane Kirkpatrick dominated the meeting of the UN Security Council on 6 September. The delegates to the council were treated to recordings of the Soviet fighter intercepts. According to these tapes, the Soviet fighters had fired no warning shots and had not tried to warn the Korean crew in any other way. The performance was impressive, and it clearly influenced the proceedings. Five days later the State Department issued corrections and additions to the tapes that supported the Soviet point of view, but the propaganda advantage already had been won.[63] Following the debate in the Security Council, representatives of the United States, NATO member states (the United Kingdom, France, the Netherlands, and Canada) Japan, South Korea, Australia, and New Zealand started to work on a draft resolution.

The strongly worded draft condemned the Soviet Union for shooting down KAL 007, demanded appropriate compensation, and asked for two independent investigations, one by the ICAO and one by the UN secretary-general. The U.S. delegate insisted upon sponsorship of the resolution by all nine countries, as the United States was unwilling to take the lead on its own. To obtain another propaganda victory the United States had to ensure that at least nine members of the Security Council supported the resolution, thereby forcing the Soviet Union to use its veto. Support on as broad a scale as possible was necessary.

The U.S. delegation in New York mobilized all its allies (in and outside NATO) to obtain the nine votes. The nonaligned states would tip the balance one way or the other. Consequently, the draft resolution had to be watered down considerably before the ninth vote could be counted upon. For a few days a major Western embarrassment seemed to be in the offing as diplomats in New York lobbied for support. Finally, Malta decided to support the resolution as the ninth country, and consequently the Soviet Union had to use its veto. As Seymour Hersh notes, "The United States had won its worldwide propaganda victory over the Soviet Union."[64]

Three months later the U.S. government triumphed again as the ICAO presented its report on the downing of KAL 007. The report failed to answer as many questions as it did answer. For example, why the Boeing jet ended up in Soviet airspace was left unresolved. But the ICAO was unequivocal in its condemnation of the shoot down. This was the last official statement on the subject, as the Western nations decided not to present their case again in the UN General Assembly. Attention already had petered out and did not revive until the American downing of an Iranian Boeing aircraft over the Persian Gulf in 1988.

The U.S. position on the KAL 007 disaster had been based on a worst-case scenario that left no room for giving the Soviet Union any benefit of the doubt. Washington had launched a vigorous anti-Soviet campaign using unbalanced and conflicting data. "The concern seemed to be one of scoring points, exposing the adversary, being proven right, using the crisis for political gains," concluded Alexander Dallin.[65] The rhetorical overkill was not followed by harsh measures. On the one hand, the U.S. government did not want an all-out confrontation with Moscow, and, on the other, Shultz tried to bolster his own position within the administration by showing a hard line vis-à-vis the Soviet Union.

Washington used its allies to support its own position. In the first few days of the crisis the allies were merely informed of developments, but, as it became clearer that the Soviet air controllers perhaps did not know that KAL 007 was a civilian airliner and that U.S. intelligence agencies probably had monitored its flight, the Reagan administration tried to rally its allies in order to bolster its own position and to prevent a major embarrassment. But even then the information given to the allies was never as extensive as it could have been. Thus, the allies were not told about the differences of opinion among the intelligence-gathering agencies in Washington, and information supporting the Soviet point of view was withheld as long as possible. All U.S. allies were mobilized in order to force the Soviet Union to cast its veto in the Security Council.

The allies complied but voiced doubts. Canadian Prime Minister Pierre Trudeau, for example, termed the Boeing's downing "a tragic incident," and, according to Trudeau, the U.S. government "didn't have a leg to stand on" with its version of the events. His British colleague, Margaret Thatcher, never afraid to support the United States, remained silent for seventeen days before commenting on the event. These two nations probably discovered through their links with the U.S. intelligence community that the Americans had used misinterpreted data.[66]

The smaller allies were more dependent upon American information, but they also started to doubt the American accusations after a few days. The Dutch, for instance, clearly supported the American position, but doubts plagued The Hague after the information about the RC-135 was made public. The change in policy by the American administration away from a unilateralist stance toward a multilateral Western one was noticed. The Dutch stance, like that of the other Western allies, also moved away from its originally harsh condemnation and subsequently left room to hear the Soviet point of view.

Conclusion

Notwithstanding the three crises cited above, analyses dealing with the future of NATO invariably predict that the organization will survive. Similarly, analyses of the roles and the problems of the smaller countries in the alliance end predictably with the conclusion that these countries will remain faithful, perhaps a little bit critical, but nevertheless loyal members of NATO in the future.[67] This should come as no surprise as long as the central rationale for NATO's existence—the military instability of Europe— is not challenged fundamentally by the governments of the member states. Given that basic principle, small allies are still prepared to give a little and take a lot.

The way NATO has dealt with crises has not changed dramatically in forty years. When the United States is in trouble, it acts unilaterally, preferably supported by its allies, but, if need be, alone. The alliance is apparently still not equipped to deal with genuine crises. All the successes in alliance consultation that former Secretary-General Brosio was able to list in 1974 concerned long-term preparations of common positions in negotiations with the Warsaw Pact. This pattern has not changed fundamentally since 1974. In times of crises, consultations prove to be almost impossible. Consequently, no report or commentary on the alliance can reach its conclusions without recommending "improved consultations."[68]

During the Cuban crisis, America's allies, large and small, were informed only at the very last moment, with the more powerful allies receiving separate treatment through special emissaries. They were expected only to support the U.S. government. Despite serious misgivings, they backed President Kennedy. Nearly six years later, neither the Americans nor the Europeans were able to give NATO the much-needed direction after the Soviet invasion of Czechoslovakia, one of the most serious crises the Western alliance has had to face. The smaller allies tried to organize their own caucus, but their efforts soon faltered. During the crisis over KAL 007 the United States acted at first without consultation, then, as its position began to deteriorate, it tried to rally its allies to its cause. Because of its need for their support, Washington changed its position. The smaller allies, however, were still dependent upon American intelligence, and their influence was ineffective.

Dependence upon the United States, disunity, lack of mutual understanding in their ranks, and inability to make a joint stand are some of the problems that have confronted the smaller allies. In the last decade, though, there also has been a noticeable shift in emphasis in the evaluation of the role of the smaller allies. Unreserved loyalty has given way to qualified loyalty. Slowly, and despite many setbacks, the European allies have bolstered their position within the alliance.[69] Their influence has grown, albeit gradually. They no longer accept uncritically the American government's policies and proclamations.

Future analyses of the role of smaller allies in NATO, therefore, will not end automatically with the observation that they will remain loyal members of the alliance. Internal cohesion has lessened considerably. NATO's policies have become hotly debated issues in a number of states, and its role as protector of Western security is under considerable pressure. Western electorates will not put up forever with bland "Yes—but . . ." responses to Soviet proposals. Mikhail Gorbachev appears to have taken away NATO's mortal enemy, and this requires a new "flexible response" in the next decade of the alliance.

Notes

1. Memorandum, Foreign Minister Luns, 1 June 1969, Code 912.1 Secret Archives, File 1041, pt. 2, Netherlands Ministry of Foreign Affairs, The Hague (hereafter cited as NMFA).

2. Alastair Buchan, *Crisis Management: The New Diplomacy* (Boulogne-sur-Seine, France: Atlantic Institute, 1966).

3. Henry Kissinger, *The Troubled Partnership: A Reappraisal of the Atlantic Alliance* (New York: McGraw-Hill, 1965); Ronald Steel, *The End of Alliance: America and the Future of Europe* (New York: Viking, 1964); K. H. Cerny and H. W. Briefs, eds., *NATO in Quest of Cohesion* (New York: Praeger, 1965).

4. Buchan, *Crisis Management*, passim.

5. Glenn H. Snyder, "The Security Dilemma in Alliance Politics," *World Politics* 36, no. 4 (July 1984): 461–95.

6. Robert W. Russell, "The Atlantic Alliance in Dutch Foreign Policy," in J. H. Leurdijk, ed., *The Foreign Policy of the Netherlands* (Alphen aan den Rijn, the Netherlands: Sijthoff and Noordhoff, 1978), 175–78.

7. See William Park, *Defending the West: A History of NATO* (Brighton, England: Wheatsheaf, 1986), vii: "Since its inception in 1949 the evolution of the

North Atlantic Treaty Organization (NATO) has been both punctuated and propelled by crises, so much so that the alliance has had to survive since birth against the background of an almost continuous death-knell."

8. After more than ten years the best study on the origins of the alliance is still Escott Reid, *Time of Fear and Hope: The Making of the North Atlantic Treaty, 1947–1949* (Toronto: McClelland and Stewart, 1977).

9. *Papers Relating to the Foreign Relations of the United States, 1949: Western Europe* (Washington, DC: Government Printing Office, 1975), 4:222–23.

10. See Articles 4 and 7 of the Treaty of Brussels and Articles 4 and 5 of the North Atlantic Treaty. For a legally oriented assessment of the obligation to consult under the provisions of the North Atlantic Treaty, see Frederic L. Kirgis, Jr., "NATO Consultations as a Component of National Decisionmaking," *American Journal of International Law* 73, no. 3 (July 1979): 372–406.

11. Harlan Cleveland, *NATO: The Transatlantic Bargain* (New York: Harper and Row, 1970), 14–15.

12. For a general survey of political consultation in this period, see Francis A. Beer, *Integration and Disintegration in NATO: Processes of Alliance Cohesion and Prospects for the Atlantic Community* (Columbus: Ohio State University Press, 1969), 12–28; and Roger Hill, *Political Consultation in NATO* (Toronto: Canadian Institute of International Affairs, 1978), 15–17.

13. *Report of the Committee of Three on Non Military Cooperation in NATO* (Paris: NATO Information Service, 1956), 12–13.

14. Ibid., 14, 9.

15. Cleveland, *NATO*, 16.

16. Rusk, as quoted in J. G. Blight, J. S. Nye, Jr., and D. A. Welch, "The Cuban Missile Crisis Revisited," *Foreign Affairs* 66, no. 1 (Fall 1987): 170. See also, D. Dijksman and J. Hoedeman, "De Grote Knal," *De Haagse Post*, 10 October 1987; and Lawrence S. Kaplan, *NATO and the United States: The Enduring Alliance* (Boston: Twayne, 1988), 85.

17. Schiff (Washington) to Luns, 22 October 1962, and Schurmann (Paris) to Luns, 22 October 1962, Code 921.340 Secret Archives, File 2149 Cuba, NMFA. According to André de Staercke, dean of the NATO ambassadorial corps, Acheson asked the allies whether they had any objections, and they had none. Kirgis concludes: "And undoubtedly [they] would not have done so under the circumstances even if they had disagreed with the American plan." See Kirgis, "NATO Consultations as a Component of National Decisionmaking," 400.

18. Cleveland, *NATO*, 22–23.

19. Bentinck (London) to Luns, 23 October 1962, Code 921.340 Secret Archives, File 2149 Cuba, NMFA.

20. See Van Ittersum (Bonn) to Luns, 24 October 1962, and Van Roijen (Washington) to Luns, 1 November 1962, Code 921.340 Secret Archives, File 2149 Cuba, NMFA. See also Konrad Adenauer, *Erinnerungen, 1959–1963* (Stuttgart, West Germany: Deutsche Verlags-Anstalt 1968), 199–200; Frank Costigliola, "The Failed Design: Kennedy, de Gaulle, and the Struggle for Europe," *Diplomatic History* 8, no. 3 (Summer 1984): 214; Charles de Gaulle, *Lettres, Notes et Carnets: Janvier 1961–Décembre 1963* (Paris: Plon, 1986), 270–72; and Elie Abel, *The Missiles of October: The Story of the Cuban Missile Crisis, 1962* (London: MacGibbon and Kee, 1966), 102–7.

21. Van Vredenburch (Rome) to Luns, 24 and 25 October 1962; Teixeira (Brussels) to Luns, 25 October 1962; Hagenaar (Ankara) to Luns, 26 October 1962; Lovink (Ottawa) to Luns, 26 October 1962, Code 921.340 Secret Archives, File 2149 Cuba, NMFA; Ottawa embassy to Luns, 26 October 1962, Code 921.340 Dept.

Archives, Box 842 Cuba crisis Part I, NMFA. U.S. Ambassador George F. Reinhardt described Fanfani's attitude as "flabby."

22. Cabinet meeting (no. 3098), 25 October 1962, Cabinet Minutes, 2.02.05. File 676, Fiche 177, Dutch National Archives, The Hague; memorandum by Directie NAVO en WEU zaken (No. 183), 29 October 1962, Code 911.31 Secret Archives, File 1152 Cuba, NMFA.

23. Memorandum by Luns for the Cabinet, 29 October 1962, Code 921.340 Secret Archives, File 2149 Cuba, NMFA; R. K. Visser (Prime Minister's Office) to the authors, 30 November 1988. The criticism was also voiced in the NMFA yearbook. See Ministerie van Buitenlandse Zaken, *Jaarboek van het ministerie van Buitenlandse Zaken 1962/1963* ('s-Gravenhage, the Netherlands: Staatsuitgeverij, 1963), 52–53.

24. See Harold Macmillan, *At the End of the Day* (London: Macmillan, 1973), 219–20. Macmillan's observation that the other allies "had no real grievance about non-consultation" is clearly at variance with our information. Ibid., 189-90.

25. George W. Ball, *The Past Has Another Pattern: Memoirs* (New York and London: Norton, 1982), 305–6; Raymond L. Garthoff, *Reflections on the Cuban Missile Crisis* (Washington, DC: Brookings Institution, 1987), 43. See also Committee on Foreign Relations, *Executive Sessions of the Senate Foreign Relations Committee*, 88th Cong., 1st sess.; 1987, 15:103–7.

26. Van Roijen (Washington) to Luns, 24 October 1962 and Hagenaar (Ankara) to Luns, 28–29 October 1962, Code 921.340 Secret Archives, File 2149 Cuba, NMFA. Concerning the *Jupiters*, see Barton J. Bernstein, "The Cuban Missile Crisis: Trading the Jupiters in Turkey?" *Political Science Quarterly* 95, no. 1 (Spring 1980): 97–125.

27. Bernstein, "The Cuban Missile Crisis," 112–21; Bernd Greiner, *Kuba-Krise: 13 Tage im Oktober: Analysen, Dokumente, Zeitungen* (Nördlingen, (Germany: Greno, 1988), 126–27, 350–65. Regarding the *Jupiters*, a swap would probably have pleased Canada, Italy, Belgium, Greece, Denmark, and Norway. Regarding the secret *Jupiter* deal and a possible role for Fanfani, see Gregg Herken, *Councils of War* (New York: Alfred Knopf, 1985), 364.

28. For some regrets, see McGeorge Bundy, *Danger and Survival: Choices about the Bomb in the First Fifty Years* (New York: Random House, 1988), 436–39.

29. Memorandum by DNW, 29 October 1962, Code 911.31 Secret Archives, File 1152 Cuba, NMFA; Costigliola, "The Failed Design," 243. Buchan rightly concludes, however, that "if the Soviet Union had not started a diplomatic retreat . . . then the lack of any standby arrangements in Washington for high level consultation among the NATO allies would have been seen as a clear and dangerous weakness." See Buchan, *Crisis Management*, 34.

30. See Manlio Brosio, "Consultation and the Atlantic Alliance," *Survival* 16, no. 3 (May-June 1974): 116; and James A. Nathan, "The Missile Crisis: His Finest Hour Now," *World Politics* 27, no. 2 (January 1975): 279. Hill comments that "Allied consultations in this crisis were as intensive as circumstances would permit." But he also notes correctly in relation to Brosio's evaluation that "a major power may have a great deal to gain from giving the *impression* of engaging in consultations." Hill, *Political Consultation in NATO*, 19, 106.

31. Andrew Noble to Lord Home, Netherlands: Foreign Office Annual Review for 1962, (CN 1011/1), 4 January 1963, File 50147-40, vol. 3, Department of External Affairs, Ottawa.

32. De Smit (Oslo) to Luns, 13 December 1962, Code 921.340 Secret Archives, File 2149 Cuba, NMFA.

33. Georgetown University Center for Strategic and International Studies, *NATO after Czechoslovakia* (Washington, DC: Georgetown University Press, 1969), 46. Concerning Lemnitzer, see Cabinet meeting (no. 4492), 8 August 1968, Cabinet Minutes, Archives of the Prime Minister's Office, The Hague (hereafter cited as APMO).

34. Private information from Dutch military sources. Kissinger describes it as: "The West had bent over backward *not* to involve itself in Czechoslovakia." See Henry Kissinger, *The White House Years* (London: Weidenfeld and Nicolson and Michael Joseph, 1979), 116.

35. Lyndon Baines Johnson, *The Vantage Point: Perspectives of the Presidency, 1963–1969* (London: Weidenfeld and Nicolson, 1972), 488–89; Ball, *The Past Has Another Pattern*, 440–43.

36. Van Lynden (London) to Luns, 28 August 1968, De Hoop Scheffer (Paris) to Luns, 29 August 1968, Code 913.10 Secret Archives, File 1394, vol. 47, NMFA; Harold Wilson, *The Labour Government 1864–1970: A Personal Record* (London: Weidenfeld and Nicolson and Michael Joseph, 1971), 551–54. Debré's German colleague, Willy Brandt, later commented that this was an "absurd presentation" of the real facts. Willy Brandt, *Begegnungen und Einsichten: Die jahre 1960–1975* (Hamburg, West Germany: Hoffmann und Campe, 1976), 282-83.

37. Cabinet meetings (nos. 4512, 4513, and 4525), 5, 9, and 20 September 1968, Cabinet Minutes, APMO. The Netherlands had signed the NPT one day before the invasion. Italy also decided not to sign.

38. Cabinet meeting (no. 4522), 13 September 1968, Cabinet Minutes, APMO; Van Vredenburch (Rome) to Luns, 23 August 1968; de Hoop Scheffer (Paris) to Luns, 29 August 1968; Van Vredenburch (Rome) to Luns, 30 September 1968, Code 913.10 Secret Archives, File 1394, vol. 47, NMFA.

39. See Cleveland, *NATO*, 118-19.

40. Kaplan, *NATO and the United States*, 123. Brandt, in contrast, recalls in his memoirs that NATO feared "for a short time that the invasion could have further, incalculable military consequences." See Brandt, *Begegnungen und Einsichten*, 285.

41. Cabinet meetings (no. 4512, 4513 and 4525), 5, 9, and 20 September 1968, Cabinet Minutes, APMO; Report on a briefing for NATO ambassadors in Washington, 31 August 1968, Code 911.31 Secret Archives, File 898, pt. 6, NMFA.

42. Cabinet meetings (no. 4522, 4525, and 4527), 13, 20, and 27 September 1968, Cabinet Minutes, APMO. See also Cleveland, *NATO*, 122–23. From the meeting on 27 September one can learn that Lemnitzer had asked again for a higher state of alert, but this was rejected.

43. See Van Lynden (London) to Luns, 28 August 1968; Van Vredenburch (Rome) to Luns, 29 August 1968; De Hoop Scheffer (Paris) to Luns, 9 September 1968; De Beus (Bonn) to Luns, 11 September 1968, Code 913.10 Secret Archives, File 1394, pt. 47, NMFA.

44. Luns to NMFA, 21 September 1968; Van Lynden (London) to Luns, 1 October 1968, Code 913.10 Secret Archives, File 1394, vol. 47, NMFA.

45. Bentinck (Paris) to Luns, 2 October 1968; De Beus (Bonn) to Luns, 2 October 1968, Code 913.10 Secret Archives, File 1394, vol. 47, NMFA; Cabinet meeting no. 4529, Cabinet Minutes, APMO.

46. Bonn (NATO, Brussels) to Luns, 15 November 1968; Memorandum, de Ranitz, 27 November 1968; De Beus (London) to Luns, 29 November 1968, Code 913.10 Secret Archives, File 1395, vol. 48, NMFA; Wilson, *The Labour Government*, 617–18. In the course of 1969 the French even repeated their policy of "the empty chair," this time within WEU, because they considered WEU not suited for discussions of out-of-area issues.

47. Cabinet meeting (no. 4534), 11 October 1968, Cabinet Minutes, APMO; Middelburg (New York) to NMFA, 14 October 1968; Van Lynden (London) to Luns, 16 October 1968, Code 913.10 Secret Archives, File 1394, vol. 47, NMFA.

48. *Keesing's Contemporary Archives*, 7–14 December 1968, 23071. See also Cabinet meetings (nos. 4558 and 4563), 18 and 22 November 1968, Cabinet Minutes, APMO; and William G. Hyland, *Mortal Rivals: Understanding the Pattern of Soviet-American Relations* (New York: Simon and Schuster, 1987), 15–16.

49. See Cleveland, *NATO*, 20–21; and Kirgis, "NATO Consultations as a Component of National Decisionmaking," 396.

50. Kaplan, *NATO and the United States*, 123; Cabinet meetings (nos. 4497, 4498, 4504, and 4525), 21, 23, and 30 August and 20 September 1968, Cabinet Minutes, APMO.

51. Guido Vigeveno, *The Bomb and European Security* (London: Hurst, 1983), 21; Harlan Cleveland, "NATO after the Invasion," *Foreign Affairs* 47, no. 2 (January 1969): 257. Significantly, neither Brosio nor Hill mentions the Czech crisis in his survey of allied consultations in the 1950s, 1960s, and early 1970s. Brosio, "Consultation and the Atlantic Alliance," 115–17; Hill, *Political Consultation in NATO*, 19–22.

52. Cabinet meeting (no. 4550), 8 November 1968, Cabinet Minutes, APMO. Concerning Rusk, see De Beus (New York) to NMFA, 27 September 1968, Code 912.1 Secret Archives, File 1041, pt. 2, NMFA.

53. Memorandum, DWH, 11 January 1972, Code 912.1 Secret Archives, File 1041, pt. 2, NMFA.

54. Johan Jorgen Holst, "Lilliputs and Gulliver: Small States in a Great-Power Alliance," in Gregory Flynn, ed., *NATO's Northern Allies: The National Security Policies of Belgium, Denmark, the Netherlands, and Norway* (London and Sydney: Croom Helm, 1985), 259.

55. The source of the forced landing rumor has never been cleared. See, for this and for the role of the CIA, Seymour Hersh, *"The Target Is Destroyed": What Really Happened to Flight 007 and What America Knew about It* (New York: Random House, 1986), 71, 142–44; and R. W. Johnson, *Shootdown: Flight 007 and the American Connection* (New York: Viking, 1986), 76–80.

56. See Dutch embassy (Tokyo) to NMFA, 1 September 1983, Code 5, File Soviet-Russia/KAL 007, NMFA.

57. For Burt's briefing, see Dutch embassy (Washington) to NMFA, 2 September 1983, Code 5, File Soviet-Russia/KAL 007, NMFA. Concerning Eagleburger, see NMFA to Dutch Permanent Mission (New York), 6 September 1983, Code 9, File VN/VR-Korea/KAL 007, NMFA. See also the account by two former RC-135 intelligence experts, Tom Bernard and Edward Eskelson, in *International Herald Tribune*, 16 September 1983; and Martin Streetly, "US Airborne ELINT Systems. Part 3: The Boeing RC-135 Family," *Jane's Defence Weekly* 3, no. 11 (16 March 1985): 460–65.

58. See Hersh, *The Target Is Destroyed*, 82–87, 103–11.

59. Dutch embassy (Washington) to NMFA, 4 September 1983, Code 5, File Soviet-Russia/KAL 007, NMFA.

60. Dutch Permanent Mission (New York) to NMFA, 2 September 1983, Code 9 DIO-archives, File VN/VR-Korea/KAL 007, NMFA; Department of State *Bulletin* 83, no. 2079 (October 1983): 3–5.

61. See Hersh, *The Target Is Destroyed*, 161; and Alexander Dallin, *Black Box: KAL 007 and the Superpowers* (Berkeley: University of California Press, 1985), 94.

62. Dutch embassy (Washington) to NMFA, 5 September 1983, Code 5, File Soviet-Russia/KAL 007, NMFA.

63. See Johnson, *Shootdown*, 118–20. Kirkpatrick's performance closely resembled that of her predecessor Adlai Stevenson during the missile crisis. The United Nations was used in 1962 as a platform where the Soviet case could be dealt a final blow before world opinion. See Nathan, "The Missile Crisis," 277–78.

64. Hersh, *The Target Is Destroyed*, 174. Extensive documentation is found in Code 9 DIO-archives, File VN/VR-Korea/KAL 007, NMFA. For some chilling observations on the consequences of this propaganda victory, see Gordon Brook-Shepherd, *The Storm Birds: Soviet Post-War Defectors* (London: Weidenfeld and Nicolson, 1988), 265–72.

65. Dallin, *Black Box*, 95.

66. See Hersh, *The Target Is Destroyed*, 244–45; and Johnson, *Shootdown*, 129.

67. To give just one example, see Sharon Squassoni, "The Smaller Allies Face Major Problems Too: The Benelux Members of the Alliance," in Walter Goldstein, ed., *Fighting Allies: Tensions within the Atlantic Alliance* (London: Brassey's, 1986), 167.

68. " 'The habit of consultation', strongly advocated by the three wise men [in 1956], became an important part of alliance rhetoric, almost approaching theological heights. . . . Virtually no report or commentary on the alliance can reach its conclusion without recommending 'improved consultations.' " Stanley R. Sloan, *NATO's Future: Toward a New Transatlantic Bargain* (Basingstoke, England: Macmillan and Company, 1986), 45.

69. For instance, see Nikolaj Petersen, *Denmark and NATO, 1949–1987*, (Oslo: Forsvarshistorisk Forskningssenter, 1987), 43–45.

The Mediterranean

Raimondo Luraghi

The NATO group in the Mediterranean Sea is not yet, in its entirety, forty years old. Only Italy (France is more of an Atlantic than a Mediterranean power) entered the alliance in 1949; Greece and Turkey were kept waiting for three years, until 1952; and Spain, which also is not, strictly speaking, a purely Mediterranean country, was even more of a latecomer, having been admitted only in 1982.[1] It seems fair, however, to speak of forty years of the alliance in the Mediterranean, because both Greece and Turkey were, from the end of World War II, in immediate danger of Soviet pressures and Communist encroachment.[2] Additionally, Spain in 1953 signed a treaty of mutual assistance with the United States.

Forty years in the contemporary world is a long time, and the Mediterranean region has been the setting during these four decades for so many important events that to compile a thorough accounting is simply impossible without writing several volumes. Nonetheless, an effort to put this time in perspective can and must be done; otherwise, it will not be possible to focus on the problems still confronting the alliance in the Mediterranean.

With the benefit of historical hindsight, it is now possible to see that NATO in the Mediterranean during its first forty years went through two series of events that on the one hand, strengthened the alliance but, on the other, also weakened it, sometimes seriously. These developments generated new and dramatic problems not even dreamed of in 1949 when Italy, first among the purely Mediterranean powers, entered NATO.

It is now quite evident that in the 1970s and immediately thereafter the alliance in the Mediterranean had to face extensive pressures from the Soviet Union, its allies, and its more or less open associates. Combined, they exerted against NATO what amounted to a low-intensity conflict that scaled upward to highly dramatic moments of tension. In the end, this conflict closed successfully for the alliance. However, it was only part of a wider low-intensity offensive directed by the Soviet Union and its allies against NATO states, according to the openly admitted principle that détente was only a "pacific" way for defeating imperialistic powers.[3]

The storm clouds gathering in the 1960s passed into the 1970s through the formulation of the so-called Brezhnev Doctrine and the clear pronouncements from Marshal A. A. Grechko and Admiral S. G. Gorshkov that gave rise to a wave of Soviet interventionism all over the Third World.[4] This military activism brought heavy pressure to bear on NATO, with the final objective of dissolving or, at the least, paralyzing the alliance.

Soviet leaders knew only too well that NATO's central front in Europe was inviolable. Any attempt to alter the borders of the Federal Republic of Germany would have led directly to the start of World War III and an all-out nuclear confrontation, which the Soviet Union did not want. The situation along the northern and southern wings of the European front was different. There were possibilities for fighting several indirect wars on these wings. The Mediterranean region looked more promising, although the heavy-handed and, at times, shameless naval pressure against Sweden during those years should by no means be underrated.

The Mediterranean always has been, and still is, by its political nature, an unstable zone. Along its shores, Christianity, Judaism, and Islam have been confronting each other for more than one thousand years, and this by itself is enough to generate a highly explosive situation.[5] Moreover, from the two shores of this sea the advanced Western world and the less developed Third World stare at each other.

The irrepressible conflicts between Shiite and Sunni Moslems, between Maronites and Arabs, between Israelis and Moslems, and the ongoing feud between Greece and Turkey, both members of NATO, combine to create troubled waters suitable for the maneuvering of Soviet diplomatic and military policy. The strong pillars of the alliance in the Mediterranean were Italy and Turkey, two countries that would soon become high-priority targets for the Soviet low-intensity offensive.

Much has been made of the increased Soviet naval presence in the Mediterranean since 1964. Although these ships have indeed been a force to be reckoned with,[6] the Soviet Fifth *Eskadra* was just one piece on the chessboard and by no means the dominating one. Its main objective has been less direct: to turn the previous situation of hitherto undisputed Western control of the Mediterranean into one of greater naval balance, and as a major fleet to serve notice on the restrictive clauses of the Montreux Convention (1936) governing passage through the Turkish Straits.[7]

The conflict that erupted between two NATO states, Greece and Turkey, facilitated Soviet strategic objectives. The armed intervention by Turkey on Cyprus in the summer of 1974 was undoubtedly the most spectacular dimension of the conflict, which also featured an ongoing clash of interests in the Aegean Sea. The situation is complex: Since Greek islands sit a few miles off the Turkish coast and and since law-of-the-sea guidelines grant a continental shelf to islands, Greece claims the largest part of the Aegean seabed. Moreover, "should she [Greece] abandon the six-mile territorial sea limit and move to the global norm of 12 miles, she would also control virtually all Aegean waters."[8] Greece fears that by abandoning its Aegean positions it would encourage Turkey to claim possession of the Greek islands along the Anatolian coast. The discovery of oil in the northern Aegean region just prior to the Turkish invasion of Cyprus precipitated the dispute, which also includes problems with military command control and the flight information region (FIR) in the Aegean. Possible solutions to the crisis do not appear likely in the immediate future.

This imbroglio has provided constant and irresolvable problems for NATO politicians and strategists. Andreas Papandreou, leader of PASOK, Greece's Socialist party, exploited and gave direction to anti-American and anti-NATO sentiments on the road to his assumption of power in October 1981 and with some modification maintained this approach in the following years. Papandreou's populist-leftist rhetoric made the United States and NATO into bogeymen and scapegoats for any difficulty, real or imaginary, Greece had to face. Papandreou proclaimed that Greece belongs to the Third World's periphery, exploited by capitalist countries.[9] Some observers viewed these statements as steps toward a form of nonalignment during a period when many nonaligned nations were falling under the influence of the nominally nonaligned state of Cuba. The Greek need for Arab oil pushed Papandreou further into sharper words against Israel. Papandreou's rhetoric, occasionally translated into actions, created an ambiguous role for Greece in the alliance in light of the Soviet offensive in the Mediterranean.

The Greek armed forces, however, seem to have remained almost unaffected by these ventures by their government. Their relations with other NATO armies and navies have been quite good. Nonetheless, Papandreou's policy seriously damaged the alliance's stand in the Mediterranean, even more recently when, with the advent of Mikhail Gorbachev, Soviet pressures subsided.

Soviet tactics began in earnest earlier against Turkey, NATO's exposed eastern rampart, with an appalling wave of terrorist activities. Similar but far more serious terrorist tactics followed in Italy, whose collapse would have meant disaster for the alliance. In October 1971, during a secret meeting in Florence in which both Italian and international terrorist organizations participated, the master plan for a destabilizing offensive against Italy was drafted. It was perfected shortly afterward in Lebanon under the chairmanship of a Palestinian, George Habash. Meanwhile, Italian terrorists were being actively trained in several camps, including some in Czechoslovakia.[10]

Terrorist activities were already spreading all over Turkey; their victims were mostly Americans, Israelis, and moderate Turkish politicians. In 1973 the Turkish government prepared a white paper on terrorism, but it decided not to publish it because foreign powers played too prominent a role in its pages.[11] However, Italian President Sandro Pertini, outspoken and fearless, did not hesitate to point his finger toward the Soviet Union as the primary organizer of the offensive.[12]

In 1976, Turkish terrorists assassinated more than one hundred individuals; in 1978–79 assassinations increased to twenty-four hundred victims. Right-wing terrorist organizations purporting to react against the leftist groups played foolishly into the hands of those who were trying to destabilize the country. By 1979, Turkey hovered on the edge of an appalling abyss, at the bottom of which lay the final disintegration of the country. The military intervened to prevent this fate and imposed a dictatorship in 1980, a heavy price but one that paid off with a victory against terrorism. In just one year the new Turkish authorities succeeded in rounding up seventy-five thousand suspected terrorists, from both the Left and the Right, and they convicted twenty-four thousand. They also uncovered large supplies of hidden arms.[13]

The appalling proportions of the terrorism demonstrated that Turkey had indeed almost reached the brink of a generalized civil war, which would have been followed by the complete collapse of the state. For such an important NATO stronghold to have crumbled would have had far-reaching consequences: The alliance would have lost its strategic perch in the eastern Mediterranean, and Italy would have found itself on the firing line.[14]

Italy was already under attack. In 1970 the main terrorist organization, the Red Brigades, began its operations, pushing the country quickly to the edge of a major political crisis. Whereas German terrorists never succeeded in attracting more than a handful of individuals, in Italy there was enough "water" in which the terrorist "fish" could "swim." The aims of the terrorists were, on the one hand, to increase active and passive complicity from supporters and, on the other, to push the Italian government to resort to authoritarian actions in order to bring the country to a generalized civil war.

The danger was extremely serious. A clandestine coterie of intellectuals in Italy inside the universities, in the theatrical world, in some publishing houses and on the editorial staffs of a few newspapers and magazines supported the terrorists. This backing ranged from passive roles (simple apologists and sympathizers) to more active participation, such as collecting money to "help the Communist victims of persecution by the state"; protecting terrorists with a conspiracy of silence; and providing them with shelter, money, and medical care.

It is very important to understand that these relatively numerous sympathizers represented a real danger for the Italian state. They served as a bridge by which terrorists might pass out of their isolation to create a mass movement and an ultimate state of civil war. They were also the reserve army out of whose ranks came active terrorists. Starting in 1968 terrorist actions in Italy, from both the Left and the Right, amounted to fourteen thousand incidents, and assassinations in a few years reached about two hundred. Ominously, Italian police began to discover signs of collusion between leftist and rightist terrorists, and between terrorists and the Mafia.[15]

Italy, however, reacted quickly and energetically. The Carabinieri, a military police organization amounting to a small but loyal and incorruptible army trained for counterinsurgency, launched a well-conceived, two-dimensional campaign. It intended to hunt down and destroy terrorist groups and to dissuade the actual and would-be accomplices of the terrorists. This latter objective was achieved by exploiting the peculiar weakness of such people: It was made clear that they would never be allowed to play it safe, that the Carabinieri would draw out such accomplices, arrest them, send them to the courts, and have them sentenced to many years in prison. The Carabinieri used such tactics to isolate "the fish" by drying out "the water" around them. The sympathizers characteristically were ready to help terrorism but had no stomach for the actual fighting and were unwilling to suffer the penalties imposed on them for their actions.[16]

In the end, Italy succeeded in the remarkable enterprise of crushing terrorism without impairing democracy. No martial law was ever declared, and no special court was ever organized. Terrorists were arrested and tried under normal criminal law and sentenced to many years in prison for common crimes. Their claim to be considered political prisoners went unheeded, and their objective of forcing the Italian state into authoritarian practices, in order to gain support for their "struggle," was a total failure. Of course, terrorism in Italy, as well as all over the world, has not been wholly extinguished. Small groups remain, still supported by some foreign governments and still able to commit an occasional murder, but they are quite isolated.

Unfortunately, the terrorist emergency was not widely understood by some friendly and even allied countries. In France, a socialist attorney general and several judges regularly refused to extradite Italian terrorists who had found shelter there. To add insult to injury, a comparison was drawn in France between terrorist refugees and Italian anti-Fascists who had found asylum in France during Benito Mussolini's dictatorship and persecutions.

As if this were not enough, French leftists went so far as to organize a conference in an Italian city purporting to denounce repression in Italy. This activity was intended to support Italian terrorism, and might even have been organized in agreement with terrorist groups. That the Italian authorities granted permission to those people to enter Italy freely and to hold their meeting, insofar as they limited themselves to talking, effectively rebutted their accusations about Italian repression.

All in all, about three hundred Italian terrorists found shelter in France. Many are still living there, despite several Italian extradition requests for their return to be tried for common crimes, including murder. This attitude, however, was restricted to some French politicians and a few judges, because the French police collaborated closely with their Italian colleagues. One cannot but wonder about what was and, in part, still is happening in France and in other allied countries, such as Canada, where a local court flatly refused to extradite a convicted Italian terrorist actively sought by Italian police.

A far worse situation occurred in Greece. There, Papandreou's government resisted collaboration in hunting down and arresting terrorists, many of whom found shelter in Greece. Greek authorities scandalously granted freedom recently to an Arab terrorist convicted in Italy of multiple murders and allowed him to find a safer haven in Libya.

Soviet official spokesmen have always denied any involvement with terrorist activities. Yet it is well known that the Soviet Union, together with other Warsaw Pact countries, has provided the terrorists with weapons, financial aid, military training, and, occasionally, even political protection. It may be supposed that the Soviet Union has refrained from directly organizing terrorist networks (this, however, is by no means sure). Nevertheless, Soviet propaganda indicated that, as terrorists were destabilizing "imperialistic and reactionary states," they were also playing a positive part for "peace and progress." At least twelve terrorist training camps were established in Cuba under the direction of KGB Colonel Vadim Kocergin.[17]

It now seems clear that the Soviet Union during the Brezhnev-Andropov-Chernenko era, while trying to establish a careful distinction between itself and the terrorist groups, encouraged and supported them. One has only to speculate on the benefits that the Warsaw Pact would have accrued from the political collapse of Turkey or Italy or both. The Mediterranean might well have become a Soviet lake, with the U.S. Sixth Fleet forced out of it. NATO's eastern defense line might have been pushed back to the very shores of France, and Spain might never have entered the alliance.

The low-intensity offensive unleashed by the Soviet Union along the Mediterranean front, with the active collaboration of such countries as Libya, Syria, and South Yemen, was never as pervasive as it was in the "peace" movement intended to forestall the installation of *Pershing* and *Cruise* missiles in European bases. As with terrorism the pacifist movement was by no means composed exclusively of Soviet agents. However, Soviet propaganda and covert organizations succeeded in infiltrating the protest groups and in providing them with guidance, a large part of their leadership, and financial aid. The objectives of these groups coincided with those of Soviet foreign policy: a neutral, disarmed, and isolated Europe. In the long run, this program failed, too. Italy and Turkey stood firm, and the Euromissiles were installed. This triumph against both terrorists and disarmament unilateralists more than made up for the many negative policies and actions of Papandreou and his government.

These advances for NATO interests contributed to the entry of Spain into the alliance, even if Prime Minister Felipe Gonzales subsequently bowed to leftist pressures by closing the U.S. Air Force base at Torrejon. A decision was then reached to transfer American F-14 jets to an Italian base in the near future, which, in turn, resulted in the protests, albeit unsuccessful, of Italian Communists and "pacifists."

In conclusion, NATO, in its fortieth year, stands firm in the Mediterranean. When future historians study these dramatic four decades, they will, without any doubt, judge as a major achievement the successful fight by the alliance's Mediterranean countries against a powerful effort to destabilize and disintegrate them. It also can be argued that Moscow's failure to achieve its objectives in the Mediterranean has contributed to the downfall of Brezhnevism, its policy of aggression, imperialism, and expansion, and to the rise of Gorbachev's new policy.

It would be, however, a major mistake for NATO's Mediterranean countries to slacken their vigilance. Even putting aside the possibility that Gorbachev might be overthrown by some opposition group inside the Soviet Union, the Mediterranean is still too strategically significant, rich in unresolved problems, and, one might add, filled with troublemaking states; it must maintain its important position in NATO considerations.

Perhaps the worst problem in the near future will be found in the continuing crisis in Yugoslavia. Both Italy and Greece should by no means underrate it. Had Brezhnev still been in power the Yugoslav crisis might already have been transformed into an international one, and the Mediterranean might have been on the appalling brink of a total war. Will Yugoslavia survive? There are experts who are deeply pessimistic regarding this query.

No historian likes to play the prophet. Let us only say that any dramatic development in the Yugoslav crisis, be it an economic collapse or, worst of all, a civil war, cannot allow NATO to remain indifferent. It would be wise for the alliance to begin consulting its members for the drafting of a common Yugoslav policy.

Meanwhile, NATO's Mediterranean states should work to eliminate local squabbles, to help in finding solutions for the Greco-Turkish disputes, and to make the most of the Spanish military and naval presence. These actions, bearing in mind the inveterate lack of interest in Mediterranean problems on the part of NATO's central and northern states, will be very important. Closer cooperation among Mediterranean countries, for example, might have helped an Italian admiral to be nominated chairman of the alliance's military committee; instead, his candidacy was turned down in favor of that of a Norwegian general.

It would be wrong for Mediterranean powers to turn their back on the alliance. On the contrary, their duty is to stand firm and watchful, to be more united among themselves and with other NATO partners, especially the United States. These are the tasks for the next forty years.

Notes

1. For in-depth coverage of NATO's involvement in the Mediterranean, see Lawrence S. Kaplan, Robert W. Clawson, and Raimondo Luraghi, eds., *NATO and the Mediterranean* (Wilmington, DE: Scholarly Resources, 1985).

2. For details, see Bruce R. Kuniholm, *The Origins of the Cold War in the Near East* (Princeton: Princeton University Press, 1980).

3. Federico Sensi, "La politica Europea dell'Unione Sovietica," in *Strategie Sovietiche e Risposte dell'Occidente*, proceedings of the eighth NATO seminar (Venice, Italy, 1982), 21 ff.

4. See Harriet Fast Scott and William F. Scott, *The Armed Forces of the USSR* (Boulder, CO: Westview Press, 1978), 57; Sergei G. Gorshkov, *The Sea Power of the State* (Annapolis, MD: Naval Institute Press, 1979), 20 ff.; and Raimondo

Luraghi, "La guerra totale nella strategia sovietica," *Mondo Operaio*, no. 2 (1982): 40 ff.

5. André Martel and Claude Carlier, "France and the Mediterranean," in Kaplan, Clawson, and Luraghi, eds., *NATO and the Mediterranean*, 125–36.

6. See Bryan Ranft and Geoffrey Till, *The Sea in Soviet Strategy* (Annapolis, MD: Naval Institute Press, 1983).

7. The convention forbids any power to pass submarines or aircraft carriers through the straits. The Soviet Union has circumvented this restriction by claiming that its carriers are antisubmarine ships, by navigating its submarines on the surface, and by making clear to Turkey that it would consider any attempt to interfere as an act of war.

8. Ihsan Gürkan, *NATO, Turkey and the Southern Flank* (New York: National Strategy Information Center, 1980), 19. See also Thanos Veremis, "Greek Security: Issues and Politics," in *Adelphi Papers* (London: Institute for Strategic Studies, 1982), no. 179.

9. Veremis, "Greek Security," 23.

10. See Claire Sterling, *The Terror Network: Secret War of International Terrorism* (New York: Holt, Rinehart, and Winston, 1981).

11. Walter Laqueur, *The Age of Terrorism* (Boston: Little Brown, 1987), 290 ff.; Sterling, *Terror Network*, 143 ff.

12. Giovanni Bensi, *La Pista Sovietica* (Milan, 1983), 27 ff. In his New Year's message of 1980, Pertini said: "The center of terrorism is not in Italy: it is abroad." And later in an interview to a French television network, he remarked: "How is it that the greatest terrorist activity is in Turkey, a country which has a thousand kilometres of common border with the Soviet Union? How is it that terrorism is so rampant against Italy, which represents the democratic bridge between Europe, Africa and Middle East?"

13. Laqueur, *The Age of Terrorism*, 291.

14. Terrorism, of course, did not spare West Germany; however, in spite of their éclat, terrorists there never succeeded in breaking out of their isolation and in creating a widespread danger. See ibid., 285.

15. Ibid., 282.

16. The ultimate terrorist act was the attempted murder of the pope. See Bensi, *La Pista Sovietica*.

17. See Sterling, *Terror Network*; and Bensi, *La Pista Sovietica*.

NATO IN THE WORLD

Europeanization versus Atlanticism: The Search for a European Pillar in the Atlantic Alliance

Reimund Seidelmann

The "Europeanist" Approach to European Security

Reflecting the close interrelation between the foreign, economic, and military dimensions of policy, on the one hand, and the reorganization of West European power after the 1940s,[1] on the other, the extension of West European cooperation and integration efforts into foreign and security policies since the early 1980s has been termed "Europeanization" and has been regarded as the outcome of a Europeanist attitude in today's Europe. Simplistic versions of this complex and contradictory process carry the danger of mistaking Europeanization for a new isolationism, of mixing it up with anti-American sentiments, or of portraying it as a threat to the Atlantic Community and, especially, to NATO.[2] However, a careful analysis of the issues, institutions, dynamics, and long-term perspectives of the Europeanization process indicates something quite opposite. The new willingness to define, organize, and implement European security interests primarily within and through genuine European or West European institutions shows a new responsibility to international politics. If the Atlantic Community is able to adapt in a constructive way, this change will improve the quality and reach of Western policies.

The Call for Europeanization

A broad political consensus on the necessity of Europeanization emerged in the early 1980s and now belongs to the standard repertoire of West European politicians. Although Europeanization involves the buildup of a European identity,[3] European Community (EC) integration plus enlargement,[4] and intensified newly liberated Eastern Europe,[5] the following political discussion limits the term mainly to the question of how to set up a European pillar within the Atlantic Alliance.

In the Federal Republic of Germany (FRG) the debate on the construction of Europeanization is most advanced. Chancellor Helmut Kohl has called for "a common European security policy."[6] Foreign Minister Hans-Dietrich Genscher has argued that a security dimension would strengthen the European pillar to ensure an equal Atlantic partnership.[7] Leading Social Democrats such as Oskar Lafontaine are making the point that a strong and efficient "European Defense Community" would serve both European and U.S. interests.[8] These positions must be seen in the light of similar demands in party programs,[9] think tanks,[10] and academic advice.[11]

British contributions to this debate include Hedley Bull's definition of a Europeanist approach, Sir Geoffrey Howe's support of the creation of a European pillar, and Peter Unwin's idea of a "European Defense Community."[12] The French debate is characterized by Pierre Lellouche's support of improved cooperation in West European defense policies, Dominique Moïsi's formula of the "Alliance of Equals," and Prime Minister Michel Rocard's view that determined Europeanists must support the Atlantic Alliance.[13] In Italy the combination of loyalty to NATO and support of Europeanization can be found in government and opposition statements, including those of the Communist Party of Italy (PCI).[14]

Europeanization is a subject not only of national discussions but also of proceedings in European institutions as well. The European Parliament (EP) started in the early 1970s to deal with security issues. The unanimous establishment of its subcommittee on security and disarmament in October 1984 underlined its interest in the subject, receiving support from its two major factions, the Socialists and the Christian Democrats.[15] EC President Piet Dankert, a Dutch Social Democrat, summarized this position:

> Yet the current international scene provides compelling reasons for Western Europe to play a more responsible and effective international role. Such a role requires a greater degree of political coherence than exists today and, inevitably, a more independent and coordinated approach to West European security. But even before that degree of coherence can be achieved, West Europeans must begin to develop a joint approach to West European security.[16]

Altiero Spinelli's initiative in favor of a European Union (EU) argued for the necessity of completing economic and political integration, including integration of foreign and security affairs.[17] Even the generally more cautious EC Commission left no doubt about its support for a European pillar that could reinforce transatlantic relations.[18] It is obvious that the Western European Union (WEU) and the European Political Cooperation (EPC), which benefited substantially from this development, are in favor of Europeanization.[19] More important is that both regard Europeanization and the Atlantic Alliance as compatible. In recent years even NATO has accepted the notion of Europeanization, expressing a positive attitude in joint declarations and individual statements, although its reservations should not be overlooked.[20] Finally, the U.S. administration and public have expressed general support of Western European attempts to improve their security cooperation.[21] President Ronald Reagan stated:

> During the years of these negotiations, new realities have come into play—new realities that present new opportunities. In particular, in recent years we have seen the emergence among some of our European allies of a willingness, even an eagerness, to seek a larger, more closely coordinated role for Western Europe in providing its own defense. We Americans welcome this. For these four decades, NATO has in effect represented an alliance between a number of partners and one very senior partner. Yet today our European allies have risen from the ruins of war to vitality, prosperity, and growing unity as a continent. And so I would submit that now the alliance should become more and more among equals, indeed, an alliance between continents. In the words of former Secretary of State Henry Kissinger, the time has come for our country "to . . . welcome a European identity in defense, which in the end is bound to spur Atlantic cooperation."[22]

Approaches to Europeanization

Behind this general consensus, however, are different and sometimes contradictory approaches. One approach asks for Europeanization as a necessary expression of a new European identity and as a legitimate pursuit of European interests. This includes a negative and a positive dimension: Western Europe should overcome U.S. domination and play a larger role in Western foreign and security policies, concurrently developing greater unity, appropriate institutions, and European interests.[23]

A second approach is more programmatic. It calls for the completion of EC integration to provide Western Europe with full actor status in East-West and in global politics. In contrast to the early 1970s idea of the EC as a "civilian power,"[24] it aims for a supranational union in control of foreign and military as well as economic policy. Europeanization of security policies is regarded not only as a precondition for improved power but also as a major stimulus for integration in general.[25]

A third approach is mainly based on defensive, cost-benefit thinking. Shared West European management of scarce resources to overcome duplication and counterproductive national competition would produce more arms without increasing defense budgets, improve defense options in a nonprovocative way, and give West European positions more weight in international negotiations.[26]

Fourth, an institution-oriented approach has emerged. Both the EC system (EC, EP, and EPC) and the WEU have discovered the value of the

Europeanization debate to improve their legitimacy, to gain new competences, and to broaden their impact on the conduct of Western European security politics.[27] Finally, French and British hopes to use Europeanization to overcome perceived pacifism and neutralism in West Germany should be mentioned.

Until now, these approaches coexisted for two reasons. First, the absence of a concrete organization of the European pillar allowed easy consensus among protesters against policies of the Reagan administration in the early 1980s.[28] Second, national governments in Western Europe under heavy domestic pressure in security and integration matters understood that such a general debate with so little substance allowed them to present a new and promising perspective for the solution of their dilemmas without facing concrete demands of transferring national sovereignty to West European bodies. The public display of such Europeanism is politically attractive— 63 percent of the EC population is in favor of the creation of a "United States of Europe,"[29] 49 percent imagines a common defense in the year 2000, and 44 percent sees the EC on equal terms with the United States and the USSR at the end of the century.[30] The diversity of approaches, the lack of political substance, and the parallel pursuit of incompatible institutional approaches allow everybody to agree without taking action. National governments can declare policies that portray themselves as active problem solvers and West Europeans gain time against U.S. demands for better political and military burden sharing by promising future changes.

Political Relevance of Europeanization

A careful analysis of the political impact of these approaches shows that Europeanization could harm Atlantic relations. First, a European Union with its own economic and military power base would challenge U.S. global domination and leadership in the Atlantic Alliance. The transition from an alliance asymmetric in structure and power to one of globally engaged equals would bring numerous conflicts about style, substance, and power, which would weaken cohesion and determination to fulfill alliance obligations.[31] Second, major structural changes within NATO as a consequence of setting up a European pillar would intensify the old decoupling trauma of nonnuclear European powers. Redefinition of U.S. nuclear and conventional engagement, currently under way,[32] together with politically sensitive reductions of American troops in Europe, would put significant strain on trust in U.S. security guarantees for Europe. Third, global competition between the United States and a European Union could add further problems to an international system that is already unstable as a result of major structural and regional conflicts. Although Atlantic relations in the past have never been without conflicts, Europeanization would change basic structures of the past. It would considerably reduce U.S. leverage on Western Europe, and it would extend the pattern of competitive partnership, which characterizes the economic relations of today, into other areas of the relationship.

On the other hand, successful Europeanization presents far-reaching possibilities for European and American interests to coincide. The gradual establishment of regional peace and order would lessen both the risks and the burdens of a military confrontation between East and West in Europe. Such a development, for which the Conference on Security and Cooperation in Europe (CSCE) would be a useful framework,[33] could make the use of military force in European affairs as unthinkable as it is in intra-NATO relations. It would lead to a drastic reduction of the costly and risky U.S. military involvement in Western Europe and accelerate democratization in Eastern Europe. Given the European consensus about the general idea, structure, and mechanism of the CSCE, the combination of economic power, political attractiveness, and a common and determined security policy of the EC would significantly speed up this process without any major military or political risks for the West.[34] Furthermore, the presence of a democratic and unified EC in world politics would provide the United States with a stronger and more effective partner in the solution of global and regional problems. Assuming a general need for sensitive and democratic global control and for constructive solutions to problems such as pollution, hunger, indebtedness, and regional tensions, and assuming also that U.S. resources are limited, such an alliance of willing and able equals could reestablish effective Western control of international politics.[35]

An evaluation of the positive and negative effects of Europeanization, however, also must include a look at the inner limits of this process. Today it is obvious that neither the traditional European nation-state nor its regional order is adequate to solve such major European problems as security, welfare, and human rights development. But the analysis of the present Europeanization process shows three competing solutions: bilateral or trilateral cooperation as in the Franco-German and the Benelux examples; multilateral cooperation such as WEU and EUREKA (Western Europe's response to SDI); and integrated or semi-integrated cooperation along the lines of EC, EPC, and NATO. Although bilateral or multilateral cooperation can be regarded as the first step toward integration, it is quite often nothing more than an attempt of a nation-state to keep anachronistic sovereignty instead of transferring it to supranational bodies.

A closer look at West European cooperation structures, however, reveals not only conflicting institutional approaches but also an extremely complicated regional pattern. Table 1 provides an overview of the most important frameworks for cooperation, the variable geometry that creates another source of problems for the Europeanization dynamic. This regional

Table 1. West European States: Membership in Regional Frameworks (1989)

Country*	Council of Europe	Political Frameworks — European Communities/European Political Cooperation	Political Frameworks — Subregional Organizations	Economic Frameworks — European Communities	Economic Frameworks — European Monetary System	Economic Frameworks — European Free Trade Association	Economic Frameworks — Subregional Cooperation
Iceland	x			fta		x	
Norway	x	(?)	Nordic Council	fta, (?)		x	
Sweden	x		Nordic Council	fta		x	
Finland	x		Nordic Council				
Denmark	x	x	Nordic Council	x	x		
Netherlands	x	x	Benelux framework	x	x		Benelux framework
Belgium	x	x	Benelux framework	x	x		Benelux framework
Luxemburg	x	x	Benelux framework	x	x		Benelux framework
Ireland	x	x		x	x		
Great Britain	x	x		x	(?)		
France	x	x	German-French Cooperation	x	x		
West Germany	x	x	German-French Cooperation	x	x		
Portugal	x	x		x	(?)		
Spain	x	x		x	(?)		
Italy	x	x		x	x		
Greece	x	x		x	x		
Switzerland	x			fta		x	
Austria	x	(?)		fta, (?)		x	

Security Frameworks

NATO Political Structure	NATO Military Structure	NATO Euro Group	NATO Independent European Program Group	Subregional Cooperation	WEU	Other Type of Cooperation	CSCE/CBM	Military Status
x	x	o					x	no major armed forces
x	x	x	x		mud		x	icp
						NN Cooperation	x	armed neutrality
							x	armed neutrality
x	x	x	x		mud		x	icp
x	x	x	x		x		x	icp
x	x	x	x		x		x	icp
x	x	x	x		x	ECJEPC Cooperation	x	no major armed forces
							x	unarmed neutrality
x	x	x	x	British-French Cooperation	x		x	icp, USb, nuclear power
x	Cooperation		x	German French Cooperation	x		x	(i)cp, nuclear power
x	x	x	x		x		x	icp, USb
x	x	x	x		x		x	icp, USb
x	Cooperation	x	x		x		x	(i)com USb
x	x	x	x				x	icp, USb
x	x	x	x				x	icp, USb
x						NN Cooperation	x	armed neutrality
							x	armed neutrality

*Turkey is not included

x   = full member
(?) = future membership to be expected
fta = free trade agreement

mud = membership under discussion
icp = integrated conventional power
USb = major US bases or troops
o   = observer

and institutional complexity, combined with numerous historical conflicts, explains why Europeanization has been more a reaction to outside challenges and less the result of an inner direction. Consensus for those national package deals on the path to further cooperation or integration is easier to obtain in response to foreign pressures than through a process of rational enlightenment. Thus the gas-pipeline deal and the subsequent conflict between the Reagan administration and West European governments stimulated more Europeanization efforts than any intra-European consensus on East-West trade.

If this hypothesis of an outside-pressure inducement for Europeanization is valid, one has to reevaluate the role of transatlantic conflicts. Consequently, politicians in favor of Europeanization could exaggerate or prolong transatlantic conflicts in order to have West European governments move toward closer cooperation and further integrative steps. If more conflicts occur in the near future, the question arises whether existing institutions for Atlantic conflict management, such as the World Economic Summit meetings or NATO itself, will be able to resolve successfully these disputes or whether new or additional mechanisms will have to be developed.[36]

Aspects of Europeanization

Lack of a master plan, external pressures, and internal contradictions have prevented a systematic, coherent, and comprehensive Europeanist approach. Instead, these tendencies have shaped a pragmatic Europeanization process. In this multi-issue and multi-institution approach, issues are often but not always related to specific institutions. A political advantage of this approach is that it can overcome stagnation or setbacks in one issue by shifting priorities to another more promising one, thus providing a politically flexible framework. Table 2 gives an overview of this distribution of labor in security policies.

Political Dimension of Security

Europeanization of the political dimension of security started in the late 1970s, when the broad Atlantic consensus on the grand strategy of East-West policies laid down in the Harmel Report dissolved.[37] The debate about détente (or the differing evaluations of Soviet behavior from a global and from a regional, European perspective)[38] and the conflicts about CSCE (or variant views on the role of the human rights issue in Western CSCE policies) explain why EC foreign ministers agreed to deal with political dimensions of security in EPC. But in spite of EPC initiatives in the areas

Table 2. Issues and Institutions of Europeanization

	EC Framework			WEU Framework	COCOM*	NATO Framework		Bilateral Frameworks	
	EC	EP	EPC			Euro Group	IEPG	German-French	British-French
Political dimension of security	x	x	x	x		x		x	
Economic dimension of security	x	x			x	x			
Arms industries	x	x		x			x	x	x
Out-of-area				x					
Arms control		x		x		x		x	
Military dimension of security				x		x		x	x

*Coordination Committee for East-West Trade, Paris.

of CSCE, the Middle East, and détente, this aspect of Europeanization generally has had more symbolic than practical meaning. Although substance and competence were added to the EPC, these efforts produced concrete results only when they led to cooperation and compromise with the United States. EPC's Middle East initiative failed because of its divisiveness, while its CSCE efforts, such as those at the Stockholm Confidence and Security Building Measures (CSBM) Conference,[39] succeeded because EPC acted as an EC pillar within the NATO framework: Issues were brought up in EPC meetings, harmonized with U.S. positions in NATO, and then presented to CSCE.[40]

Economic Dimension of Security

Closely related to the political dimension of security, the economic dimension covers issues such as trade embargoes, technology transfer, and security effects of economic dependencies. Thus the first Europeanization efforts began with the changes in U.S. trade policies toward the Eastern bloc in the late 1970s. They were followed by a unified West European stand on the gas-pipeline sanctions. But apart from this unity in response to outside pressure, a second line of Europeanization emerged. The agreements signed since 1988 between the EC and COMECON, on the one hand, and between EC and individual East European countries and the USSR, on the other, mark three new developments. First, they establish the EC as an influential actor in East-West relations.[41] Second, the indirect but clear linkages between EC's economic cooperation with the East and its demands for human rights improvements and arms control compromises underline the willingness of the EC Commission and EP to extend their reach into security issues.[42] Third, this development is caused by internal dynamics and not by outside pressure. Similar to EC, EPC, and EP Latin America activities, it indicates an EC foreign policy that primarily exploits the economic strength of the EC. For future Atlantic relations, this situation shows the potential both for intensified economic competition and, if adequate Atlantic management is provided, for a forceful division of labor between U.S. and EC global politics.

Arms Industries

The establishment of a potential common EC market for military goods and services—that is, open access to national bidding within the EC and common regulations for arms trade between the EC and other countries—is stimulated more by the outside challenge than by internal dynamics. EP efforts in that direction, discussions within the EC Commission, WEU activities, and the call of Independent European Program Group (IEPG) for a common arms market are more reactions to the hypothesis of U.S. market domination than the result of rational cost-effectiveness thinking.[43]

Nonetheless, the Europeanization of EC arms industries is on the way, and the establishment of a common arms market can be expected in the early 1990s. One reason for this assumption can be found in the legal situation. The Treaty of Rome excludes military goods, but this paragraph could easily be eliminated without touching the general EC framework. Agreements on the single European market for 1992 could be extended to the armaments sector without major problems. Second, U.S. burden-sharing pressures, internal defense budget problems, and shortages of manpower are forcing West European governments to reduce costs. A common market would provide for common research, development, and production. Third, arms industries, especially those in the high-tech sectors, are increasingly interested in and are now preparing for an EC common market.[44]

It is obvious that such Europeanization would drastically increase U.S.-EC competition in global markets, make U.S. penetration and domination of the EC arms market more difficult; lead to numerous disputes like those over Airbus and Ariane; and intensify the conflict over perceived protectionism.[45] In turn, the strengthening of EC arms industries through Europeanization opens financially and militarily attractive possibilities for a new type of transatlantic cooperation, a two-way street and a division of labor, that would increase political cohesion[46] and enhance military deterrence[47] without raising defense budgets.

Out-of-Area Problems

With the gradual globalization of EC interests and activities, out-of-area problems have become part of the Europeanization process. EC and EP activities in Latin America and East Asia have become more coherent and more effective. Extensive use of economic means, political cooperation, and transfer of democratic know-how have significantly contributed to the reduction of the potential for regional and domestic conflicts and to the establishment of peaceful regional cooperation patterns in Latin America.[48] In addition, WEU efforts in the Gulf war of 1988 resulted in European naval support for the U.S. task force, marking an important step in the Europeanization of out-of-area policies. Although the naval support was multilateral (there was no integrated European command), reactive to U.S. unilateralism, and ad hoc in character, this activity differed significantly from the ill-fated intervention of West European armed forces in Lebanon. Furthermore, national military efforts in support of West European interests, such as those of the French in Africa, the British in Asia, and the German lead in the assistance program for Turkey, offer another model of European out-of-area engagement.

Due to military restrictions and strong national sensibilities, the Europeanized response will continue to follow past patterns. Military engagement will be either national or ad hoc multinational and will be coordinated more within the WEU and the NATO framework than in the EC system; the result may be friction between military and economic strategies. If they are closely coordinated, major conflicts between U.S. and West European activities will not occur. In the long run, however, EC's preference for economic and political methods will conflict with the American tendency toward military interventions. Again, the intensity and amount of such transatlantic conflicts will depend heavily on the willingness and the ability of the Atlantic Alliance to come up with a new formula for global burden sharing and conflict solution.

Nonissues

Current Europeanization efforts are characterized by nonissues as well as by issues. Arms control, defense, and military issues have been left to NATO. Although EP and the WEU Assembly have dealt with arms control from time to time, and WEU has its own small arms control institution,[49] important regional issues such as CSBM, Conventional Stability Talks (CST), and intermediate-range nuclear forces (INF) were excluded from Europeanization efforts.

Another problem, even more important for a stronger European partnership within the Atlantic Alliance, is the nuclear question. This involves the will and the ability of the French and the British to enlarge their respective nuclear sanctuaries to cover the whole of Western Europe and to accept some sort of joint target planning. Yet the very fact that arms control and nuclear deterrence, two essential components of security policy, are not part of the political Europeanization debate indicates the limited political relevance of these developments and the continued strength of national thinking. Nuclear and arms control issues are not only the main problems for the European security community but also the major sources of permanent dissension within NATO, and this highlights the limited scope of the present Europeanist approach. Excluding these issues from Europeanization avoids conflict but perpetuates the patterns that the West Europeans wish to change. They reveal the inner contradictions of the Europeanization approach and the unwillingness to begin the necessary steps toward an effective European pillar in the essential elements of security policies.

Institutions of Europeanization

The Europeanization process is also hampered by the so-called parallel approach toward institutions.[50] Graph 1 illustrates the problem already detailed in Table 1: West European security policies are managed in a multitude of institutions and frameworks with completely different membership and levels of cooperation. A comparative analysis of the function, structure, and dynamic of each institution shows unorganized duplication, uncontrolled political competition, and counterproductive structures, all of which further limit the possibility of establishing the wanted European pillar.

European Political Cooperation (EPC)

The EPC, which now attempts to harmonize the foreign policies of EC member countries within the EC framework established in 1970, started to deal officially with political aspects of security in 1981 and acquired institutional structures through the Single European Act (SEA) in 1986. A major review and overhaul are planned for 1992.[51]

Today, EPC is limited in three respects. First, it is a cooperative effort of sovereign nation-states and not an integrated supranational organization. Second, its competences in the political dimension of security are "today limited,"[52] according to Article 30, 6 SEA. Third, it officially recognizes existing alliances, including NATO and WEU, and it respects NATO's primacy.

Internal and external management has been successful. EPC has developed a modus vivendi with Irish neutrality,[53] resulting in the full participation of Ireland in decision making on the political aspects of security and eliminating concerns of potential neutral member countries such as Austria and Sweden. In addition, EPC has established constructive working relations with NATO, reducing tensions and distrust to a minimum and managing successful conflicts of substance, such as those concerning CSCE policies.[54] But EPC's relevance for Europeanization lies less in its present activities, which are quite limited, than in its future. The prerogatives, membership, and role of its secretariat could be easily enlarged, and, if the political will emerges,[55] EPC could be transformed into a fully integrated part of the EC Commission supervised by EP. Thus, EPC is not only a model for a new type of Atlantic relations, for which Europeanists are looking, but also a constructive step toward a common EC foreign policy.

Membership of West European States in Military Organizations*

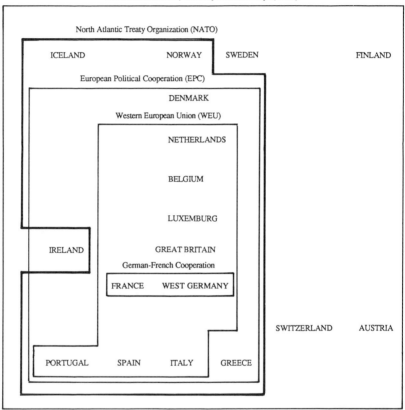

Conference on Security and Cooperation in Europe (CSCE)

North Atlantic Treaty Organization (NATO)

ICELAND   NORWAY   SWEDEN   FINLAND

European Political Cooperation (EPC)

DENMARK

Western European Union (WEU)

NETHERLANDS

BELGIUM

LUXEMBURG

IRELAND   GREAT BRITAIN

German-French Cooperation

FRANCE   WEST GERMANY

SWITZERLAND   AUSTRIA

PORTUGAL   SPAIN   ITALY   GREECE

*Turkey is not included

EC Commission

The commission changed its role from an interested observer to an active player in the Europeanization process in 1988, when it signed cooperation agreements with COMECON and a number of East European countries.[56] Although the agreements are restricted to economic, financial, and technological issues, EC Commission representatives left no doubt about the political conditions of this cooperation: progress in human rights and concessions in arms control talks. There are far-reaching possibilities, if one bears in mind the enormous attraction that economic cooperation with the EC has for Eastern *perestroika* policies. If the EPC becomes fully integrated, the EC Commission will be in command of both the political and economic aspects of security. EC-U.S. relations will then need a major overhaul concerning conflict management, burden sharing, and an equitable division of labor, not only in East-West but also in North-South and global politics.

European Parliament (EP)

Limited in its authority and legitimacy, the EP nonetheless has played an important supportive role in the Europeanization process. The EP was an early supporter of general Europeanization and of certain aspects of security, such as arms control. It has promoted the development of a European identity and the harmonization of party federation views on security. EP delegations, particularly those in Eastern countries, also have pioneered improvements in East-West relations. Further, EP serves as a major political education body. Returning to National politics, its members carry the message of EC integration and experience with intra-EC cooperation.

Although cooperation between EP and the U.S. Congress has started, it has limited prospects. Differences between the European and the U.S. party-parliamentary system are too fundamental, and EP traditionally exploits public criticism of U.S. politics to gain political attention, to overcome internal heterogeneity, and to gain influence in EC and EPC activities. Therefore, despite all declarations, EP's Europeanism is not promoting Atlantic consensus.

Western European Union (WEU)

In contrast to the EC system, the WEU displays a multinational but not a supranational approach. Its revitalization at the end of 1984 can be explained primarily by clusters of national interests. Thus, the French desire to play a greater role in West European security policy but to avoid reintegration into the military framework of NATO. West Germany, on the other hand, hopes to draw France into a web of bilateral and multilateral cooperation. WEU not only was able to set up an effective working structure of foreign and defense ministers but also produced in 1987 a joint charter on West European security,[57] defining such objectives for Europeanization as a common arms market. Unsuccessful in major arms cooperation projects, WEU had its first political success when it proved able to organize and coordinate West European military efforts in the Gulf war.

WEU's new political attractiveness was underlined when Spain and Portugal became members in 1988. WEU membership is also being discussed in Denmark and Norway. WEU's open challenge of NATO's competence and legitimacy has made it one of the most outspoken supporters of Europeanization and has also allowed member countries to play the European card to demonstrate independence from U.S. leadership while maintaining their commitment to NATO. Having established itself as a major force for Europeanization, WEU is today developing a more pragmatic approach to NATO and to the EC system that is marked by increased WEU-NATO communication and by ideas to merge the WEU Assembly with the NATO Assembly or with EP. But refusal to discuss integration of its members' foreign and military policies limits WEU's Europeanization to multinational approaches.

NATO's EUROGROUP and Independent European Program Group (IEPG)

It is ironic that those organizations best suited for the establishment of a unified European pillar were both unable to make the necessary steps in the 1970s and unwilling to join actively the Europeanization process in the 1980s. The Informal Group of NATO European Defense Ministers (EUROGROUP) has not only been handicapped by the lack of any sufficient institutional structure, but it also has reproduced exactly the pattern of U.S. domination and West European disunity. IEPG, motivated by competition with EC and WEU, developed new initiatives toward arms industry cooperation.[58] But, instead of implementing its recommendations and establishing working structures for EC-WEU-IEPG cooperation in arms industries and common procurement, NATO proved to be unable to take advantage of these efforts. NATO's passivity concerning Europeanization and the establishment of an equal European pillar is largely the result of West European unwillingness to transfer national sovereignty to supranational bodies in exchange for greater unity, effectiveness, and influence. It also can be explained by ambiguities in U.S. policies toward European integration. For the United States, there are long-term advantages in a new formula for the Atlantic Alliance as an alliance of equals. The disadvantages—conflict, dissent, and competition between the United States and a unified Western Europe, together with the costs of adjustment—are short term. Day-to-day U.S. policies indicate no major interest in the establishment of an effective European pillar.

The Question of New Security Policies

The present Europeanization debate concentrates on a vague call for West European unity—on a redistribution of political responsibilities and on institutional questions, or a new West European "security architecture." Few problems of political substance are discussed: What kind of a security policy should be pursued? What political priorities should be given either to arms control or to the improvement of defense capabilities? What kind of grand strategies should be developed? None of these questions play a major role in the debate.

Five different and conflicting types of new Europeanized West European security policies can be foreseen at the moment. The first is traditional security policy with its heavy emphasis on strong, effective defense, including a significant and diversified nuclear component. Although they are in the minority, proponents of this type of policy can be found in the Margaret Thatcher government and in a number of national defense establishments. A second type is a more moderate traditional security policy, willing to restrain armaments and to limit its own military options if an adequate response from the Warsaw Pact is assured. Again, this view accepts nuclear deterrence as a major and indisputable part of security policy. The François Mitterrand governments provide examples of this more moderate position, which attracts greater acceptance within Western Europe than does a policy of purely military strength. Besides these traditional concepts, a more modernized version of security policy has emerged, strongly influenced by the FRG's foreign minister, Hans-Dietrich Genscher. This third concept nominally gives equal weight to defense and détente, but primarily seeks to use détente, including arms control, to ease the defense and security burdens and risk. Fourth, an even more recent concept, which emphasizes arms control and the complete denuclearization of Europe, can be found in most of the Social Democratic parties in Western Europe and, especially, in the Green parties and peace movements. Finally, a fifth concept, found in the EC Commission's East-West policies, gives priority to economic policies.

This variety of concepts contributes to intra-European dissent and conflict as well as to differences with most recent U.S. security policies. Given the present arrangements, a common West European security policy would probably be based on the third concept, which emphasizes arms control, CSCE, and sufficient defense, along with an effective minimal nuclear deterrence. But even this could create a political agenda and priorities in conflict with U.S. policies. Conflict might result from different views on the future of CSCE, the extent and intensity of economic cooperation with Eastern Europe and the USSR, and priorities in arms control negotiations. Again, such conflicts between the American and the European pillars of the Atlantic Alliance should not be overestimated. If the Bush administration's line of active arms control, close cooperation with NATO allies, and constructive East-West policy is continued, these disputes will be limited in scope and intensity.

Given the present lack of conceptual thinking in the Europeanization debate and the potential differences between a future U.S. and a common Western European security policy, NATO faces a challenge. Avoiding the past mistake of not responding early and adequately to Europeanization needs, NATO could try to play a major role in the development of an acceptable common West European security policy. Stimulating a substantive debate, assisting in the formulation of a common concept for a European pillar, and managing and solving American-European conflicts about security policy will not contradict but rather reinforce both sides and give NATO a new political role.

Europeanism versus Atlanticism

Numerous proposals for the change of NATO's institutions,[59] its military strategy,[60] and its political raison d'être are indications that not only the actual conditions but also the political structures have shifted since the alliance's establishment forty years ago. First, Western Europe has changed from a dependent, economically and politically weak group of allies into an economically strong and dynamic power. Globalization of EC policies and Europeanization efforts reflect this new strength and self-consciousness. Second, the actual burdens and perceived risks of the military confrontation in Europe have created major political and financial problems for the continuation of traditional security policies. Third, the socioeconomic and political attractiveness of Western Europe, including its integration process, constitutes a drawing card that has been a magnet for newly liberated European societies. Fourth, if Gorbachev's reforms become structural—still an open question—and the Soviet military threat is permanently removed, NATO could lose the primary purpose of its mission and dissolve. In sum, both the political conditions and the political functions of NATO as the most important institution of the Atlantic Alliance have basically changed, and the improvement of East-West relations has created the opportunity and the necessity for an adequate reappraisal.

Assuming that the establishment of a European pillar not only is necessary and, in terms of cost-risk calculation, beneficial for the West but also is an adequate answer to the need for change, two questions remain. First, should and how can the present disorganized and contradictory Europeanization process be focused and streamlined? Second, should and how can the new Europeanist attitude be combined with a renewal of the Atlantic Alliance?

Despite all present and future deficiencies of the EC system,[61] the continuation of EC integration will provide EC and EP with more influence in European security policies. EC's economic power and inner dynamic may force and attract WEU into closer cooperation or even affiliation with it, thus changing the triangular competition among the EC, WEU, and NATO frameworks into an EC versus NATO constellation. This process may take years and face setbacks and stagnation, but it could lead finally to common foreign and security policies with global scope. Such a reemergence of Western or EC Europe as a world power will not take place without numerous Atlantic disputes and conflicts. Together with the change in threat perceptions, this process could lead to a gradual erosion of the Atlantic Alliance, if West Europeans and Americans alike do not take precautions.

The continuation of the Atlantic Alliance is a matter not only of basic values but also of common global concerns. Both Europeans and Americans have a fundamental interest in peaceful Western democratic control of global politics, including the management and solution of structural problems and regional conflicts. The emergence of the EC as a global power with adequate economic, military, and political means will lead to further economic and political competition with the United States. If this competition can be controlled and a partnership of equals can be established, this might provide the Atlantic Alliance with innovative concepts, additional means, and new credibility. Present structures are insufficient to allow such a redefinition and the successful management of these many conflicts. NATO's preoccupation with defense, U.S. domination of the alliance, and Europe's inability to form adequate two-pillar structures and mechanisms constitute major obstacles. NATO's role in East-West peacekeeping, intra-West European cooperation, and the reestablishment of democracies in Greece, Portugal, and Spain, however, reinforce the need to keep and to reform NATO.

Changes should concentrate on three points. First, NATO's functions should be enlarged; with economic, foreign, and security policies bearing equal weight. This reorientation, however, would require a global reach for NATO and the improvement of Atlantic consensus building. Second, institutional mechanisms to allow and stimulate West European integration, especially the Europeanization of security policies, should be established.

They could define and manage consensus and the distribution of labor, risks, and burdens among West Europeans, and they could prevent either U.S. or West European unilateralism. Third, the Atlantic Alliance should define some global problems to be resolved by joint U.S.-European efforts, thus setting new and realistic tasks for constructive cooperation and a new role in international relations.

Thus, the new Europeanism can be integrated in a constructive way into a new Atlanticism that reflects both historical changes and the need for new efforts in constructing global order. This long-term and explicitly idealistic view cannot and will not prevent future conflicts within the Atlantic Alliance, conflicts partly caused and exploited by those promoting Europeanization through limited dissociation from the United States. But it can set political perspectives both for Europeanization and for the renewal of the Atlantic Alliance. The question is thus less that of Europeanization versus Atlanticism and more that of the establishment of a unified European pillar within a reformed Atlantic Alliance.

Notes

1. In contrast to Paul M. Kennedy, *The Rise and Fall of Great Powers: Economic Change and Military Conflict from 1500 to 2000* (New York: Random House, 1987), this position does not accept the hypothesis of power decline but rather the hypothesis of the reemergence of European power.

2. S. Hedley Bull, "European Self-Reliance and the Reform of NATO," *Foreign Affairs* 61, no. 4 (Spring 1983): 874–92. Compare with this the argument that the establishment of a single European market would mean protectionism and a "fortress" Europe in terms of the arms market in Joseph Fitchett, "National Security Gives Protectionists a Weapon," *International Herald Tribune*, 16 December 1988.

3. Such an identity does not yet exist. EC integration and the Europe-wide community of Europeanists have not been able to create it. Even the basics, as for example a European media and Europarties, are still missing.

4. It is assumed that Austria, Norway, and Sweden will become EC members, whereas Switzerland will find a way between full membership and association.

5. This involves political cooperation among North America, EC, neutral-nonaligned nations, East Europeans, and the USSR in the CSCE process and economic cooperation between EC, on the one hand, and COMECON and Eastern countries, on the other.

6. From Helmut Kohl's statement to the German Bundestag, 10 September 1988, *Bulletin der Bundesregierung*, no. 86, 11 September 1988.

7. From Hans-Dietrich Genscher's statement to the German Bundestag, 11 November 1988, *Pressemitteilungen des Auswärtigen Amtes*, no. 1224/1988.

8. See Oskar Lafontaine, "Europäische Sicherheitspolitik. Rede vor der National Defense University, Washington, am 23. September 1987," *Die Neue Gesellschaft/Frankfurter Hefte*, no. 11 (1987): 976–82. However, compare Oskar Lafontaine, *Angst vor den Freuden. Die Atomwaffenstrategie der Supermächte zerstört die Bündnisse* (Reinbek, Germany: Rowohlt, 1983).

9. For the Christian Democrats, see Christdemokratische Union, "Beschluss des 36. Bundesparteitages der CDU. Unsere Verantwortung in der Welt. Christlichdemokratische Perspektiven zur Deutschland-, Aussen-, Sicherheits-, Europa-, and Entwicklungspolitik," *CDU-Dokumentation*, no. 19 (1988); for the Social Democrats, see Sozialdemokratische Partei Deutschlands (SPD), *Entwurf für ein neues Grundsatzprogramm der Socialistischen Partei Deutschlands. Entwurf, Irsee, Juni 1986* (Bonn: SPD, 1986).

10. The most prominent are Konrad-Adenauer-Stiftung (KAS), Friedrich-Ebert-Stiftung (FES), and Stiftung Wissenschaft und Politik (SWP).

11. See Lothar Brock and Mathias Jopp, eds., *Sicherheitspolitische Zusammenarbeit und Kooperation der Rüstungswirtschaft in Europa* (Baden-Baden: Nomos, 1986); Reimund Seidelmann, ed., *Auf dem Weg zu einer westeuropäischen Sicherheitspolitik* (Baden-Baden, Germany: Nomos, 1989); Forschungsstelle der Evangelischen Studiengemeinde (FEST)/Hessische Stiftung für Friedens- und Konfliktforschung (HSFK)/Institut für Friedensgund Sicherheitspolitik Hamburg (ISFH), *Friedensqutachten 1988* (Heidelberg: FEST, 1988); and David Greenwood, "Errichtung der Europäischen Säule: Fragen und Institutionen," *NATO-Brief*, no. 3 (1988): 15–19.

12. Bull, "European Self-Reliance," 875; Sir Geoffrey Howe, "The European Pillar, *Foreign Affairs* 63, no. 2 (Winter 1984–85): 330–43; Peter Unwin, "Britain's Foreign Policy Opportunities. Part 2: The European Community," *International Affairs* (London) 57, no. 3 (1981): 394–406. See also Greenwood, "Errichtung der Europäischen Säule," 12.

13. Pierre Lellouche, "Europe and Her Defense," *Foreign Affairs* 59, no. 4 (Spring 1981): 813–34; Dominique Moisi, "Less America in Europe Should Mean More Europe in NATO," *International Herald Tribune*, 2 March 1988; Dominique Moisi, "French Foreign Policy: The Challenge of Adaptation," *Foreign Affairs* 67, no. 1 (Fall 1988): 151–64; interview with Michel Rocard, *Die Welt*, 23 November 1987.

14. Compare Valerio Zanone, "Die Rolle Europas in der NATO," *NATO-Brief*, no. 2 (1988): 9–13.

15. See the statement of the European People's party (EPP) in favor of a "European Security Union," Brussels, 31 May 1988; and Hans-Gert Poettering, "Deutschlands und Frankreichs Interesse an einem europäischen Sicherheitspolitik," *Aussenpolitik* 37, no. 2 (1986): 175–85. For the Socialists, refer to the statement of the Confederation of Socialist Parties of the EC (CSPEC), *Pressemitteilungen der SPD*, no. 571/88, 5 July 1988. More details are given by the chairman of the subcommittee, Hans-Gert Poettering (EPP), and his deputy, Klaus Hänsch (CSPEC), in *NATO-Brief*, no. 4 (1988): 4–5. For an overview of EP's activities, see Reimund Seidelmann, "European Security and the European Communities," *Journal of European Integration*, nos. 2–4 (1984): 221–51.

16. Pieter Dankert, "Europe Together, American Apart," *Foreign Policy*, no. 53 (Winter 1983–84): 18. Compare Niele Jorgen Haagerup, "Die europäische Sicherheitsdimension," *Europa-Archiv* 38, no. 1 (1983): 273–78.

17. Altiero Spinelli, "Die Parlamentarische Initiative zur Europäische Union," *Europa-Archiv* 38, no. 24 (1983): 744.

18. Christopher Tugendhat, "Europe's Need for Self-Confidence," *International Affairs* (London) 58, no. 1 (1982): 10.

19. See Reimund Seidelmann, ed., "Special Issue on European Security," *Journal of European Integration*, nos. 2–3 (Winter-Spring, 1986). See also Giovanni Januzzi, "Die Europäische Politische Zusammenarbeit: Auf dem Weg zur engeren Integration," *NATO-Brief*, no. 4 (1988): 13–18.

20. See "Final Communiqué of NATO's Summit Meeting in Brussels, 2 and 3 March 1988," *Europa-Archiv* 43, no. 7 (1988): D 201–8; Lord Carrington, "Das Nordatlantische Bündnisse und Verteidigung Europas," *Europa-Archiv* 40, no. 6 (1985): 155–64; and Manfred Wörner, press statement at the 34th meeting of the NATO Assembly, 17 November 1988, Hamburg: "European cooperation measures, which tend to exclusivity and which might be perceived as the establishment of a 'club within a club,' could have negative political consequences and should be avoided. Independent of its form, European cooperation in security and defense should be characterized by transparency and compatibility with the Alliance's goals." This statement is available in NATO press release, 17 November 1988, NATO Press Service.

21. Examples are Henry Kissinger, interview, *International Herald Tribune*, 7 December 1986; and Flora Lewis, "Disarmament Jitters," *New York Times*, 22 December 1987.

22. Ronald Reagan, "Speech to the U.S. Military Academy West Point," *U.S. Policy Information and Terms*, no. 197 (29 October 1987): 16.

23. Horst Ehmke, "Eine Politik der Selbstbehauptung Europas," *Europa-Archiv* 39, no. 7 (1984): 195–204 (this is a shortened version of a SPD document written by Ehmke); Ernst-Otto Czempiel, "Die Zukunft zur Atlantischen Gemeinschaft," *Aus Politik und Zeitgeschichte*, no. 12 (1983): 21.

24. See Johann Galtung, *Kapitalistische Grossmacht oder Die Gemeinschaft der Konzerne?* (Reinbek: Rowohlt, 1973); and Max Kohnstamm and Wolfgang Hager, eds., *Zivilmacht Europa—Supermacht oder Partner?* (Frankfurt, Germany: Suhrkamp, 1973).

25. See Karl Kaiser et al., *Die EG vor der Entscheidung: Fortschritt oder Verfall?* (Bonn, Germany: Deutsche Gesellschaft fuer Auswaertige Politik, 1983).

26. See Robert Rudney and Luc Reychler, eds., *European Security beyond the Year 2000* (New York: Praeger, 1988).

27. See Panos Tsakaloyannis, ed., *The Reactivation of the Western European Union—The Effects on the EC and its Institutions* (Maastricht, the Netherlands: European Institute for Public Administration, 1985); and Panos Tsakaloyannis, ed., *Western European Security in a Changing World: From the Reactivation of the WEU to the Single European Act* (Maastricht, the Netherlands: EIPA, 1988).

28. Compare this with the gas pipeline deal discussion in Reimund Seidelmann, "Energy Trade Relations between the Federal Republic of Germany and the USSR," in Robert Lieber, ed., *Will Europe Fight for Oil? Energy Relations in the Atlantic Area* (New York: Praeger, 1983): 71–103.

29. See Commission of the European Communities, "Public Opinion in the European Community. Europe 2000," *Eurobarometer* (March 1987). The question was "Are you personally for or against the European Community developing towards becoming a 'United States of Europe'?"; the answers were: 23% "for—very much," 40% "for—rather," 13% "against—rather," 7% "against—very much," and 17% "don't know."

30. Ibid. The question was "Now let us try to imagine Europe in the next, 21st, century. For example let us try to pretend that it is now January in the year 2000. Could you tell me if you think the following things will have actually come about by then or not?" Common defense: 49% yes, 30% no, 21% no answer; equal terms: 44% yes, 35% no, 21% no answer.

31. See Eliot A. Cohen, "The Long-Term Crisis of the Alliance," *Foreign Affairs* 61, no. 2 (Winter 1982–83): 325–43; and Michael Howard, "A European Perspective of the Reagan Years," ibid. 66, no. 3 (Spring 1987): 942–57.

32. Examples are the no-first-use debate and the discussion about discriminate deterrence.

33. See Reimund Seidelmann, "European Security and the CSCE-Process," *Journal of European Integration*, nos. 2–3 (Winter-Spring, 1986): 209–42.

34. A contrasting view holds that this process might lead to a semicolonization of Eastern Europe by the West.

35. The idea of a renewed Western global responsibility does not exclude a trilateral approach, that is, the inclusion of Japan. However, Japanese willingness and experience concerning international engagement should not be overestimated.

36. Within NATO circles the idea of adding new political roles to NATO is already under discussion.

37. See Pierre Harmel, "Vierzig Jahre Ost-West-Beziehungen: Hoffnungen, Befürchtungen und Herausforderungen," *NATO-Brief*, no. 4 (1987): 3–11.

38. A more globalized EC would have acted differently and more in line with U.S. policies.

39. See Ingo Peters, *Transatlantischer Konsens und Vertrauensbildung in Europa* (Baden-Baden, Germany: Nomos, 1987).

40. This differs from the U.S. leadership role, which is underlined for the years before 1975 by John Maresca, *The Road to Helsinki: The Conference on Security and Cooperation in Europe, 1973–1975* (Durham, NC: Duke University Press, 1985).

41. Since the collapse of the Communist system in the former Warsaw Pact nations, the successor governments in 1990 are all seeking relationships with the EC as a major step toward a free market economy. In the fall of 1988 the situation was: EC-Romania: negotiations to enlarge an already existing trade agreement. EC-Hungary: negotiations since 1987 for an agreement on trade and industrial cooperation; successful conclusion is expected soon. EC-Czechoslovakia: negotiations since 1987 for an agreement on trade of industrial products; successful conclusion is expected soon. EC-Poland: first contacts in 1987 for an agreement on trade but major obstacles. EC-Bulgaria: same as Poland. EC-German Democratic Republic: first contacts in mid-1988 for an agreement on trade. EC-USSR: first contacts in March 1988 for a major agreement on trade and industrial cooperation. EC-COMECON: negotiations since 1986 on a joint statement for the establishment of official relations; conclusion and signing act in mid-1988; major obstacles for trade and cooperation agreements.

42. The EC Commission and EP have established an informal but highly effective division of labor for negotiations with the East. Furthermore, there are close informal contacts between Social Democrats and Christian Democrats on this matter.

43. For details see Seidelmann, ed., *Auf dem Weg*. See also Brock and Jopp, eds., *Sicherheitspolitische Zusammenarbeit und Kooperation*.

44. A good example is Daimler-Benz's merger policies, which have merged automobile, high-tech aircraft, electronics, and arms enterprises.

45. See Fitchett, "National Security."

46. The overall political effect of the reintegration of France would be much higher than any major increase of defense budgets.

47. See the demands of John V. Galvin, "Kooperation in der Rüstungsproduktion: Ein Kernelement der Abschreckung," *NATO-Brief*, no. 5 (1988): 19–23.

48. For example, the Contadora approach and Arias peace plan for Central America.

49. This is a leftover from the early Brussels treaties restricting West Germany's armament and arms production.

50. The parallel approach means to engage WEU, NATO, and EPC as well; this position can be found especially in West German, British, and Italian official documents and statements.

51. For details see Seidelmann, *Auf dem Weg.*

52. See Januzzi, "Die Europäische Politische Zusammenarbeit."

53. See Peter J. Dundy and Dermot McAleexe, *Ireland and the European Community* (Cambridge, England: Cambridge University Press, 1984).

54. Thus, Wörner's remark about the dangers of a club within the club (see note 20) does not refer to the EPC.

55. For an evaluation of future developments, see Rudney and Reychler, eds., *European Security*; and Christopher Hill, ed., *National Foreign Policy and European Political Cooperation* (London: G. Allen and Unwin, 1983).

56. For further details, see Reimund Seidelmann and Thomas Meyer, *Eine neue Ostpolitik für die Europäische Gemeinschaft* (Freudenberg: Friedrich-Ebert Stiftung, 1988).

57. See Alfred Cahen, "Neubelebung der Westeuropäische Union Auswirkungen auf das Atlantische Bündnis," *NATO-Brief,* no. 4, (1986): 8–14.

58. See Vredeling report, *Towards a Stronger Europe: A Report by an Independent Study Team Established by Defence Ministers of Nations of the Independent European Program Group* (Brussels: Independent European Program Group, 1986).

59. For example, see Henry Kissinger, "Ein Plan für die Umstrukturierung der NATO," in Henry Kissinger, *Weltpolitik für morgen* (Munich, Germany: DVA, 1986), 255–73.

60. For example, see Jonathan Dean, "Military Security in Europe," *Foreign Affairs* 66, no. 1 (Fall 1987): 22–40.

61. For a comprehensive catalog of deficits and proposals for solutions, see Werner Weindenfeld et al., *Europäische Defizite, europäische Perspektiven—eine Bestandsaufnahme für morgen* (Gütersloh, Germany: Bertelsmann Stiftung, 1988).

The United States, NATO, and the Third World: Dominoes, Imbroglios, and Agonizing Appraisals

Scott L. Bills[*]

For big powers the Third World has long been a kaleidoscopic mise-en-scène: a coat of many colors, a pond for leapfrogging, a strategic gameboard, a laboratory for new or recycled theories of imperial pacification, a burial ground for the weary or unwary. For the superpowers, after 1950 the Third World offered a new arena for Cold War contention, for the struggle for hospitable clients, far-flung outposts, tough proxies, and hearts and minds. However, this new terrain, it became increasingly apparent, lacked attributes that contribute to decisive victories: stability, familiarity, and common assumptions about paths and goals. The colonial rimlands did not easily accommodate American anxieties about the Communist threat.

Jefferson Caffery, the U.S. ambassador to France in the later 1940s, typified the instinctive skepticism of American Cold Warriors who examined indigenous nationalist movements in overseas dependencies. In June 1946, looking across the Mediterranean at French North Africa, Caffery painted a scene of looming Soviet challenge. The key problem, he asserted, was that "it is extremely difficult in such relatively backward countries as Algeria, Tunisia and Morocco, to distinguish between Communists, autonomists and those natives advocating full independence. It would seem, on the contrary, that these various movements, which should

* Archival research for this article was funded by grants from the Stephen F. Austin State University Research Council. In addition, I would like to thank Jimmi Fischer and Lee Sullenger of the Steen Library, SFASU, for their assistance in obtaining source materials.

in theory be quite separate and distinct, are on the contrary confused and interwoven at the base, with a few leaders at the top giving the appearance of separate and distinct movements." Caffery did not believe that the obvious contradictions between communism and Islam were a major obstacle to the spread of Soviet influence in Africa or the Middle East. "The Embassy, viewing the situation from Paris, believes that Communist doctrine in North Africa is purposely kept exceedingly fluid, ill-defined, and that according to Leninist-Stalinist theory it has been tailored to adapt itself to the loose and as yet uncrystallized nationalist aspirations of these areas and towards the exploitation of the misery and subnormal standards of living which for several years have prevailed in North Africa." Communism, wrote Caffery, wore "a cloak of nationalism and local autonomy."[1] This thesis of Soviet tactical fluidity and pronationalist posturing—strongly held by the State Department Europeanists who dominated policymaking during the early Cold War period—continued to shadow and distort American analysis of the colonial situation.

Furthermore, U.S. policymakers in general had long been reluctant to accept the notions that 1) radical (that is, revolutionary) change was necessary to reform the global colonial network or to legitimate native aspirations, and that 2) violence of any sort could be a forerunner of positive change in colonial societies. Michael H. Hunt has traced America's jaundiced view of anti-imperial movements to an underlying foreign policy ideology: an inherited mind-set that propelled the United States into an assertive, aggressive use of police power.[2] This mind-set has been particularly resilient with regard to the Third World, where revolutionary regimes have rankled, where U.S. virtue has been questioned, and where the American agenda has often been frustrated. Juggle all the accumulated adjectives—savage, primitive, backward, undeveloped, underdeveloped, less developed, dependent, emergent, colonial, neocolonial, exotic, and alien—this has been the Third World vista to Americans. Some foreign countries are more foreign than others.

The term "Third World," it frequently has been noted, is marvelously imprecise and wonderfully inclusive. The belt of former colonies, protectorates, and mandates stretches across the southern rim of Eurasia, curved, perhaps an arc, sometimes called a crescent. The Third World was saddled with the artificial creatures of treaties and commissions, settling as the chaff from brutal wars of extermination and dominance on the rimlands of clashing empires. The only unity suggested by the term "Third World" is that of suppression, dislocation, and outside rule. But even here, at the points of origin, the different colonial spheres developed disparate characteristics. Franklin Roosevelt, like other Americans during the war years, identified some European allies as better imperialists than others, suggesting that there was a beneficent tutelage to be performed by those

Western nations that could handle the responsibility and act fairly in their relations with lesser peoples.

As unrivaled parvenu of the First World, the United States emerged in 1945 as the chief guarantor of the status quo. Washington, it seemed, had everything to gain by the quieting of colonial discontent, the expansion of the Open Door, the reconstruction of compliant allies in Europe, and the leashing of Soviet aspirations. Challenges certainly might come, but America had extraordinary resources to meet them. What was unexpected was that challenges might be mounted over which extraordinary resources would not prevail.

War's End

The excitement was genuine, the hopes expansive. Along the wide-ranging perimeter of war, among the scattered hunter-gatherers of the Office of Strategic Services (OSS), the notion of a greatly expanded U.S. role in world affairs was axiomatic. Wartime operations had demonstrated the significance of colonial locales, and, once extended, the long arm of the American power could hardly be withdrawn. Major A. W. Schmidt, an OSS mission chief in British West Africa, argued forcefully "that the United States, having finally emerged as a major world power . . . must of necessity be interested and continue to be interested in important developments in every nook and cranny of the world." The value of information, observed Schmidt, was a vital lesson from the war: "Who would have thought in the year 1935 that the gauge of the track of the Benguela railroad [in Angola] or the condition of its rolling stock would be important to United States interests in case Rommel had been successful at El Al[a]mein? . . . In the same year who would have thought that the defenses at Dakar were of particular importance to people of the United States?"[3] Data were a lever for influence: topography, average rainfall and temperature, crop yields, manufacturing indices, mineral resources, harbor depths, tide schedules, demographic statistics. What did foreign peoples believe and want? Were they friendly, unfriendly, or indifferent? Were they Christian, Muslim, or Buddhist? How badly did they want independence? Were they going to fight for it if they didn't get it? How well and for how long could they fight? Were nationalist leaders anti-Western? Would they embrace communism?

"War telescopes social time," wrote Gabriel Kolko, "bringing together new forces and new interactions with traditional institutions, producing predictable as well as original mutations in human experience and social systems."[4] In 1944–45 no one more intuitively understood this precept than OSS agents working among the native populations of Africa, the Near East, India, and Southeast Asia. The war had greatly encouraged dreams of

self-determination through such documents as the Atlantic Charter and
(even more so) through the devastation and conquest that marked the
collapse of racial myths and the weakening of the administrative tendons of
empire. Throughout the colonial rimlands, there arose an aggressive rhythm
of self-expression. As OSS officer Edmund Taylor advised from his post in
Southeast Asia, "The importance of this theater, in my opinion, arises
mainly from the fact that after the war it is going to be a power vacuum, or
partial vacuum, and therefore a storm center."[5] From V-E Day through the
end of 1945, the storm centers multiplied: Sétif, Beirut, Damascus, Hanoi,
Saigon, Batavia. During 1945–46 unrest, armed conflict, and big-power
discord flared across the colonial landscape, from the former Italian
territories of Cyrenaica and Tripolitania through Iran and Palestine, from
British India through much of Southeast Asia, from divided China out onto
the Korean peninsula. But events in the colonial world were not permitted
to intrude unduly upon plans for a unified Western bloc to counter Soviet
prowling and probing.

For President Harry S. Truman, as well as for top-ranking officials in
the State Department, self-determination applied only to peoples who were
ready to handle their own affairs, in the Western manner. Few colonial
populations appeared sufficiently mature. Nationalist leaders in colonial
areas were advised to be patient, cautious, and understanding. Rome could
not be unbuilt in a day. Armed struggle would generate political chaos,
exacerbate class differences, arouse sleeping peasantries, disable economies,
and ultimately benefit only those forces who sought the undoing of
civilization. Yet, real threats to national security needed to be
acknowledged and met. As Secretary of State James F. Byrnes remarked in
February 1946: "Our diplomacy must not be negative and inert. . . . Though
the status quo is not sacred and unchangeable, we cannot overlook a
unilateral gnawing away at the status quo. . . . We cannot allow aggression
to be accomplished by coercion or pressure or by subterfuges such as
political infiltration."[6] Within several years, such references to external
pressure and fifth-column subversion had become the bedrock theses of
containment.

Byrnes had spoken to the basic fear of an imperial power: slippage,
erosion, an insidious gnawing away at domain and prestige. When enemies
abounded, friends became more dear. The process of consolidating spheres
appealed to both superpowers in 1946–47, and it soon proceeded apace.
Western Europe was utterly dependent on the United States, but theirs was
hardly an enthusiastic and uncritical dependence. Privately, for instance,
London officials complained about the "ancient grudge" evidenced in the
periodic rise and fall of anti-British sentiment in the United States. Too
often and too unfairly, Britain's empire had been chastised as the epitome of
a self-centered, oppressive colonialism. Analyst J. C. Donnelly, of the

Foreign Office's North American Department, complained of the difficulty in anticipating what kinds of policy proposals might emerge from the "vapour" of American politics. Frederick Puckle, an adviser with the British embassy in Washington, contended that Americans "have little patience with any situation which looks to them like a senseless mess and traditionally cling firmly . . . to the belief that there is always a short cut to a solution of any practical problem." Americans had "simple minds," he believed, and they would have to be educated continually about geopolitical realities.[7]

Diplomat Ivone A. Kirkpatrick, visiting the American offices of the British Information Service in late 1946 and early 1947, described the United States as "a nation where people are apt to live on word spinning." Although Britain had been much abused and misunderstood in America, he found that public opinion was not yet ready to assign England the status of an expired, second- or third-rate power. In fact, said Kirkpatrick, there was quite a bit of American interest in British affairs, because "the Americans are thrilled by strife. Strife is news."[8] Strife remained news, and "word spinning" was a fitting description for the adroit but empty American invocation of its anticolonial heritage.

The North Atlantic Treaty

The years from 1947 to 1949 marked the trial flight of containment and its concomitants, a Eurocentric foreign policy that treated colonial affairs as background noise. With few exceptions, State Department officials agreed that Western Europe was the preeminent frontier of U.S.-Soviet rivalry. As Henry L. Deimel of the Office of Near Eastern and African Affairs later commented, "I think Europe first was necessary, because a world without Europe would be a world dead for us, a world in Russian hands."[9] The ascendance of what Thomas Paterson has called the "peace and prosperity idiom" was complete: U.S. postwar aid targeted Western Europe as the politicoeconomic workshop that could be most rapidly rebuilt and stabilized as an anti-Communist sphere. The restoration of economic vigor was to be the precursor of political calm and renewed self-confidence.[10] The end of despair and desperation in Western Europe would provide the opportunity to use the ties of empire to revive productivity in overseas territories. Prosperity in the heartland would percolate outward to the southern rimlands, quelling the native unrest generated by poverty and powerlessness. The evolution of an Open-Door world, it was assumed, would liberalize colonial rule, expand economic interdependence, and raise all peoples to a higher standard of living. The timetable was necessarily indefinite, but the pattern appeared to be sound.[11]

The Eurocentric view seemed simply commonsensical. Clearly, not all geostrategic areas were created equal. The Soviet challenge, however exaggerated, was most acute in heartland Europe. Upheaval through the colonial crescent was uncomfortable, to be sure, in large part because of the fearsome imagery of aroused, unwashed masses uncoiling into a powerful political and economic dagger. Still, this visceral anxiety remained a secondary concern compared to the more direct damage that would be done by Communist control of Europe. Problems in the colonial world, presumably, could be charted and somewhat ameliorated by astute American consuls. Harmful trends could be later arrested. It seemed unlikely that there would be any irreversible hemorrhaging of American prestige and power in the Third World, while Washington concentrated for several years upon reconstructing European industry, armies, navies, and self-esteem.

The negotiation of the North Atlantic Treaty (NAT) during 1948–49 capped the initial phase of containment. Amid charges that the alliance tied the United States too closely to imperialism, Senator Tom Connally argued that "the North Atlantic Treaty seeks to protect the following status quo: The United Nations; a common heritage of civilization; freedom; the principles of democracy; the rule of law; peace, and security. I fail to find anything evil or hopeless or objectionable about that kind of status quo." Signing the pact did not signify any sort of American imprimatur upon the colonial policies pursued by other treaty members. "I agree 100 percent with those who argue that this treaty should not be either the front door, the side door, or the back door through which the United States might be drawn into family quarrels between the signatory parties and their overseas territories in Africa, the Far East, or other parts of the world." It was apples and oranges, argued Connally. The alliance had nothing to do with colonialism and its fellow travelers.[12]

Still, the North Atlantic Treaty contained clauses and presumptions that might pull the United States into colonial affairs. It was important, for example, to consider the impact of the alliance on attitudes abroad. Senator Henry Cabot Lodge, Jr., observed that there must be a "proper explanation" of the need for this military accord. Otherwise, he remarked, "it will lend color to the theory that we are the warlike country. It will lose us a lot of good will among the humble and obscure people in the world."[13] These were not people that Lodge knew very well, but their views seemed worthy of consideration. Furthermore, since the alliance was designed primarily to meet fifth-column threats to European order, it was logical that the treaty's founding fathers would consider using the pact to suppress subversive challenges outside Europe. Two issues were pertinent. First, should the northern departments of Algeria be included within the geographical sweep of the treaty (Article 6)? The French were insistent that no pact would be signed without coastal Algeria appended. American reactions were mixed. While Senator Arthur Vandenberg termed it a "pretty lousy inclusion . . . in executive session" both Lodge and Connally accepted the colony as an integral part of the French Union. As much so, remarked Lodge, "as 14th Street and Pennsylvania Avenue is a part of Washington." This compromise could be tolerated. "I am not going to commit suicide over this," said Vandenberg.[14]

There was a second question as well. Within the treaty area, what kind of violence would trigger the "armed attack" provision in Article 5? Would revolutionary unrest in Europe or North Africa lead to the commitment of U.S. troops? Questioned by the Senate Foreign Relations Committee in March 1949, Secretary of State Dean Acheson averred that Article 5 would not apply to a "purely ideological offensive." "If you have a combination of the use of force with an internal fifth column," he said, "of course it would [apply]." A bit later he commented: "Whether you would reach the same conclusion if the thing were entirely generated from inside, with external stimulation, is another question." A few days later, however, during a press conference, the secretary was more certain that revolutionary uprisings supported by an outside power would be an "armed attack."[15] Thus, the territorial scope of the pact and the outcome of the debate concerning its military functions effectively signaled U.S. policy priorities in favor of an expansive role for NATO.

The most perceptive public criticism of the NAT's impact on imperial relationships came from W. H. Hunton of the Council on African Affairs. During Senate hearings on the treaty, he criticized the colonial policies of the European members of the alliance and charged that the United States "is today the most powerful colonial power of all time." Noting the eruption of warfare in outlying zones, Hunton contended: "In these colonial areas lies the real threat to world peace. Colonialism has been and continues to be a major cause of the world's wars. The North Atlantic Pact is designed to perpetuate this evil instead of erasing it."[16] Shorn of its explicitly antialliance contents, Hunton's commentary on the long-range impact of imperialism could have been Franklin Roosevelt's.

At the signing ceremonies, on 4 April 1949, British Foreign Minister Ernest Bevin provided a reminder that the new alliance did not lessen Western attentiveness to what later became known as out-of-area events. "Although this Pact is called the Atlantic Pact and is defined as covering the Atlantic area," said Bevin, "I must repeat what I said recently in the British House of Commons, that it does not minimise either our interest in or determination to support others not included in this Pact with whom we have had long years of friendship and alliance."[17] The same was certainly true for the United States, especially given its much greater economic and military power. Theodore Achilles, head of the Division of Western

European Affairs during the alliance negotiations, recalled many years later that there had never been any intent, in formulating the treaty articles, to limit NATO interests only to the European theater.[18]

During the treaty debate, Senator Lodge had identified a root ambivalence concerning the colonial question and Euro-American partnership: "This is one of the fundamental contradictions in terms of this whole thing; because we need . . . these [European] countries to be strong, and they cannot be strong without their colonies and yet we do not like their colonies, and that is a contradiction in terms."[19] But not liking colonies was different from taking active steps to ensure their self-government. There was ample evidence, for instance, that Algerian nationalist groups opposed the treaty terms, and their criticism was clearly separate from routine Communist opposition to the pact as a whole.[20] Being uncomfortable with a second- or third-hand imperialism was not the same as being anticolonial. Words can be slippery. Intent sometimes can be taken for substance, but only if the United States had actively sought the empowerment of indigenous nationalist movements—whether they operated against or in tune with the actions of powerful allies—could U.S. foreign policy reasonably have been called "anticolonial."

As the 1950s opened, the horizon was heavily dotted with potential and actual Third World troubles: Algerian unrest, fractured Libya, ripe oil fields, increasingly militant Islam, the conundrum of Egypt and Suez, violence in Palestine, religious strife in India, guerrilla warfare in Southeast Asia, the political cauldron in Central America. Everywhere along the arc of the southern rimlands there were similar tales of nationalism on the rise, armed insurrection, the coming firestorm that was soon called "wars of liberation." Yet, the European priority still held. As Acheson told Congress in September 1950, "The beginning and the center of everything we do is really the building up of the strength of the North Atlantic forces."[21]

Watching the Map

In January 1950, William L. Clayton, former assistant secretary of state for economic affairs, spoke about the troubled legacy of the Second World War. "Hitler failed, it is true," said Clayton, "but as he went out he slammed the door so hard it jarred the universe." After the Allied victory, the United States had been forced to confront desperate difficulties in the Cold War, facing a shrewd ideological foe guided by "Oriental cunning" and using new techniques of "boring from within" to subvert freedom and undercut American power. The challenge and the danger could be depicted easily:

If we had before us here today a map of the world, drawn to outline the progress and developments in the cold war—black for communism and white for freedom, this is what it would show: Most of continental Asia in black and the rest of it resting under a very dark shadow; most of the European Continent in black right up to and west of Berlin and much of the rest of it sustained by subsidies from the United States; the United States still in white, of course, but caught midway between Europe and Asia in a sort of huge economic vise or pincers, the pressures of which are fast becoming unbearable. Those pressures will grow and grow.

The "economic problem," said Clayton, was "the heart and soul of the cold war." "One of Stalin's most effective weapons is the fear which he instills into the ranks of democratic governments, causing them to spend excessively for armaments, and the fear which he instills into private people, causing them to withhold the capital upon which free enterprise depends." Americans legitimately worried, according to Clayton, that Stalin was winning the Cold War. "The Communists are closing in on us. . . . The truth of the matter is that communism is catching on in the world. It feeds on cold, hunger, and hopelessness. There is entirely too much of that kind of food in the world today and too little of the kind that nourishes the body, the heart, and the spirit." The West's beacon was now only a glimmer: "The Communists are awakening the masses, and make no mistake about it, the masses are listening."[22]

The Atlantic Union hearings of January 1950, held before the House Foreign Affairs Committee, revealed the interconnected threads of U.S. foreign policy during the first few years of the Cold War:

1) the stark, apocalyptic language that routinely·portrayed the conflict as a mortal struggle between two titans, one good and one evil;

2) the progress of Euro-American cooperation, as evidenced by frequent references to the Marshall Plan and the North Atlantic Treaty; mixed, however, with

3) concerns about the West's appeal to Asians and colonial peoples in general; and

4) the shredding of the bipartisan consensus that previously had underwritten American support for the United Nations and the Europe-first priority.

At these hearings, Clayton argued strongly that the United Nations was not a vehicle for fighting the Cold War, since Soviet use of subversive tactics had rendered it ineffective. Others disagreed. Overall, his call for a supranational union of Euro-American peoples generated little but skepticism. More disturbing was his claim that the Soviet Union was winning the Cold War, at dizzying speed; here, several committee members voiced similar concerns. China lobbyist Walter H. Judd called for a broader offensive, "with China gone, and other parts of Asia almost certain to follow and with Africa riddled with Communist propaganda. . . . Personally, I think that is their [Soviet] strategy, to keep us preoccupied in western Europe while they get control of the sources of raw materials in the world. We bleed ourselves to death trying to supply western Europe, or let it go down and stand alone with the world lined up against us."[23]

Grim scenarios abounded on the world map. The danger of subversion was omnipresent and expanding. True, American resources needed to be well marshaled. The pell-mell dispatch of troops and equipment here, there, and everywhere was not the best way to apply vigilant counterforce. The United States, said Undersecretary of State Robert Lovett, must overcome its penchant for jumping into situations "without looking."[24] And yet the urgency of Cold War decision making seemed to require a willingness to take periodic leaps into the policy abyss. This urgency was not diminished by the apparent stability of the European theater. A Central Intelligence Agency analysis of February 1950 foresaw an expanded Soviet propaganda effort in the Far East—the opening of a revolutionary "second front."[25] As was soon proven in Korea, the signing of the North Atlantic Treaty did not inhibit the willingness or the ability of the United States to intervene militarily in distant ports of call. Paradoxically, the war in Korea made more explicit the U.S. commitment to imperial Europe. Furthermore, NSC-68-style Cold War planners did not share Clayton's fears about overspending, and they soon forgot their fears about overcommitment of American resources.[26]

Once it became clear that Europe was divided and would remain so for the foreseeable future, the colonial rimlands became more openly and obviously the new great game. Secretary of State Acheson acknowledged this reconfigured Cold War rivalry on 14 January 1952, when he addressed the Senate Foreign Relations Committee in executive session. Performing the ritual obeisance to containment doctrine, the secretary noted the pervasive Soviet threat, affirmed the vitality of the Atlantic Alliance, and emphasized the strategic importance of West Germany and Japan. He next observed: "We then find that there is another great area of the world, geographically, and from the point of view of our relations with the Soviet Union, and that is the area of struggle. It is the area chiefly of nations which have just come into existence or peoples who are pressing for independence."[27] Later, this would be called the Third World: North Africa, the Middle East, the Indian subcontinent, and Southeast Asia. Its battlefields would become synonymous with distant thunder, public ambivalence, and bitter and brutal guerrilla encounters. The only exception to this pattern was the Korean conflict, a limited conventional war, the last rim-of-Asia face-off akin to the "good war." But even in Korea there were hints of the frustration and ambiguity that would haunt later administrations.

The Containment Tangle

In the process of shifting outward from the European center, the Cold War acquired an ever-expanding roster of intangibles: image, prestige, credibility. British historian D. C. Watt has suggested that "the illusions of the mighty can assume a pseudo-reality by virtue of the strength of those who hold them." Certainly, the superpowers sought to impose their own versions of reality on the rest of the world, sometimes violently, often heavy-handedly. As it turned out, however, the superpowers frequently found themselves held hostage to shaky notions of grandeur, "emotional and psychological factors not reducible to practical or concrete terms or calculable as mundane national interests."[28] Containment was irrevocably altered by the accumulation of these imponderables, eerie accompaniment to the clash of real security interests. Another remarkable result of the expanding U.S.-Soviet conflict in the Third World was the utter confusion of ends and means, of vital and peripheral interests. In the process, the Atlantic Alliance found itself twice divided on out-of-area issues: first, over Anglo-French military action and, second, over American interventionism.

The Truman and Eisenhower administrations both sought to imitate NATO by forging a ring of interlocking alliance systems along the Soviet perimeter. The acronyms were somewhat reminiscent of the Atlantic Pact, but was a NATO-CENTO-SEATO world truly secure? Was "massive retaliation" the only glue holding together the Western security system? Outside Europe, it soon became clear, containment was a ramshackle tangle of pacts and treaties rather than a self-sealing cordon sanitaire. Third World nations and protectorates resisted the regimentation of the two-camp struggle. They sought to preserve their freedom of action, to garner the greatest possible levels of assistance, and to protect their own elites.

The developing world became a recognizable political force in April 1955 during a conference in Bandung, Indonesia. Billed as a meeting to enhance Asian-African unity, it attracted representatives from nearly thirty independent nations. In his opening remarks, Sukarno of Indonesia predictably denounced colonialism and announced that Afro-Asian countries were "no longer the tools of others and the playthings of forces they cannot influence."[29] The gathering provided an international forum for the doctrine of nonalignment, and it offered an opportunity for Zhou Enlai to further a more activist diplomacy on behalf of the People's Republic of China. American fears that the conference would establish the groundwork for an anti-Western bloc proved to be unfounded; such U.S. allies as

Turkey, Pakistan, Iran, and the Philippines contributed ringing anti-Communist rhetoric and a spirited defense of regional security arrangements. The final communiqué of the Bandung meeting condemned "colonialism in all its manifestations," allowing each superpower to feel unthreatened by the ever-rising nationalist ferment in the rimlands.

While Third World unity remained elusive in succeeding years, the Indonesian conference served notice that the developing world demanded greater attention from the big powers. The promise of the conference was redeemed only by the steadily expanding list of Third World members of the United Nations. But the Suez crisis of the following year delivered a complementary message: 1) the West European imperial powers were no longer able to act independently in out-of-area colonial wars, reinforcing the verdict of Dienbienphu; 2) the Soviet Union now had an entry in the Middle East, the way opened by two prominent NATO nations; and 3) the United States was now without guideposts in its Third World policy—the model of a resuscitated Western Europe using empire and commonwealth to foster economic modernization within a liberalized colonial administration was no longer viable. This model had underlain the U.S. mobilization from 1947 to 1949. Clayton had said that "we cannot start with the whole world. We have to start with those countries which think as we do about life and government. Those that have the same ideas and the same ideals."[30] Thus were empires to be transformed from bothersome outposts of atavism into potential wheels of fortune. Then came the Suez invasion, a stupid, effete stroke from the American standpoint. With Third World opinion aroused, the British and the French reconjured the image of aggressive empires while demonstrating their own unalterable weakness. Previous concerns revived about the United States becoming too closely identified as a member of an elite transatlantic club. President Dwight D. Eisenhower thus came to favor unilateral action to sustain the status quo, and this was soon demonstrated in Lebanon and South Vietnam. The Suez fiasco marked the fading interest of France and Britain in Third World adventures.

The period from 1945 to 1956 was an important era of new mythmaking among Third World peoples. The new myths had a hardy, steely countenance, produced by long years of imperial conquest and expropriation, of Western racism and arrogance. They were fed by the raw emotions of the dispossessed and the heady enthusiasm of the newly independent and nurtured in the hothouse environment of guerrilla struggle and revolutionary coups. The new myths transformed the United States from wartime redeemer to the new Rome, the cynical guarantor of the ancien régime, the puppet master of empire. Soviet rhetoric, on the other hand, was incautiously supportive of this mythmaking, openly revolutionary, spurning the past, demanding a settling of accounts with the imperialists. Even if they did not understand how much they encouraged reactionary as well as radical nationalists, Soviet leaders were able to tap a deep well of anti-Western/anti-American sentiment by the late 1950s. The Soviet appeal to Third World leaders was further boosted when the orbiting of *Sputnik* in October 1957 proclaimed the ability of the USSR to mobilize physical and human resources on a spectacular scale. Technocratic prowess combined with bravura diplomacy to create in the Third World a strong sense of Soviet expertise and ideological surety.[31]

In part, however, the Suez crisis exaggerated U.S.-West European tension. While the French and the British appeared to be the powers most irrevocably wed to outdated imperial attitudes, it was American antipathy toward revolution that most threatened to split the alliance and involve it in out-of-area conflict. NATO performed a largely unsung purpose through the 1950s in enabling both Britain and France to come to terms with their reduced status within an alliance system that shielded them from devastating armed threat.[32] Both countries were free in 1956 to fight and lose abroad without endangering their security at home, although certainly not without impact upon national self-image and political careers. Later, in the 1960s, NATO provided the starting point for the reassertion of European confidence and power, enabling France to husband sufficient resources to pursue its *force de frappe* and providing the infrastructural precedent for the development of the Common Market. Yet, throughout the fall and rise of Europe, there was little lessening of American Cold War messianism. As former diplomat J. Rives Childs pointed out, it was a long-established U.S. trait "to be cursed by the spirit of proselytism which leads us to endeavor to make the world over in our own image."[33]

The Pax Americana incorporated many hegemonies: mean-spirited and dogmatic ones, ones powered by Open Door dreams and others primarily paternalistic and benign, porous and nonporous spheres of influence, "moral imperialism," "welfare imperialism," and "expansion with limitations."[34] If American policymakers were moved by the crescendo of crises to assume greater burdens and wider powers than anticipated, who could blame them? Invulnerability encouraged wide vistas. As David Calleo has observed, both the New and the Old World profited from the unequal relationship. The United States proudly walked the earth as the mightiest power and the leader of the Western world—its dominance "packaged in the multilateral hocus-pocus of NATO"—while Britain and France secured a permanent U.S. garrison in Europe and borrowed American power for use in policing their Third World clients.[35] But by May 1954 the borrowing had failed in French Indochina, and it failed again, even more dramatically, at Suez in 1956. The colonial world lay open to a ruthless, predatory communism. American unease increased exponentially as more colonies achieved independence and charismatic leftist leaders arose to taunt the West with charges of impotence and decline.

Vietnam: The Fatal Attraction

The presidential campaign of 1960 highlighted the rising Soviet challenge
through the southern rimlands. Senator John F. Kennedy asked often what
the next decade would bring, so that he could provide his own answer:
challenge toe-to-toe competition with the Soviet Union. "How can we," he
asked, "over a long period of time, maintain our position, our strength, our
leadership, relative to that of the Communist world?" The Soviet Union
was working hard to increase their range of influence. "Mr. [Nikita]
Khrushchev spends a month at the United Nations and he is a busy man. . . .
He knows that in the next decade people in Latin America and Africa and
Asia are going to begin to make a judgment as to which side they are going
to take, which side represents the best hope for them, which system travels
better, communism or freedom?" Already, he said, there were Communist
inroads in West Africa, a leftist regime in Cuba, crisis in the former Belgian
Congo. "What I am concerned about is in 1970 I don't want to see
independent country after independent country [in the developing
world] . . . go where Cuba has already gone, because . . . they feel that the
Communists represent the future, they feel that we are identified with the
past, they feel that we are identified with colonialism, they feel that we are
identified with the kind of future which they do not want. Why? After all,
what we want is their independence."[36] Why did they dislike America? The
question was readily answered: The U.S. formula for the gradual
devolution of empires, under Western tutelage, had been undercut by the
Cold War. Communism cloaked as nationalism stalked the rimlands like a
disease, an epidemic, a cancer on the global community. A *New York Times*
editorial of 1 January 1961 pondered the impact of two radical Communist
regimes, those of newly minted Cuba and the People's Republic of China.
Would Cuba "infect other Latin-American countries with the distemper of
Castroism"? Would Red China "run amuck" [*sic*] in Asia? "On every
hand," cautioned the editorial, "there are hopes and doubts." The same day,
correspondent Robert Whalen asked: "What is the balance sheet on 1960?
How do both sides in the cold war stand as they move into 1961? . . . As for
the communists, the feeling is that they have succeeded in seizing and
holding the initiative at point after point in the cold war." Especially
prominent were Soviet successes in the Third World.[37]

Watching the map since 1950 had been for many a sobering experience,
and 1960–61 brought no respite from Cold War incidents and accidents.
The First World as well as the Third World was in disarray marked by the
stormy U-2 affair, Soviet claims about intercontinental ballistic missiles
(ICBMs) rolling off the assembly lines, *Strelka* and *Belka*, the "missile gap,"
the Bay of Pigs, the Berlin wall. That Khrushchev's bravado and a more

flexible, pragmatic Soviet foreign policy were already creating a nostalgia for the bad old days of the early Cold War was acknowledged by Secretary of State Dean Rusk in February 1961. "The Stalinist approach, . . . the rough, direct, simple pressure of the Stalinist period, was relatively easy to understand, and it was relatively easy to mobilize opinion and effort against it," he remarked. "In the 1950's the Communists have begun to get smart. They are moving with energy, with sophistication, with subtlety, and with considerable effectiveness all over the world in a kind of competition which is extremely difficult to meet." The Soviet Union had recognized, said the secretary, that "the contest is shifting" from Europe to the rimlands. "The battles for Africa, Latin America, the Middle East, [and] Asia are now joined, not on a military plain in the first instance, but for influence, prestige, loyalty, and so forth, and the stakes there are very high."[38]

To meet this challenge came a more determined global activism backed by a massive arms buildup, expanded economic assistance efforts, and better packaging of burden sharing within NATO. There was no need to proclaim a "year of Europe" during the avowedly Europeanist Kennedy administration. Nor was there any need to search diligently through multiple public pronouncements to discover the bold Cold War tenor of Kennedy's foreign policy. It was "a buoyant reenactment of NSC-68."[39] In his inaugural address, Kennedy warned "those peoples in the huts and villages of half the globe" not to trade one colonial master for "a far more iron tyranny." America, he promised, would provide help against misery, because it was right and humane, not because it was politically expedient. And, while the new president advised that there might be "beach-heads of cooperation" pushing back "the jungle of suspicion,"[40] it seemed very unlikely, with freedom so threatened, that superpower rapprochement could be near. The Soviet Union and Communist China would find themselves facing eager New Frontiersmen along both the far and the near perimeter. American hegemony in the Western Hemisphere would be retained by aid and CIA operations. Wars of liberation in the Third World would be met by American counterguerrillas. Castro's Cuba would be contained as communism on one island. The nuclear balance would remain tipped in favor of the United States.

Yet the American empire was beset. The splendid piping of the Pax Americana had lost some of its luster. The United States needed at least a symbolic victory over Communist forces, one beyond its hemispheric backyard and one suggesting that the nation's wide-ranging influence was still considerable, that its government was still led by innovative and daring men who would guard the marches and uphold virtue. The mantle of American globalism was passed by default in 1963 to the struggle in distant Vietnam, a country that became synonymous by decade's end with a massive failure of vision and strategy, due to the duration and intensity of the American involvement, the economic impact of the war, the full playing-out of flawed theories about falling dominoes and demonic communism, and the collapse of the domestic consensus favoring U.S. intervention abroad to deal with "cosmic geo-political-military matters"[41] derived from Cold War exigencies. The Americanization of warfare in Southeast Asia also focused the criticism that had been mounting within NATO: charges of neglect of central interests and fears that Western Europe would be deprived of its conventional force tripwire in order to feed the steady escalation of the Vietnam conflict.

The short-term successes of militarized containment in the 1950s—Korea, Iran, Guatemala—had established among American policymakers a peculiar ebullience that was grafted onto the Kennedy-era enthusiasm for counterinsurgency. When that failed, the Johnson administration shifted to a more straightforward military strategy—with worse results. Military intervention could not cure political disorders. Resolute resistance, deep-rooted hostility toward the United States, and a changing international correlation of forces combined to make old-style containment obsolete.

"If we are to be a great power," said Secretary Byrnes in February 1946, "we must act as a great power." But how does a great power act? Or, more to the point, how does it act intelligently and responsibly? Instead of shoring up U.S. credibility, the widening ripple effect of the Vietnam War severely undermined international confidence in American leadership. Illusion triumphed over capability. The *guerre civilisatrice* sputtered and then went out during the Nixon administration, amid efforts to right the balance and undo the skewed tilt of convoluted strategic thinking. "The abstract, generalized mode of domino theorizing" functioning "as a substitute for thought" was at last to be adjusted somewhat to political reality. But only somewhat. "The final lesson of Vietnam," said President George Bush on 20 January 1989, "is that no great nation can long afford to be sundered by a memory."[42] The moth to the flame, the noble to the absurd, this was the American experience in Vietnam. As Walter Lippmann noted in the midst of the Second World War, "Upon the effects of foreign policy are staked the lives, the fortunes, and the honor of the people, and a free people cannot and should not be asked to fight and bleed, to work and sweat, for ends which they do not hold to be so compelling that they are self-evident."[43] For the United States and its NATO allies, the matter of ends and means was part and parcel of the debate over nuclear deterrence and "flexible response" throughout the 1960s. However, it was American policy toward the Third World that raised the matter most persistently and provocatively.

Ends and Means

"I think one of the great problems everybody faces in dealing with foreign affairs," commented Dean Acheson in September 1969, "is that not only is the future clouded but the present is clouded." He continued:

> What are the facts? Nobody knows what the facts are. The facts are really a matter of interpretation of a very limited segment of data that one gets. If you add more data the interpretation would be different. But what the true data are nobody knows. The poet says things are not what they seem. The great trouble is sometimes they are what they seem. The question is are they or aren't they what they seem? This is inherent in the problem. That is what makes government, particularly foreign affairs, an art and not a science.[44]

What are the true data, and what are the misleading bad sums, wrong analogies, and half-baked theses? American OSS agents had hunted for the right data during the final months of 1945 and had found it: Western colonialism was crumbling, indigenous nationalists were intent on replacing foreign controls with self-rule, and an empathic United States had much to gain. Nevertheless, U.S. policymakers ignored what they suspected to be true, that colonial peoples were becoming disillusioned with America, because they believed that it was necessary to first hold the line against Communist rabble-rousers in Europe. Aligned in NATO with seasoned imperialists (the usual suspects), American leaders struggled to maintain their credibility as an anticolonial power. However, it was not the NATO connection that most determined the course of U.S.-Third World policy; rather, it was the conservative anticommunism of a Washington unwilling to move beyond simplistic assumptions. As former Senator Joseph H. Ball wrote in 1945, "There is no controversy or difficulty over fine objectives. Everyone is for them."[45]

American foreign policy thus has been, since 1945, an art unevenly conceived and poorly articulated. Good hearts and good intentions have not paved the way to success. Nor have thick-headedness and cynicism always meant failure. Too quickly, America's postwar optimism was replaced by pessimism and anxiety coupled with arrogance. In the process, there was a "failure of analysis," a "hypnosis of doctrine."[46] In 1943, Lippmann concisely posed guidelines for U.S. planners. The republic's foreign policy must become "solvent"; its foreign commitments must be in accord with its means to sustain those commitments, tangible as well as intangible. Failure would be measured by the recurrence of conflict. "Insolvency in foreign policy will mean that preventable wars are not prevented, that unavoidable wars are fought without being adequately prepared for them, and that settlements are made which are the prelude to a new cycle of unprevented wars, unprepared wars, and unworkable settlements." A more recent work, by John Lewis Gaddis, has argued likewise and equally persuasively for the alignment of ends and means.[47] But pragmatism may seem unkind, and nonintervention may not appear heroic. This is the political dilemma posed by solvency.

Born-again Détente

As Lawrence S. Kaplan has pointed out, the worldview for NATO's first generation was framed by the Truman Doctrine: "The doctrine itself in the 1950s and 1960s appeared to have been etched in stone, a permanent part of America's political life." Then came Vietnam, a war "that seemed to make a mockery of containment."[48] But failure in Vietnam brought on the Nixon Doctrine, a doctrine born of weakness and defeat rather than ebullience and the scent of hegemonic power. Détente was containment writ small, based upon the realization of U.S.-Soviet nuclear parity and the onset of serious systemic problems in American society. The collapse of détente, undercut by a string of Third World crises in the final two years of the Carter administration, left Ronald Reagan with a relatively free hand to reconstruct or ignore policy precedents. He did both. Richard Nixon had promised a more orderly, less violent world, ruled by practical, if cynical, men. Gerald Ford promised relief from Nixon's intrigue. Jimmy Carter offered a less imperial foreign policy, suggesting that an effort would be made to accommodate Third World nationalism. Even after the November 1979 seizure of the U.S. embassy in Tehran, Carter was willing to say that America had "neither the ability nor the will to dominate the world, to interfere in the internal affairs of other nations, to impose our will on other people whom we desire to be free."[49] But the drumbeat of apparent Soviet victories and the reality of the Soviet arms buildup overwhelmed all sentiment for continued détente, as self-proclaimed Marxist regimes won control in Angola, Nicaragua, and Ethiopia, and as the Red Army installed a client government in Kabul in December 1979.

President Reagan cast his rhetorical net back toward the Truman/Eisenhower era of the Cold War, declaring in a 1982 speech that "a new kind of colonialism stalks the world today and threatens our independence. It is brutal and totalitarian. It is not of our hemisphere, but it threatens our hemisphere and has established footholds on American soil for the expansion of its colonialist ambitions." The American hemisphere, he said, faced the "expansion of Soviet-backed, Cuban-managed support for violent revolution in Central America," with Nicaragua serving as a new platform for mounting assaults against unstable regimes. There would be no "new Cubas," warned Reagan. In what could easily have been the first taste of a new doctrine, the president remarked: "Let our friends and our adversaries understand that we will do whatever is prudent and necessary to ensure the peace and security of the Caribbean area."[50] But this was not to be the "Reagan Doctrine." That came later, in 1985, in less abrasive remarks.

The spawning ground for nearly every doctrine since 1947 has been a Third World crisis, whether a brief flare-up or a more prolonged series of events:

Truman Doctrine (1947)	Eastern Mediterranean
Eisenhower Doctrine (1957)	Middle East
Johnson Doctrine (1965)	Latin America
Nixon Doctrine (1970)	Vietnam
Carter Doctrine (1980)	Persian Gulf
Reagan Doctrine (1985)	Third World

It has been observed that U.S.-Soviet involvement in the Third World is "perennially out of sync," with a mood favoring retrenchment among the leadership of one power corresponding with a penchant for activism among the leaders of the other.[51] The ebb and flow of Third World issues also have been a continuing cause of intra-NATO dissonance. The volatility of out-of-area confrontations—with unsettled regional powers, revolutionary regimes, or stubborn irredentists—has distinguished these encounters from all other points of East-West contention. While it is true that Europe has remained the central theater and that arms control/reduction has remained the key problem in U.S.-Soviet rivalry, Third World issues have assumed ever greater importance since the 1950s.[52] At times rimland clashes have commanded wide audiences and consumed vast resources, yet consistently there have been no decisive victories.

In his book *The Price of Empire*, former Senator J. William Fulbright offered apparently conflicting advice about the current state of international relations. He called upon the superpowers to cooperate more effectively in reducing the frequency of conflict among smaller nations, but he also contended that the big powers could not shape and control events in the Third World. "Small countries wish to find their own ways, make their own mistakes," he wrote.[53] But how many mistakes should they be allowed to make? What if they find their own way into persistent, pervasive regional conflict? Fulbright's comments reflect a persistent paradox of the postwar world, certainly the world of the 1970s and the 1980s—the urge to control and the inability to do so. This has affected not only the rhythm of U.S.-Soviet relations but also the character of intra-NATO politics. Since the signing of the North Atlantic Treaty, there has been a shared sense that the Western powers should work together outside the alliance area, cooperating to tamp down brushfires and to strengthen overall the strategic integrity of the pact. But solidarity has been more threatened than buttressed by Third World intervention.

Senate hearings in 1982 on NATO's future featured conflicting testimony on out-of-area responsibilities, most notably that of former Undersecretary of State George W. Ball, a top-level official in the 1960s, and former Undersecretary of Defense Robert W. Komer, influential in the national security establishment during both the 1960s and late 1970s. Ball identified the "central danger of our time" as the escalation of Third World warfare, downplaying the impact of Soviet intervention and emphasizing instead the indigenous causes of instability. He believed that the alliance played an important role in dealing with such problem areas: "It is artificial that NATO should be detached from dealing with these local conflicts." While the smaller NATO countries obviously would have little to contribute, the alliance could nonetheless "be used as a common forum for strategy and for mobilizing resources." Robert Komer, on the other hand, was not sanguine about NATO's ability to undertake joint operations beyond the European continent. It was natural, he argued, for the United States as a global power to accept extensive out-of-area commitments. The European partners of NATO did not possess the same capability and could best supplement U.S. policy by better providing for their home security and thereby releasing American forces in Europe for action elsewhere, possibly in the Persian Gulf. "We will get more from our European allies," he said, "more bang for the buck if you will, if we get them to take on more of the mission of home defense because it is easier for them."[54]

Overall, the Third World has not been kind to interventionists during the last forty years. Temporary advance has seldom meant permanent gain in client regimes. The Vietnam War proved so many theories wrong that we are still unable to sort it out. Heavy Soviet involvement in Afghanistan faltered amidst the fragmented but feisty opposition of the mujahideen. Even pinprick intervention has produced uneven results, as in the invasion of Grenada, the bombing of Tripoli, and the mission to Beirut. The Third World resists easy categorization as effectively as indigenous governments and peoples resist external control. More questions need to be asked: Why do we so frequently treat small countries as pawns in the global struggle? Why do we so fear leftist regimes in the Third World? Why do we pursue demons abroad when there are so many at home? Surely the domestic tranquility is in such tatters that policymakers of all branches can read the runes of despair, fear, and mounting hate and indifference. In which of the two major political parties might a grand strategy of American *perestroika* take root?

A New Era?

Much of the Cold War ethos has evaporated; much of the ideological baggage of the 1940s and 1950s was jettisoned during Nixon-era détente. Still, the Third World has remained a zone for superpower maneuvers, as evidenced by Soviet-Cuban activity in Africa and U.S. intervention in Central America in the 1980s. The recrudescence of ideology during the first Reagan administration obviously did not preclude the sudden, startling changes in U.S.-Soviet relations of the past several years. By and large, however, these changes did not result from American initiatives. Indeed, one prominent characteristic of the 1980s was the lack of any systematic, sustained U.S. foreign policy goals beyond the Reagan administration's early embrace of a revitalized Cold War. To paraphrase Ronald Steel, a stance is not a policy.[55]

By 1987–88, despite the fact that the cramp and press of international events had overshadowed trite aphorisms, there had been only limited efforts to reevaluate basic policy assumptions. American foreign policy had become a swirling pool of eddies, countercurrents, and random splashes. The so-called Reagan Doctrine was a mélange of previous desiderata and fitful impulses toward global activism. It mattered little if the activity itself was responsible or irresponsible, effective or ineffective, deadly or benign, foolish or opportunistic. Aid to the contras constituted a halfway house for right-wing ideologues frustrated by the subterranean flux of indigenous revolution and the stubborn drive of the Central American peasantry for a more stable, less murderous life. The Strategic Defense Initiative remained a problematic pipe dream, simplistic and quixotic. The Third World remained a battleground of bruised, ill-nourished societies, scarred by decades of covert operations and proxy wars, still infested with the tendrils of Communist conspiracy, and armed by Soviet and East European factories.[56]

Of course, the Reagan era is over. Perhaps the policy jumble of static musing, ideological calisthenics, and trenchant moralism will be cleared away. Maybe the empty, formulaic rhetoric that substituted for political analysis will be replaced by a resolute pragmatism and humanism. It would be comforting to believe that American policymakers might regain a sense of purpose, even a sense of bipartisanship on major issues. After all, the "duel of infinite duration" may be coming to an end. Marshall Shulman has described the current U.S.-Soviet competition as one between two creaky, "overmilitarized" systems, a "dance of the dinosaurs." For E. P. Thompson, the national security elites of East and West have become "heavy dancers," out of sync with their own people as well as world events.[57] Threadbare symbolism, rote shibboleths, and the resuscitation of "credibility" may no longer move either public opinion or government planners. What does this mean for Euro-American partnership?

NATO after Forty Years

"I come before you and assume the Presidency at a moment rich with promise," said George Bush in his inaugural address. "We live in a peaceful, prosperous time but we can make it better. For a new breeze is blowing and a world refreshed by freedom seems reborn; for in man's heart, if not in fact, the day of the dictator is over. The totalitarian era is passing, its old ideas blown away like leaves from an ancient, lifeless tree." It was a day for mixing and rejuvenating tired metaphors. Bush evoked the gentle image of the future as "a door you can walk through—into a room called Tomorrow."[58] His innocent enthusiasm recalled advertising slogans from the early postwar era, when technological marvels bespoke broader and grander horizons, a shiny, metallic future of opportunity and prosperity. His imagery recalled Harry Truman's proclamation of 16 August 1945, in the fresh, exciting light of total victory over the Axis: "This is the end of the grandiose schemes of the dictators to enslave the peoples of the world. . . . This day is a new beginning in the history of freedom on this earth."[59]

Bush purposely evoked the halcyon days of Cold War consensus: "A new breeze is blowing—and the old bipartisanship must be made new again." It was an opportune moment for bland optimism and generic hope, energized by the whirlwind video of two Communist giants in twin turmoil. "Our nation is on the eve of a new international era," wrote Henry Kissinger and Cyrus Vance in the summer of 1988. This new diplomatic season required 1) a reevaluation of U.S. commitments abroad, 2) a reexamination of America's ability to shape world trends, 3) a rededication to executive branch-congressional cooperation, and 4) a determined effort to resolve lingering structural weaknesses in the U.S. economy that threatened to limit American activism in foreign affairs.[60]

Similar concerns animated speakers who appeared before members of the Atlantic Council in June 1988. While much of the discussion focused upon the recently concluded Moscow summit and the signing of the Intermediate-range Nuclear Forces (INF) Treaty, other important issues were also addressed. Presidential candidate Michael Dukakis affirmed the importance and durability of the Atlantic Alliance. Former National Security Adviser Zbigniew Brzezinski asserted that while the international situation remained "inherently ambiguous," it was nonetheless true that "something mysterious has tipped in the scale of history." In fact, he claimed, "the Soviet Union and its associates are going on the historical defensive."[61] If it was not a brand-new era, it was surely a different one. Amid the confusion and uncertainty, American security had to be protected. What was to be done, undone, or otherwise revised and edited?

Doctrines have come and gone, shunted from one policy room to another, hopscotching from crisis to trouble spot. The issues have remained much the same: containment, collective security, growth and competition, burden sharing, and the response to Third World upheaval. Whither intervention? Forecasting the time and place for successful military action in the Third World has been among the most thorny of NATO's perennial problems. Calls for collective action outside the North Atlantic Treaty area have been virtually abandoned. Those who feared American inconstancy could take heart that the Third World remained a mass of unruly and unapologetic peoples, of wily, difficult cults and cultures. Colonial peoples would have continued to be eminently forgettable except that their terrain covered such valuable natural resources and offered such an excellent staging ground for superpower competition. With the semipermanent division of Europe into two opposing camps, Cold War contention moved outward to the rimlands. In the process the easy assumptions about ideological purpose and purity were quickly and quite effectively obscured. The reigning metaphors of falling dominoes and monolithic blocs were based on untenable assumptions stretched over the jutting, broken polity left in the wake of devastating global war. Proxy imbroglios provided geopolitical thrills but netted few friends and minimal long-term advantage. By the mid-1980s the USSR as well as the United States had become a status quo power.[62] Agonizing appraisals and reappraisals altered neither the European priority nor other basic policy rationales.

The "kaleidoscopic circumstances" of the present comprise an appropriate fin de siècle spectacle: The international stage is in such ferment that the birth of a new postwar world system seems at hand.[63] That such considerations may be premature and damage the integrity of the Atlantic Alliance, opening the way for an ironic, *glasnost*-induced Finlandization, was the concern of several long-time observers by the spring of 1989. James Schlesinger, for example, commented ruefully on rising intra-NATO discord and declining public support: "Nothing, apparently, fails like success."[64] Yet these worries coincided with the high-profile celebration of the alliance's fortieth anniversary as the mainstay of postwar peace in Europe—as therefore the indirect cause of the reorientation of Soviet policies. In Kennanesque terms, the Soviet Union had been contained and, in the process, had mellowed and been forced to begin internal restructuring. In a dramatic speech in Brussels on 29 May 1989, President George Bush spoke openly about a postcontainment Europe. Two days later, in Mainz, West Germany, he sounded a similar theme, talking of breaking through the "frozen tundra of the Cold War" and forging a Europe "whole and free."[65]

Whether this future will work or not is still unknown. There remains no alliancewide consensus on such issues as rimland revolutions, Arab-Israeli relations, and antiterrorism campaigns. The persistence of discord has made it tempting to agree with President Bush that there should be a statute of limitations on difficult and controversial problems, a moment at which dilemmas might vanish from the political and historiographical fray. But the fortieth anniversary gathering of NATO leaders showed clearly that concern about Third World problems had ebbed considerably. Once again the centrality of Europe to East-West relations was affirmed. The alliance has remained viable throughout its very real Third World-generated crises and strains because its main purpose was, and is, security in Europe. If NATO is phased out—either dramatically or, like SEATO, with a whisper—it will be because its primary function is no longer required, not because of internal tensions sparked by Third World-related disagreements and imbroglios. Too many dominoes have fallen for it to be otherwise.

Notes

1. Jefferson Caffery to secretary of state, 26 July 1946, RG 59, 851R.00/7-2646, Decimal Files, Department of State, National Archives (hereafter cited as DSNA). Caffery restated his thesis in a note of 27 August 1946, 851.R.00/8-2746, ibid. Steven P. Sapp, "Jefferson Caffery, Cold War Diplomat: American-French Relations 1944–49," *Louisiana History* 23, no. 2 (Spring 1982): 190–92, characterizes Caffery as "a committed Europeanist and staunch anti-Soviet" who effectively lobbied the State Department in favor of strong support for a "Centrist solution" in France without regard for French colonial policies.
2. Michael H. Hunt, *Ideology and U.S. Foreign Policy* (New Haven: Yale University Press, 1987), 41–42, 107, 117, 159, 170, 174–75.
3. A. W. Schmidt, acting divisional deputy, African Division, Secret Intelligence Branch, Office of Strategic Services, to Lieutenant W. T. M. Beale, executive officer, SI, OSS, 7 September 1944, "Report of Field Conditions," folder 140d, box 29, Mediterranean Theater of Operations, Africa Division, entry 99, RG 226, Military Reference Branch, National Archives (hereafter cited as MRB). See also Michael Vlahos, "The End of America's Postwar Ethos," *Foreign Affairs* 66, no. 5 (Summer 1988): 1096.
4. Gabriel Kolko, *Anatomy of a War: Vietnam, the United States, and the Modern Historical Experience* (New York: Pantheon, 1985), 4.
5. Edmund Taylor to William J. Donovan, OSS director, 25 April 1945, folder 2092, box 115, entry 154, RG 226, MRB. See also Taylor's two books, which discuss his OSS experience: *Richer by Asia*, 2d ed. (Boston: Houghton Mifflin, 1964), and *Awakening from History* (London: Chatto and Windus, 1971).
6. James Byrnes, ". . . We Have Pinned Our Hopes to the Banner of the United Nations," Department of State *Bulletin* 14 (10 March 1946): 355–58, italics in original (hereafter cited as *Bulletin*). For other official or semiofficial statements asserting that the United States was not (or should not be) a status quo power, see

John Carter Vincent, "The Post-War Period in the Far East," ibid. 13 (21 October 1945): 644–48; and idem, "Our Far Eastern Policies in Relation to Our Overall National Objectives," in John Carter Vincent et al., eds., *America's Future in the Pacific* (New Brunswick, NJ: Rutgers University Press, 1947), 4–5. See also Harry S. Truman, *Memoirs*, vol. 1; *Year of Decisions* (Garden City, NY: Doubleday, 1955), 237–38.

7. Donnelly minute, 23 March 1945, F.O. 371, AN929/22/45, Foreign Office Correspondence, Public Record Office, London (hereafter cited as PRO); Frederick Puckle, adviser on Indian Affairs to the British embassy in Washington, to P. J. Patrick, India Office, 25 April 1945, F.O. 371, AN1561/24/45, PRO. "According to the Foreign Office," wrote Terry H. Anderson in *The United States, Great Britain, and the Cold War, 1944–1947* (Columbia: University of Missouri Press, 1981), 85, "the United States was a lumbering giant, a powerful nation but a novice in foreign affairs, lacking leadership, aimlessly wandering down international paths."

8. I. A. Kirkpatrick, "Visit to the B.I.S. in America," 10 January 1947, F.O. 371, AN187/1/45, PRO. Kirkpatrick arrived on 27 November 1946 and left on 4 January 1947. In thirty-eight days he visited Washington, New York City, Chicago, Los Angeles, San Francisco, Dallas, Houston, and New Orleans. He also spent one day at the State Department.

9. Deimel oral history interview, 5 June 1975, p. 67, Harry S. Truman Library, Independence, Missouri (hereafter cited as HSTL). See also a similar comment by Abbot Low Moffat, first head of the Division of Southeast Asian Affairs, in U.S. Congress, Senate, Committee on Foreign Relations, *Causes, Origins and Lessons of the Vietnam War: Hearings before the Committee on Foreign Relations*, 92d Cong., 2d sess., 1973, 165–66.

10. Thomas G. Paterson, *Meeting the Communist Threat: Truman to Reagan* (New York: Oxford University Press, 1988), 26.

11. For sample discussions of the Europe-first priority, see Harold M. Vinacke, *The United States and the Far East, 1945–1951* (Stanford: Stanford University Press, 1952), 3–5; Russell H. Fifield, *Americans in Southeast Asia: The Roots of Commitment* (New York: Thomas Y. Cromwell, 1973), 70–71; George McT. Kahin, "The United States and the Anticolonial Revolutions in Southeast Asia, 1945–1950," in Yonosuke Nagai and Akira Iriye, eds., *The Origins of the Cold War in Asia*, (New York: Columbia University Press, 1977), 343, 347–48; Joseph M. Siracusa, "FDR, Truman, and Indochina, 1941–1952: The Forgotten Years," in Joseph M. Siracusa and Glen St. John Barclay, eds., *The Impact of the Cold War War: Reconsiderations* (Port Washington, NY: Kennikat, 1977), 173; Robert J. McMahon, *Colonialism and Cold War: The United States and the Struggle for Indonesian Independence, 1945–1949* (Ithaca, NY: Cornell University Press, 1981), 14; Scott L. Bills, "The United States, NATO, and the Colonial World," in Lawrence S. Kaplan and Robert W. Clawson, eds., *NATO after Thirty Years* (Wilmington, DE: Scholarly Resources, 1981), 149–64; and Geir Lundestad, *East, West, North, South: Major Developments in International Politics, 1945–1986*, trans. Gail Adams Kvam (Oslo: Norwegian University Press, 1986), 67–68.

12. See Connally speech, 5 July 1949, U.S. Congress, Senate, *Congressional Record*, 81st Cong., 1st sess., 95, pt. 6:8814–16. For the text of the treaty, see ibid., 8744–45.

13. Lodge statement, 11 May 1948, U.S. Congress, Senate, Committee on Foreign Relations, *The Vandenberg Resolution and the North Atlantic Treaty: Hearings Held in Executive Session*, 80th Cong., 2d sess.; 81st Cong., 1st sess., 1973, 31.

14. Lodge and Vandenberg comments, 18 February 1949, ibid., 117, 121.

15. Acheson statement, 8 March 1949, ibid., 155–56; Acheson press conference of 18 March 1949, *New York Times*, 19 March 1949.

16. Hunton statement, 12 May 1949, U.S. Congress, Senate, Foreign Relations Committee, *North Atlantic Treaty: Hearings before the Committee on Foreign Relations*, 81st Cong., 1st sess., 1949, vol. 3:963–64.

17. Memorandum by Edward T. Wailes, 17 June 1949, transmitting copies of speeches delivered at the signing ceremonies, 840.20/7-1249, DSNA.

18. Luncheon remarks, 16 April 1980, "NATO after Thirty Years" conference, Kent State University, Kent, Ohio (author's notes).

19. Lodge remark, 2 June 1949, *Vandenberg Resolution and the North Atlantic Treaty: Hearings Held in Executive Session*, 256.

20. See, for example, a dispatch from George Bogardus, U.S. vice-consul in Algiers, 22 March 1949, 851R.00/3-2249, DSNA.

21. Acheson remarks, 11 September 1950, U.S. Congress, Senate, Committee on Foreign Relations, *Reviews of the World Situation, 1949–1950: Hearings Held in Executive Session*, 81st Cong., 1st and 2d sess., 1974, 340.

22. Clayton remarks, U.S. Congress, House, Committee on Foreign Affairs, *Atlantic Union: Hearings before the Committee on Foreign Relations*, 81st Cong., 2d sess., 1950, 3–4, 20, 21–22. For similar remarks see also speech texts titled "Atlantic Union—The Road to Peace in an Atomic World," 17 January 1950, folder: Speeches & Statements—1949–50, box 80, Papers of William L. Clayton, HSTL; and "What Atlantic Union Means to You and to Me," 27 September 1949, ibid.

23. Judd comment, *Atlantic Union: Hearings*, 15.

24. Lovett comment, 5th National Security Council (NSC) meeting, 13 January 1948, box 203, President's Secretary's File, HSTL.

25. "Review of the World Situation as It Relates to the Security of the United States," 15 February 1950, CIA 2-50, box 207, ibid.

26. See John Lewis Gaddis, *Strategies of Containment: A Critical Appraisal of Postwar American National Security Policy* (New York: Oxford University Press, 1982), chap. 4, "NSC-68 and the Korean War."

27. Acheson testimony, 14 January 1952, U.S. Congress, Senate, *Executive Sessions of the Senate Foreign Relations Committee* (Historical Series), 82d Cong., 2d sess., 1952 (Washington, DC: Government Printing Office, 1976), 4:2–3. See also a similar comment of 5 August 1949, in U.S. Congress, House, Committee on International Relations, *Selected Executive Session Hearings of the Committee, 1943–50*, vol. 5, *Military Assistance Programs* (Washington, DC: Government Printing Office, 1976), pt. 1:230.

28. D. C. Watt, "American Anti-Colonial Policies and the End of the European Colonial Empires, 1941–1962," in A. N. J. Den Hollander, ed., *The Impact of American Dissent on European Life* (Leiden, The Netherlands: E. J. Brill, 1973), 109; Russell D. Buhite, *Soviet-American Relations in Asia, 1945–1954* (Norman: University of Oklahoma Press, 1981), 229–30.

29. *New York Times*, 18 April 1955. See also Scott L. Bills, "The World Deployed: U.S. and Soviet Military Intervention and Proxy Wars in the Third World since 1945," in Robert W. Clawson, ed., *East-West Rivalry in the Third World: Security Issues and Regional Perspectives* (Wilmington, DE: Scholarly Resources, 1986), 83–85.

30. *Atlantic Union: Hearings*, 18.

31. On the impact of *Sputnik*, see Walter A. McDougall, *The Heavens and the Earth: A Political History of the Space Age* (New York: Basic Books, 1985), 6–8, 132–34, 248. A summary of many of McDougall's main themes appeared in his article "Technocracy and Statecraft in the Space Age—Toward the History of a

Saltation," *American Historical Review* 87, no. 4 (October 1982): 1010–40. See also Lawrence S. Kaplan, *NATO and the United States: The Enduring Alliance* (Boston: Twayne, 1988), 80, 89.

32. See Colin Gordon, "NATO and the Larger European States," in Lawrence S. Kaplan and Robert W. Clawson, eds., *NATO after Thirty Years* (Wilmington, DE: Scholarly Resources, 1981), 82. See also David Calleo, *Beyond American Hegemony: The Future of the Western Alliance* (New York: Basic Books, 1987), 36–37.

33. Childs, *Diplomatic and Literary Quests* (Richmond, VA: Whittet and Shepperson, 1963), 19. See also Richard J. Barnet, *Intervention and Revolution: The United States in the Third World* (New York: World Publishing, 1968), 78.

34. The terms are borrowed, respectively, from Thomas G. Paterson, *On Every Front* (New York: W. W. Norton, 1979, 35; Watt, "American Anti-Colonial Policies," 125; Ronald Steel, *Pax Americana*, rev. ed. (New York: Viking Press, 1970), 16–17; and Geir Lundestad, *America, Scandinavia, and the Cold War, 1945–1949* (New York: Columbia University Press, 1980), 193–97, 335. Calleo, *Beyond American Hegemony*, 35, has referred to the "European craving for independence" following World War II and contended that West Europeans "preferred outright American hegemony." Lawrence S. Kaplan, "Western Europe in 'The American Century': A Retrospective View," *Diplomatic History* 6, no. 2 (Spring 1982): 117, characterized U.S. hegemony within NATO as essentially benign and short lived.

35. Calleo, *Beyond American Hegemony*, 37, 42. For a discussion of the divisiveness of out-of-area matters during the mid-1950s, see Kaplan, *NATO and the United States*, chap. 4.

36. Kennedy speech, Southern Illinois University Stadium, Carbondale, Illinois, 3 October 1960, in U.S. Congress, Senate, Committee on Commerce, *Freedom of Communications*, pt. 1; *The Speeches, Remarks, Press Conferences, and Statements of Senator John F. Kennedy, August 1 through November 7, 1960*, prepared by the subcommittee of the Subcommittee on Communications, 87th Cong., 1st sess., 1961, 459–62.

37. *New York Times*, 1 January 1961; Robert G. Whalen, "The Year in Review," ibid.

38. Rusk comments, 28 February 1961, U.S. Congress, Senate, *Executive Sessions of the Senate Foreign Relations Committee*, 87th Cong., 1st sess., 1961, vol. 13, pt. 1:187.

39. Vlahos, "End of America's Postwar Ethos," 1099. Paterson, *Meeting the Communist Threat*, 199, wrote of the members of the Kennedy administration, that "theirs was a Trumanesque, NSC-68 view of the world."

40. Kennedy inaugural address, 20 January 1961, *Public Papers of the Presidents of the United States: John F. Kennedy, 1961* (Washington, DC: Government Printing Office, 1962), 1–3 (hereafter cited as *Public Papers* followed by the president and year).

41. The phrase is from Richard J. Walton, *Cold War and Counterrevolution: The Foreign Policy of John F. Kennedy* (New York: Viking Press, 1972), 30. For summaries of historical writing concerning the legacy of the American involvement in Vietnam, see the following: David Fromkin and James Chace, "What Are the Lessons of Vietnam?" *Foreign Affairs* 63, no. 4 (Spring 1985): 722–46; George C. Herring, *America's Longest War: The United States and Vietnam, 1950–1975*, 2d ed. (New York: Alfred A. Knopf, 1986), chap. 8; Gary R. Hess, "The Military Perspective on Strategy in Vietnam," *Diplomatic History* 10, no. 1 (Winter 1986): 91–106; George C. Herring, "Vietnam Remembered," *Journal of American History* 73, no. 1 (June 1986): 152–64; George C. Herring, "America and Vietnam: The

Debate Continues," *American Historical Review* 92, no. 2 (April 1987): 350–62; and Robert A. Divine, "Vietnam Reconsidered," *Diplomatic History* 12, no. 1 (Winter 1988): 79–93.

42. Byrnes, ". . . We Have Pinned our Hopes," 355–58; Theodore Draper, "Falling Dominoes," *New York Review of Books* 30 (27 October 1983): 18; Bush inaugural address, *New York Times*, 21 January 1989. See also Gaddis, *Strategies of Containment*, chap. 8.

43. Walter Lippmann, *U.S. Foreign Policy: Shield of the Republic* (Boston: Little, Brown and Company, 1943), 86.

44. "Conversation with Dean Acheson," 28 September 1969, in Eric Sevareid, *Conversations with Eric Sevareid: Interviews with Notable Americans* (Washington, DC: Public Affairs Press, 1976), 72.

45. Joseph H. Ball, "There Is No Ivory Tower for Us," *New York Times Magazine*, 14 January 1945, 36.

46. The quoted phrases are from Melvyn P. Leffler, "From the Truman Doctrine to the Carter Doctrine: Lessons and Dilemmas of the Cold War," *Diplomatic History* 7, no. 4 (Fall 1983): 261; and Arthur Schlesinger, Jr., "Foreign Policy and the American Character," *Foreign Affairs* 62, no. 1 (Fall 1983): 13.

47. Lippmann, *U.S. Foreign Policy*, 82-84; Gaddis, *Strategies of Containment*, passim.

48. Lawrence S. Kaplan, "NATO, the Second Generation," in Kaplan and Clawson, eds., *NATO after Thirty Years*, 4.

49. Carter press conference, 28 November 1979, *Public Papers: Jimmy Carter, 1979* 2:2173. See also Walter LaFeber, "From Confusion to Cold War: The Memoirs of the Carter Administration," *Diplomatic History* 8, no. 1 (Winter 1984): 1–12; Paul M. Kattenburg, *The Vietnam Trauma in American Foreign Policy, 1945–75* (New Brunswick, NJ: Transaction Books, 1980), 324; and Bills, "The World Deployed," 97–98.

50. All quotes are from "Remarks on the Caribbean Basin Initiative to the Permanent Council of the Organization of American States," 24 February 1982, *Public Papers: Ronald Reagan, 1982* 2:213–14.

51. Michael T. Klare, "Marching to a Different Drummer: U.S. and Soviet Interventionism in the Third World," in Daniel N. Nelson and Roger B. Anderson, eds., *Soviet-American Relations: Understanding Differences, Avoiding Conflicts* (Wilmington, DE: Scholarly Resources, 1988), 156, 159, 164–65.

52. See comments by Francis Fukuyama, "Military Aspects of U.S.-Soviet Competition in the Third World," in Marshall D. Shulman, ed., *East-West Tensions in the Third World* (New York: W. W. Norton, 1986), 182; Richard H. Ullman, "Containment and the Shape of World Politics," in Terry L. Deibel and John Lewis Gaddis, eds., *Containing the Soviet Union: A Critique of US Policy* (New York: Pergamon-Brassey's International Defense, 1987), 122; and Michael Mendelbaum, "Ending the Cold War," *Foreign Affairs* 68, no. 2 (Spring 1989): 20. See also Robert E. Hunter, "NATO's Future: The Out-of-Area Problem," in Stanley R. Sloan, ed., *NATO in the 1990s* (New York: Pergamon-Brassey's International Defense, 1989), 315–33.

53. J. William Fulbright with Seth P. Tillman, *The Price of Empire* (New York: Pantheon, 1989), 41, 169.

54. Ball statement, 9 June 1982, U.S. Congress, House, Committee on Foreign Affairs, *NATO's Future Role, Hearings before the Subcommittee on Europe and the Middle East*, 97th Cong., 2d sess., 1982, 118–20; Komer remarks, 20 May 1982, ibid., 39. In support of Komer, see Peter Foot, "Beyond the North Atlantic: The

European Contribution," *Aberdeen Studies in Defence Economics*, no. 21 (Spring 1982): 29–30, 32–34, 39, 49, 61.

55. Steel, *Pax Americana*, 155.

56. For negative assessments of Reagan-era policymaking, see Walter LaFeber, "The Two—or Three?—Phases of U.S.-Soviet Relations," in Morris H. Morley, ed., *Crisis and Confrontation: Ronald Reagan's Foreign Policy* (Totowa, NJ: Rowman and Littlefield, 1988), 13–45; and Bruce Cumings, "American Hegemony in Northeast Asia: Security and Development," in ibid., 80–106. For a more positive portrait of basic policy themes during the Reagan years, see Robert W. Tucker, "Reagan's Foreign Policy," *Foreign Affairs* 68, no. 1 (special annual issue, 1988–89): 1–27. For a discussion of the practical limits of the Reagan Doctrine, see Stephen S. Rosenfeld, "The Guns of July," ibid. 64, no. 4 (Spring 1986): 698–714; and Ted Galen Carpenter, "Benign Realism: A New U.S. Security Strategy in the Third World," in Ted Galen Carpenter, ed., *Collective Defense or Strategic Independence? Alternative Strategies for the Future* (Lexington, MA: Lexington Books, 1989), 215.

57. Marshall D. Shulman, "The Superpowers: Dance of the Dinosaurs," *Foreign Affairs* 66, no. 3 (special annual issue 1987–88): 494; E. P. Thompson, *The Heavy Dancers* (New York: Pantheon, 1985), xi, 12. Thompson drew his metaphor from the poem "Prophecy," by Thomas McGrath. The phrase "duel of infinite duration" is from George Kennan's "The Sources of Soviet Conduct," reprinted in *Foreign Affairs* 65, no. 4 (Spring 1987): 862.

58. George Bush, inaugural address, *New York Times*, 21 January 1989.

59. "Proclamation 2660: Victory in the East—Day of Prayer," *Public Papers: Harry S. Truman, 1945*, 223.

60. Henry Kissinger and Cyrus Vance, "Bipartisan Objectives for American Foreign Policy," *Foreign Affairs* 66, no. 5 (Summer 1988): 900–901, 911.

61. Dukakis speech, 14 June 1988, *Atlantic Community Quarterly* (Special Issue/July 1988): 7–19; Brzezinski remarks, 14 June 1988, ibid., 40–42. Brzezinski's comments foreshadowed his analysis in *The Grand Failure: The Birth and Death of Communism in the Twentieth Century* (New York: Charles Scribner's Sons, 1989).

62. See Elizabeth Kridl Valkenier, "East-West Economic Competition in the Third World," in Shulman, ed., *East-West Tensions*, 166, 170, 178; and Fukuyama, "Military Aspects of U.S.-Soviet Competition," 191.

63. The quoted phrase is from Paul Kennedy, "Can the US Remain Number One?" *New York Review of Books* 36 (16 March 1989): 36–42. On the birth of a new order see Vlahos, "End of America's Postwar Ethos," 1106–7; Kissinger and Vance, "Bipartisan Objectives for American Foreign Policy," 900–901; Mendelbaum, "Ending the Cold War," 18, 36; Walter Lafeber, "We Need Fresh Scholarship to Understand Changed World Realities," *Chronicle of Higher Education* 35 (24 May 1989): A40.

64. James Schlesinger, "Preserving the American Commitment," *NATO Review* 37, no. 1 (February 1989): 14.

65. Bush remarks excerpted in *New York Times*, 30 May 1989; ibid., 1 June 1989.

NATO AND SECURITY ISSUES

NATO and Détente:
Cycles in History

Anton W. DePorte

It is a truth almost universally acknowledged that East-West tension has always been the cement of the Atlantic Alliance, and East-West détente its potential solvent. But is this true, or is it one of those items of common wisdom that turn out to be more common than wise? We should be able to answer this question one way or the other by examining the history of NATO. It has existed, after all, for forty years, and it has been studied and has had its strengths and weaknesses probed, diagnosed, and prescribed for almost that long. The answer to the question should lie in the record.

The record, unfortunately, is very imperfect. There are few, if any, histories of the Atlantic Alliance or even of the behavior of the allies with respect to the main facets of its activity: planning how to deter or resist Soviet attack or pressure, dealing with changes in Soviet policies or image, and addressing the out-of-area and economic issues that impinge on the effectiveness of the alliance. This is not to say, of course, that even the most complete history would give us what policymakers and students of the subject want most: a dependable guide to understanding and dealing with the next problem to come along in one or another of these policy areas. To know why and how the alliance survived a dozen debates about as many kinds of problems does not guarantee that the thirteenth challenge will fall into the same pattern as those that preceded it. Nonetheless, it would be better, to the extent that it is possible, to understand that there have been patterns in these matters than to face each episode with the wonder of a newborn babe.

So what are we to do? What are we to advise policymakers to do? For one thing, we should encourage the writing of the history of the alliance overall and of its principal areas of concern and activity. In the meantime, we can only try to look at its problems in as detached a way as we can, laying out the historical framework as well as possible and examining each problem to the extent that our understanding of the imperfectly organized record permits us. At no time has it been more important to do this with care and precision than now, when we have entered a period of marked relaxation of tension between West and East that may turn out to have unique implications for the alliance, if only because of the unprecedented changes that are occurring.

To help structure this discussion, which can only be a brief introduction to a vast terrain, it seems useful first to set out certain definitions and admit to certain judgments even before the relevant record has been reviewed. First, it is a fact that the level of East-West or U.S.-Soviet tension has not remained uniform over the past forty and more years. There have been periods of more tension and of less. It has become conventional to call at least some of the periods of lesser tension by the name of détente. There seems to be some benefit in the practice and no harm, provided it is understood that the terms "tension" and "détente" are used here descriptively, to denote states of fact but not moral judgments (for example, that the former is bad and the latter good). Judgments have differed from time to time and among various governments and peoples as to whether more or less tension between West and East advanced or set back the purposes and objectives of the alliance and of the policies that the individual allies pursued within and outside it.

Second, the most extreme level of tension never led to war in Europe or to a successful exertion of Soviet pressure short of war to the serious detriment of the alliance or any member. No major crisis has arisen in Europe since October 1962, although tension has declined and mounted more than once.

Third, the periodic or episodic ebbing of tension has not led to the dissolution of NATO or to the dismantling or invalidating of its established structures and policies or even to the withdrawal of any member. We would be interested in this topic now only as history, if the alliance had not survived and gone about its business over the last four decades, even as it has continued to be characterized by rounds of lesser tension as well as more.

Fourth, each cycle or round of tension and détente left behind a particular impact on the relationship between the two superpowers and their two blocs in Europe. The residual effects of each cycle have not added up to a straightforward cumulative downward pattern of tension once a high point had been reached and passed. The pattern is more complex than that. But each round has left some mark on the relationship that affected later phases of tension and détente.

Primal Tension and the First Pause

The Atlantic Alliance was created in April 1949 as a direct result of the tension that began the Cold War in Europe after World War II. It came to birth in the midst of the crisis connected with the decision in 1948 by the three Western occupying powers—the United States, Great Britain, and France—to create the Federal Republic of Germany (FRG), followed by the Soviet blockade of Berlin. Moscow called off the blockade a few weeks after the treaty was signed and within a few days after the FRG's establishment. At least in Europe, tension was manifestly less in the year that followed May 1949 than it was in the year that preceded, despite the Soviet Union's testing of its first nuclear device and the "loss of China" to "international communism."

This first cycle of tension and détente in the history of the alliance proved instructive to contemporaries and even more so in retrospect. The Soviet Union failed to dislodge the Western allies from Berlin or to intimidate them or the West Germans into backing off from the establishment of the Federal Republic. Neither the period of high tension nor the diminution of tension that followed shook either the Western orientation of the nascent FRG or the commitment of the United States, or that of any other ally, to the alliance.

At the same time, the United States had shown that it was not willing to use its nuclear weapons in a case such as this, although the Soviet Union then had none. Nor was it willing to use conventional forces, given the risks that general war entailed, when the airlift provided an alternative way to relieve Berlin. The Soviet Union also was not willing to use force, notwithstanding their local preponderance.

In this first alliance crisis the rules of deterrence and mutual military restraint that characterized the East-West confrontation in Europe thereafter began to be invented and applied. Their application lowered the level of tension rather than escalating it to conflict. The handling of this first crisis set a precedent, if not an example, for those to come.

From War to Thaw

The outbreak of war in Korea in June 1950 had even more important effects on the alliance, half a world away, than did the Berlin crisis. The United States did not use nuclear weapons in the Korean War, although the Soviet Union had very few, and its prescription for strengthening deterrence against a possible Soviet attack in Europe included the creation of NATO's military arm, command structure and political system, the rearming of most of the European allies, and the arming of the Federal Republic. These responses were not made easily or quickly. There were feverish debates, in the United States about whom and where to fight and in France about rearming the Germans. But once they were made, the decisions were not reversed when a truce and then, in June 1953, an armistice were agreed to in Korea.

The end of fighting in Korea coincided with the death of Joseph Stalin in March 1953 and a major change in internal Soviet politics. The "thaw" within the Soviet Union was matched by an easing of tension between West and East, a negotiated Soviet withdrawal from Austria, which thus recovered its independence, and the first summit meeting to be held in ten years, at Geneva in July 1955. This first period of what might be called self-conscious or structured détente reached its peak, perhaps, with Nikita Khrushchev's accounting of Stalin's crimes—and the failures of the system that allowed them—to the 20th Congress of the Soviet Communist party in February 1956.

The frozen surface beneath which there had been practically no diplomatic contact between West and East for years was broken, and it would never freeze over to the same extent. Efforts toward what Khrushchev called peaceful coexistence between the blocs continued. Most important, from the Geneva summit emanated the idea that the nuclear powers now recognized that their competition could not be allowed ever to become total, that they had at least one interest in common: the avoidance of nuclear war. From this joint judgment, in turn, came the effort to curtail nuclear testing that, for all the talk of "massive retaliation" in the United States and Khrushchev's truculence after the launching of the first Soviet *Sputnik* in October 1957, was to lead in 1963 to a major landmark of détente: the three-power treaty ending nuclear testing in the atmosphere.

High Tension Again

The thaw turned out to be a pause between two periods of high tension. East-West tensions rose again with Soviet bloc arms sales to Egypt, the attempted Hungarian revolution, and the Suez war. Relations became most aggravated, however, when Khrushchev threatened in 1958 to turn over to the German Democratic Republic (GDR), which the allies steadfastly refused to recognize, the obligations of the Soviet Union with respect to Western rights of access to Berlin. During this period, as it has been before and since, contrary to the common wisdom, the Western allies were as divided about how to respond to Soviet provocations as about how to respond to lowered tension. The Americans and British were more inclined to try to defuse the situation by negotiating with the Soviet Union than were the French and West Germans. In the end, all were willing to talk to the Russians in order to avoid having to talk to the East Germans. Although Khrushchev welcomed those talks, little progress was made toward the achievement of his ostensible objective

High tension centering on the vulnerabilities of the Western position in Berlin was punctuated by ambiguous episodes of détente, negotiations, and summitry and then, when these produced no results, by renewed tension.

Khrushchev gave the West a "reprieve" in exchange for an invitation to visit the United States in September 1959, where he engendered, not entirely with President Dwight D. Eisenhower's approval, the "spirit of Camp David." This spirit, however, lacked substance. Khrushchev gave a second reprieve as the Big Four powers prepared, albeit reluctantly on the part of the Western three, for their Paris summit of May 1960. The Soviet leader disrupted this process by his almost comic outcry against the admitted U.S. use of spy planes over his country. Even so, he granted a third reprieve until the next American president had been elected.

Tension then increased sharply. President John F. Kennedy's administration attempted and failed in April 1961 to topple the Fidel Castro regime in Cuba, the Soviet Union and its East German allies succeeded in almost completely halting the massive exodus of East Germans to the West by constructing the Berlin wall in August 1961, and, finally, Moscow decided, for reasons still debated, to deploy missiles in Cuba that would be capable, as no other Soviet missiles then were, of delivering nuclear bombs onto American territory. The vigorous American response to this in October 1962 ended with Soviet retreat from its exposed position in Cuba and the quiet evaporation of Soviet threats concerning Berlin. The Cuban missile crisis was the closest approach there has ever been to war—and perhaps nuclear war—between the two superpowers. It marked the highest point of tension ever reached between the two blocs and, as such, the climax of the Cold War or even, depending on one's definition, the end of it.

In the more than twenty-five years that followed this crisis there have been many U.S.-Soviet and East-West confrontations and another long period of tension between 1979 and the mid-1980s. But the prospect of a direct U.S.-Soviet military clash, and particularly of a nuclear exchange, has been minimal since October 1962. The confrontation in the early 1980s resembled that of the 1950s in its global, ideological, and rhetorical scope. Yet it was much less passionately waged in Europe, the original heartland of the Cold War, than it was in areas of ambiguous alignment elsewhere. It often led to unsatisfactory results for one or the other superpower or for both in regions such as the Horn of Africa, Lebanon, Central America, Afghanistan, and southern Africa. In Europe the structural status quo established by the mid-1950s was not only maintained but also scarcely challenged, doubtless because it continued to reflect the realities of the broad balance of power between the blocs and within them. That balance was reaffirmed, even while it was being modified, by the many East-West agreements and arrangements that were the main fruit of the long period of détente between 1963 and the mid-1970s. Thus, two thirds of the Atlantic Alliance's life span to date falls after the end in 1962 of the last real threat of conflict in Europe.

The sharp recrudescence of tension that followed the long period of détente was no more permanent or definitive than the preceding period of détente proved to be. Tension and détente, more or less intense and extended, have continued to alternate since 1962 as they did before. This might have disappointed those who had hoped either that the West might prevail once and for all over its Eastern antagonist or that the two sides could settle their main disagreements once and for all by negotiation. But it should not have surprised those who understood that the relations of these two Great Powers, like those of all other Great Powers before, would be bound at best to take the form of "competitive coexistence," to borrow a useful term from the 1960s. Those relations would be sometimes more acutely competitive, sometimes more self-helpfully coexistent, as long as the world offered the two superpowers the scope or the occasion for trying to extend their own influence and to limit that of the other. This is the oldest tale in the politics of nations, however unique the circumstances of the U.S.-Soviet competition since 1945.

The Long Détente

The United States gave the signal and sanction for beginning the next phase of U.S.-Soviet and East-West relations after the missile crisis with President Kennedy's American University speech on 10 June 1963, which called for a new approach to relations with the Soviet Union. The first conspicuous manifestation of this new approach was the signing on 5 August 1963 by the United States, the United Kingdom, and the Soviet Union of a treaty to end the atmospheric testing of nuclear weapons. The United States continued to pursue arms control negotiations with the Soviet Union even as it became more and more preoccupied with its war in Indochina. The arms control effort bore fruit in the Nuclear Non-Proliferation Treaty in March 1968 and then, after Richard M. Nixon became president, in the opening of a systematic effort to reconstruct the American-Soviet relationship.

The French Opening to the East

The United States presumably intended to lead the Western march toward this reconstruction, as it had led the West during periods of tension. But the very magnitude of the American success and the Soviet setback in the missile crisis, and of the prompt relaxation of tension that followed, gave rise to a widespread perception in Europe and elsewhere that the bonds of alliance could safely be loosened, and along with them the habit of allied deference to American leadership in security and other fields. In these circumstances President Charles de Gaulle of France found the occasion, although certainly not the motive, to pick up the ball of détente and run with it as far as he could on behalf of French independence and leadership. His objective was to "overcome Yalta," the French code for the postwar division of Europe into blocs dominated by the superpowers, and to build a new European system "from the Atlantic to the Urals." This creation gradually and eventually would replace the outdated two-bloc system by building "détente, entente, and cooperation" between the countries of the Eastern and Western blocs.

An intense intra-alliance fracas between the United States and France characterized, perhaps not surprisingly, this phase of East-West détente. The American government and much of public opinion criticized de Gaulle's policy on many grounds. Controversial issues included his building of a national nuclear force (perceived as providing a dangerous incitement to West Germany to do the same and weakening American ability to manage the alliance during crisis or war), his withdrawal of the French armed forces from integration in NATO's military wing (although he did not take France out of the alliance), and his trips to Eastern Europe and elsewhere to preach the virtues of overcoming the postwar system. To many Americans this program appeared likely to weaken the alliance, particularly if others followed France's example, and to foster not real détente but illusions that would be dangerous in face of the Soviet Union's strength and policies.

As events turned out the Soviet Union, by invading Czechoslovakia in August 1968, confirmed American doubts about the prospects for the radical change in the postwar European system that de Gaulle wanted. Concurrently, however, the Americans themselves were pursuing arms control negotiations with the Soviet Union. The idea that some improvement in relations was possible began to find followers elsewhere in Europe, and above all in West Germany. Konrad Adenauer had left the chancellorship in October 1963, and power had passed to younger leaders more open to reexamining fixed policies from which both the United States and France, each in its own way, were moving away. Many American and European leaders understood that at the least they should not leave the political benefits of pursuing détente to de Gaulle while they remained frozen in Cold War postures. They agreed on the need, if the alliance was to retain public support, to offer an alternative approach for the limiting of tension and the building of "détente, entente, and cooperation" between West and East in Europe.

The "Second Leg" of the Alliance

These considerations led the allies to try to arrive at a common position aimed at adapting their policies, and the alliance itself, to the prospect of continuous negotiations with the Eastern countries and, beyond that, to a new kind of relationship with them that would still ensure, but no longer be confined to, preserving the security of Western Europe. This was not a problem that the founders of NATO would have foreseen. They might have expected an ebb and flow of tension as the Soviet Union moved forward in one place or another, to be "contained" each time and forced to draw back, only then to resume its forward movement again. They do not seem to have anticipated that a time might come when there would be a need to manage other kinds of dealings with the Soviet Union, that is, détente as well as deterrence, and at the same time. Yet, that is the situation the allies faced from the mid-1960s on.

To meet this new challenge the North Atlantic Council, on the initiative of Pierre Harmel, the Belgian foreign minister, appointed a committee to draft a report on "The Future Tasks of the Alliance." The council, including the French representative, reviewed and adopted this document on 14 December 1967. The report noted that important changes had taken place in the international environment since the founding of NATO in 1949, in part because of its very existence. The threat of Communist expansion in Europe had been stopped. There was no longer a monolithic world Communist bloc, and the proclaimed Soviet policy doctrine of "peaceful coexistence" had "changed the nature of the confrontation with the West but not the basic problems." As a result of these developments, the alliance not only had to maintain and improve its ability to deter aggression but also now had "to pursue the search for progress towards a more stable relationship in which the underlying political issues can be solved. Military security and a policy of détente are not contradictory but complementary." The allies quite properly spoke of "a policy of détente," meaning that it likely was not a goal but a means. "The relaxation of tensions is not the final goal but is part of a long-term process to promote better relations and to foster a European settlement."[1] The allies also took this occasion to affirm their agreement in principle (however various their practice had been and would be) to the proposition that the alliance was not isolated in the world, even though it was geographically delimited, and that developments anywhere could affect its well-being and functioning inside the treaty area.[2]

The Harmel Report became the charter for what came to be called the alliance's "second leg," the commitment of the members to pursue a changed relationship with Eastern Europe. Each remained free to make its own policies but all agreed to engage "in frank and timely consultations" with the others to avoid splitting the alliance.[3] Such a commitment, or the need for it, would have been unimaginable at the time of the alliance's creation and for a long time afterward as a realistic objective of allied diplomacy or even as a propaganda diversion. This new focus of alliance attention was seen as supplementing but not replacing its original purposes. New circumstances had created new needs, but old problems persisted. The allies, therefore, would maintain their arrangements aimed to deter or, if necessary, meet what they continued to perceive as a Soviet threat to their security, even as they explored the possibilities of curtailing or removing the sources of that threat or some of its consequences. The success of the alliance in its original purposes, as well as other changes on the international scene, seemed to create possibilities for doing so.

This carefully balanced policy did not mean the same thing to all the signatories. But it prepared the way, just in time, for achieving a reasonably common allied approach and reasonably well-coordinated policies in the high summer of détente that was soon to blossom from the seeds planted after the Cuban missile crisis. Ironically, de Gaulle, whose unilateral and, to many, provocative initiatives had done so much to oblige the allies to focus on how to pursue détente without jeopardizing essential alliance solidarity, did not benefit from the harvest. It did not take place in the ways he had hoped for or under his, or France's, leadership, and it would not have the outcomes of which he had dreamed.

Détente in Practice

The Warsaw Pact invasion of Czechoslovakia and the proclamation of the Brezhnev Doctrine signified that the Soviet Union was not ready to allow its bloc to unravel, whatever France or others did in and to the Western bloc. If there was to be relaxation of tension, it would have to be developed, at least in the beginning, not by trying to overcome the two-bloc system in Europe but by accepting and even reaffirming it, because the Soviet Union, without which nothing could be done, would not take part unless the process and the outcome were consonant with the consolidation and re-recognition by the allies of its bloc. That response was not what de Gaulle had in mind. Indeed, what ensued might have seemed to him a reaffirmation of Yalta rather than even a first step toward overcoming it. Some saw more than that in the agreements reached in the 1970s, others did not. But by the time this process of détente got under way, de Gaulle had been forced from the French presidency as a delayed consequence of the events of May and June of 1968. By the time the outcome of this round of détente began to be clear, he was dead.

The lead now fell into the hands of Richard Nixon, who was elected president of the United States in November 1968, Henry Kissinger, his adviser for national security affairs, and Willy Brandt, who in October 1969 became the first Social Democratic chancellor of the Federal Republic. During the next three years an extraordinary volume of negotiations took place in varying patterns among the United States, the FRG, and the other Western allies, and between them and the Soviet Union and its allies. These initiatives resulted in a remarkable volume of important agreements. The

Western allies were able to pursue their distinct but convergent policies in the spirit of the Harmel Report, but the main agreements that defined this high tide of détente, extensive as they were, failed in the end to define a stable period of East-West relations. Instead, a new phase of acute tension followed.

Both the United States and the Federal Republic of Germany had reasons to want to put relations with the Soviet Union on a more nearly contractual basis than what had been defined up to then by the tensions of the Cold War and the fruitful but intermittent lessons and limits produced by the periods of thaw and peaceful coexistence. U.S.-Soviet arms control negotiations had developed momentum and supportive clienteles. The Nixon administration saw a possibility of strengthening its hand in the inevitable disengagement from Indochina by carrying out a rapprochement with the Soviet Union and China. Beyond that, some members of the administration conceived the possibility of curtailing Moscow's expansionism by weaving a web of mutually profitable but confining economic and other ties with and around the Soviet Union.

The West Germans were ready by 1969 to write off their long-professed official hope of being able to achieve the unification of their divided country by way of a Western "situation of strength" and to give up their resistance to recognizing and dealing with the "other" German state. Practical amelioration of their relations with the states of Eastern Europe, not in defiance of but in cooperation with the Soviet Union, was now considered desirable in itself in the near term and as offering the only long-term prospect of eventually wearing away the barriers between the two parts of Europe and of Germany.

France, Great Britain, and the other allies all showed interest in consolidating a lowering of tension in Europe, although not in such a way as to endanger the structures of the alliance that still seemed, to most of them, essential to their security and, indeed, to the ability of the Western states to negotiate concrete measures of détente with the East. They generally shared the American concern that the West Germans might become so entranced by the potential of a breakthrough in their relations with Eastern Europe as to be tempted into taking steps that would jeopardize NATO. The European allies also shared a concern that the United States might be tempted to make bilateral deals with the Soviet Union about arms control and Indochina while neglecting or blocking any benefit the Europeans themselves might hope to derive from the new situation. The Germans, French, and others were alert to the risk that the reaffirmation of the structural status quo in Europe might degenerate into a reimposition of Yalta by the superpowers on their allies.

The convergence of these complex and diverse considerations on both sides of the Atlantic required and produced a remarkable degree of policy coordination among the players. This was not achieved without suspicions and hesitations. But on the whole the authors of the Harmel Report should have been satisfied that the "frank and timely consultations" they had called for, when the moment came for a round of serious negotiations between East and West, had taken place and had been successful.

This coordination became especially important as the subject matter of the various negotiations became woven into a web of linkages in which no part of the whole was likely to be carried to fruition unless the others were. Each major participating government, West and East, had its own prime objectives and required some satisfaction of them if it was to agree to satisfying the wants of others. It is remarkable that all of them were so well satisfied.

The main results of the negotiations were as follows:

1) Treaties between the Federal Republic and the Soviet Union (1970), Poland (1970), and the German Democratic Republic (1972) by which the FRG in effect accepted the postwar frontiers drawn in Eastern Europe and, under the formula of "two states in one nation," recognized and established diplomatic relations with the other German regime.

2) Agreement among the United States, Great Britain, France, and the Soviet Union (1971) reaffirming the rights of the Western powers with respect to Berlin and defining the relations between the part of the city they occupied and the FRG.

3) A U.S.-Soviet treaty limiting the number of their antiballistic missiles (ABM) and an interim agreement (SALT I) limiting the numbers and types of strategic missiles they would build.

4) Agreement by the Western governments to a long-standing Soviet proposal to convene what was eventually called the Conference on Security and Cooperation in Europe (CSCE), which, when it met at Helsinki in July 1975, in effect reaffirmed the European territorial status quo (the original Soviet objective); laid out a framework for establishing closer ties between the two parts of Europe in economic, cultural, and other matters; and (at Western insistence) included commitments by all the signatories to observe principles of human rights that the Soviet Union and its allies were notoriously known to flout.

5) Agreement by the members of NATO and the Warsaw Pact to enter into negotiations aimed at bringing about mutual and balanced force reductions (MBFR) of their conventional forces in Europe.

This linked set of agreements reaffirmed the postwar territorial status quo, including the legitimacy of the East German state and the reality of Soviet domination over Eastern Europe. It opened the door to more nearly normal state-to-state relations between the FRG and its eastern neighbors, above all the German Democratic Republic. There seemed to be good reason to hope that as normalization progressed, even within the constraints of the enduring two-bloc system, some of the tensions of the past could be reduced. If the MBFR negotiations led nowhere initially, they at least kept on the international agenda the prospect or goal that the two blocs might someday, in more favorable political circumstances than those of the 1970s and 1980s, come to the view that they could provide for their security needs at a lower level of armament in Europe. If the follow-up conferences to the CSCE did not have an immediate effect on human rights in the East European states, they at least helped to keep that issue, too, on the international agenda, pending a time when it would be taken more seriously, both within the West and between the blocs, than it ever had been taken before.

The reaffirmation of the territorial status quo gave the Soviet Union something it had consistently wanted. This did not signify that the West had given up anything except what its own behavior up to that time had shown that it did not possess, that is, the ability or intention to roll back Soviet control from Eastern Europe or to draw some of the Soviet allies out of the Eastern bloc or to unite the two German states in the face of Soviet opposition. The Soviets and their allies were not alone in being pleased that the FRG agreed to accept normalization of its eastern frontiers and relations with its eastern neighbors in this manner.

The general perception that this batch of agreements diminished the prospects of conflict or tension did not have the effect, as some had feared, of inducing "détente fever" in the Western countries or undermining the solidarity or effectiveness of the Atlantic Alliance. What had been accomplished was welcomed in most European countries for its benefits, but it was also accepted by most people as having reached the limits of what could be achieved at that time. If they hoped for more and better developments in the future, that did not give any allied government, during the many contentions that divided NATO in the next decade, reason or pretext to rupture or fatally diminish its ties with the alliance.

This climax of negotiated measures in the direction of East-West détente did not succeed, however, in putting the global competitiveness of the two superpowers on a permanently lower level of tension. After a decade or more of movement toward détente and even some measure of cooperation, tension began to rise again between the United States and the Soviet Union even before the Helsinki Conference met.

The Faltering of Détente

The issues that slowed, interrupted, and then reversed the process of détente were mainly non-European. The East-West agreements that had removed most European issues as major sources of tension held firm even as U.S.-

Soviet tension outside Europe increased. Détente, contrary to some American judgments in the dark year of 1980, turned out not to be indivisible; at least its fruits in Europe proved firmly enough based in power realities and common interests, including American interests, to survive the ending of the impetus toward seeking new agreements.

Nonetheless, the slogan about the indivisibility of détente meant that the superpowers could not advance further along that path in Europe when out-of-area issues gave rise to heightened tensions between them. The establishment and reaffirmation in the early 1970s of the territorial, political, and ideological status quo in Europe was insufficient to lead the Soviet Union and the United States to structure their competitive relationship elsewhere by imitating the understanding that they had reached there. Nor could they simply give less importance and intensity to their competition in Asia, the Middle East, Africa, and Latin America, if only to shelter their European understandings and their arms control negotiations from the negative fallout of their Third World rivalries.

The superpowers agreed on a global statement of the principles that were to animate their relationship, but surely neither believed that the other really intended by that gesture to leave it a free hand to extend its influence in the inviting, but treacherous, sands of Third World conflicts and alignments. The United States had no more reason to refrain from taking advantage of the Soviet debacle in Egypt in 1973, for example, than the USSR had to abstain from supporting those groups in the newly liberated Portuguese colonies of Angola and Mozambique that were most hostile to the United States. Neither superpower was prepared to let the other's protégé (newly swapped) prevail in the Somali-Ethiopian war.

The United States, in addition, seemed to believe that it was strong enough vis-à-vis the Soviet Union to be able to use not only the economic benefits that the latter hoped to achieve from détente but also arms control negotiations as levers to force the Soviet Union to grant concessions on emigration policy and human rights abuses, if not on its activities in the Third World. The Soviet Union, seeking in détente to have its "parity" with the United States recognized, rejected these efforts. The Jackson-Vanik amendment failed in the short term in its ostensible purpose of improving the prospects for Soviet emigration (indeed, it had quite the opposite effect), putting an end to whatever prospects there were at the time for binding the Soviet Union to détente over the long term by ties of economic interest.

Meanwhile, a rising level of criticism in the United States about the substance of arms control and even of the process itself (on the grounds that it was inherently disadvantageous to the West because it lowered Western guard against Soviet expansiveness) became entangled in the politics of the 1976 presidential election. As a result, President Gerald Ford chose not to submit the second Strategic Arms Limitation Treaty (SALT II) agreement, completed by him personally at Vladivostok in December 1974, for ratification by the Senate. In the 1976 campaign, hard-pressed by Ronald Reagan's bid for the Republican nomination and its consequences even after he had been nominated, Ford even backed off from the use of the term "détente."

Fourth Cycle, First Phase: Neo-Cold War

The long development of movement toward détente and specific agreements between West and East that had begun after the Cuban missile crisis ended somewhere in the mid-1970s, even as some of the negotiations to which it had given rise were still in progress. In the latter part of the decade came a sharp upsurge of U.S.-Soviet tension. This never reached the level of October 1962, but it was more intense than any time of stress since then. It is remarkable that during this period the prospect of an actual U.S.-Soviet military clash was always practically nil (notwithstanding talk in the United States of a "window of vulnerability"). Nonetheless, a shocked and frightened United States abandoned détente as a process, although not the arms control and European improvements already obtained, when the Soviet Union followed up on its objectionable behavior in eastern and southern Africa by invading Afghanistan in December 1979.

This uniquely provocative action, the first time the Soviet Union had sent its troops outside its bloc since World War II, occurred just as the seizure of the American embassy and its occupants in Tehran reminded the United States not only of the collapse of its strategic position in the Persian Gulf and beyond with the downfall of the shah of Iran but also of its humiliating impotence in face of such provocation by a lesser nation. American opinion saw the two events as linked parts of a Soviet drive to the Indian Ocean. If in these circumstances President Jimmy Carter said that he at last understood the Soviet Union's policies, his successor, Ronald Reagan, spoke for many when he made clear that he had never been under the least illusion about the aggressive character of what he would later term the "evil empire."

The revival of acute tension between the superpowers after so many years of relative relaxation created serious strains within the alliance, but less serious ones than might have been expected. At first it appeared that the Europeans were considerably out of step with the anguish overtaking the United States in 1980. They did not perceive their own security, permanently threatened as it was by the Soviet presence on the Elbe, as any more threatened by events in Iran and Afghanistan. West German Chancellor Helmut Schmidt said that the invasion of Afghanistan created an East-South problem (that is, bad Soviet relations with Muslim and other Third World countries) but not an East-West problem affecting Europe.

France's President Valéry Giscard d'Estaing met Leonid Brezhnev in Warsaw in May 1980 with the hope of showing that Western Europe did not see things the same way as the United States and that the fruits of détente in Europe should not be sacrificed on the altar of the notion, much discussed in America without much reflection about its implications, that "détente was indivisible." American efforts to convince the allies to adopt strict economic sanctions against both Iran and the Soviet Union and to withdraw from the 1980 Moscow Olympic games met with only limited success. Americans were, for a time, outraged: "Where are the allies when we need them?"

That the Soviet actions remained outside the NATO treaty area highlighted once again one of the deepest fault lines in alliance solidarity: Repeatedly, the United States and some of the European allies failed to see eye-to-eye on developments in the Third World, and many Americans resented that their interpretation of what was happening there and what needed to be done was not accepted by the allies. For a time, many seriously feared that the concern of West Europeans about being dragged by the United States into what they saw as unnecessary and dangerous tensions with the USSR and the outrage of Americans at being left alone to defend what they defined as Western interests under attack outside Europe might lead to a genuine rupture between the two sides of the alliance. Certainly this interlude resulted in one of the three or four most serious episodes of intra-alliance strain since 1949.

The muscular rhetoric of the incoming Reagan administration toward the Soviet Union, rhetoric of a kind unheard for more than a decade, seemed to increase the prospects of a major transatlantic clash. It foreshadowed the emergence of a global American strategy for dealing with the worldwide problem presented by the Soviet Union. This strategy entailed severe restrictions on East-West trade (which the allies would be expected to adopt), a readiness to use force in Third World conflicts (which the allies should at least sanction), a massive weapons buildup to which the allies should contribute, and the cessation of arms control talks. These negotiations were deemed not only incapable of leading to agreements benefiting the West but also dangerous in themselves—like détente altogether, of which they were the centerpiece—because of the illusions they bred among the public about the gravity and permanence of the Soviet threat.

Here, it seemed, was the occasion that would lead at last to that tightening of American leadership over the allies to which the United States had intermittently aspired for years or, failing that, to an American break in the direction of unilateral action aimed at the USSR and the Third World toward which it also had aspired more than once in certain phases of the national mood. In the latter case there might well follow the rupture of the alliance structure, which some Europeans thought too dangerous and some Americans, including those who came to office in January 1981, thought too restrictive of their country's freedom to deal with the Soviet problem. This thesis, widely held in the heady early days of the Reagan administration, turned out to be mistaken, for two main reasons. First, West European opinion, public and official, proved to be less hostile to the changes in U.S. policy and leadership and more willing to temporize with or even support them than had seemed likely. France, the surprise bellwether in this respect, was headed by its first Socialist president and the first Socialist-led cabinet in a quarter century, a cabinet that also included Communist ministers for the first time since 1947. This government had been expected to be, if not leftist-neutralist and anti-American in its foreign orientation, at least Socialist-Gaullist and anti-American. It proved to be neither.

François Mitterrand and his associates recognized and reflected the drastic decline of Marxism from its long-time centrality among French intellectuals and the accompanying "Solzhenitsin syndrome" among the population. They perceived that Giscard d'Estaing's gesture toward Brezhnev in May 1980 had not been popular with the voters. If the French were less concerned about the implications for their security of events in Iran and Afghanistan, they seemed much more concerned by the outlawing of the Solidarity union in Poland and even more so by the Soviet military buildup. The non-Communist French seemed almost unanimous in their support for countering the buildup in the way the alliance had prescribed: by deploying intermediate-range nuclear force (INF) missiles in the Federal Republic and four other countries (but not in France). The left side of German politics mounted an ever more vigorous campaign against deployment, with nationalist overtones of disengagement and neutralism, making German commitment to the deployment policy, and to the alliance and the United States, that much more appealing to the French. The climax of this remarkable trend in French and alliance policy was Mitterrand's advice to the German voters during his visit to the FRG in January 1983 to vote in the upcoming elections for those parties that favored deployment— not the Social Democrats.

If French opinion, paradoxically in light of recent history, appeared to be the most pro-INF in Europe, adequate majorities also were found in the FRG, Italy, Belgium, and the Netherlands to allow their governments to implement deployment in the face of strong Soviet objections. It is true that the willingness of the United States to enter into negotiations with the USSR to limit or reverse deployment strengthened the position of its supporters. Few, however, expected those negotiations to lead anywhere. The alliance demonstrated a remarkable degree of unity in this, the sharpest East-West clash in Europe in the 1980s, and it did so at a time when other developments soured relations between the United States and at least some of the allies. The best explanation seems to be that many Europeans shared, in diverse ways, American concern about Soviet power. Many, in addition to the French Socialist government, welcomed and praised the U.S. military buildup.

The second reason why dreams and fears of a U.S.-European rupture did not become realities as tension replaced détente was that the U.S. government did not implement the global anti-Soviet policy that many had expected of it. Nor did it press the allies to the point of rupture to conform even with the few aspects of such a policy that it did try to carry out, as, for example, in the matter of the agreements made by Britain, France, the Federal Republic, and Italy to bring Soviet gas to Western Europe. The United States did not ask the allies to renounce the fruits of 1970s détente in Berlin or elsewhere. It did not try very seriously to prevent the FRG from continuing and expanding economic relations with the GDR, even after the declaration of martial law in Poland in December 1981 and even though this policy, once opposed by the Christian Democratic party, was taken up by it when it returned to power in October 1982. American willingness to engage in INF negotiations with the Soviet Union, even if only for tactical reasons and without expectation of reaching agreement, was nevertheless a step away from rigorous rejection of all arms control negotiations. Furthermore, American policies in the Third World were in general not of such a nature, nor was the U.S. call for European support of them so imperative, as to rupture the alliance.

Fourth Cycle, Second Phase: Neo-Détente

The phase of East-West tension that had opened in the late 1970s and took such intense form after 1980 might have seemed destined to last for a very long time, if one judged by the official American rhetoric of those years. It did not seem then that the renewed development of Western "positions of strength," to use the language of the 1950s, was intended to lay a basis for reopening negotiations with the Soviet Union on arms control or much of anything else. As was the case thirty years before, Western strength seemed intended to lead not to negotiations with the Soviet Union but to forcing it to withdraw from the positions it had asserted in the Third World and eventually those in Eastern Europe, too, if not, indeed, to its internal collapse.

Yet, this phase of high tension, like those before it, was followed by a period of renewed relaxation of tension. Neo-Cold War has given way to neo-détente. After burying no less than three Soviet leaders, the Reagan administration decided to negotiate not only INF deployments but also strategic arms control. The atmosphere was much more cordial than merely businesslike with a Soviet regime that it had denounced for disrupting the

Middle East, Africa, and Central America, for being the center of world terrorism (if not also world drug trafficking), for shooting down a civilian airliner, and for plotting the murder of the pope.

How is this turnabout to be explained? Were the hard-line policies and rhetoric meant from the start to lay the foundation and provide credibility with the public for moving to détente later? Historians will have an interesting task identifying who among the personnel of the Reagan administration was able to conceive and carry out so deep a policy. Was it a matter of personalities? Or of domestic politics? Were the growing signs of Soviet retrenchment abroad and reform at home under Mikhail Gorbachev so appealing as to be irresistible to policymakers and to politicians who appreciated the impact of Soviet behavior on the public, American as well as European? Détente, after all, has proved to be as popular with the American people as "standing up to the Russians," although only at the right moments, which have usually come along after a phase of high tension.

Is There a Pattern?

This pattern of alternating and mutually generating phases of tension and détente as a feature of American politics since the 1940s can perhaps be found on the larger international stage as well. The foregoing review of the three complete cycles of tension and détente that the allies have experienced since 1949, as well as the first round and the beginnings of a second round of a fourth cycle, gives some reason to believe that every phase of tension generates policies and responses that produce a reaction toward a lessening of tension, and every phase of détente generates policies and responses, and unrealistic hopes, that lay the groundwork for a new phase of tension.

This impression seems supported by the plain fact that the Atlantic Alliance has continued to survive and function throughout these many years. The other plain fact, however, is that on the "relaxation" side of all or most of these phases of tension and détente the question was raised whether the alliance would or should survive as the threat of conflict or crisis in Europe declined. Three factors together explain why the alliance was formed in 1949 and why it has survived since:

1) Throughout all the years since the 1940s the Soviet Union has continued to act in such a way as to appear to most European governments most of the time to pose a threat of some kind to their security. Military attack, intimidation, or subversion were the literal fears in the early years. Even when those concerns lost their acuteness, there remained a lower-level but enduring fear based on Western Europe's unchanging proximity to the power, whatever people thought from one time to another about the intentions, of an immense, heavily armed, totalitarian state whose ideology

and postwar policies in Europe bespoke expansionism. No thaw or détente has changed either the Soviet military and hegemonic presence in Central Europe from 1945 until today or the concerned perceptions of the West European governments of the implications of that stark fact for the well-being of their countries.

2) The European countries sharing this enduring concern about Soviet power and proximity were too weak and divided in 1949 to deal by themselves with the perceived Soviet threat. They therefore solicited and welcomed the American guarantee provided in the North Atlantic Treaty and its embodiment in the continuous elaboration of the alliance structure, military and civilian. The European allies have at no time since then been sufficiently strong or united to deal by themselves with the threat they continued to sense from Soviet power and proximity, nor have they perceived themselves to be, despite their extraordinary economic development and political and social stabilization since the 1940s. Furthermore, to judge by their behavior toward the United States and the alliance through much internal discord and clash of perceived interests over forty years, the Europeans, including even General de Gaulle, have never ceased to value the U.S. guarantee and the alliance system.

3) In 1949 the United States gave a security guarantee to the countries of Western Europe as a central part of its broad policy of containing the further expansion of Soviet and Communist power and influence. Since then it has never departed in principle from containment as the centerpiece of its relationship with the only other world power on its own scale. It has never ceased to act on the assumption that Western Europe remains a highly important area (whatever the claims of other areas on its attention) in which the containment of Soviet power and influence should be pursued. And it has never found a better means to pursue this goal than to maintain the Atlantic Alliance, notwithstanding almost permanent disappointment, exasperation, and even outrage over various actions and failures to act of the European allies.

Americans may have had what seemed to be good reasons over the years for wanting to reduce their material or even political commitments to the security of Western Europe. But their own prevailing perceptions of Soviet strength and relative West European weakness have prevented them from doing so. Because these perceptions have corresponded with those of the allies themselves, the alliance has continued to appeal to the partners on both sides of the Atlantic as the most effective, least costly and least dangerous means available to them for promoting their common interests in the independence, social and political stability, and economic prosperity of Western Europe.

Thoughts about the Future

The current phase of détente has moved at such a rapid pace and taken such forms in 1989 as to raise the question of whether the adversarial confrontation between West and East, the United States and the Soviet Union, may not this time, at last, undergo a diminution of tension and an eradication of its causes so far-reaching as to bring the pattern of the ebb and flow of tension to an end. The issues that gave rise to the confrontation and have maintained it, at least in Europe, might be settled or take on new forms. The Cold War could be over.

However, the end of the system brought about by World War II would not be the end of interstate relations between and among the nuclear superpowers and the countries of Europe. Nor is it likely that their relations, whatever the structure they are given, would cease to be competitive or even adversarial in the familiar way of European interstate relations since time immemorial. The Russian state, long dominant or aspiring to domination in Eastern Europe, is likely to remain an important part of any European state system. The Soviet ideology and system of rule might disappear. The Soviet Union might even fall back for a time to an inward-looking Russia, which, as in the Brest-Litovsk period, would undertake to rebuild its strength in semi-isolation at the eastern end of Europe. But a Russian state populated, endowed, and located as it is, whatever its ideology and institutions, would seem destined over the long term to remain, after the Communist episode as for centuries before it, a permanently great and even ambitious player in the European state system.

That system might differ from the bipolar system we have known in that Russian power for a while, and perhaps for a long time, would weigh rather less heavily on the rest of Europe than it has since 1945. Some of the other European players, particularly Germany, would for that reason have greater freedom of action and would therefore weigh rather more heavily than they have. Possibly the balance of power within Europe would become such that the United States could prudently, with the agreement of its present allies, drastically reduce, if not terminate, its security role.

Perhaps some of the allies would prefer that that not happen. What seems like the free-fall of the Soviet Union will eventually level out, and it may do so in such a way that some of the Western allies would continue to welcome a counterbalancing structural tie with the United States in face of a still powerful, and still nearby, Russia. One conclusion we may remember from the pattern of tension and détente over the last forty years is that the West Europeans have maintained the alliance for decades after they lost their fears of imminent Soviet attack and after the last serious threat of conflict in Europe. Perhaps, in the same way, the perceptions they will hold of their relationships vis-à-vis the Soviet Union will change less than might be expected even in the face of the present drastic changes in the Eastern bloc, at least until, or if, a more united Europe west of Russia thinks itself more able than it has ever been to deal with a vast state that—whether it be liberal democratic, socialist or Russian nationalist—might still be, or become again, so much more powerful than any other European state. Some of the allies might grow more inclined in this direction if the normalization of the European system caused by changes in Moscow's policy allowed it to engage more actively in European diplomatic maneuvering than the rigidity of the Cold War system permitted, thereby creating new concerns in some countries as it aligned itself with others.

In that case, as well as for other reasons, the United States might still wish to supplement its permanently important economic ties with Europe by maintaining a political-security presence there, and, therefore, it might respond positively to those allies that want it to do so. Thus, some kind of Western security-political-economic system might still be desired on both sides of the Atlantic even if, or even because, the mellowing of bolshevism into oblivion were to be followed by the remergence from its ossified shell of a new "old Russia."

In the post-Cold War Europe, then, there will still be something on the one side including Russia, with or without allies, coerced or otherwise, and on the other a balancing grouping of states comprising some of those to the west of Russia plus the United States. This Western group would still be more or less U.S.-led or U.S.-centered, depending on the policies of the new Russia and the strength and unity of the European states in face of that threat. This part of the new European state system might even still be called the Atlantic Alliance, which title remains available, together with many economic and other institutions, for the purpose. The relations between this U.S.-European grouping and Russia might even display a shifting pattern of greater and diminished tension not unlike that which we have known for the last forty years. It is prudent, however, to leave to future historians the task of judging whether some such European system, deideologized and more nearly multipolar than bipolar, will be largely continuous in its structure and dynamics with the post-1945 system of European state relations.

Notes

1. "The Future Tasks of the Alliance (Harmel Report)," in Lawrence S. Kaplan, *NATO and the United States: The Enduring Alliance* (Boston: Twayne, 1988), 223–25.
2. Ibid., 225.
3. Ibid., 224.

Arms Control and Disarmament

Luc Reychler

The Arms Control Imperative

The future of NATO depends on its arms control behavior. There is an overwhelming international expectation and enthusiasm for the success of détente and its major expression, arms control talks and agreements. The activities of the Euro-doves and the reactions of the political establishments have meant that high-profile initiatives in arms control have become a political necessity.[1] To a majority of Europeans, arms control is perceived not only as a solution for redressing their security problems but also as the only solution. To paraphrase Winston Churchill, there is a growing belief that arms control may be the worst solution, except for all others.[2]

To convince public opinion that NATO has done well is not an easy task, first of all because both hawks and doves are inclined to be arms control skeptics. Doves tend to complain about the slowness of negotiations: three years for Strategic Arms Limitations Talks I (SALT I), four years for SALT II (which was not ratified), and fifteen years for mutual and balanced forces reductions (MBFR), which delivered no agreements at all. When these negotiations overlapped changes in the U.S. presidency, real discontinuity resulted, because each new president was inclined to discard what his predecessor had done and to start afresh. Meanwhile, new and often destabilizing technologies have complicated the process.

A second complaint is about the disproportionate attention paid to quantitative rather than qualitative factors. Arms negotiators seem to have become latter-day scholastics, arguing over how many warheads can dance on the head of an intercontinental ballistic missile.[3] By focusing on nuclear or conventional parity, negotiations have discouraged directing attention toward nuclear sufficiency or conventional stability, which are more difficult to count or measure.

A third criticism concerns the "leveling up" impact of negotiations. Since neither side wants to destroy any of its own weapons, limits tend to be set as high or higher than the actual level of armaments. These ceilings may thus stimulate participation in the arms escalation on the part of the side that sees itself behind, instead of constraining the arms race for the benefit of all participants. A related criticism is that arms control negotiations have legitimated the arms race rather than stopping it.

Fourth, there is the so-called balloon effect. As George Rathjens has pointed out, negotiating restrictions is like squeezing a balloon: constrict it in one place, and it pops out somewhere else. For example, the amount of nuclear tests increased after the Limited Test Ban Treaty (LTBT) took effect, and there was an enormous increase in the overall number of warheads on both sides after SALT I.[4]

A fifth and major observation focuses on the negative impact of the belief in bargaining chips and leverage. Bargaining chips are by definition intended to be traded. The United States, for example, might offer to eliminate the MX in return for Soviet agreement to cancel an equivalent missile. By contrast, bargaining leverage is based on the assumption that one has more influence during negotiations if one enters them from a position of strength. Such leverage does not tend to produce concessionary behavior, for a state that is confident in its military power has little incentive to negotiate, whereas a state that is insecure about its military capabilities may be equally reluctant to negotiate seriously, believing itself to be in an inferior bargaining position. The SALT I agreements probably would have been impossible had the Soviet Union not finally approached nuclear parity with the United States.[5] Furthermore, the bargaining chips argument does not always live up to its promises. Not only does it sometimes lead to the development of unneeded or militarily less desirable weapon systems (MX), but it also may delay the withdrawal of such obsolete and redundant weapons as the U.S. *Titan* and the Soviet SS-4 and SS-5.[6]

Finally, hawks point out that two decades of arms control have failed to improve national security. A former assistant secretary of defense under the Reagan administration, Richard Perle, claimed that arms control agreements tend to foster a false sense of security and thus anesthetize the public need for constant vigilance and a posture of military strength: "Democracies will not sacrifice to protect their security in the absence of a sense of danger. And every time we create the impression that we and the Soviets are cooperating and moderating the competition, we diminish that sense of apprehension."[7] Advocates of this position point to the large Soviet nuclear buildup during the 1970s as proof that détente was a dangerous illusion.

These criticisms could lead to the conclusion that NATO's arms control efforts have not been very successful. This conclusion, however, does not take into account the selective perceptual disposition of hawks and doves.

Forty years of arms control provides a huge number of examples that could be highlighted to support any criticism or praise. An objective and balanced analysis of NATO arms control behavior is difficult. It requires the discipline of detachment and access to historical data, of which a great deal is still inaccessible. Despite some interesting research on the politics of arms control, the Soviet Union remains largely a black box,[8] at least through the first forty years of NATO's history.

History of NATO Arms Control

Historical Sketch

In the forty-year history of NATO arms control, six periods can be distinguished.[9] The first period (1949–1954) has been described as the era of largely ritualistic gestures, rhetorical battles, and arms control buildups. In the second period (1954–1957) both alliances failed, perhaps only narrowly, to agree on significant and comprehensive disarmament.[10] The third period (1957–1968) left behind the general and comprehensive disarmament approach. Out of the impasse that developed by the end of the 1950s, there emerged a body of ideas that Hedley Bull called "new thinking,"[11] the belief in the mutual interest in the regulation of arms between adversaries and a determination to destroy the illusions of disarmament, while nonetheless remaining optimistic about the contribution of arms control to improving the prospects of peace and security. Both alliances undertook limited arms control negotiations to constrain their nuclear competition and produced several collateral agreements, such as the LTBT of 1963. The fourth period (1969–1980) was characterized by the two SALT agreements, a greater focus on conventional arms control, and a move from predominantly bilateral to more multilateral negotiations, including MBFR and Conference on Security and Cooperation in Europe (CSCE). The secret diplomacy of the negotiating table increasingly was complemented by public discussion intended to put pressure on the governments by mobilizing public opinion and parliaments. The fifth period (1981–1986) was marked by the fireworks of the new Strategic Arms Reduction Treaty (START), the Strategic Defense Initiative (SDI), and Mikhail Gorbachev's vision of a nuclear-free year 2000—and also by the collapse of arms negotiations. By the mid-1980s the two superpowers found themselves on the brink of a new round of arms competition that neither could afford and from which neither was likely to profit militarily.

We are now in the sixth period, which began in 1987, a watershed year for many reasons. First, there was Black Monday, the day when the New York stock market lost more than 20 percent of its value. It became clear that the United States was badly overextended economically, needed to make budget cuts, and might have to consider scaling down its military commitment to Europe. Second, 1987 was also the year in which the Gorbachev "revolution" reached the world. Many deeds have followed his words and his rhetoric thus cannot be dismissed as propaganda. He signed the intermediate-range nuclear forces (INF) agreement; he allowed START negotiations to make progress; he recognized areas of asymmetry in the conventional strengths of NATO and the Warsaw Pact, allowed more verification, and withdrew militarily from Afghanistan. The major negotiation forums have been START, the Conference on Forces in Europe (CFE), and the Conference on Confidence and Security Building Measures and Disarmament in Europe (CDE). This seems to be a period poised for progress.

Some Trends

Looking back at these forty years of arms control, several trends can be distinguished. First, one notices considerable advances. Although the first two decades brought only limited progress in restricting arms, the next twenty-five years produced several important arms control agreements. Indeed, fruitful negotiations characterize the most recent years.

Second, one notes a move from essentially bilateral negotiations, with the United States and the Soviet Union as the predominant actors up until 1970, to a more multilateral approach. West Europeans in the 1970s began to play a more vital role in arms control dynamics (see Figure 1).[12] Correlated with this multilateral process is a rise in political consultation within NATO. Ten years ago, Luc Crollen, who evaluated NATO's first thirty years of arms control behavior, wrote that "over time these consultations evolved from a purely informative stage in the fifties and early sixties, to exchanges of views prior to national decision making (for instance in meetings of the NATO Senior Political Committee with disarmament experts), to harmonization of policies (CBM's—Confidence-Building Measures), and even to collective decision-making and binding guidance in the case of MBFR."[13] His prediction that the influence of the Europeans was bound to grow was correct.

Third, one notices the increasingly public character of arms control negotiations. The most recent and intensive form of the cross-impact of diplomacy and public debate has been displayed from the time NATO took its "double-track" decision in 1979 right up to the ongoing debate about the modernization of tactical nuclear weapons. The next round of negotiations on conventional arms control is likely to give additional stimuli to this trend toward increasingly "public" arms control negotiations, because the numerous links with various political areas are likely to produce significant public articulation of divergent interests. Additionally, Gorbachev's dynamic style is calculated to maximize support at home and in the West. In earlier years, attempts in the East and West to influence each other's public opinion were asymmetric.[14] The Soviet Union and its allies were able to use the media in the West to mobilize individual groups and parties within the pluralistic structure of Western democracies in favor of its arguments. Western governments did not have the same facilities to influence the East. With *glasnost*, however, public communication is no longer a one-way street. It is therefore probable that the dynamics of mutual influence will intensify and characterize future arms control behavior.

A fourth trend indicates changes in the scope of the negotiations. There have been moves from efforts at general and comprehensive disarmament, to partial, predominantly nuclear arms control negotiations, and then to parallel negotiations in distinctive but interdependent areas of arms control: conventional, chemical, and different types of nuclear weapons. Simultaneously there has been a gradual shift from a narrow to a broader definition of arms control.[15] In the narrow definition, the focus is mainly on the direct control of the military instrument, military decision making, and military doctrine. The broad view distinguishes itself through a shift from a direct to an indirect approach to arms control. Rather than trying to control the military instrument directly, this tactic attempts to shape political and economic incentives at both international and domestic levels to reduce the instrument's usefulness. An example of the broad definition, which is complementary to the narrower approach, is the CSCE process. West Europeans especially strongly believe that both approaches, if successfully pursued, could considerably increase European security.

A fifth, and final, trend is the delegitimation of nuclear deterrence, which has been in progress for several years. Karl Kaiser has observed that the political forces working in that direction span the entire political spectrum and range from President Ronald Reagan (in justifying SDI) and the Catholic bishops of America to the antinuclear protest movements of Western Europe. "A reversal of priorities is involved here: the priority of war prevention as a consequence of the incalculable risk of nuclear war is replaced by the priority of damage limitation dictated by the enormous destructiveness of modern nuclear weapons. And so a more probable conventional war becomes more acceptable than an unprobable nuclear war."[16] In tandem with this trend is a shift to a more reassuring defense approach. One of the key words in the recent European security debate, "reassurance," seems to refer to 1) reassuring one's own people through bolstering confidence in the security policy and 2) reassuring the opponent by the development of a deterring but nonprovocative defense policy. Proposals concerning self-imposed restraints and the coordination of force posture and strategy changes with likely Soviet reactions deal with the

second aim of reassurance. Much of the discussion focuses on the
iatrogenic aspects of present security policy and explores ways to escape the
security dilemma. The confluence of all of these changes is making arms
control negotiations a very complicated and challenging process.

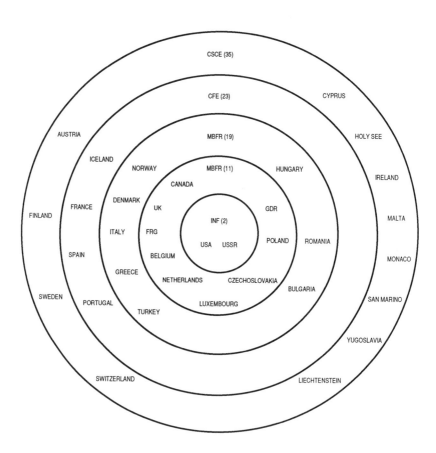

Figure 1.   European Negotiation Forums in the 1980s

Evaluation of Forty Years of Arms Control Efforts

To evaluate the past forty years of arms control efforts, one must look at both formal arms control agreements and informal measures, either tacit or unilateral. Although the former tends to receive most of the attention, the importance of the latter efforts should not be underestimated. Thomas Schelling complains of an underestimation of tacit and informal, unilateral or reciprocated restraints, and a hardening of the belief among diplomats and the public that arms control has to be embedded in treaties.[17] Among the many examples of informal arms control is the development of fail-safe devices. The risk of accidental nuclear war has, if anything, receded with the perfection of electronic safety locks. Nuclear weapons have become more immune to unauthorized use with the centralization of the nuclear release decision by both sides.[18] Another example is the French assurance that they will behave as if they were signatories of the Non-Proliferation Treaty, although they were not willing to sign it. Equally significant was the Reagan administration's de facto adherence to SALT II despite the president's opposition to the 1979 treaty.

Some Results

Negotiations and agreements are largely responsible for advances in arms control. Nearly twenty agreements have been signed dealing with nuclear weapons:

1) limitations on the testing of nuclear weapons: Partial Test Ban Treaty (1963), Threshold Test Ban Treaty (1974), Peaceful Nuclear Explosion Treaty (1976);
2) conventions establishing nuclear free zones: Antarctic Treaty (1952), Outer Space Treaty (1967), Treaty of Tlatelolco (1969), Non-Proliferation Treaty (1970), Seabed Treaty (1971);
3) treaties imposing limits, reductions, and even the elimination of certain nuclear weapons: SALT I ABM Treaty (1972), SALT I Executive Agreement (1972), SALT II Treaty (1978), INF (1987); and
4) agreements to communicate, avoid misunderstandings, and build confidence: Hot Line Agreement (1963, with upgradings in 1971 and mid-1980s), Nuclear Accidents Agreement (1971), High Seas Agreements (1972), Agreement of Basic Principles (1972), Nuclear War Prevention Agreement (1973), the Ballistic Missile Launch Notification Treaty and the creation of the Nuclear Risk Reduction Center (1987).

Agreements have focused on other weapons areas, too. Thus, in 1972 a Biological Weapons Agreement was signed, prohibiting the development, production, and stockpiling of biological weapons. Chemical weapons talks have been conducted in Geneva. Limited progress has been made on conventional weapons, which consume a lion's share of the defense budgets. The MBFR negotiations lasted fifteen years and died in 1988 without tangible results. Some confidence-building measures, however, resulted from the CSCE in 1975 (Helsinki accords) and the CDE, which ended in 1986.

At the moment, several important negotiations are going on with respect to strategic weapons (START), weapons in space, chemical weapons, and conventional forces. The latter takes place in two forums: the CFE between the sixteen NATO nations (including France) and the seven Warsaw Pact states, which concentrates on the whole of Europe; and the follow-on CDE among all thirty-five CSCE participating states.

Meaning of Arms Control

What have these efforts achieved? Have they been successful in controlling arms? The answer depends on what is meant by "controlling arms." Despite an identity crisis in the field of arms control, there exists a considerable consensus about its goals.[19] Traditionally, arms control measures have been expected to reduce 1) the chances of war, 2) destruction in case of war, and 3) security costs. Most authors, however, add that all of this should be achieved while maintaining or increasing national security at objective and subjective levels. Subjective security refers to the perceived probability of a system's survival. A situation can only be described as secure when both subjective and objective security are present. A situation is very risky when people feel secure in an objectively insecure environment. Equally undesirable is an objectively secure situation in which people feel insecure and thus tend to engage in greater defense efforts than are needed. Not only are such efforts expensive, but they also reinforce an image of aggressiveness.

Arms Reduction and Disarmament

If the meaning of arms control is arms reduction and disarmament, then success has been minimal. Although the INF agreement contributed to an abrupt reversal of "vertical proliferation" (the continued multiplication and elaboration of the nuclear arsenals of the superpowers), it only eliminated about 3 percent of the nuclear arsenal. Successful START negotiations could eliminate another 25 to 50 percent, but the world still would be left with an ample stock of nuclear weapons. A single submarine of the *Trident* class, armed with twenty-four missiles, carries within its hull the equivalent in destructive force of eight wars on the scale of World War II.[20] Nuclear, conventional, and chemical weapons are being modernized. Controls on qualitative improvements are practically nonexistent. What exists now is a large arms control net with very big holes. This net is woven at a glacial pace. Doves do not even see progress; they criticize arms control because they believe that it has no impact whatsoever upon the arms buildup of any state.

The conclusion that arms control has proceeded at a glacial pace, creating a net with very large holes, is correct, but it overlooks some of the more positive results. Arms control has established limits on certain kinds of vertical and horizontal proliferation and has produced some reductions.[21]

Stability

People who ignore the positive results tend to confuse the concepts of arms control and disarmament. The latter aims for a reduction of armaments down to the basic minimum for domestic policing. In contrast, arms control is concerned with constraint and stability—crisis stability, arms race stability, and political stability.[22] Crisis stability requires a lack of incentive to strike first, arms race stability a lack of incentive for either party to expand or modernize its arsenal. Political stability is determined by the effectiveness of deterrence in reducing incentives for major coercive changes. From this point of view, one can distinguish regions where arms control has been more successful and others where it has been less. Some areas have become peace islands, or "pluralistic security communities," including Western Europe and North America. The term "pluralistic security community" refers to a group of countries in which the expectation of peace and peaceful change among them is considered a given. Whereas Gorbachev's "European house" is still a vision, the "Atlantic house" is a given. Allowing it to decay would mean a regression in history.

Other areas of the world are characterized by armed peace and by détente. For over forty years there has been no war between NATO and Warsaw Pact countries, and, in Schelling's words, "we have realized what ought to be an important source of reassurance, a confidence-building experience: 40 years of nuclear weapons without nuclear war."[23] Although it has been customary to see arms control as the handmaiden of deterrence, designed to make deterrence more effective and to cost less, it also is appropriate to see deterrence itself as a major arms control endeavor, particularly deterrence based on nuclear weapons, when the ultimate goal is never to have to use them.[24] Several arms control measures have considerably increased deterrence and crisis stability: NATO has established, tacitly as well as explicitly by agreements, a network of communications and rules of behavior that allows a remarkable and unparalleled degree of crisis management. Also, with respect to conventional weapons, a whole series of confidence-building measures has been approved or is being discussed.

The Stockholm Conference in 1984 was different from most arms control negotiations in that it addressed not the capabilities for war—the number of weapons and troops—but rather the most likely causes of war: flawed judgments and miscalculations derived from fears of sudden attack and uncertainty about the military intentions of an adversary.[25] Although the recent MBFR talks have not led to arms reductions, they have succeeded in preventing unilateral reductions by the United States that would have jeopardized the solidarity and military capability of Western Europe and the stability of central Europe. Furthermore, as the conference served as a de facto multilateral standing consultative committee within and between alliances to exchange information and to question suspicious deployments, it may have helped to defuse destabilizing situations.[26] Perhaps the most important benefit of arms control talks is that they have reduced uncertainties about the strategic thinking and the weapons programs of adversaries. The reduction of uncertainty and the enhancement of predictability in the armament programs of the two alliances has weakened the arguments for worst-case analyses and provided more room for better-case analyses.

Bordering on the peace islands and areas of détente on the world map, there are regions that still convey an icy Cold War atmosphere, such as North and South Korea. Moreover, a large part of the globe is characterized by violence. At the end of 1987, thirty-six major armed conflicts were being waged.[27] Fortunately, a third world war has not occurred, but there have been many Third World wars. By contrast, NATO's arms control efforts have been successful; even if they have not brought large-scale arms reduction, they have secured the stability of the northern part of the world.

Subjective Security

Arms control has accomplished more in the past two decades than is sometimes realized by those who point to the absence of deep reductions. Objective security is partially reflected in subjective public opinion; 86.3 percent of the Belgians, for example, do not feel threatened by the Soviet Union.[28] Paradoxically, however, a large part of public opinion continues to feel threatened and tends to attribute a major part of the responsibility for this to NATO. This does not mean that support for NATO is dwindling. The autumn 1988 figure in West Germany favoring NATO membership was 86 percent. This is equally true of the younger generation, which otherwise holds markedly different views on almost all political issues: In the autumn of 1988, 78 percent of those sixteen to twenty-four years old were in favor of staying in NATO, as against 15 percent who wanted the country to quit.[29] The alliance is still strongly supported, but its supporters have become critical.

Perceptions of the Soviet Union no longer appear to be the primary determinant of support for Western policy toward the Soviet Union. Rather, the key factor appears to be attitudes toward military power, Soviet or Western.[30] The growth of military power is often considered to be the primary threat to security. More arms are believed to enhance the chances of conflict. People tend to focus more on how NATO policy may threaten peace and less on the military requirements for maintaining security. There seems to be a conviction that NATO, which has provided security, remains simultaneously necessary and, in and of itself, a possible source of insecurity. The result is a strong preference for arms control measures over defense improvements in most member states, including the United States.[31]

Several conditions have reinforced the negative appraisal of NATO's past arms control behavior. First, during a period of tightening national finances, arms control as a method of coping with burden sharing and budget problems looks very attractive. Second, the lack of a widely accepted *gesammtkonzept* with respect to arms control tends to force the alliance into a reactive approach at a time when a great deal of public opinion would like to see a more active policy. Finally, public opinion is impatient and unfamiliar with the complexities of international relations. The negative image of NATO is, in Lawrence Freedman's opinion, partially self-inflicted. If Gorbachev's concessions to Western demands are eroding popular support for NATO's security policies, it is, according to Freedman, because of the way these policies were sold. It has often been easier to sell a "threat" than to explain the complexities of international affairs. Consequently, there has been a dangerous swing from Cold War belligerence to the euphoria of détente.[32] A better understanding of international politics, in general, and arms control, in particular, would considerably reduce the attribution of most of the responsibility for insecurity to NATO. A thorough analysis of forty years of arms control by NATO would provide a better understanding not only of the constraints under which the decision makers operated but also of the available opportunities.

Arms Control Enhancing and Inhibiting Conditions

Looking back at the past four decades of arms control experience, it is possible to distinguish arms control enhancing and inhibiting factors. They can be clustered into seven groups.

First Cluster: Outer- and Interalliance Relations

POWER SYMMETRY. One of the greatest obstacles to disarmament and arms control is the fact that nations are less concerned with what they are than with what they would like to be.[33] Most nations do not like to be in an inferior position. Negotiations between NATO and the Warsaw Pact about the limitation of nuclear weapons did not succeed as long as the USSR occupied an inferior position. 1969 was a turning point in arms control negotiation, because in that year the Soviet Union approached numerical parity in strategic delivery vehicles.[34]

DÉTENTE. NATO's interest in disarmament and arms control can be traced back to the first thaw in East-West relations. Distrust and tension are major obstacles confronting arms control and disarmament. The United States, in particular, has insisted over the years that arms control is dependent upon the peaceful resolution of political disputes. The Soviet invasion of Afghanistan in December 1979 contributed to the derailing of SALT II, and the continuing crisis in Iran distracted the Carter administration from the issue of SALT II ratification. It is difficult to decouple regional and other conflicts from the arms control process. "Admittedly, a high level of distrust generated by political differences," according to Lloyd Jensen, "is hardly conducive to creating the sort of environment necessary to reach a consensus on disarmament issues, but low levels of tension reduce the incentives for doing anything about the arms problems."[35]

PREDICTABILITY OF DEVELOPMENTS IN OUTER-SPACE ARMS CONTROL AREA. The Soviet Union made it clear that it was unwilling to begin SALT negotiations until the NATO negotiations were completed. It wanted to make sure that other countries, such as West Germany or Japan, did not acquire such weapons.

PERCEPTION OF COMMON THREAT. The diffusion of arms to the Third World, including the threat of nuclear proliferation, and the spread of long-range ballistic missiles, will make that part of the world considerably more dangerous. The imminence of that common danger could drive both alliances to act together to inhibit further developments.[36]

Second Cluster: Military Strategic Thinking

WAR WARINESS AND ALARMING EXPERIENCES. The memories of recent alarming experiences tend to boost arms control efforts. The 1962 Cuban missile crisis, for example, produced the hotline and focused attention on nuclear arms control.

AWARENESS OF THE LIMITS AND POSSIBLE DANGERS OF THE MILITARY INSTRUMENT. Several factors have contributed to this awareness. First, the diffusion of military power over the world has reduced the effectiveness of the use of weapons. Second, the growth of nonmilitary threats to national security, and the inability of military power to cope with these threats, has diminished some of the military's perceived usefulness. Finally, East and West alike are more aware of the danger of uncontrolled arms races. The recent use by NATO Secretary-General Manfred Wörner of the term "common security" is a clear indicator of the awareness that survival requires cooperation.[37]

DOCTRINAL CHANGE. Richard Nixon's replacement of "superiority" by "sufficiency" prepared the terrain for SALT. Gorbachev's call for radical arms control also can be seen as the culmination of an evolving Soviet doctrine on nuclear and conventional wars.[38] Progress in controlling arms, as during the 1970s, was enabled by the shared convictions that neither country could hope to maintain a meaningful military advantage and that the limitation of U.S. and strategic nuclear forces was therefore both possible and desirable.[39]

MEASURING AND COMPARING MILITARY POWER. The lack of agreed-upon data and the difficulty of measuring and comparing forces can also pose major obstacles to successful negotiations.

BIPOLAR THINKING IN A MULTIPOLAR WORLD. In his analysis of arms control between the United States and the Soviet Union, Coit Blacker observes that bipolarity has tended to promote rigid thinking that narrows the range of options considered by policymakers. The United States, for example, was slow to perceive the unraveling of the Sino-Soviet alliance in the late 1950s and even slower to explore how the split between Moscow and Beijing might enable it to improve relations with both. The Soviet Union, for its part, initially resisted the diplomatic overtures of West German Chancellor Willy Brandt in the late 1960s directed toward normalizing relations between Bonn and Moscow, overtures that eventually led to the conclusion of a series of mutually advantageous agreements between the Federal Republic of Germany and the countries of Eastern Europe, including the Soviet Union.[40]

Third Cluster: Technological Developments

Although technology might enhance arms control by providing better verification techniques, technological change is often an impediment to successful negotiation. The belief that one might develop the ultimate weapon or the ultimate defensive system leads decision makers to reject restraints on military research and development. This tendency, coupled with the fear that the opponent may break out of any agreed arms control restraints, generates conservatism in arms control policy as decision makers seek to keep their options open. Moreover, technology may contribute to peaceful activities as well as military purposes, making negotiations on arms control exceedingly difficult. Past attempts to control nuclear energy have made this abundantly clear.[41]

Fourth Cluster: Verification

Edward Luttwak has noted that arms control without confidence in verification is a contradiction in terms. In the absence of adequate verification procedures, arms control may increase rather than reduce incentives for force building and the risk of conflict.[42] Breakthroughs in verification technology and the increased willingness of the Soviet Union to accept more extensive and intrusive verification has considerably facilitated the negotiation of agreements.

Fifth Cluster: Domestic Variables

OPEN DEMOCRATIC POLITICAL SYSTEMS. The current democratization of the Warsaw Pact countries is a most effective confidence builder. Without progress in internal détente (that is, democratization of the relations within and between the East European countries), external détente efforts would never have been able to produce full détente.

GOVERNMENT CONSENSUS ABOUT SECURITY POLICY. Progress on arms control is complicated by the fact that positions taken are often dictated by the domestic political situation. Nixon's distractions over Watergate paralyzed the SALT II negotiations. Lack of consensus about security policy also inhibits progress. The most difficult negotiations on arms control often occur within governments rather than between.

PUBLIC PRESSURE. The balance of public pressures among hawks, doves, and owls is also a major variable. For example, the environmental consequences of nuclear test explosions mobilized public opinion against the above-ground testing of nuclear weapons. Peace organizations are now better organized, nationally and internationally, and have a significant impact on policymaking.

SUCCESSOR GENERATIONS. Recent political changes in Europe cannot be understood without taking into account the world views of the successor generation, for whom Munich, Pearl Harbor, and the genesis of the Cold War are merely lessons learned in a diplomatic history course.

ECONOMIC CONSIDERATIONS. Economic pressures in Eastern and Western Europe demand that military security be provided in a more cost-effective way. In Western Europe, defense budget increases are politically close to impossible. In Eastern Europe those economic pressures are called *perestroika*.

DEMOGRAPHIC DECLINE. Taking NATO as a whole, by the year 2000 several member states will see the number of their eighteen- to twenty-year-old men decline by over 20 percent. While the underlying reasons for working toward mutual manpower reductions are not identical, it is in the interest of both East and West to reach such an accord over the next decade.[43]

Sixth Cluster: Negotiation Machinery and Approach

NEGOTIATING INFRASTRUCTURE. The creation of the Arms Control and Disarmament Agency (ACDA) in the United States in 1961 provided the necessary infrastructure for preparing and evaluating negotiations. NATO also has seen a gradual strengthening of its arms control machinery. As a consequence of the 1967 Harmel Report, the Senior Political Committee (SPC) was created in 1968. During the same year a new section was established at NATO's international secretariat to deal with disarmament and arms control matters.[44] Since then, this negotiating machinery has been considerably expanded.

THE ABSENCE OF RHETORIC. American adherence to the privacy rule during the SALT I negotiations apparently impressed the Soviet Union. Privacy helps to minimize the rhetorical and propaganda content of negotiating positions and maximizes their flexibility in changing and compromising. Moreover, proposals that take into account the security interests of all concerned parties and that try not to freeze them into inferior positions tend to have a higher rate of success.

THE EXISTENCE OF A NEGOTIATION HABIT. The development of a "negotiation habit" is a positive arms control asset. Success in Geneva or in Vienna would increase chances for more far-reaching arms control in the future.

Seventh Cluster: Intra-alliance Consensus Achievements

In a pluralistic security community such as NATO, consensus building is a slow process. The interests of the different parties within and among the member states are multifaceted and often divergent. Stakes and risks are often too high for bold initiatives or clever proposals to surface. Consequently, initiatives as well as agreements often reflect the lowest common denominator.[45] The tedious process of consensus building is greatly responsible for NATO's cautious response toward Gorbachev's barrage of arms control proposals. An overwhelming popular majority endorses the values that NATO represents. But the present conjunction of real changes, uncertainties, and expectations is without precedent since the creation of the alliance.[46] Consequently, NATO's arms control behavior has become the focus of intense debate, and the demand for a new and integrating arms control concept is unrelenting.[47] Observing these lively and sometimes overheated debates, one analyst writes of widening gaps in strategic cultures.[48] Also indicative of discord is the increased construction of intellectual taxonomies for the debates.[49]

Conclusion

The achievement of a new arms control consensus is urgent. Western leadership, or the lack of it, will make the difference between using or missing arms control opportunities that have now appeared between the Soviet Union and its allies and NATO. Successful arms control has been related in no small measure to the interests and persuasiveness of top leadership. Presidents John F. Kennedy and Jimmy Carter were arguably the most enthusiastic about arms control, but Nixon with the assistance of Henry Kissinger was among the most successful as he negotiated the SALT I agreements and ushered in an era of détente. President Reagan and his advisers, on the other hand, were the most hostile toward arms control until the Reykjavík summit and INF Treaty in the last years of their administration.[50]

Until now, NATO has been a caretaker and not a mover, a role that Gorbachev seems to have accepted. The rather passive, reactive role of the Western countries is partly due to their uncertainty about what direction they should be taking. It would be a great mistake for them to continue to react to new arms control proposals without having first decided what their strategy should be in this new era of international relations.

The arms control challenge to the alliance is, first and foremost, to create a viable security and arms control concept and to rally public support around it. Only when the alliance has achieved this new security consensus will West European leaders be able to lead public opinion to support a sound arms control policy.[51] The greatest challenge for the alliance will be to build a "European house" without destroying détente and the "Atlantic house."

Notes

1. James H. Wyllie, *European Security in the Nuclear Age* (Oxford, England: Basil Blackwell, 1986), 5, 77.
2. Robert A. Levine, *NATO, the Subjective Alliance* (Santa Monica, CA: RAND Corporation, 1988), 171.
3. David P. Barash, *The Arms Race and Nuclear War* (Belmont, CA: Wadsworth, 1987), 249.

4. George Rathjens, "The Dynamics of the Arms Race," *Scientific American* 220, no. 4 (April 1969): 15–25. See also D. Coit Blacker and Gloria Duffy, eds., *International Arms Control*, 2d ed. (Palo Alto, CA: Stanford University Press, 1984).

5. Lloyd Jensen, *Bargaining for National Security: The Postwar Disarmament Negotiations* (Columbia: University of South Carolina Press, 1988), 81–85.

6. Ibid., p. 84.

7. Barash, *The Arms Race*, 250–51.

8. David Holloway, *The Soviet Union and the Arms Race* (New Haven: Yale University Press, 1983); Congressional Research Service, Library of Congress, *Soviet Diplomacy and Negotiating Behavior, 1979–88: New Tests for U.S. Diplomacy* (Washington, DC: Government Printing Office, 1988), 1–876.

9. See D. Coit Blacker, *Reluctant Warriors: The United States, the Soviet Union and Arms Control* (New York: W. H. Freeman, 1987).

10. Thomas C. Schelling, "What Went Wrong with Arms Control?" *Foreign Affairs* 64, no. 2 (1985–86): 219–33; Blacker and Duffy, eds., *International Arms Control*, 94.

11. See Hedley Bull, *The Control of the Arms Race: Disarmament and Arms Control in the Missile Age* (London: International Institute of Strategic Studies, 1961).

12. Jane Sharp, "Conventional Arms Control in Europe: Problems and Prospects," in *SIPRI Yearbook 1988: World Armaments and Disarmament* (Oxford, England: Oxford University Press, 1988), 315–37.

13. Luc Crollen, "NATO and Arms Control," in Lawrence Kaplan and Robert Clawson, eds., *NATO after Thirty Years* (Wilmington, DE: Scholarly Resources, 1981), 236.

14. Karl Kaiser, "Conventional Arms Control: The Future Agenda," *The World Today* 44, no. 2 (February 1988): 22–27.

15. See John Barton and Ryuckicki Imai, eds., *Arms Control II: A New Approach to International Security* (Cambridge, MA: Oelgeschlager, Gunn and Hain, 1981); and R. Rudney and Luc Reychler, *European Security beyond the Year 2000* (New York: Praeger, 1988), 292–93.

16. Kaiser, "Conventional Arms Control," 23.

17. Schelling, "What Went Wrong with Arms Control?" 219–33.

18. Christoph Bertram, "Europe's Security Dilemmas," *Foreign Affairs* 65, no. 5 (Summer 1987): 943–57.

19. Luc Reychler, "Arms Control Evaluation: A Joint Search for Objective Criteria" (Paper for Institute of International Peace Studies, Kyung Hee University, Korea, 1986).

20. Blacker, "Reluctant Warriors," 1.

21. Harvard Nuclear Study Group, *Living with Nuclear Weapons* (Cambridge, MA: Harvard University Press, 1983).

22. Joseph Nye, "Farewell to Arms Control," *Foreign Affairs* 65, no. 1 (Fall 1986): 1–20.

23. Schelling, "What Went Wrong with Arms Control?" 219–233.

24. Patrick Morgan, "Arms Control in International Politics: Some Theoretical Reflections" (Paper for Center for International and Strategic Affairs, University of California, Los Angeles, 1988).

25. Wyllie, *European Security*, 134–35.

26. William P. Boyd, "The Once and Future Quest: European Arms Control— Issues and Prospects," in Robert Kennedy and John Weinstein, eds., *The Defense of*

the West: Strategic and European Security Issues Reappraised (Boulder, CO: Westview Press, 1984), 375–412.

27. Kenneth Wilson and Peter Wallensteen, "Major Conflicts in 1987," in *SIPRI Yearbook 1988*, 285–300.

28. Public opinion polls published in *HUMO* (Brussels), 6 April 1989.

29. *German Tribune*, no. 1361 (5 March 1989): 2.

30. Gregory Flynn and Hans Rattinger, eds., *The Public and Atlantic Defense* (London: Croom Helm, 1985), 370–78.

31. Ibid., 372–73.

32. Lawrence Freedman, "Managing Alliance," *Foreign Policy*, no. 71 (Summer 1988): 65–85.

33. John Stoessinger, *Why Nations Go to War*, 2d ed. (New York: St. Martin's, 1978), 237.

34. Blacker and Duffy, eds., *International Arms Control*, 220.

35. Jensen, *Bargaining for National Security*, 250.

36. Philip Schrag, "The New Age in Arms Control Negotiations: The Case for a Multilateral Ballistic Missile Treaty," *Georgetown University Law Center Magazine* (Fall 1988): 8–9; Lord Zuckerman, "The World without INF," *New York Review of Books* 35 (2 June 1988): 36–40.

37. Pierre Harmel, *L'Alliance Atlantique et la Sécurité de l'Europe* (Paper presented at the Western European Union, 20 February 1989).

38. Mary C. Fitzgerald, "The Strategic Revolution behind Soviet Arms Control," *Arms Control Today* (June 1987): 16–19.

39. Blacker, *Reluctant Warriors*, 134.

40. Ibid., 21.

41. Jensen, *Bargaining for National Security*, 250.

42. Edward Luttwak, "Why Arms Control has Failed," *Commentary* 65, no. 1 (January 1978): 24.

43. Susan L. Clark, "Who Will Staff NATO?" *Orbis* 37, no. 4 (Fall 1988): 521–39.

44. Crollen, "NATO and Arms Control," 215–36.

45. Boyd, "The Once and Future Quest," 395.

46. François Heisbourgh, "The Three Ages of NATO Strategy," *NATO Review* 37, no. 1 (February 1989): 24–29.

47. Robert Blackwell, "Conceptual Problems of Conventional Arms Control," *International Security* 12, no. 4 (Spring 1988): 28–47; Jonathan Dean, *Watershed in Europe* (Lexington, MA: Lexington Books, 1987).

48. Robin Ranger, "Contrasting Models of Arms Control in European Security," in Davis S. Yost, ed., *NATO Strategic Options: Arms Control and Defense* (New York: Pergamon, 1981), 63–84.

49. See Michael Krepon, *Strategic Stalemate: Nuclear Weapons and Arms Control in American Politics* (New York: St. Martin's, 1984). A particularly interesting analysis is Robert A. Levine, *NATO: The Subjective Alliance* (Santa Monica, CA: RAND Corporation, 1988).

50. Jensen, *Bargaining for National Security*, 57.

51. James Thomson, *The Arms Control Challenge to the Alliance* (address to the North Atlantic Assembly in Plenary Session, Oslo, 25 September 1987), 1.

Defense, Deterrence, and the Central Front: Around the Nuclear Threshold

William H. Park

When analyzing NATO's military arrangements, it is tempting to be guided by the logic of strategic thinking, or "strategism" as it has been called.[1] Yet force levels, capabilities, structures, and deployments, and the threat perceptions that lie behind them, typically emerge from a wide range of sometimes crosscutting determinants. Economic, organizational, political, societal, and historical factors may partially explain why a given military force structure is what it is. The scope for military and strategic incoherence is even greater where alliances are concerned, for not only will such factors be operating within each member state in turn, but also there can be little guarantee that the armed forces of the various member states will harmonize or that their security interests and perceptions will coincide. Of course, the very fact that an alliance exists suggests counterpressures militating against absolute divergence. Furthermore, the internal dynamics, needs, and norms of an alliance may erode any awkward diversity. Nevertheless, it remains true that neither NATO's current strategy nor the composition of its aggregated forces reflect a rational arrangement. The strategy is a compromise, the forces are a composite, and any current analysis of NATO must work with the legacies of past debates, decisions, and developments. It is unlikely that anyone trying to create a more ideal political and military posture for NATO would want to start from here, from where we are today. It is also unlikely that NATO's overall posture in the future will ever mirror some strategically determined ideal, or even that there will be a consensus on what such an ideal might look like.

These points are especially germane to NATO's central European posture. In many respects the alliance grew out of the circumstances of central Europe at the close of World War II, for here the threat seemed greater and the stakes higher. NATO's most important European members, the Federal Republic of Germany (FRG), France, and Great Britain, were all crucially involved, as were some of its smaller adherents. For all of Washington's early dominance, NATO's disposition on the central front was bound to be characterized by the intermeshings of an alliance of sovereign states. No one state's perception of the threat, nor of what could or should be done to meet it, could enjoy omnipotence.

Additionally, the closed and centralized nature of the Soviet system and the geographical and political asymmetries between NATO and its eastern counterpart ensured that NATO would begin life on the defensive, at least in central Europe and where conventional forces were concerned. The Soviet Union did not demobilize at the same heady pace and to the same extent as did its wartime allies in the West, and those of its forces that did return home enjoyed a greater geographical proximity to the middle of Europe than did U.S.-based American forces. Moscow was also in a position to impose on its new "allies" in Europe more substantial military efforts than their economies could healthily afford. That the imbalance in conventional forces between NATO and what was to become the Warsaw Pact was overstated, probably grossly so, has been known to analysts of NATO strategy at least since the findings of U.S. Defense Secretary Robert McNamara's staff became public during the 1960s and the 1971 publication of Alain C. Enthoven and K. Wayne Smith's *How Much Is Enough?*.[2] Nevertheless, what to do about the perceived conventional force threat in central Europe was the first major problem confronting NATO's force planners at the alliance's inception.

The collective response to this problem, seemingly made more urgent by the outbreak of the Korean War in 1950, was the Lisbon force goals of February 1952. These objectives called for the creation of ninety-six divisions to be available in Europe within thirty days of an order to mobilize (M+30). About thirty-five ready divisions were required in Europe, and, of these, twenty-five were to be stationed on the central front. It was anticipated that these forces, to be achieved by 1954, would be capable of holding off a force between two or three times as large without resorting to nuclear weapons.[3] Yet in October 1953, National Security Document 162/2 (NSC-162/2) declared that the U.S. government would be prepared to use tactical nuclear weapons (TNWs) in any major conflict in Europe. This readiness was echoed by the full North Atlantic Council in December 1954. Around this time a buildup of TNWs in Europe began, which was to reach a total in excess of seven thousand by the mid-1960s. It is worth noting that the Lisbon force goals were abandoned in December 1953, before the issue of German rearmament had been settled. This is not an insignificant detail, given that the German armed forces were planned to expand to five hundred thousand and thus become NATO's largest force in Europe. As the crisis in Korea subsided, NATO lost the sense of urgency that had fueled the massive rearmament effort following the outbreak of the Korean War. Washington reverted to its "long haul" concept of force planning, which implied long-term competition with the Soviet Union rather than imminent war.[4] Defense programs elsewhere in NATO were stretched out and budgets cut. The British government, for example, announced cuts in its defense program on the very day the Lisbon Conference opened in 1952. Thus, with the waning of the Korean scare and the death of Joseph Stalin in 1953, the mood in NATO became rather relaxed with respect to the imminence of war in Europe and hence to the immediate significance of its own conventional military inferiority.

Thus NATO's endeavors, if they can be called that, to provide the capabilities and strategy to defend Europe without resort to nuclear weapons were short-lived and half-hearted. NATO was born more or less simultaneously with the nuclear age, and from the outset the strategies of the alliance have reflected that fact. Indeed, from Washington's perspective, the function of NATO's conventional forces was initially to hold up the Soviet hordes only for as long as it took America's effective nuclear monopoly to bombard the Soviet Union into submission. The preferred option was that the Europeans should provide the bulk of these nonnuclear assets. However, the British were hardly tardier than the Americans in shifting toward a nuclear emphasis; nor was French thinking so far behind. The position of the Federal Republic was from the outset sensitive and pivotal: It was on the front line, denied the nuclear option, and expected to provide a lion's share of the conventional capability to an alliance whose leading members had moved very early to a pronounced faith in nuclear weapons.

The effect on NATO's overall posture of the Eisenhower administration's New Look and the thinking associated with it was profound and confusing. This focus on the attributes of nuclear weapons and on the cost and substitutability of conventional forces served to undermine further the will of the Europeans to make inordinate sacrifices in a seemingly forlorn effort to close the perceived force imbalance with the Eastern bloc. If a major conflict with the Soviet Union had broken out during the 1950s, Washington likely would have resorted to a large-scale use of nuclear weapons at a fairly early stage. NSC-162/2, adopted as national policy on 30 October 1953, asserted: "In the event of hostilities the United States will consider nuclear weapons to be as available for use as other munitions."[5] Numerous statements to the same effect were made by American officials, not least the president, throughout the 1950s. There seemed little point in the European allies preparing to fight a long war, and this mood was reinforced by the expanded availability of TNWs. Even as the threat to launch nuclear strikes against the Soviet homeland appeared to lose credibility as the 1950s progressed, reliance on the battlefield use of nuclear weapons mounted.

Many factors drove the development of TNWs, and indeed of the New Look as a whole, but clearly their introduction into the European theater can be explained only partly by NATO's assumed relative weakness in nonnuclear forces. Many in the American and other NATO armed services were attracted by the supposed military utility of TNWs. They could either destroy attacking forces or require them to disperse, thus weakening their offensive punch. President Dwight D. Eisenhower remarked that, if TNWs were used on strictly military targets and for strictly military purposes, he saw no reason why they should not be used just exactly as one would use "a bullet or anything else." TNWs were to be deployed to deter war from occurring—which had particular appeal to Europeans, on whose territory war would be fought—and they were to be substituted for conventional forces to fight war more effectively and cheaply should it break out. There was a kind of circularity to NATO's position at this time that never quite disappeared: Nuclear weapons were needed to make up for NATO's conventional force shortfall, and it was possible to live with the conventional inferiority because TNWs could fill the gap. The activities of military and scientific lobbies, and the possibly mistaken assumption that TNWs offered defense on the cheap, seem to have contributed to a rather loosely supervised production and deployment momentum imperfectly related to any centrally determined overview of military requirements. TNWs were developed and thus produced. Once produced, they had to be deployed, and Europe became the home for an ever-increasing number of them.

The 1955 inclusion of the Federal Republic in NATO, while bringing with it the undoubted benefit of that country's armed forces, also burdened NATO with the militarily thorny problem of forward defense. It could no longer be NATO's policy to regard Germany, East as well as West, as little more than a killing ground, a battlefield. German membership highlighted and complicated the issue of the use of TNWs. Could it make sense to use them on territory that NATO was committed to defend? The famous, or infamous, Carte Blanche exercise of 1955 raised serious doubts, at least in West Germany.[6] And, if the answer were to be yes, at what stage in the battle should their use be contemplated? The stockpiling of TNWs in Europe, which began in the 1950s and which an almost blind momentum seems to have carried into the 1960s, took place with little reference to these dilemmas.[7] There was considerable heart-searching in the Federal Republic, though, whose double misfortune it was to provide a large chunk of the battleground and to begin its conventional rearmament "at the height of the age of nuclear euphoria."[8] This unease continues to find expression in West Germany.

McNamara, Deterrence, and Defense

It fell to Robert McNamara, the defense secretary of the new John F. Kennedy administration, to put these issues on NATO's open agenda. He sought to make sense of the complicated and confused relationship between NATO's assumed conventional force inferiority and its growing bias toward nuclear weapons, and he raised the issue of the relationships between conventional and nuclear war fighting and between deterrence and defense. His attempts to clarify these uncertainties and to put NATO strategy on a more coherent military basis uncovered quite substantial differences of opinion within the alliance that have continued to bedevil NATO's military and strategic debates ever since. His most complete statement on TNWs was a draft presidential memorandum of 1965 on the "Role of Tactical Nuclear Forces in NATO Strategy."[9] First, the document argued, given the likelihood of a two-sided use of TNWs and the high levels of attrition that would result, it was far from clear that TNWs could somehow compensate NATO for any conventional force inferiority. Second, the only clear "firebreak," or threshold, was that between nuclear and nonnuclear forces. The consequences of any nuclear use were uncertain, probably uncontrollable, and possibly devastating. Third, McNamara did not believe that Washington's European allies would be prepared to see even a limited nuclear war fought on their territory. Their declaratory stance had to be distinguished from their likely behavior in a conflict. Finally, he saw no reason to be depressed by the East-West balance in conventional forces and believed that they might be sufficient even in the absence of the largely qualitative improvements for which he called. Furthermore, conventional forces should be maintained at whatever level was required to render resort to nuclear weapons unnecessary.

The ideas contained in the memorandum were featured in many of the speeches and statements made by McNamara and members of his staff during the early 1960s. Although the TNW stockpile in Europe continued to expand and Washington stopped well short of either proposing its removal or forswearing its use, the reaction in Europe to the voices emanating from Washington was fierce, although far from uniform or united.[10] Only the French went so far as to withdraw from the alliance's military structure as a consequence of the debate over flexible response, but French thinking had powerful echoes in London, Bonn, and elsewhere.

The furor surrounding McNamara's ideas revealed that NATO had multiple military objectives and that these objectives were not necessarily consistent.[11] All members of the alliance shared the objective of deterring any war in Europe. For Europeans, however, geography, historical experience, and the advent of the nuclear age had made deterrence an absolute consideration. Even a successful conventional defense by NATO would leave large areas of the European battlefield in ruins.[12] During the 1950s and into the 1960s, Europeans had become attracted to, and dependent on, the view that the best way to ensure the continued deterrence of the Soviet Union was to deny Moscow the option of a conventional-only war, which would leave Soviet territory untouched. Thus, the preferred strategy threatened an early resort to nuclear weapons and a rapid escalation to nuclear strikes against the territory of the superpowers, thus profoundly raising the costs to the Soviet Union of conventional aggression in Europe. If Americans were becoming uneasy about the prospect of losing New York in the defense of Bonn, then by the same token Soviet leaders might hesitate if confronted with the possible loss of Leningrad in an attempt to acquire Cologne.

Washington, through its expression of concern at the destructiveness and uncontrollability of nuclear war, was hinting at the possibility of self-deterrence in the event of a major crisis. Europeans were inclined to the view that, so long as NATO did not convey its unease to Moscow, the same destructiveness and uncontrollability would deter Soviet adventurism. As just one manifestation of these differences, it was reported that Washington had to insist on the exclusion of targets in western Russia in an early stage of the war from proposals on the use of nuclear weapons in Europe put forward by the defense ministers of the Federal Republic and Great Britain in 1969.[13] Later European interest in the deployment of American intermediate-range nuclear forces (INF) in Europe had its roots in similar concerns. The determination of both London and Paris to provide and maintain national nuclear deterrent forces was boosted by this transparent expression of American queasiness, which also largely explains the German interest in the multilateral force (MLF). Europeans have continued to favor a low nuclear threshold for its presumed deterrent effect, hoping that this would inhibit any Soviet temptation to attempt a quick and low-cost victory in Europe.

Although they shared the European preference for avoiding war altogether, Americans had begun to think about what would happen should deterrence fail. NATO strategy and capabilities seemed to make escalation unavoidable and uncontrollable, which in the coming era of mutual vulnerability would put American cities at risk. As a result, Washington began its quest for options, for more centralization, predictability, and control, even though McNamara and numerous Pentagon officials since have had little faith in the military utility of TNWs or in the chances of successfully preventing uncontrollable escalation if the nuclear threshold, the "firebreak," were crossed. Nonetheless, the stakes were high enough to warrant substantial improvements in the command and control of all nuclear weapons systems.

In Europe, this American emphasis on controlled response smacked of a preference for confining a war to Europe, which in itself might weaken deterrence by holding out to the two superpowers the prospect that their homelands could be preserved from nuclear attacks. As Manfred Wörner, the former West German defense minister and current NATO secretary-general, once said: "A separation of tactical nuclear weapons from the strategic nuclear theory is absolutely unacceptable for us Europeans. The territory of the USSR cannot be allowed, in theory or in practice, to become a sanctuary in the nuclear phase of a conflict in Europe."[14]

From McNamara's perspective, however, it would have been better still to avoid resorting to nuclear weapons altogether, and this meant maintaining a conventional capability sufficient to block a Warsaw Pact advance, thus placing the onus of escalation onto Moscow's shoulders. The Pentagon's assertion that the gap in conventional forces was small and could be closed fell on mostly deaf European ears, as the task and cost of closing the gap would fall primarily on European shoulders.

The best recent illustration of the durability of this transatlantic division of opinion was the "no first-use" proposal put forward in 1982 by four very eminent Americans (dubbed the "Gang of Four"), including McNamara, and the reply to it penned by four equally eminent Germans.[15] More interesting, at least for our present purposes, than the pros and cons of the "no first-use" proposal were the differing views regarding the deterrent role of nuclear weapons. While the four Americans quite correctly drew attention to the continuing failure to develop a plausible scenario for the widespread use of TNWs in Europe, their European protagonists familiarly emphasized the dire consequences of any war in Europe, nuclear or otherwise, and the continuing overwhelming necessity of preventing war from breaking out in the first place. The echoes from two decades earlier could hardly have been more resonant.

Nonetheless, these transatlantic differences should not be exaggerated. The four German authors, for example, expressed their support for "an energetic attempt to reduce the dependence on early first use of nuclear weapons." Indeed, the intense discussions within the alliance in forums such as the Nuclear Planning Group have helped to thrash out positions with which all sides can reasonably live and have provided an opportunity to appreciate and respect the various positions held by the member states of the alliance. A voluntary gathering of sovereign states can hope to survive only through this readiness to accommodate, compromise, and listen. The European position has never rested on the complete absence of restraint in the use of nuclear weapons in Europe. Indeed, Bonn has been persistent in its attempts to obtain a veto, or at least the right to be consulted, on the use of nuclear weapons based on its own territory or likely to cause damage there and has been generally nervous whenever the subject of nuclear use in

Europe has been raised. For West Germans, in particular, and for Europeans, in general, the competing requirements of deterrence and defense create a probably irresolvable dilemma. McNamara had a point when he distinguished between the declaratory preferences of the European allies and their likely response should war break out. The Germans especially have been far from cavalier with respect to the operational capabilities of their armed forces.

Nevertheless, the adoption of flexible response in 1967 did not reflect a triumph of the American view because, as McNamara noted in 1983, "the substantial raising of the 'nuclear threshold' as was envisaged when 'flexible response' was first conceived, has not become a reality."[16] The European failure to provide the requisite conventional force levels has in effect vetoed full implementation of flexible response in its pristine form. The implicit European strategy has been to make a military contribution sufficient to dampen the persistent American frustration with the distribution of alliance burdens and to head off any precipitate reduction of the American presence in Europe, while simultaneously maintaining a lower nuclear threshold than Washington finds ideal. To be sure, by the late 1960s, American insistence on greater conventional effort had waned, and it has never since been as forcefully articulated as it was during the early years of McNamara's stay in office. But it has never completely died, and a steady stream of American military commanders (notably NATO's former Supreme Allied Commander General Bernard Rogers, who in 1983 likened NATO's strategy to "delayed tripwire"[17]), congressmen, officials, and commentators of various kinds have continued to bemoan Europe's inadequate military contribution to its own defense and NATO's excessive reliance on an early resort to nuclear weapons, which is its inevitable consequence. Positions, or at least the manner in which they are expressed, may have moderated, but they have not fundamentally altered. On the other hand, circumstances have changed and continue to change, and this is encouraging a reconsideration not only of the main contours of NATO strategy but also of the characteristics of its military instruments.

TNWs in NATO Strategy

Two explanations can be forwarded for the intensification of the debate about NATO strategy. First, McNamara's attempt to revise NATO strategy was prompted by his recognition of the consequences of the looming emergence of Soviet strategic nuclear parity with the United States. Not only has parity at this level long since been attained, but also the development of Soviet military capabilities across the board has served, in the eyes of many, to undermine the flexible response approach. At each rung of military power, the onus of escalation is on NATO, but NATO would stand to lose at least as much as the Soviet side by any such escalation. The INF Treaty of 1987 further complicated the implementation of the strategy. The strategic context has changed. Second, so too has the political context. The emergence, or reemergence, of the antinuclear movement in Europe, largely in response to the neutron bomb debate and the INF deployment but reinforced by the advent of Mikhail Gorbachev, signaled a widespread unease about NATO's current strategy and posture. Antinuclear sentiments have found their way into left-of-center political parties throughout Europe, and in some countries—most significantly the Federal Republic—they have a wider currency still. How permanent this phenomenon will be is difficult to foretell, but for the time being at least it has rekindled interest in the relationship between conventional and nuclear forces in Europe. Curiously, Washington, which over the years has shown itself generally less enamored of overreliance on nuclear weapons in Europe, has borne the brunt of the anger of the protestors.

To determine the role of TNWs in NATO's posture and strategy, one must first consider the characteristics of the stockpile. Since the stockpile emerged from a process essentially unguided by any overarching definition of military requirements, it is not surprising that some elements of the stockpile have seemed singularly inappropriate to the European theater. Defense Secretary James Schlesinger, who probably had more faith in the possibility of fighting limited nuclear wars than did most incumbents of that office, once colorfully referred to NATO's TNW arsenal as "a pile of junk."[18] Changes have been made to this arsenal over the years.[19] With the decision to deploy INF systems in Europe, an equivalent number of TNW warheads were withdrawn, leaving a total of around six thousand. In 1983, at Montebello, NATO decided to refine the arsenal further by withdrawing, by 1988, fourteen hundred additional warheads, particularly in the short and medium-range categories. Many of these systems (for example, the surface-to-air *Nike-Hercules*) are being replaced by conventional alternatives. Some systems, such as the Dutch F-16 aircraft, are reverting to conventional-only missions. There have been other changes, too, particularly in the fields of miniaturization and accuracy, although substantial variations in each of these categories persist. Yields range from artillery shells of one-tenth of a kiloton to bombs of up to five hundred kilotons. There have also been improvements in the permissive action links, or electronic locks, that are fitted to the various systems to prevent unauthorized release. Security and point defense at the one hundred or so TNW storage sites scattered around Europe have also been somewhat patchily enhanced. As a result of these improvement programs, NATO's TNW arsenal is now smaller, more survivable, more secure, less destructive, and, it would seem, altogether more appropriate to the European theater than was the case twenty years ago. Should modernization programs eventually go ahead, or should TNWs be caught up in the arms control process, NATO's TNW arsenal would be still further refined.

Doubts remain, however. Many of these center on the release procedures and the command, control, communications, and intelligence (C^3I) capabilities and facilities associated with the arsenal. Catherine McArdle Kelleher has argued that "NATO has failed to develop a comprehensive system integrating conventional and nuclear C^3I,"[20] which leaves scope for serious doubt concerning the likelihood of unobstructed passage of TNW release requests or permission up and down the NATO command chain. On the other hand, the Nuclear Planning Group has devised elaborate procedures governing authorization for the release and use of TNWs in Europe, in an attempt to prevent unauthorized, unwanted, or overhasty resorts to nuclear use.[21] The emphases have been on controlled use and escalation and on damage limitation, but the details of the general political guidelines for TNW use remain shrouded in secrecy, and it has proved difficult to move beyond the formulation of generalities.

A request from a field commander for permission to use TNWs could take up to sixty hours to be granted or refused, by which time it would probably be too late. A request by the Supreme Allied Commander, Europe, (SACEUR) either to release warheads to units in the field or to use them, whether on his own initiative or in response to requests from his subordinated commanders, should be passed up to his political masters in either the Atlantic Council or the Defense Planning Committee. The willingness of either of these bodies to arrive at a quick and unanimous decision cannot be guaranteed. On the other hand, these cumbersome release procedures could be bypassed in favor of bilateral or even unilateral decision making. Except for the small British and French capabilities, the warhead arsenal is American-owned and controlled. Thus, the permission of the U.S. president would be necessary. The delivery systems for around half the warheads are also American. Given that SACEUR doubles as Commander in Chief of U.S. Forces, Europe (USCINCEUR), who is subordinate to his president, there is scope for the unilateral release and employment of TNWs in Europe by the United States regardless of the positions taken up by the allied governments.

Delays in the granting of permission to use nuclear weapons could rapidly result in destruction of the stockpile, defeat of NATO's forward-based forces, and capture of TNW systems before permission to use them has been granted. The success of initial Warsaw Pact thrusts could inundate the command, control, and communications (C^3) network with requests for TNWs by field commanders facing imminent defeat. At a minimum, there would probably be substantial pressure on the authorities to accede to the early dispersal of TNW warheads from their storage sites. The logic of the nuclear battlefield points toward early dispersal, decentralization, and even predelegation. Yet this logic is accompanied by its own set of difficulties, for greater decentralization weakens the scope for restraint and control: TNWs would be used in the absence of any appreciation of the broader picture and in response to the immediate circumstances faced by NATO forces in small sectors of the front. A widespread uncoordinated resort to TNWs would be likely.

If the use of TNWs were to commence, all sorts of problems would come into view. The nuclear battlefield would be two-sided. The Soviet arsenal is believed to consist of larger and "dirtier" warheads than its NATO counterpart and to place less emphasis on control and limitation. The close proximity of opposing forces and the inaccuracy of targeting intelligence in a fast-moving and confusing battle are two more imponderables from a very long list. Given the crowded conditions of central Europe, it is not surprising that most forecasts of the outcome of a TNW battle there have predicted massive civilian casualties and unprecedented physical damage. Much of the affected area is territory that NATO is pledged to defend. It is questionable whether TNWs can be sensibly used, even more moderately, on or around heavily populated territory that it is the intention to defend.

There seems to be little confidence that any set of TNW release guidelines would be able to surmount the inherent conflict between the political requirement for central control and the military requirement for easy accessibility. Nor is there much faith in avoiding uncontrollable escalation if the nuclear threshold were crossed. It is hoped that the Warsaw Pact forces would be defeated, or that Moscow would succumb to intrawar deterrence and terminate its aggression, at some point short of a nuclear holocaust. Not everyone is convinced, however, that a Soviet Union undeterred before the nuclear threshold had been crossed would become deterred following the initial use of nuclear weapons.[22] It is not surprising that Kelleher concludes that, for all the welcome improvements in the characteristics of NATO's TNW arsenal and in the processes of alliance consultation, "the risk of uncontrolled escalation remains," while simultaneously there is a "significant probability that . . . these weapons will never be available for use."[23]

Many Americans believe, and not without cause, that Europeans have generally been happy to live with the risk of uncontrolled escalation. As an American official put it in 1974, "The NATO doctrine is that we will fight with conventional forces until we are losing, then we will fight with tactical nuclear weapons until we are losing, and then we will blow up the world . . . indeed, that is what the Europeans think it ought to be."[24] This observation rather colorfully conveys some of the frustration with NATO's current strategy. Insofar as Europeans have been happy with this state of affairs, it is because they have distinguished, in an intellectually messy and paradoxical way, what they think would happen from what they think will happen. Europeans are as capable as Americans of recognizing that chaos and massive destruction would ensue from a war in Europe. For Europeans, though, because it would be intolerable, it has become unthinkable. Because it is unthinkable, it has become unlikely. As David Calleo has put it, a Soviet attack in central Europe "would be the most elaborately anticipated and least expected invasion in Europe's history."[25]

The relationship between anticipation and expectation is symbiotic. Familiarly, the form that the anticipation has taken has reduced the expectation; that is, deterrence has worked. But, more subtly, the low expectation of war has influenced the form that the anticipation of, or preparations for, war have taken. Europeans have been able to live with an implausible military strategy because they consider the outbreak of war itself implausible. To overstate and to oversimplify somewhat, contemplating the consequences of a breakdown of deterrence in Europe has been not only unthinkable but also not worth thinking about. This is akin to what McGeorge Bundy referred to as "existential deterrence," the view that nuclear weapons deter by their very existence and that any overelaboration of posture and strategy is not really necessary or desirable.

Is this somewhat messy situation sustainable? Left to themselves, and given the Soviet threat as it has manifested itself in the past, most European governments would probably prefer to leave NATO's arrangements much as they are. They are not, however, left to themselves. In addition to the steady erosion of the escalatory structure of flexible response—a process speeded up by the INF Treaty—they have to contend with an increasing American frustration with the distribution of burdens, a mood that could lead to a gradual American disengagement.[26] The collapse of the Warsaw Pact as a military force has exacerbated the unease felt by significant numbers of European voters about continuing to rely so heavily on the deterrent threat to use nuclear weapons. The prospect of far-reaching arms control alone threatens the military status quo.

Thus, Europeans sometimes share with their American allies an unease regarding NATO's current posture, and they are now probably more inclined than ever before to think about what might happen should nuclear deterrence fail. For Europeans, however, TNWs do not represent a barrier between the failure of deterrence and nuclear annihilation. For those living in the path of a TNW battlefield, the short-range nuclear systems are the instruments of annihilation. Accordingly, many politicians, defense experts, and officials on both sides of the Atlantic doubt whether it would really be rational and in NATO's own interests to initiate the use of nuclear weapons.[27] The specter of self-deterrence refuses to leave in peace even those who enjoy the most profound faith in the continuing successful operation of nuclear deterrence. If NATO is not fully convinced of the credibility of its own posture, can it be safely assumed that the Soviet Union might not one day be tempted to call its bluff?[28] Incorporating TNWs into NATO's war-fighting forces, so as to enhance the credibility of the nuclear-use threat, increases the likelihood that they would be used. If there really is a distinction between NATO's (or NATO-Europe's) deterrent preferences on the one hand and actual war-fighting preferences on the other, this arrangement is dangerous, because it could result in a use of nuclear weapons that nobody desired.[29] For all of these reasons, and because of the potential of modern technology, recent years have witnessed a burgeoning interest in NATO's conventional force levels and posture.

The Conventional Balance

Since the very inception of the alliance, the role of NATO's nonnuclear forces has been inextricably bound with assessments of the conventional force balance. Although enthusiasm for the military and economic virtues of TNWs alone would have driven their introduction into the European theater, NATO's presumed inferiority in conventional forces clearly motivated and rationalized its growing reliance on nuclear weapons. Yet this faith in the deterrent or war-fighting capabilities of nuclear weapons may have discouraged efforts to enhance the West's nonnuclear forces. This thought provided much of the basis for the "no first-use" proposal in 1982. Nonetheless, there has never been any real consensus on the extent or even the existence of the alliance's conventional weakness vis-à-vis the Soviet bloc.[30]

Counting rules are particularly important in understanding how, at the outset of its existence, NATO was so able to convince itself of its massive conventional inferiority. First, the balance of forces was typically presented as being between, on the one hand, all Soviet bloc forces, wherever they might be and regardless of their state of readiness, and, on the NATO side, only those ready divisions deployed in Europe. Second, the balance in ground forces was crudely expressed in numbers of army divisions. No account was taken of the readiness, morale, equipment, or size of those divisions. On these assumptions NATO officials were for over a decade able to pit 175 Soviet divisions against 30 or so for NATO, even though in 1954 NATO's then SACEUR, General Alfred Gruenther, claimed that the alliance had almost 100 divisions in varying degrees of readiness. In fact, in that same year NATO probably had more, and certainly not significantly fewer, men under arms than did the Soviet Union and its "allies."[31] Much of the military strength of the major NATO powers was deployed outside Europe. Whether these forces would and could have been brought to bear in Europe in time in the event of war or tension was an interesting question that seems never to have entered into the official and public assessments of the balance on Europe. The poor state of readiness and the distance from the front of many Soviet bloc divisions should also surely have been taken into account, although intelligence gathering was less precise then than it is today.

Not until McNamara's arrival at the Pentagon was NATO's official pessimism regarding the conventional balance officially questioned. The questions asked by McNamara's staff seem obvious in retrospect: How big is a Warsaw Pact division? How combat-ready are they? How good is their equipment? How do air forces compare?[32] It immediately became evident that the crude "bean counting" approach that had previously characterized the Pentagon's and NATO's assessments of the East-West military balance had created a widespread and largely unjustified pessimism. In scrutinizing the quantitative indicators more closely, and in taking into account qualitative and intangible factors, McNamara's Pentagon staff produced a substantially more positive estimate of NATO's nonnuclear capabilities. Although Washington's newfound optimism fell on generally stony European ground during the 1960s, it nevertheless remains true that NATO has since learned to live without some of its more extreme pronouncements of Warsaw Pact superiority. Indeed, "dynamic analysis"—the attempt to incorporate intangible factors into calculations of the conventional military balance—is now quite commonplace, at least among independent commentators. Still, NATO and its constituent national governments continue to push out figures that rely heavily on bean counting, resulting in unhappy assessments of the state of military balance.

There are varying degrees of unhappiness in the West regarding the degree of Warsaw Pact superiority, and there are still no agreed-upon rules even on how to conduct a bean count. Thus, the British, American, and West German defense ministries and the independent International Institute for Strategic Studies use profoundly different counting procedures to produce widely divergent figures relating to the conventional balance. They disagree on such crucial matters as the numerical levels of various military systems, the scale and progress of modernization programs, whether and what reserve forces and stocks to count, how many and what aircraft to include, the appropriate geographical area to consider, and states of readiness. Nor can we safely assume that identical counting procedures are adopted for both NATO and the Warsaw Pact.[33] Nevertheless, these largely quantitative estimates coincide in awarding numerical superiority to the Soviet bloc and in concluding quite firmly both that NATO needs to do more, even if how much and of what remains unclear, and that there is no immediate alternative to placing its faith in nuclear deterrence.

Whereas bean counting can only imply combat outcomes (that is, the numerically weaker side is generally assumed to be weaker in battle), the whole raison d'être of dynamic analysis is that it endeavors to incorporate likely combat outcomes into its assessments of the balance.[34] However, the list of factors that could plausibly be taken into account are legion, including political and military leadership qualities, the morale and discipline of troops, mobility and survivability, sustainability, terrain, reinforcement rates, force-to-space ratios, the availability and capability of operational and other reserves, command and control, the military strategies of the two sides and their relationship to each other, and weapons quality. There are two immediate difficulties with such complex and multifaceted forms of analysis. First, how does one balance the intangible factors against the more traditional, and more measurable, quantitative indicators? Not surprisingly, those analysts who reject excessive reliance on bean counting often do so because they attach less credence to its results than do those analysts who persevere with it. Yet it could be argued that there is a virtue in staying with data that are measurable, even if this means qualifying one's findings.[35] Second, how does one balance intangible factors against each other? How does one calculate the likelihood, and impact, of NATO's political indecision resulting in a delayed mobilization?

Thus, dynamic analysis sows the seeds of its own destruction through the introduction of subjective and scenario-dependent factors in the hope that a more accurate picture of the military realities will emerge. It might be more realistic to take these factors into account, but there is no guarantee that more consensus will develop regarding the precise state of the NATO-Warsaw Pact military balance, that combat outcomes will be more reliably predicted, or that we will ever know which prediction is truest. Furthermore, much depends on the assumptions about battle conditions. It has been recently argued that most current assessments of the military balance in Europe assume unstable combat conditions, in which the process of battle itself magnifies small initial imbalances.[36] Thus, even a moderate initial weakness on NATO's part might result in a substantial military defeat. A successful blitzkrieg by the numerically weaker side offers a perfect example of unstable combat conditions. If unstable combat conditions are assumed, and given the existence of so many imponderables with respect to the initial balance (for examples, the role of the French, the rate and extent of each side's mobilization, the amount of warning time and NATO's response to it), then the availability of greater resources in peacetime may do little to offset a disastrous initial weakness at the onset of war. In other words, some of NATO's problems are better understood as those of the defender rather than those of the weaker side.

Given that the more sophisticated attempts to measure the balance of conventional forces in Europe tend toward a greater optimism than is traditional, and given, too, the dim prospect of substantially increased resources being devoted to NATO's conventional forces, it is comforting to be able to argue that additional resources would do little to rescue a defense that would not succeed in any event. Notwithstanding the fragile consensus that seems to have emerged in NATO in favor of more robust conventional capabilities, the devotion of still greater resources to defense is unlikely. The mood in the United States, too, has shifted against even the maintenance of its existing defense burden in Europe, let alone additional costly commitments.[37] At the very best, Americans look set to spend less and Europeans unlikely to spend more. Barry R. Posen has reminded us that, according to U.S. Defense Department figures, NATO outspent the Warsaw Pact for each year of 1965 to 1985. In the last of these years, NATO spending exceeded that of the Warsaw Pact by 36 percent.[38] If NATO really is as weak as the pessimists claim it is vis-à-vis the Warsaw Pact, then these vast resources must have been appallingly utilized, and there is surely little point in calling for still higher defense spending if that, too, is to be misdirected.

Conventional Defense: Scope for Improvement?

Once we begin to shift away from simple calls to spend more, and instead focus on how NATO might enhance its defensive capabilities and prospects, we are again in danger of being buried by an avalanche of often conflicting advice. Yet the options do sort themselves out quite neatly. Those who are fairly optimistic concerning NATO's chances of mounting a successful defense generally favor incremental improvements in NATO's defensive posture.[39] Their essence is to ensure that NATO does not lose out in the initial exchanges: It should not be caught by surprise, and its forces should be able to plug any gaps and parry any breakthroughs that might occur. These proposals attempt to shift expected combat conditions from unstable to stable or at least neutral. This would deny the Warsaw Pact the option of a quick, low-cost victory resulting from a successful blitzkrieg attack and instead would draw it into an ever more costly and drawn-out war of attrition. Thus, NATO is often exhorted to enhance its sustainability by improving ammunition and reserve material stocks. It is also often argued that NATO does not sufficiently exploit the inherent advantages of defense, through such measures as the better preparation of defensive strong points, the construction of obstacles and fortifications of various kinds, the improved air defense of airfields, storage depots, C^3I facilities, and the like, and the proper deployment of NATO's forward defense forces. In the same context, calls for more, and more effective, operational reserves have become commonplace. These are needed to bolster weak points in the forward defensive line, to prevent the Warsaw Pact from taking advantage of any breakthroughs, and to replace exhausted frontline forces as the battle drags on. They need firepower, mobility, and effective C^3I, as well as numerical strength.

Optimists believe that a mobilization race need not necessarily favor the pact, which not only might take longer than NATO to deploy battle-ready forces into the theater but also could find itself relying more and more on poorly trained, poorly led, poorly motivated, and poorly equipped forces. John J. Mearsheimer has drawn attention to the significance of force-to-space ratios, which place upper limits on the ability of the pact to concentrate more and more forces on a confined area in an attempt to achieve a force ratio sufficient for a successful offensive against a well-armed and well-deployed defense.[40] It has been argued, however, that NATO's greatest vulnerability is the possibility of political indecision in the event of a major military crisis;[41] nonetheless, lowering its mobilization threshold probably represents the alliance's most problematic task in this area. This is an essentially political rather than military issue, owing to the tendency to regard early mobilization as provocative rather than deterring.[42]

This emphasis on the need for a sustainable defense in central Europe raises some complicated issues. Measures that reduce the likelihood of a successful surprise attack can attract widespread support. They represent a strengthened commitment to forward defense and might deter Soviet adventurism and risk-taking fired by the hope of quick and easy victories, thus further enhancing deterrence by putting back onto the Soviet Union some of the onus for escalation of conflict. Increased sustainability, on the other hand, could be perceived as offering Moscow the prospect of a conventional-only conflict and as unintentionally signaling an overwhelming reluctance on NATO's part to resort to the use of nuclear weapons. In these circumstances, NATO might be in danger of blurring the distinction between no early first-use, with which Europeans can agree, and absolutely no first-use. It could be argued that the price to the Soviet Union of eventual victory on the battlefield would be made high, but not suicidally so. Yet improved sustainability need not be interpreted as meaning anything more than the achievement of NATO's thirty-day planning guidance levels for war reserve stocks and ammunition. These targets can be approached with little fanfare and at relatively little cost, and thus they may emit only the most muted of signals. In fact, some studies suggest that stocks may already be at or near the guidance levels, and improvements are continuing.[43] The complicating factor here is the ambiguity surrounding NATO's nuclear threshold. If it is not clear where it is or is supposed to be, then it is not clear what level and type of conventional force improvements are required.

Military reformers have proposed alternative, although not necessarily mutually exclusive, methods of improving NATO's prospects of mounting a successful forward defense in central Europe. Chief among them is the follow-on forces attack (FOFA) concept, which was adopted as a Planning Guideline by NATO in 1984, the essence of which is to undermine the

Warsaw Pact's capacity to fight a sustained campaign. The SACEUR, General Bernard Rogers, was reasonably confident that NATO's frontline defense could withstand an initial Warsaw Pact onslaught given timely mobilization and improvements in war reserve stocks. He was less sanguine, however, about the chances of holding back subsequent waves of attacking forces.[44] FOFA was seen as a method of utilizing new technology to destroy Warsaw Pact forces, bases, transportation networks, and C^3I facilities located two hundred kilometers or more from the forward edge of the battle area. Although a portion of NATO aircraft have long been earmarked for strike missions deep into Pact territory, the higher priority of deep strike, which FOFA represented, has been encouraged by the emergence of a range of new technologies and weapons systems that have appeared to make it an altogether more viable strategy. Using emerging technology, targets could be more quickly located and identified and could be hit with greater accuracy and lethality.

One problem with emerging technology, however, is precisely that—it is emerging. Some of the systems may never be developed, others may fail to live up to their research-stage promise. Sophisticated technology is usually expensive, and, although there is no consensus surrounding the likely cost of many of the new systems, there is also little likelihood of significantly expanded defense budgets. This is linked to the concern in Europe that most of the systems will originate in the United States, so that a major European reequipping program could reinforce still further the current one-way street in the transatlantic arms trade. Skeptics point to additional drawbacks of a more military nature. The C^3I facilities, upon which much of the new technology would heavily rely, could be highly vulnerable to direct attacks and to countermeasures, as could some of the weapons themselves. Also, in a world of finite budgets, money spent on glamorous, sophisticated, and state-of-the-art technologies could be at the expense of frontline defenses. A defeat of the pact's second-echelon forces would be a Pyrrhic victory, if it were accompanied by an easier breakthrough by first-echelon forces. In any case, those who are more impressed by the pact's capacity for surprise attack, and who believe that a rapid, low-cost victory is the only one to which Moscow would be at all attracted, argue that excessive concern with subsequent attacking waves is misplaced.[45]

Nevertheless, technology does progress incrementally. Even if we are not to witness a revolution in military tactics and doctrine in the near future, it is clear that new weapons will generally possess high lethality and will provide new military options. The high lethality of modern, "smart" weapons is felt by some to favor the defense over the offense. Large-scale tank breakthroughs and the achievement of air superiority will become things of the past. NATO could benefit from these changed circumstances if it is prepared to revert to a more purely defensive defense.[46] These arguments dovetail neatly with the apprehension that FOFA and related approaches have offensive, preemptive connotations and could have a destabilizing effect on the military confrontation in central Europe. Sentiments such as these are particularly widespread in the Federal Republic, and they have fueled a strong interest in concepts such as "defensive defense," "area defense," and "alternative defense."[47] Although there are many variants of these by no means mutually consistent ideas, most reflect a faith in the capacity of relatively immobile, lightly armed, well-concealed forces to deny territory to a tank-heavy aggressor. Most, too, reflect an unease with NATO's present reliance on a nuclear response in central Europe. They also, however, are subject to a number of political and military criticisms. It has been argued that the requisite technology is not yet available, that there would be too much reliance on vulnerable C^3I facilities, that so dispersed a defense might easily fragment, and that the pact could counter with a shift toward initial infantry engagements or airborne assault.

Although many of these "defensive" proposals are German in origin, the consequences for the Federal Republic could be especially profound. German territory would more clearly become the battleground if pact forces were drawn in to become entangled in NATO's defenses. The initial defense might in any case weaken, due to the emphasis on nonprovocation, the increased reliance on mobilized forces, and the shift of resources toward the area defense forces. Bonn would probably find itself bearing a bigger proportion of the burden of defense of central Europe than is the case at present. Above all, the absence of forces structured to conduct counteroffensive operations would make it impossible to dislodge pact units that break through the more forward defensive layers. Furthermore, "alternative defense" ideas go beyond any other sets of proposals in reducing or removing NATO's battlefield nuclear weapons. They represent a clear faith in deterrence by denial rather than by punishment. Although there is much that is interesting and even applicable about this wave of thinking, there is also an air of unreality about it. There is little chance of a consensus coagulating around many of these ideas, even in West Germany. It is not easy to see how NATO would set about what could amount to a massive restructuring of its present forces. Furthermore, these ideas do not really address the complexities of forward defense. Perhaps their best chance of success lies in future Conventional Forces in Europe talks with the Warsaw Pact, which might shift both sides toward such concepts. In 1990 these outcomes seem to lie in the near distant future and, in any case, will raise the question of whether there is any threat at all to NATO and its allies.

Conclusion

NATO's first forty years have been replete with crises, prompting in roughly equal measure calls for substantial reform and predictions of imminent demise. Over the years the alliance's military preparations have constantly raised the question of just how much military and strategic untidiness, and how much doctrinal difference of perspective and opinion, a political-military alliance of sovereign states can take. Is there a bottom line? And, if so, where is it likely to be drawn? Strategic analysts, susceptible as they sometimes are to the affliction we have already identified as "strategism," also are among those most prone to impatience with NATO's internal wranglings and military imperfections. Yet the alliance's remarkable record of survival and growth caution against any rushes of blood to the head when considering its future.

It is nevertheless difficult to resist the suspicion that, in its fortieth year, NATO really has reached a watershed. The perception of a more or less unambiguous Soviet threat, the faith in nuclear deterrence, and NATO have been inseparable elements of the total Atlantic picture of the past four decades. Now, Gorbachev's redirection of internal and external Soviet policies, and the disintegration of the Warsaw Pact, is causing even the most skeptical and world-weary observers to wonder whether, this time, the threat really is evaporating. Related to this, but driven by its own internal moral, political, and military concerns, is a clear Western drift in the direction of a reduced reliance on, and faith in, nuclear deterrence. This inchoate process takes many forms—Strategic Defense Initiative (SDI) and Reykjavík as well as the peace movement—but is currently felt most dramatically in the Federal Republic. The INF Treaty has shifted the burden of theater nuclear deterrence onto the remaining short-range systems, and these are disproportionately located in and targeted on the two German states. Right or wrong, Germans have come to feel that if deterrence fails it will be they who will most suffer the consequences and that they might even suffer them more or less exclusively. Both deterrence and defense could be undermined by the combination of the Gorbachev peace offensive and the fear of nuclear weapons.

What are NATO's prospects if the other two parts of the familiar picture change so profoundly? For the moment, there is a looming, enveloping sense that NATO is at a point of relative historical discontinuity, when the past may be a less helpful guide in pondering the future than we expect it to be in more normal times. Nowhere might this be more true than where the alliance's military preparations are concerned. We might well ask ourselves: When peering into the future, which is most relevant, the past forty years or forty months?

Notes

1. Richard K. Betts, "Conventional Strategy; New Critics, Old Choices," *International Security* 7, no. 1 (Spring 1983): 149.
2. See Alain C. Enthoven and K. Wayne Smith, *How Much Is Enough? Shaping the Defense Program, 1961–1969* (New York: Harper and Row, 1971). For a brief consideration of the imbalance in conventional forces during these early years, see William Park, *Defending the West: A History of NATO* (Boulder, CO: Westview Press, 1986, and Brighton, England: Wheatsheaf, 1986), 21–29.
3. See Roger Hilsman, "NATO: The Developing Strategic Context," in Klaus Knorr, ed., *NATO and American Security* (Princeton: Princeton University Press, 1959), 11–36.
4. For discussions of the "long haul" see Warner R. Schilling, Paul Y. Hammond, and Glenn H. Snyder, *Strategy, Politics and Defense Budgets* (New York: Columbia University Press, 1961), 62–69; Robert E. Osgood, *NATO: The Entangling Alliance* (Chicago: University Press, 1962), 87–91.
5. NSC-162/2, 30 October 1953, *Papers Relating to the Foreign Relations of the United States, 1952–1954* (Washington, DC: Government Printing Office, 1984), 2:593.
6. See Gordon A. Craig, "Germany and NATO: The Rearmament Debate," in Knorr, ed., *NATO and American Security*, 240–41.
7. For a discussion of the forces behind this momentum see Jane E. Stromseth, *The Origins of Flexible Response: NATO's Debate over Strategy in the 1960s* (Oxford, England: MacMillan, 1988), 88–95.
8. Catherine McArdle Kelleher, *Germany and the Politics of Nuclear Weapons* (New York: Columbia University Press, 1975), 282.
9. The following discussion is closely based on Stromseth, *The Origins of Flexible Response*, 58–64.
10. For further discussion of the initial reactions in Paris, London, and Bonn see Stromseth, *The Origins of Flexible Response*, 96–174; and Park, *Defending the West*, 127–34. The following passage draws heavily on these two sources. See also Carl H. Amme, *NATO Strategy and Nuclear Defense* (Westport, CT: Greenwood Press, 1988), 19–43.
11. For this point see Stephen J. Cimbala, "Theater Nuclear and Conventional Force Improvements," *Armed Forces and Society* 11, no. 1 (Fall 1984): 115–29.
12. Ibid. See also Gregory F. Treverton, "Managing NATO's Nuclear Dilemma," *International Security* 7, no. 4 (Spring 1983): 93–115.
13. Amme, *NATO Strategy and Nuclear Defense*, 23.
14. Quoted in David S. Yost and Thomas C. Glad, "West German Party Politics and Theater Nuclear Modernization since 1977," *Armed Forces and Society* 8, no. 4 (Summer 1982): 328. Stephen J. Cimbala also makes much of this European unease in "Flexible Targeting, Escalation Control, and War in Europe," *Armed Forces and Society* 12, no. 3 (Spring 1986): 383–400.
15. McGeorge Bundy, George F. Kennan, Robert S. McNamara, and Gerard Smith, "Nuclear Weapons and the Atlantic Alliance," *Foreign Affairs* 60, no. 4 (Spring 1982): 753–68; Karl Kaiser, Georg Leber, A. Mertes, Franz-Josef Schulze, "Nuclear Weapons and the Preservation of Peace: A German Response to No First Use," ibid. 60, no. 5 (Summer 1982): 1157–70.
16. Robert S. McNamara, "The Military Role of Nuclear Weapons: Perceptions and Misperceptions," *Survival* 25, no. 6 (November-December 1983): 261–71.

17. Bernard W. Rogers, "Greater Flexibility for NATO's Flexible Response," *Strategic Review* 11, no. 2 (Spring 1983): 16.

18. See Josef Joffe, "Allies, Angst, and Arms Control: New Troubles for an Old Partnership," in Marsha McGraw Olive and Jeffrey D. Porro, eds., *Nuclear Weapons in Europe: Modernization and Limitations* (Lexington, MA: D. C. Heath, 1983), 33.

19. For recent descriptions of the stockpile see Catherine McArdle Kelleher, "Managing NATO's Tactical Nuclear Operations," *Survival* 30, no. 1 (January/February 1988): 159–78; and James M. Garrett, "Nuclear Weapons for the Battlefield: Deterrent or Fantasy?" *Journal of Strategic Studies* 10, no. 2 (June 1987). The following passage is loosely based on these two sources.

20. Kelleher, *Germany and the Policy of Nuclear Weapons*, 68.

21. For the work of the Nuclear Planning Group see Paul Buteux, *The Politics of Nuclear Consultation in NATO 1965–1980* (Cambridge, England: Cambridge University Press, 1983).

22. A point made by, among others, Amme, *NATO Strategy and Nuclear Defense*, 13.

23. Kelleher, *Germany and the Politics of Nuclear Weapons*, 75-76.

24. Morton Halperin, in U.S. Congress, Senate, Committee on Foreign Relations, *Hearings on Nuclear Weapons and Foreign Policy*, 93d Cong., 2d sess., March-April 1974, 44.

25. David Calleo, *The Atlantic Fantasy: The U.S., NATO, and Europe* (Baltimore: Johns Hopkins University Press, 1970), 30.

26. A point made by, among others, Jeffrey Record and David B. Rivkin, Jr., "Defending Post-INF Europe," *Foreign Affairs* 66, no. 4 (Spring 1988): 735–54.

27. Stressed by Treverton, "Managing NATO's Nuclear Dilemma."

28. This quite familiar point is central to European arguments for greater conventional capability. See, for example, John Baylis, "NATO Strategy: The Case for a New Strategic Concept," *International Affairs* 64, no. 1 (Winter 1987–88): 43–59; and Norbert Hannig, "Failure of NATO Defense Policy—Need for New Solutions," *Armada International* 1 (15 February 1985).

29. Baylis, "NATO Strategy: The Case for a New Strategic Concept," emphasizes this point.

30. For a brief discussion of NATO's earliest assessments of the conventional balance see Park, *Defending the West*, 21–26.

31. Ibid. Also see Lord Ismay, *NATO: The First Five Years, 1949–1954* (Utrecht, The Netherlands: Bosch, 1954), 40, 110–12.

32. See Enthoven and Smith, *How Much Is Enough?*

33. See Anthony H. Cordesman, "Fatal Flaws in Presenting the NATO/Warsaw Pact Balance," *Armed Forces Journal International* (July 1988).

34. See Joshua M. Epstein, "Dynamic Analysis and the Conventional Balance in Europe," *International Security* 12, no. 4 (Spring 1988): 154–65; and Kim R. Holmes, "Measuring the Conventional Balance in Europe," ibid. 166–73. Simon Lunn, "The East-West Military Balance: Assessing Change," and Dr. James A. Thomson, "An Unfavourable Situation: NATO and the Conventional Balance," both in "The Changing Strategic Landscape: Part II," *Adelphi Papers* no. 236 (Spring 1989), are also highly sophisticated considerations of the balance.

35. Betts, in "Conventional Strategy," and elsewhere, comes close to arguing this point.

36. For this interesting argument see Stephen D. Biddle, "The European Conventional Balance: A Reinterpretation of the Debate," *Survival* 30, no. 2 (March-April 1988): 99–121.

37. For this pessimism see Stephen J. Flanagan, "Emerging Tensions over NATO's Conventional Forces," *International Defense Review*, no. 1 (1987): 31–34, 37–39.

38. Barry R. Posen, "Is NATO Decisively Outnumbered?" *International Security* 12, no. 4 (Spring 1988): 200-202.

39. See, for example, Epstein, "Dynamic Analysis and the Conventional Balance in Europe"; and John J. Mearsheimer, "Numbers Strategy and the European Balance," *International Security* 12, no. 4 (Spring 1988): 174–85.

40. See, for example, John J. Mearsheimer's studies, "Why the Soviets Can't Win Quickly in Central Europe," *International Security* 7, no. 1 (Summer 1982): 3–39; and *Conventional Deterrence* (Ithaca, NY: Cornell University Press, 1983).

41. See U.S. Congress, House, Defense Policy Panel of the Committee on Armed Services, *Soviet Readiness for War: Assessing One of the Major Sources of East-West Instability*, 100th Cong., 2d sess., 5 December 1988. See also Betts, "Conventional Strategy."

42. See Holmes, "Measuring the Conventional Balance in Europe."

43. For a generally upbeat assessment of NATO's current military preparedness, see David M. Shilling, "Europe's Conventional Defence: Solid Progress but Challenges Remain," *Survival* 30, no. 2 (1988): 122–23.

44. See, for example, Bernard Rogers, "Greater Flexibility for NATO's Flexible Response," *Strategic Review* 11, no. 2 (Spring 1983); and idem, "Follow-On Forces Attack: Myths and Realities," *NATO Review* 32, no. 6 (December 1984): 1–9.

45. For a cool assessment of ET and FOFA see Fen Osler Hampsen, "NATO's Conventional Doctrine: The Limits of Technological Improvement," *International Journal* 41, no. 1 (Winter 1985–86): 159–88. The Report of the European Security Study (ESECS), *Strengthening Conventional Deterrence in Europe: Proposals for the 1980s* (London: Macmillan and Company, 1983), of course represents an altogether more positive view.

46. See Hannig, "Failure of NATO Defense Policy," for a strong expression of this view.

47. For an excellent analysis of these alternative ideas see Jonathan Dean, "Alternative Defense: Answer to NATO's Central Front Problems?" *International Affairs* 64, no. 1 (Winter 1987–88): 61–82.

THE FUTURE OF NATO

The Future of NATO: An Insider's Perspective

S. I. P. van Campen

Nobody knows the future. In the opinion of certain people even the future is not what it used to be. Others do not wish to know it, because it resembles too much the past; some take the opposite view. In discussing the future of NATO, I will not be so bold as to commit myself to what I am going to present here. As a preliminary I would like to warn anyone against committing himself or myself to necessarily speculative thoughts about a somewhat uncertain subject.

My second warning is no less imperative. You are entitled to know something about the man addressing you. I have a number of convictions:

1) power plays an essential part in international and national affairs;
2) morality plays no role in national or international affairs;
3) the United States is somewhat ridiculous, as Thomas B. Macauley said of the British public, in having from time to time fits of morality and subjecting people to them;
4) contrary to the practice of the United States, we should stick to our old friends, proven in war and peace; and
5) the objectives of foreign policy must be essential interests, concrete and tangible, not uncertain and immaterial, like democracy or human rights.

It is not that I do not care about democracy or human rights. Yet I find that in general these terms are used without definition, and everybody seems to cover with the term "human rights" any complaint or grievance he or she might have against something or someone. Do we really want to imitate one of the smaller alliance member nations, the Netherlands, which proclaimed that human rights form its principal objective? In the field of foreign policy, I find it difficult to believe that is the truth. It would be more serious if this were the main objective of the foreign policy of the United States. Here again, I do not like the statements made recently in the American press. Nonetheless, it may seem that we are entering a period where such aims are, in fact, fundamental. If so, I predict that our awakening will be rude and fearful and that nobody will draw any benefits from these policy objectives except those who do not fall into such traps. The intent of these remarks is not only that you may know your man but also to describe these objectives' impact on the future of the alliance.

The facts that may determine the future of the alliance are of two kinds: external and internal. The future of the alliance may depend on the outcome of Mikhail Gorbachev's proposals to the West. I have not been asked, fortunately, to discuss Gorbachev, but his effect on the West directly influences our subject. To the extent that the West frivolously accepts his views and proposals, and to the extent that he demonstrates his capacity to stay in power and to overcome internal resistance and conservatism, we may predict a future full of trouble for NATO. I feel strongly about this subject not because I am against Gorbachev but because there are unknown factors in his words and deeds that concern me. For example, we do not know who will succeed Gorbachev, nor do we know when this will occur or under what circumstances.

Most European members of NATO are willing to attach belief to Gorbachev's pronouncements and to draw conclusions from them, as in the case of West Germany's opposition to the modernization of nuclear weapons. This is not astonishing. There is a long tradition of such responses and an equally long list of events to support them. It will not break the alliance, for apart from West Germany, Britain, and France, none of the European members is in a position to influence decisively the future of the alliance.

A more important problem stems from the example of the United States. Here I am not pleased by what is happening. It seems to me that the American public is somewhat overanxious to accept Gorbachev's pronouncements, and the concessions he proposes, at face value. Americans are not prepared to look behind his statements for underlying motives and considerations.

Moreover, is it really in our interest for Gorbachev to succeed in restructuring the Soviet economy, to make it function more smoothly than before? Is it really in our interest that Gorbachev, who, according to his statements, wants more freedom in the Soviet political system, succeeds in this enterprise? Remember the example of the British Empire in the nineteenth century, the greatest expansionist achievement previously known in the history of the world: This took place while England was a relatively open society with an active parliamentary system that became increasingly democratic as the empire expanded. Does this example not show that expansion of the Soviet (or Russian) state might be the consequence of an improvement in the Soviet Union's political and economic systems?

Do I conclude from this that we must actively oppose Gorbachev? I do not. But neither am I willing to attach too much importance to what he says and what he does. I would recommend that we adopt toward President Gorbachev and all his deeds a policy of masterly inactivity, as the British would have it. Certainly I would recommend that we, as an alliance, keep our military forces up to date and capable of carrying out missions assigned to them. But Gorbachev has had considerable success in some parts of the West, and it remains to be seen whether the chickens in the West will not readily fall into the trap that the Russian fox is setting for them. The future of the alliance, as a security organization, at the very least looks uncertain because its own members do not want protection any more when this protection is, in their view, not necessary. The history of the alliance should teach us that, if and when the Russians strike in an expansionist movement against the West (which I do not expect at all in the present circumstances), the alliance cannot be recreated on the day hostilities begin. Then it will be too late.

Many years ago I proposed to NATO's secretary-general, Manlio Brosio, that the International Secretariat be reduced by at least 50 percent and that NATO be transformed into a sleeper organization designed for organizing military maneuvers, keeping up militarily, and coming out of its winter sleep, so to speak, should an actual military need arise. In my thinking the sections of the International Staff that devote time and effort to political and other consultation, and concentrate on such subjects as the "Challenges to Modern Society," were far from ineffective, but they are not necessary. My proposal was made when political consultation among the allies was at its lowest ebb; I therefore felt that the whole Political Division should be abolished. I need not go further into my proposals, because Brosio did not accept them, no doubt for very good reasons.

I recall these events because they directly concern our subject today. If we do not succeed in reorganizing the alliance, if we do not succeed in convincing the various public opinions that NATO is important, or if we do not succeed in getting national parliaments more interested in alliance decisions, the publics of the member nations may feel that the future of the alliance is not worth very much. It follows, therefore, that NATO should follow the example of the European Economic Community, where there is, at least in theory, decision making by majority, a practice that does not exist in NATO. The system of unanimity or consensus has been justified as being completely in tune with the national sovereignty of member states. This is not the first time that I have publicly expressed regret about this system, but I do not expect full national sovereignty to be canceled or abolished in NATO.

Nevertheless, I predict that, unless NATO does something about this system, the future of the alliance looks bleak indeed. In the long run, people will be reluctant to permit member state X or Y, unwilling to contribute much to the common defense expenditure, to lecture others on what they should do. The present treaty allows us to do away with the whole system of sovereignty and to introduce a supranational system without changing the wording in the text of NATO's charter, but it is unlikely that this opening will be exploited.

The same might be said of the parliamentary organization known as the Consultative Atlantic Assembly. Admittedly, its importance is less than that of the other elements, but, unless the alliance succeeds in getting parliamentarians to attend its meetings and its committees, we cannot hope for national parliaments to increase interest in what we strive to achieve. The present secretary-general should do something to enhance the standing of the Consultative Atlantic Assembly. The word "consultative" has no further reason to exist. I understand the difficulties that such action implies. I also understand the difficulties that must be overcome in those countries that, in a mistaken urge to retain the sovereignty system's original purity, cannot see any reason to denude our present system of national sovereignty and to clothe the parliamentarians with greater responsibilities. All of the secretaries-general that I have known have tried to do this; all have failed. Nonetheless, this must be undertaken if the alliance is to get a better hearing in national parliaments for its concerns. The alliance at present constitutes an intergovernmental organization, with the government of each member-state responsible to its parliament, and this precludes progress toward solving NATO's problems.

Other factors may determine the future of the alliance. Most important among these are the age-old policies of alliance nations, on the one hand, and the policies of the International Staff, on the other. If we suppose for a moment that Gorbachev means what he says and that he will achieve full success, we also can suppose that the protective alliance (the security organization for which NATO was intended in the first place) will crumble.

Nonetheless, consultation among countries of the West must still take place, but where? The International Staff, through the director of the private office, has often expressed its preference that this consultation should take place in the North Atlantic Council. In fact, during the thirteen years that I was director of the private office of Secretary-General Joseph Luns, I composed a great number of memorandums defending this point of view that were read by him at the weekly luncheons of ambassadors.

Ambassadors listened to the secretary-general politely enough, but they did not take any further action, undoubtedly on instructions. This reaction should not surprise us. Most countries are so embedded in their own sovereignty that they do not want to consult at all; they only consult in panic, during crises. Since fear is less operative now than it was before, due to Gorbachev's words and deeds and the reactions of the United States, the greatest and most powerful of alliance members, it follows that consultation may be less than it was before. The impression I received from the ambassadorial luncheons with the secretary-general was that countries, in the long run, have mistaken but, in the short run, seemingly right reasons for not wanting the alliance to meddle in their own policies. Nor should we be quiet about the blame that is attached to the United States in this matter: Washington did transfer what rightfully should be discussed in the North Atlantic Council to other institutions, where they could meet directly with their opposite numbers in the Common Market organization.

The best example of this mistaken attitude, which in the long run will contribute to the demise of the alliance, is the pipeline dispute, which in its security aspects belonged in the North Atlantic Council and nowhere else. The International Staff did not fail to point this out to the secretary-general, who brought it to the attention of the ambassadors, but all was in vain.

If the alliance cannot transform itself into a clearinghouse of Western policies, and if the security organization represented by NATO is no longer necessary, it is difficult to predict a bright future for the alliance. If NATO is left without any task of real content and magnitude, the future of the alliance looks pessimistic indeed.

My own conclusions are therefore as follows:

1) As a security organization, the alliance stands and falls with the fortunes of President Gorbachev. On the other hand, if the alliance rejects Gorbachev's seducing words against the wishes of public opinion, it also may be in trouble.
2) As a consultative organization, as an organization with a political role, or as a clearinghouse for Western policies, the future of NATO looks none too promising. This is wholly the fault of the Western governments and nations concerned; Gorbachev cannot be blamed.

If the alliance fails to reorganize itself, there may be no future for NATO. I would bitterly regret it if NATO were to weaken or disappear altogether, because it has served our cause faithfully and sincerely. But as I have warned, we do not know the future, and it is in the habit of playing the most unexpected tricks on us. There are, in the history of the alliance, events that could not have been predicted. Human beings are obviously not clever enough to predict exactly what is going to happen. Of one thing, however, we may be sure: Member nations will never put a formal end to the alliance, because too many interests are involved. But current trends point to the increasing irrelevance of NATO, which will make formal dissolution unnecessary.

NATO, the Superpowers, and the European Problem*

Ronald L. Steel

NATO, in more ways than one, is not unlike a modern marriage. Born in high excitement, stimulated by thrills and danger, posing a united front to outsiders, convenient and eminently practical, a warm shoulder to fall back on when temptations deceive or disappear, its self-absorption disturbed by unexpected dependents and responsibilities, its *longueurs* relieved by periodic quarrels and reconciliations, the Atlantic Alliance has served far better and far longer than its matchmakers could have imagined. The question now is whether the two partners, America and Western Europe, both having changed profoundly during the four decades of their conjugal connection, will decide to stick with a relationship that, for all it lacks, is at least familiar—or whether it is time to call it a day and hope to salvage a good friendship out of a crumbling marriage.

There is much to be said for staying with the discomfort that we know rather than plunging into the possible perils of the unknown. In many ways NATO has been remarkably beneficent and successful. It has provided, through the famous American shield, the means by which Western Europe has grown prosperous and safe and has endowed itself with the comforts of a welfare state. Indeed, some European states are richer, safer, and enjoy more public welfare than does the United States itself. NATO has allowed the greater part of Germany to rearm without arousing the fears of its western neighbors, and it has helped to integrate the Federal Republic into a wider Western community. It has squelched whatever temptations the

---

* This paper, originally entitled "Increasing Fractures in the Alliance," was delivered at the Cato Conference, "NATO at 40: Confronting a Changing World," held on 3–4 April 1989. Reprinted by permission of the Cato Institute, Washington, DC.

Soviet Union might once have had about spreading its domain westward. It has done all of these things so effectively that these numerous virtues are hardly ever commented upon.

In addition, the alliance has given the United States much influence over its allies' military forces, and thereby over their foreign policies. This situation is remarked upon, for obvious reasons, less frequently in America, where it is enjoyed, than in Western Europe, where it is resolutely repressed. NATO also has provided, unintentionally, a justification, or an excuse, for the Soviet occupation of Eastern Europe and thus has contributed to the continued division of the European continent. But then its intention never was to alleviate that division, only to make it safer.

NATO has helped to keep Germany to a manageable size at which it neither dominates nor threatens its neighbors. In this way it has provided a solution of sorts to the age-old "German problem." It has allowed both superpowers, to use the comic book phrase, to define the world in terms of their respective spheres of influence. And it has permitted the United States, over the past twenty years, to engage in ever more fanciful acts of deficit financing, debt accumulation, and currency manipulation in order to pursue foreign policy goals beyond its means, or at least beyond its willingness to pay for in real money. The European allies have obligingly bought U.S. Treasury bills, suffered the inflation of their own currencies, and covered the American deficits as a normal part of their dependent relationship. Such are the virtues of hegemony.

NATO thus has provided considerable benefits for both parties. It is tempting to assume that an organization that has endured so long and survived so many crises of credibility not only must be charmed but also will endure forever. Or, if not quite forever, at least long enough so that we may pass on to another generation the challenges and comforts of addressing what is by now the eternal question: Whither NATO?

NATO's ability to survive its various vicissitudes over the years has been such an inspiring example of bureaucratic hardiness that it would be unwise even to hazard a guess over its likely longevity. Yet the problems the alliance has encountered have been framed within a familiar pattern of Soviet obduracy, European dependency, and American prosperity and energy. This pattern is now being changed in quite fundamental ways, with the result that any discussion about the future of NATO must be viewed within different dimensions.

First, there is the dimension of economics. The United States, having for years refused to tax itself to pay for its foreign policy—whether for the imperial adventure in Vietnam or for the credit-card military buildup of the Ronald Reagan era—is in serious economic trouble. Only a few years ago it was the world's major creditor, a position of economic strength on which the Atlantic Alliance was built; it is today its leading debtor. Persistent trade and budget deficits have made it increasingly difficult to sustain the great costs of maintaining a large land army in Europe. What was in the past first a bagatelle and then an easily manageable burden has now become a serious, and even threatening, drain on American resources. The commitment to NATO, although fundamental, can no longer be taken entirely for granted. Consuming nearly one half the U.S. defense budget, some $150 billion per year, it has to be weighed against competing demands on American resources and the necessity to reduce budget deficits. These deficits raise the question of whether NATO, like so many other programs from an age of seemingly unlimited resources, may be another example of how America is living beyond its means.

Searching for ways to cut budget deficits, it is not surprising that critics of fiscal overstretch have focused on NATO. They have accused the European allies of being "free riders" and have demanded that they pay more for NATO, presumably on the theory that thereby the United States can pay less. How this would work exactly, they do not explain. Should the Europeans increase their military budgets by the infamous $150 billion? Should they reimburse the United States for its expenses? In this case, should the GIs be viewed as latter-day Hessians in reverse? None of this is quite clear, although the general feeling of irritation with NATO Europe is unmistakable.

Complaints range from calls for greater burden sharing to demands that the United States pull its troops out of Europe and let the allies shift for themselves. Although NATO-bashing can be found at both extremes of the political spectrum, and while the ultimate effect may be similar, the litany differs somewhat. Right-wingers are angry at Europeans for resisting American political direction. They want to punish the allies for having independent interests, whether it be the right to buy Soviet natural gas or to go wild over Gorbachev. Although they talk a lot about money and about what NATO is doing to the American defense budget, one wonders, judging by their support for such fantasies as the Strategic Defense Initiative (SDI) or Star Wars, whether it is the cost of NATO that troubles those on the political right or that Europeans seem to have a political agenda of their own not dictated from Washington.

Left-wingers are equally critical of NATO, although for somewhat different reasons. They think that the United States should spend its money at home, building up the kind of welfare state that most north Europeans already enjoy. As a general principle, they would like to cut military spending, and NATO is an obvious place to start. They are annoyed that the British and the French insist on maintaining their own nuclear arsenals, which in their view merely embroil America further in the dangers of nuclear war. Moreover, they resent that the allies, as in the *Pershing II* affair in the early 1980s, push the United States to deploy even more nuclear weapons in dangerous places. In such cases, nuclear strategy seems to be driven not by concerns about Soviet intentions or capabilities but by the allies' anxieties about American fidelity. The American complaints may or may not be well taken. But whether they come from the resentful right or the romantic left, they share one thing: a deep-seated American proclivity toward unilaterialism.

While the burden sharers have a serious economic case, they are reluctant to accept the full implications of their analysis. Unilateralists, whether on the Right or on the Left, desire the United States to have full freedom of action in the world—to disengage from Europe, to defy the Soviet Union with impunity, or to sign deals with them with alacrity— without paying any political price for it. They believe that they can give up control over Europe's defense and yet still somehow, whether through gratitude or habit, maintain a serious measure of control over the diplomacy of the allies.

Even the reformers in the center, as distinct from the abolitionists at the extreme, share this problem. They do not want to pull out of NATO, or even to withdraw most of the GIs from the Continent. They merely want the Europeans to pay more. In other words, they want someone else to pick up the bill, but the political balance within the alliance to remain the same. They, too, assume that the Europeans, having given up the benefits of American largesse, will still allow Washington to call the political tune. But this is not the way things generally work. The problem with the burden sharers, in the center and at the far edges, is that they are unwilling to carry through the full implications of their logic.

Second, there is the military dimension. From the very beginning the alliance has rested on an American nuclear guarantee and an American threat to be the first to use nuclear weapons. This promise to protect the European allies—known as extended deterrence—rested on an immense American military advantage. The United States, with a virtual monopoly of nuclear weapons during the early years of NATO, could strike the Soviet Union from bases in and around Europe, but the USSR could not touch the United States. That, of course, was a shaky foundation that could not hold. The Soviet Union built up its nuclear arsenal and delivery systems, and by the 1960s this put both the United States and the nuclear guarantee at risk. The Eisenhower-Dulles threat of "massive retaliation" with atomic weapons if the Soviet Union so much as put a toe across the line was soon revealed as either too dangerous a strategy or too empty a bluff. John F. Kennedy and Robert McNamara replaced it with the more complicated, and presumably more credible, doctrine of "flexible response." This suggested that the United States would counter Soviet, or Soviet-inspired, or generically Communist provocations with various levels of force: from

Green Beret SWAT teams, to so-called battlefield nuclear weapons, to the instruments of Armageddon.

This strategy, while perhaps more flexible, also has been not only enormously dangerous but also costly. To provide credibility, it has required both a large standing American army in Europe, which is to say mostly along the front in West Germany, and the deployment of U.S. nuclear weapons on European soil. The earlier strategy had offered deterrence on the cheap; flexible response opened the floodgates to an immensely costly and open-ended arms race.

Despite these handicaps the strategy was designed to pose barriers to the descent into nuclear war. It would do this through a buildup, dependent largely upon the Europeans, of conventional land forces. But this strategy had obvious flaws. Matching the Soviet Union on the ground not only would require an immensely costly and politically difficult buildup, but also might undermine the very force that seemed to have kept the peace: fear of nuclear war. Even a conventional war, as recent evidence has demonstrated, would leave Europe in a state of ruin. Furthermore, even a "tactical" or small nuclear war would be "strategic" and close to total as far as the Europeans, and particularly the Germans, were concerned. Europeans preferred to brandish the "ultimate weapon" on the assumption that this threat would make any kind of war, nuclear or conventional, less likely.

The inherent strategic dilemma of extended deterrence was a political even more than a military problem, for it rested on clear disparities between the United States and its European allies. On one level, risks did not seem to be fully shared and perhaps could not be fully shared. Americans complained that the Europeans favored a policy that could lead to nuclear war, while the Europeans charged that the Americans wanted to confine any fighting, and any damage, to European soil. Over the years, various attempts have been made to resolve this dilemma, from the Multilateral Force, a kind of Noah's ark of missile-carrying NATO cargo ships in the 1960s, down to the deployment of the *Pershing II*s in the early 1980s. In every case the issue has been essentially one of confidence and reassurance, in other words, one of psychology, but the attempted solution has been one of hardware. These attempts to impose military solutions on what are essentially political problems have not been notably successful.

Third, the political problems that confront NATO, although urgent, have not been confronted, precisely because they are so fundamental. The *Pershing II*s are a good case in point, for they represented the expression of a political anxiety. The European allies sought reassurance and some measure of control over American strategy. The INF Treaty resolved some of the military anxieties by securing the removal of the Soviet *SS-20*s, along with the U.S. *Pershing*s. It did little, however, to alleviate the underlying political anxieties that flow from the disparity between Europe's economic strength and its military-political weakness.

Western Europe has its own political agenda, which is not necessarily identical with that of the United States. Europeans would like to secure greater control over American decision making insofar as the alliance is concerned, while at the same time they wish to pursue their own political and economic agenda in Eastern Europe, the Soviet Union, and indeed elsewhere in the world. They do not, in other words, want their military dependency to inhibit their diplomatic freedom of action: They desire all the conveniences of protection by a powerful ally and none of the inconveniences associated with military dependency. For this reason they complain about American hegemony, but they try not to let it get in their way, and they certainly do little to remove its major cause by relieving the United States of the burden of their defense.

It is understandable that they want this. Why should they not? But this is not quite the bargain that they, or the United States, undertook in joining NATO. That bargain was that the Europeans would relinquish diplomatic autonomy in return for American military protection. No one ever put this into writing, to be sure, but that was the bargain. General Charles de Gaulle understood this perfectly well, inveighed against it frequently, and pulled France out of NATO's integrated command because he wanted to pursue a diplomacy directed from the Elysée and not from the White House. For this, he was pilloried by American officials as an egotist and an ingrate.

In a sense he was, a condition not unknown among heads of state. But what U.S. officials really resented was France's pretense at independence and its questioning of the terms of the alliance. NATO was meant to be an American show. If it was not, why should the United States undertake such enormous economic costs and run such terrible dangers of nuclear devastation? Serious measures were taken to put de Gaulle in his place, and he has been, so far, the last to issue such an open challenge to Washington. His successors, in France and elsewhere, have been more circumspect, but their objective is no different. Nor, from a European point of view, should it be.

Discord is NATO's middle name, and certain tensions are endemic to the alliance. These lie in the disparity of power between America and its European allies, the inequality of risks among the members, the fact that the allies have no common diplomacy or clear purpose outside the NATO area, the determination of the United States to maintain political direction of the alliance, and the unwillingness of the Europeans to abide by their vows of diplomatic chastity.

It is an axiom of alliances that their cohesion depends on a sense of danger: the more of the latter, the better the health of the former. Like most axioms, there is some degree of truth in this, although NATO's pan-throwing sessions have usually been succeeded by kiss-and-make-up reconciliations. But the alliance has never before had to deal with a phenomenon quite like Mikhail Gorbachev, nor with the changes that his policies are unleashing in both the Soviet Union and the Soviet empire. Gorbachev's efforts to liberalize Soviet society, his withdrawal from Afghanistan, his scrapping of the SS-20 missiles, his announced unilateral cuts of Soviet forces in Europe, his peacemaking efforts in the Third World, and his avowals to cut nuclear arsenals and negotiate political differences— all have had a profound effect on European politicians. Bizarre as it may seem, Gorbachev is probably the most popular politician in Europe, and it is just as well that the "common house" has not yet been built, for he would be a strong candidate for president.

Two years ago it was considered daring to say that the time has come to rethink the fundamentals of the Cold War. Today it has become a veritable cliche to say that the Cold War is over. Even Margaret Thatcher has said so. What was once seen as a struggle unto death now appears to be evolving into something far more familiar and manageable: a power rivalry among states. In this rivalry the weapons are not ideology but productivity quotients, and the stakes are not control of the world but prosaic spheres of influences and balances of power.

The cataclysmic ideological struggle for the soul of the world now seems overblown and improbable. Few any more take seriously the pretensions of communism, or even capitalism, for that matter. Almost everyone worships at the market. The problem is that of management, and the Europeans believe that they do this not only better than the Communists, which is undisputed, but also better than the Americans. On both sides of the Iron Curtain the issue is how to make the market economy work efficiently. On the diplomatic level the confrontation between what used to be called the free world and the Communist world has evolved into the daunting task of managing the transition of the Soviet Union from an autarkic pariah into an honorary member of the European state system.

The Soviet threat has been redefined. For Europeans, the task is to prevent Moscow from sliding backward from the changes engineered by Gorbachev, to assist politically and economically the evolution of Eastern Europe toward greater autonomy, and to protect the European economy from an American policy based on insolvency, indebtedness, and fiscal irresponsibility. In the eyes of many Europeans, U.S. economic policy poses as great a threat to European well-being as does Soviet military policy.

In the United States as well, threats to national security can no longer be defined exclusively, or perhaps even primarily, in terms of the Soviet Union. The United States is faced with the daunting tasks of restoring its economy to health and making it fully competitive within the world system, ending the trade and budget deficits that cause such turmoil among our allies and partners, and incorporating a demoralized, antisocial, and drug-ridden underclass into the American social compact. Increasingly, the dangers facing the American republic at home seem far more pressing and intractable than those emanating from Moscow.

The erosion of the Cold War consensus has left NATO with a problematic future. While its demise is hardly imminent, and indeed its prospects are better than those of the Warsaw Pact, its continued relevance is open to question. The most familiar and easiest approach to this issue is essentially to do nothing much and to hope for the best. But, although inaction is easy, maintaining the current system is not, for it is unstable, resting on an outdated condition of U.S. hegemony that the American taxpayer is increasingly unable and unwilling to support, and that Europeans consider outmoded. Greater burden sharing, which is really an attempt to shore up the present system by shifting the weight around a bit, sounds good from Washington's point of view, for it means that Europeans will pay more for the alliance and Americans less. If that is all that it means, it is not much of a bargain for Europe. And if it means more—that is to say, greater European control of the alliance—then it will lead to even greater tensions between the transatlantic partners, not fewer.

Once again, as in the case of the *Pershing II*s in the early 1980s, we see nuclear weapons being used to address a political problem. This time it is the short-range missiles based in West Germany that Washington, together with London and Paris, wants to "modernize" with greater range and destructive power. The Germans resist this. The issue is not firepower but the relationship of the Federal Republic of Germany to its eastern neighbors. The *Lance* missiles are seen as a way of anchoring Bonn to its Atlantic partners, and thus acceptance of them has a high symbolic value. But if there is a political problem within the alliance, it will not be resolved by a nuclear fix. Pressure on the Germans to accept new missiles not only increases tensions among the allies but also is quite at odds with the political evolution in the East that is dramatically transforming the relationship between the two blocs.

If the current paste-and-patch approach to NATO's problems is unlikely to provide much in the way of a solution, can we find inspiration in a far greater European role within the alliance, that is, in "devolution," to use the accepted phrase? This would mean a European commander for NATO, much more European decision making, and probably even some form of independent European nuclear deterrent. A pillar and a pedestal would be wondrously transformed into two equal pillars. This would have the virtue of more accurately reflecting the current political and economic balance within the alliance, and thus it seems eminently logical. The problem is that partial devolution—more European control, fewer U.S. troops—will not resolve European anxieties over the reliability of the American nuclear deterrent. By combining the British and French forces, the United States almost certainly would withdraw its own nuclear commitment. No American Congress can be expected to accept commitment without control.

Thus, devolution may be more of a conundrum than a solution. If it means only more European troops and money, it offers little to the Europeans. If it means a European nuclear force, it threatens the transatlantic connection. A European deterrent may be an idea whose time has passed, requiring not only enormous political will and cooperation but also an overwhelming sense of danger. Both are lacking in Europe today, and so long as the Soviet Union continues its benign political evolution, the emphasis will be placed on engagement rather than on confrontation with the East. Devolution is a way of restructuring the balance within the alliance, but it does not address the issue of the relation of the alliance to the Communist countries to the East. Who speaks for NATO? In the past it has been, for all practical purposes, the United States. A successful devolution would give more weight to the European voice. But which Europe, and which voices within Europe? Western Europe does not yet have the political authority and cohesion to engage in a serious dialogue with Moscow. Through devolution it might eventually develop this authority, but the result would be a NATO without the United States, something that would not be NATO at all.

The problem with both burden sharing and devolution is that they address themselves to NATO's structural problems but not to its existential ones. What is it, after all, that NATO is supposed to do? Judging from the current debate, it would seem that mere survival is enough in itself. But that is not why the alliance was created, and if that has become its reason for being, then even its survival prospects are not bright. The purpose of NATO, it is worth recalling, was to help bring about the conditions that would make its existence no longer necessary. Its goal, in other words, was neither perpetual life nor devolution, but rather ultimate dissolution. It was supposed to help tide the West over until an evolution of forces in the East made it possible to negotiate a settlement of the Cold War. Integral to such a settlement was the breaking down of the barriers between the two parts of a divided Europe and the restoration of the Continent to itself.

Rather than focus on how best to cement NATO together, it is more important to know whether NATO has fulfilled its historic role and should dedicate itself to shedding a no longer functional identity. NATO is not now superfluous, but its goal must be to become so. But can NATO be expected to negotiate away its own existence? Bureaucracies, after all, are among the more enduring works of man, and survival is their guiding principle.

Can the nations of the alliance move beyond NATO to address their common interests and use the alliance itself to further those interests? Can NATO, rather than being an end, become a means? To be an effective means, it must evidence both cohesion and leadership. Yet the "general correlation of forces," as the Russians are fond of saying, is working in the other direction. NATO is becoming less cohesive, and the ability of the United States to lead the alliance effectively is diminishing. This results not from any lack of will but from all the reasons that already have been discussed.

The game is not over, however. America is still the dominant force in NATO and retains the ability to negotiate on behalf of its ally-dependents. NATO is a trump that the United States still holds, which it could use to achieve the goal that both it and its European partners desire: a political settlement with the Soviet Union over the future of Europe. Only Moscow and Washington can conduct such negotiations, for only they have the power to bargain. It is not a power that will last indefinitely.

The United States and the Soviet Union have common interests to protect. Both their political and their economic positions in Europe are growing increasingly weak. Their quite extraordinary period of hegemony, which has lasted most of these past forty years, is now in its final days and cannot be resuscitated. Even were *perestroika* to be scrapped and the Kremlin to become more militant, the economic balance of forces in the world has changed profoundly. Key decisions are no longer being made exclusively in Washington and Moscow but in Brussels and Tokyo as well.

The two powers that once contended for the leadership of the world, but who are now resigning themselves to more modest goals, have parallel objectives. Americans want Europe not to be endangered by the threat of Soviet attack or intimidated by Soviet pressure and to cease to be a drain on the U.S. Treasury. The Soviet Union wants a prosperous and generous Western Europe to pull them out of its economic sinkhole and bail out its satellites, yet still allow Moscow a sphere of influence in the East European states. Both sides need a settlement in Europe. A policy of drift and procrastination will resolve nothing. Its only result will be a continued erosion of the ability of the two Great Powers to achieve a workable settlement.

Is this not, some might object, an issue that should be resolved among Europeans? No, it is not. The West Europeans do not have the military strength and cohesion to back up their diplomacy, even if they had one. NATO has been the institutionalized means for their abdication from diplomacy. A coherent diplomacy requires not only greater political unity than Western Europe yet has but also an ability to address the still unresolved German question, a problem that no longer can be avoided as German reunification becomes a reality. There are a number of ways of dealing with the issue, for the question is really a part of the larger European question and can be addressed only within that context.

Resolving the European question requires great-power involvement and cooperation. The last time such cooperation was seriously attempted was at Yalta in 1945. There it seemed that the Soviet Union had accepted a sphere of influence in Eastern Europe that did not involve political servitude, and to many the path seemed open toward the reconstruction of a Europe that would be a threat to no one, including itself. At the time, John Foster Dulles saluted the Crimea conference as opening a "new era" in which the United States would abandon the aloofness that it had been practicing for many years and the Soviet Union would permit joint action on matters that it had the power to settle for itself.

These hopes were soon dashed, and a rigid line of demarcation cut through the center of Europe as a result of growing mutual hostility, for which the Western side is not totally blameless. Once that division became cemented into place, NATO played a creative role in building a strong and secure Western Europe. But in so doing it has ignored the greater objective that its founders originally envisaged: a Europe dominated neither from within by any of its members nor from without by the Great Powers on its flanks.

Ironic though it may seem, the objective of a restored and self-reliant Europe cannot be achieved by the Europeans themselves. It requires the cooperation of the two Great Powers that still serve as their guarantors. Herein lies both the utility and the opportunity of NATO. Rather than accept the continued dissipation of its influence over the alliance and the consequent diminishment of the alliance as an instrument of East-West entente, the United States, in the declining days of its hegemony, should use NATO to achieve a settlement with the Soviet Union of the wider European problem. There is nothing esoteric about the outlines of such a settlement. It would provide for the gradual withdrawal of both Soviet and American armies from Europe, a guarantee to the Soviet Union of its security position in Eastern Europe, a ban on the reintroduction of foreign troops into Europe, and the evolution of the internal affairs of the European states along lines to be decided by citizens of those states themselves.

The Cold War, as we have known it, is over. We are in a period of transition, when all that we have known as solid is suddenly fluid and uncertain. In this twilight of the superpowers, they have the opportunity to draw to a close, on terms that protect both their interests, the great confrontation in Europe. To dissipate that power in its declining days would be to lose control over the settlement, and perhaps also to lose the stability that the rival alliances, in their own way, have produced. The transition from détente to entente is one that Europeans cannot make by themselves. It requires an accord by the superpowers that will result in the demise of their rival alliances. Only then will the Cold War be completely over.

NATO at Middle Age: An Unexpected Midlife Crisis

Thomas H. Etzold

Anniversaries such as NATO's fortieth, celebrated in 1989, are times for reflection on what has gone before. They are, however, equally appropriate moments to consider what might—or could—come next. In NATO's case, it is particularly important to consider past and future in tandem for, ironically, this anniversary year also has been one of the most far-reaching change in European and East-West security, economic, and political relations since the earliest years following the Second World War. Although NATO's forty years are rich in experience and lessons, the next several decades will exhibit significant change in the political, military, and economic topography of Western security and prosperity. In fact, and without hyperbole, NATO faces in the 1990s tests of solidarity, strategy, and structure greater than any it has encountered since the mid-1960s crisis over nuclear policy and the role of France in the military dimensions of the alliance. While the "wise men" approach to papering over differences (which produced the Harmel Report of 1967) will surely be tried again, and soon, it will have to produce more substantial results this time around than the "lowest common denominator" that committee reports and alliance communiqués tend to produce.

While long anticipated, the end of a period that began with the Second World War, the Marshall Plan, and the doctrine of containment has finally arrived. Some individuals may regret this; it surely remains in the interests of Western democracies to limit the influence of the Soviet Union outside its borders. Yet forty years is a long time for a policy—or an alliance—to last, and there is no need to criticize past policies because changing conditions call for alterations in the structure of strategic relationships established in the first years after World War II. In this regard, despite the self-congratulatory speeches and pronouncements of NATO officials and Western leaders, the missing theme as the celebration rolls on is the current absence of concrete alliance goals. This is a troubling fact, for clear and shared objectives—not to say commitments—seem on the face of things an absolute requirement for the nature and extent of partnership that the Western democracies must nurture and employ in coming decades.

In the context of these preliminary thoughts, the present essay will address briefly the questions of a) why the alliance has worked so far; b) what is changing that bears on how, and how well, the alliance has and will work; and c) what to expect with regard to the alliance's nature, significance, and effectiveness in the next several decades.

Why the Alliance Worked

The NATO alliance has worked for the forty years since World War II, however imperfectly at times, for three central reasons: 1) perceptions of threat more shared than not; 2) the economic preeminence of the United States for most of the years since 1945; and 3) the transatlantic cultural and social ties nurtured in the latter nineteenth century and reinforced by the world wars and other critical common experiences of the twentieth century, together with the shared aspirations for the world's political and economic development to which these in part led.

For most of the postwar years, the nations of the North Atlantic Treaty Organization have shared, never exactly but in general, a perception of threat—or threats—to their security, stability (both external and internal), and prosperity. Conveniently, it seemed for most of this period as though this combination of complex threats had a common origin in the power of the Soviet Union, in terms of both the Red Army and the Communist ideology and economic systems instituted, maintained, and defended by that same superpower, whether in Europe, in Asia, or in parts of the Third World experiencing the wrenching changes following the devolution of European imperium as it had been known since the fifteenth century. It must be remembered that for many, if not most, European members of the alliance, the stability and direction of domestic politics were shaped considerably by the powerful Communist parties of states such as Italy, France, and still others. Early postwar Soviet and Chinese Communist efforts to accelerate decolonialization and to support "wars of national liberation" as a logical and justified extension of Communist fraternalism lent credibility to security concerns in Europe itself while posing sustained, and at times almost insurmountable, political problems for governments and even, from time to time, for the alliance itself.

The second principal reason why the alliance worked so long and so well was America's economic preponderance in the first three postwar decades, coupled with a new American commitment to play a considerably larger international role than it had previously. At the end of the Second

World War, the United States owned nearly half of the world's wealth, as such things were then calculated. As the 1940s drew to a close, America's gross national product amounted to nearly one quarter of the world's, and its foreign trade accounted for roughly 22 percent of world trade. The much-debated Soviet offer in 1946 to accept a $6-billion loan from the United States "in order to prop up its economy" (a loan requested on unusually preferential terms for the era) seems laughable in retrospect, despite efforts of revisionist historians to claim that U.S. mishandling of the request was a major source of Soviet-American antagonism early after the war.

The simple truth was that only the United States had the resources to rebuild Europe's war-riven societies and economies and to cushion the economic as well as political shocks accompanying the loss of empire, economic independence, and military effectiveness. It will probably always be impossible to estimate with confidence just how different East-West relations, including security concerns, could have been had the Soviet Union and its East European satellite states accepted America's invitation to join in the great rebuilding of Europe initiated under the Marshall Plan. One can only note that the startling and rapid "decommunization" of Eastern Europe late in 1989 has afforded unexpectedly saddening indications of the underlying weaknesses in the East European economies presumed to be among the strongest and most advanced, such as that of the German Democratic Republic.

The third chief reason for the alliance's durability and—from time to time—effectiveness since 1949 lay in the shared cultures, experiences, and values of the governing and policy elites of most NATO nations. This century's two world wars and the Great Depression between them imprinted a generation of leaders in the West with the conviction that extremism, whether of the Right or of the Left, was dangerous to the security, political stability, and economies of democratic states. In many respects, these shared experiences both expanded on and made up for the slow decline in calculated British-American alliances of family and fortune. So much has been written about this remarkable transoceanic set of relationships that little more need be said here. Suffice it to say, for present purposes, that the enduring influence of such men in the United States as Paul Nitze, George Kennan, and Dean Acheson, to name but a few, as well as that of their counterparts in key allied countries, did much to preserve a commonality of viewpoints on these matters that otherwise might have been either intermittent or unattainable.

What Is Changing the Alliance's Ability to Work as Before?

Each of the factors critical to alliance functioning since the Second World War is changing in considerable measure. Perceptions of threat seem to be less and less shared, even amid wide consensus that the danger of military confrontation in Europe may be diminishing. The United States has lost its economic dominance in the West, and its economic preeminence in the world, at least by certain measures. And new generations of Americans, Europeans, and natives of other regions and nations are assuming positions of leadership in government, industry, academia, and popular culture, generations whose experiences are more differentiated than common.

Although much has been written about the strategic premises of the Cold War, including some chapters of the present volume, more still must be set out, partly because the Soviet side of the equation remains inadequately expounded, and, more important, because the abandonment of the Cold War's strategic premises *by both sides* has proven to be an essential precondition for the "new politics" now so widely hailed. Hence, the space here devoted to this central subject.

In the 1990s the superpowers, their allies, and important regional powers will undertake—or at least undergo—the most significant adjustment of security policies, relationships, and related military forces since the late 1940s. The very magnitude of change lying ahead makes it imperative to recapitulate briefly the central premises of West and East since the Second World War, together with a summary of critical differences in them as things stood in the late 1980s, when it became clear that important aspects of the postwar order were passing.

Despite frequent attempts to rename U.S. strategic doctrines and to re-explain Western strategic perspectives, large continuities showed in security policy and associated strategy from roughly 1947 through 1985.

1) In this context, U.S./Western strategy was a) strategically defensive; b) primarily based on deterrence of conflict, especially that directly affecting the possibility of bringing the superpowers into head-on collision; and c) politically determined to restore peace on favorable terms (usually defined as the status quo ante). This broad strategy rested on a posture composed of collective defense commitments, forward deployments of U.S. forces to the first lines of defense in Europe and Asia (partly to serve as tripwires), and flexible force structure to provide at least some options for lesser contingencies than those involving the Soviet Union.

2) Deterrence of the use of nuclear weapons against any state, in any region, but especially between the Soviet Union and the United States (and their respective allies) held highest priority. This priority contributed greatly to early Western determination to build nuclear variants for use by virtually every combat arm and major combat system and in virtually every combat situation, from relatively close ground engagements to intercontinental range. In turn, this variety of nuclear systems encouraged stockpile growth to the very large sizes existing in the latter 1980s.

3) In conventional forces the United States and its allies showed strong preferences for maintaining naval superiority worldwide, sustaining air forces intended to secure air superiority in combat areas, and pursuing quality over quantity in allocating resources.

NATO's adoption of "flexible response" strategy in 1967 explicitly coupled these nuclear and nonnuclear elements of military power. To keep nuclear deterrence valid, and the nuclear threshold relatively high without eroding the case for having nuclear weapons at all, "alliance flexible response doctrine [was] always . . . . to walk that fine line between perceived strength and vulnerability."[1]

Over time, this approach left strategic legacies that became increasingly uncomfortable, especially for Americans: 1) disproportionate confidence in nuclear weapons to deter across the entire conflict spectrum; 2) a propensity, at least in theory and in doctrine, to escalate from disadvantage; and 3) an overreliance on the United States not only for naval and strategic air power (which was the original commitment called for from the United States in NATO's earliest military planning),[2] but also for men and supplies from CONUS to tip the European military balance in the earliest days of war.

The paradoxes of this strategic approach in large part underlay the periodic—almost decade by decade—revisitation of strategic doctrine and alliance security policies, discussions that so often sparked comment on the supposed disarray of the alliance. By 1980, indeed, even experts and officials formerly committed to the postwar Western security structure were remarking that "the largest question in this debate (over the viability of Western security) is whether time and circumstance have outrun the 30-year old American paradigm of deterrence and alliance and whether a new orientation is required."[3]

Soviet/Eastern strategic premises differed considerably from those in the West, as did the forces, doctrines, and operational posture of Soviet and Warsaw Treaty Organization (WTO) forces. Soviet officials considered themselves to be strategically on the defensive, but they developed doctrine and fielded forces for initial offensive operations as deep into Western territory as they could get, and as quickly; they also viewed nuclear weapons as likely to be decisive in any future war and certain to be used in one involving the United States or (later) Great Britain or France. Over time, they joined these nations in doctrines of preemption for nuclear, nonnuclear, and mixed conflict. Perhaps most important, Soviet leaders viewed their primary strategic task as defending against intrusion into or disruption of the USSR's security zone, the buffer states over which the Red Army had advanced control in the last years of World War II. (Interestingly, in the fall of 1989, Polish leaders attempted to distinguish between the Soviet "zone of security" and its "sphere of influence," with Poles being willing to remain in the first but less inclined to stay within bounds of the second.[4])

These premises led Soviet/WTO leaders to strategies, postures, and investments in some cases parallel to those of the West, but in others strikingly different:

1) Soviet leaders gave top postwar priority to development and fielding of fission and fusion weapons in militarily significant numbers. Their response in this regard was effective enough so that by the mid-1960s they could have some confidence that their forces would deter Western leaders from starting at the higher end of conflict; by 1969, when the first efforts to negotiate strategic arms reductions began, there was for all practical purposes parity in Soviet and American strategic forces. Remaining disparities in numbers of deliverable shorter range and smaller yield weapons were also rapidly offset on the Soviet side.[5]

2) In nonnuclear forces the Soviet Union gave priority to land forces—primarily the army—both as the defender of the homeland and as the guarantor that war, should it come, would take place on enemy territory, not in the Soviet Union. Other land-based forces, especially those devoted to air defense, also received early and continuing priority. Naval forces came to prominence only in the early 1960s, and for a time slowly, first as a forward interference and shortly thereafter as a partial analog to Western undersea nuclear missile forces.

3) Soviet strategists, in contrast to their Western counterparts, accorded more importance to quantity than to quality, at least as seen from the West. In part, this reflected Russian experience in prolonged warfare against powers of commensurate status, experience summed up by Vladimir I. Lenin in the phrase, "At a certain point quantity becomes quality." It also reflected the continuing Soviet need to hedge against Western technological superiority. Finally, it was a simple necessity, because Soviet transportation and other infrastructure did not permit timely movement of large forces from West to East, or vice versa, and the Soviet Union had considerable fear of Chinese and Japanese military potential, along with the possibility of large-scale war on two fronts. In effect, the USSR had to have forces for use in Asia in addition to those available for use in the West.

4) Soviet interest in power projection options and forces appropriate to them evolved much more slowly than in the United States. To be sure, the USSR had its hands full just in maintaining effective control of its East European sphere of influence; this was in one sense, perhaps, similar to its long efforts to consolidate the results of the 1917 October Revolution. Unlike the United States, the Soviet Union did not find itself involved in the internal politics, security affairs, and range of regional issues that complicated American foreign and security policy continuously after war's

end. When, in the mid-1960s, Soviet forces showed some evidence of growing interest in power projection as it was understood in the West, it proved to be largely flag-showing and capabilities to support its own forces in operation at militarily significant levels. The invasion of Afghanistan in December 1979 was the first major effort to use Soviet forces as the West long had done. The experiment proved both unwise and unpleasant; as of the latter 1980s, when Mikhail Gorbachev withdrew Soviet forces from Afghanistan, it seemed unlikely soon to be repeated.

5) The foregoing premises and developments led to large disparities in the size and composition of the forces of East and West. Ironically, these disparities were troubling to both sides, though as time went on more so to the West. The size of Soviet nonnuclear forces caused many in the West to conclude prematurely that effective nonnuclear defense of Europe might not be possible. The Soviet penchant for quantity as a good in itself, when manifested in missile throw-weight, posed mighty threats and obstacles to negotiation when warhead fractionation became possible for the Soviet Union as well as for the West. Soviet emphasis on armored formations and strike aircraft induced years of Western worry about short-warning attack, a replication of the stunning and unmeetable blitzkrieg with which the Second World War had opened. The Soviet Union saw the Western forward position as provocative, surely no less so than the offensive configuration of its land armies. The West's refusal to adopt a common position with the USSR on "no first use" of nuclear weapons encouraged exploration of preemptive options, especially as the likely destructiveness of such weapons came to be appreciated on each side. Inability to reach comprehensive peace treaties recognizing the Soviet absorption of the Baltic Republics and the Northern Territories in the Pacific, and settling once and for all the status of Berlin, the legitimacy of East Germany, and the permanent division of Europe, left the Soviet Union uneasy about Western intentions. The containment formula, with its implication of isolating the Soviet Union while the West maintained global maritime superiority and thus access to all the rest of the world, kept alive a strategic as well as political dimension to perennial Soviet concerns about the recognized legitimacy of its revolution and the regime it established.

These and other divergences in Western and Soviet/Eastern premises and perspectives resulted in strategic differences so fundamental that, at least until the mid-1970s, East-West relations seemed destined to revolve forever around managing threats; around worst-case planning; around the focal point of confrontation, the center of Europe; and around the increasingly menacing and publicly troubling possibility of nuclear weapons use. For the allies of the two superpowers, as well as for Third World states in all parts of the world, it also seemed to foreclose any possibility of preventing Soviet-American confrontation in third areas, or of turning the influence, resources, and efforts of the greatest powers toward increasingly large and urgent problems not then directly affecting the central strategic balance.

Perhaps most important to realize amid all that is changing is the growing role of economic influence—whether based on growth, current account surpluses, role in finance, or sectoral economic or technological strength/advantage. The new importance of economic influence in large extent is determining which states will be constant players, as mentioned above. It will predispose the ways and means through which problems are defined and resolved. And it will require increasingly sophisticated understanding of the relationships between internal political and economic matters and external affairs.

With these considerations in mind, a few of the more important specific trends can usefully be set out:

1) The next decade or more will be characterized by slowing/slow/no growth in the more mature economies, including those of South Korea, Taiwan, Hong Kong, and Singapore. Even Japan's much-praised and studied economy may perform less impressively by traditional measures.

2) This stagnation will coincide with a period of maximum need in Third World countries for debt restructuring (in large part forgiveness, deferral, and lowered interest rates) and development assistance.

3) Relatively few states will hold convertible reserves and account surpluses sizable enough to make significant differences in dealing with the Third World's economic needs, not to say crises (Japan, Germany, South Korea, Taiwan, and—not to be forgotten—the United States).

4) Increasingly, regional crises and conflicts of the sort that formerly enmeshed the superpowers in local affairs will have economic origins. In this regard, the Soviet Union as early as 1986 put "Third World debt" number three on their list of possible causes of superpower conflict in the next several decades, a point with implications the West has been slow to appreciate. Notably, by the late 1980s, 68 percent of the American public had come to view the Japanese economic "threat" as more significant to U.S. interests than Soviet military power, further confirming this point.

5) Western Europe will increase its cohesion and independence from the superpowers in political, economic, and military matters. Over time, East European states (either bilaterally or through multilateral arrangements and agencies) will participate in the opportunities and benefits of this development. The question of German reunification introduces significant and to some extent contradictory prospects here. The mere prospect of reunification hastened European efforts toward integration as early as December 1989, especially among the members of the Economic

Community; this reinforced the tendency of Western Europe to move toward greater independence from the superpowers, as did East European efforts to secure development aid and direct investment from the West and from international organizations. But the prospect—and the pace at which discussions of reunification were proceeding—also stirred security and stability concerns that kept alive the prospect that the superpowers, not to say the Four Powers victorious in the Second World War, might feel compelled to assert or maintain a role that none of them would have anticipated before 1989.

6) Developing countries will accelerate pressures to reorient the international political, economic, and military agendas, and they will meet with increasing success, though far short of the "new economic order" sought formally since 1977. Issues such as the decline of Communist parties as formal state rulers, assaults on drug production, trafficking, and finance, the environment, and energy supply will require and receive increasing attention at the expense of more traditional sphere-of-influence and balance-of-power matters, with their clear-cut military dimensions. (This also implies continuing interest in defining new missions for such military forces as are maintained in the traditional powers.)

7) In effect, two triangles will emerge, one primarily economic, the other primarily military. Economically, the United States, Japan, and a combined Western—possibly central—Europe will stand out if not entirely dominate. Militarily, the most powerful states will be the United States, the Soviet Union, and probably China. Of note, only the United States will rank in both triangles.

8) A number of these developments will erode confidence in the usability of force without undue escalation risk or cost and in the appropriateness of military power as a response to problems arising either in central or peripheral strategic areas and relationships. Thus they will soften long-term public support for military modernization and the maintenance of forces even on the basis of some principle of "sufficiency" (presumably a less demanding criterion than either East or West has formally applied through most of the post-World War II years).

For the next several decades, therefore, it will be

1) possible to be an economic power without being a military power;
2) possible to wield great political influence without the corresponding military weight traditionally needed to do so; and
3) difficult, if not impossible, to be economically weak and militarily strong as well as politically influential.

Under the conditions sketched here, both the United States and the Soviet Union, and many other nations, face formidable challenges. For the

United States, the question is how to preserve traditional interests in limiting Soviet influence, maintaining secure access to all parts of the world, and supporting the viability and independence of friendly countries and democracies around the world *despite a decline in military power both absolute and relative and a slumping economy.* Increasingly, it seems, influence abroad depends greatly on how much money a state is willing to provide in aid and trade, either directly or through multinational organizations. In times of economic constraint, it is almost a reflex for Americans to cut back on foreign aid, and the emergence of new internal concerns—such as health care costs in an aging and AIDS-infected population—provides serious competition for discretionary funds.

The Soviet leadership under Gorbachev has apparently concluded that a favorable international environment can only be created on the basis of an accommodation with the United States and a tolerance of liberalizing forces that will permit internal restructuring. This in turn over several decades should produce a Soviet Union better equipped than its predecessor regimes to deal with the politics, economics, and military aspects of the international environment in the twenty-first century.

Conclusions: What to Expect in Coming Decades

In the next two decades the Cold War premises of East and West will largely be abandoned in the face of economic, technological, and political change. Contracting forces, "new politics," and "new thinking" will rapidly invalidate most of the war and contingency planning done in the strategic renaissance of the 1980s.

There will probably be a substantial shift in planning focus from worst case (central front war involving the Soviet Union, with large nuclear escalation potential) to likely case (middle- and low-intensity warfare in other areas). Whether or not this shift occurs, or occurs cleanly, problems of and requirements for conflict in Third World areas will receive increasing attention and will no longer be subsumed as "lesser included threats" under a U.S.-USSR planning perspective. U.S. and Soviet influence on the whole range of coming security, economic, and stability issues will be greater when they cooperate than when they compete.

There will continue to be powerful long-term incentives for a more cooperative superpower relationship. Much of this cooperation will remain tacit and will take place in the form of unilateral, reciprocal steps both in and beyond arms control. The governing principles will be a perception of shared interest in strategic stability, managed change, and the avoidance of inadvertent conflict or confrontation over less than vital matters. Even if there should be a rupture of the new harmony between the superpowers, it is unlikely that it would lead to a renewal of the Cold War.

Both in traditional alliances and in regional affairs, states are likely to act more and more independently of the United States and the USSR. The superpowers will without a doubt play a declining role in the European order of the twenty-first century, as the Europeans increasingly distance themselves from the United States and the USSR. Indeed, Europe could be much reduced in traditional importance as a U.S.-USSR area of conflict, even with a return to more competitive than cooperative superpower relations.

The large alliances of the Cold War will play a correspondingly reduced role in addressing specific contingencies, shaping the forces of the superpowers, and influencing their policies and actions in crisis or contingency operations. Withdrawal of forward-based forces will deprive allies of their virtual veto over the use of very large percentages of U.S. forces. Loss of overseas infrastructure and the development of alternatives to it in support of military reach also will make the United States—and to a lesser extent the USSR—capable of more unilateral actions or cooperative approaches that might not have appealed to allies under 1980s and early 1990s conditions. Both superpowers, as well as many other states, will increasingly rely on temporary coalitions directed at specific contingencies or problems rather than try to broaden traditional alliances in ways that would suit them to address out-of-area and new agenda issues.

Nuclear weapons will continue to exist in militarily significant, although smaller, quantities. More countries will have them available. As the superpower arsenals shrink, the forces of the United Kingdom, France, and other parties will become more truly independent and more significant politically and strategically. In this context, the United States and the USSR will eventually agree on a formula for measured, cooperative deployment of advanced defenses in some form and in phases over a considerable interval. In the next several decades, improved defenses and other force multipliers may well provide the essential measure of advantage needed to operate effectively in Third World areas. Public opposition to nuclear weapons will increase in Europe as well as throughout the Third World, and very likely in the American and Soviet publics as well. The establishment of nuclear-free zones will be increasingly likely, as will the elimination of short-range nuclear weapons from central Europe, if not "from the Atlantic to the Urals."

Both traditional allies of the superpowers and Third World countries, individually and in groups, hold the superpowers responsible for many of the more lamentable aspects of current and coming conditions. They are demanding timely and substantial contributions and involvement of the Soviet Union and the United States in addressing them. Pressure for arms reduction is intended in part to make the world less crisis sensitive and war prone but increasingly—however erroneously—also as a means of freeing up large sums of money for alternative uses on "new agenda" matters. Leaders of both superpowers have emphasized the unlikelihood of a sizable "peace dividend" from arms reductions even as they have negotiated them at ever more rapid rates. Moreover, it is a long-recognized fallacy that monies not spent by governments for one purpose automatically become available for others. Neither budgets, laws, nor economies work quite so simply.

In view of these trends, as well as for other internal reasons, the Soviet Union and the United States have moved cautiously toward consensus on the importance of "strategic stability" as a central mutual interest and goal to be sought not only through arms control but also through a cooperative approach to regional change (including in the heart of Europe), international institutions (the first U.S.-Soviet joint resolution in the history of the United Nations was introduced in the fall 1989 session in New York, calling for the strengthening of the United Nations and respect for human rights), and mutually beneficial economic ventures. In doing so, however, the superpowers have rearoused old suspicions that they may pursue condominium or otherwise seek to insulate themselves from the consequences of change rather than make a constructive and substantial commitment to bettering the general international welfare. Hence, the mixed and not wholly optimistic outlook with which the world's nations approach the 1990s.

In sum, in the coming decades NATO is likely to be

1) Militarily less capable than in the past, and
2) Politically more important as a venue for sustaining U.S. and Soviet involvement in the stability and security of Europe.

All in all, we approach the twenty-first century as the United States loses control of the security agenda in the West and the Soviet Union loses control of the political agenda in the East. Both the United States and the USSR have long since lost most control over economies other than their own, and it could be argued that, as economic interdependence has progressed, they have lost a considerable measure of absolute control even in their domestic economies.

Of one thing we can be certain: NATO's future problems and debates will resemble those of the last several decades less and less, and those of an earlier era of European politics in European terms more and more. As Henry Kissinger recently noted, "The test for stability is whether for the first time in history Europe can live in equilibrium with a Russian empire, with neither side fearing invasion by the other,"[6] Meanwhile, ministers and secretaries of various concerned governments in East and West are, as they say in Washingtonese, "laying down markers," that is, establishing or reconfirming continuing interests, especially of the superpowers, in the continuation of the alliances in some form for some as yet indeterminate purpose. Thus, Secretary of State James Baker has presented detailed proposals "for enhancing NATO's role as a political forum for dealing with its former adversaries."[7]

As we enter the 1990s, John Dryden's familiar observation has special poignancy: "Even victors may be undone by victory." The so-called winning of the Cold War has, at the moment, a certain bittersweet quality. We can improve on this flavor only if, and as, we place stronger emphasis on designing future East-West and West-West relationships and focuses, and not only on repudiating what has been done before.

Notes

1. Quoted in William Drozdiak, "NATO Weighs Nonnuclear Strategies," *Washington Post*, 26 September 1983.

2. See the NATO Defence Committee's document DC 6/1, *Strategic Concept for the Defense of the North Atlantic Area*, 1 December 1949, published with commentary in *Containment: Documents on American Policy and Strategy, 1945–1950* (New York: Columbia University Press, 1978), 335–38.

3. Earl Ravenal, *Foreign Policy* 19 (Summer 1980): 36.

4. Reported in *Washington Post*, 25 October 1989.

5. See the extended discussion of these matters by Thomas H. Etzold, "The End of the Beginning . . . NATO's Adoption of Nuclear Strategy," in Olav Riste, ed., *Western Security: The Formative Years (European and Atlantic Defence, 1947–1953)* (Oslo: Norwegian University Press, 1985), 285–314.

6. Kissinger's syndicated column, printed in *Washington Post*, 10 October 1989.

7. Remarks made at the NATO ministerial meeting in Brussels, 12 December 1989, reported in ibid., 15 December 1989.

Index

ABC-22. *See* Joint Basic Defense
Plan No. 2
Acheson, Dean, 59, 63, 267;
Adenauer and, during Cuban
missile crisis, 95; briefs North
Atlantic Council on Cuban
missile crisis, 94; Franks and,
36; on difficulties of foreign
policy, 165; on NATO, 155,
156; Third World and, 158; to
de Gaulle in Cuban missile crisis,
95
Achilles, Theodore: on NATO
defense, 155–56
Adenauer, Konrad, 85, 87, 187; FRG
and, 82–83; on Soviet Union,
86; on U.S. reaction to Berlin
wall, 94; reaction to Cuban
missile crisis, 95
Afghanistan: Marxism in, 166;
Soviet invasion of, 71, 86,
168, 194, 214, 271; Soviet
withdrawal from, 206, 259
Agreement of Basic Principles
(1972), 209
Ailleret, Charles, 66
Airborne warning and control system
(AWACS), 24
Airbus, 135
Airplane: impact of on defense
policy, 7
Air Policy Commission: report of,
7–8
Alaska, 14; defense of, 6; DEW line
and, 17
Aleutian Islands: defense of, 6; DEW
line and, 17
Algeria, 42, 149; Kennedy on
independence of, 62; NATO and,
154–55; unrest in, 156

Algerian War: effect of on France, 62;
end of, 63
Allende, Salvador: overthrow of, 104
Allied Command Europe Mobile
Force: NATO and, 23
Alphand, Hervé: on Czechoslovakia,
57; on de Gaulle's economic
policy, 65
The American Challenge, 65
Andropov, Yuri, 120
Angola, 86, 193; Marxism in, 166;
Portugal and, 104; Soviets and,
71
Antarctic Treaty (1952), 209
Antiballistic Missile (ABM) Treaty,
191, 209
Anti-imperialism: Hunt on U.S. views
of, 150
Arab-Israeli War (1973): France and,
68–69
Arabs, 116
Ariane, 135
Arms control: NATO and, 203–18
Arms Control and Disarmament
Agency (ACDA): creation of,
217
Aswan Dam, 61
Atlantic Barrier Command, 17
Atlantic Charter, 152
Atlantic Council, 230
Atlantic Declaration, 68–69
Atlanticism: NATO and, 142–44
Atomic bomb: Attlee government and
development of, 34–35;
Gaillard government and, 61;
impact of on defense theory, 7
Atomic Energy Act: revision of, 42
Attlee, Clement R., 49; atomic bomb
and, 34–35; Truman's nuclear
policy and, 37